Harriet Dyer Adams
Albany, New York
December 1972

CONSERVATION OF LIBRARY MATERIALS

A Manual and Bibliography on the
Care, Repair and Restoration of
Library Materials

Second Edition

by
George Martin Cunha
Conservator, Library of the Boston Athenaeum
and
Dorothy Grant Cunha

VOLUME II: Bibliography

The Scarecrow Press, Inc.
Metuchen, N.J.   1972

This book has been printed
on permanent/durable paper
with a neutral pH to insure
a life expectancy of at least
one hundred years.

Library of Congress Cataloging in Publication Data

Cunha, George Daniel Martin.
    Conservation of library materials.

    1. Books--Conservation and restoration. 2. Books--
Bibliography. I. Cunha, Dorothy Grant, joint author.
II. Title.
Z701.C782   025.84   77-163871
ISBN 0-8108-0427-1 (V. 1)

"The first duty of a studious librarian must be to devote his time and labor to increasing the library in his charge.... If he neglects increasing the collection, let him at least take care not to reduce it by losing the books committed to his care or letting them perish in any way. He must therefore particularly suspect and beware of those enemies of books 'fire and water.' He is to repair in the same style bindings destroyed by age, remind readers to treat books decently, keep them in a fixed and safe place, and know the names or authors of individual volumes. But if there are too many books for him to remember the numbers and names, he must make a list on a loose leaf or in a notebook (grouping them by authors)."

Instructions for the librarian by Peter von Arbon in the first catalog of the Abbey Library, Admont 1370 (in what is now northern Austria). Translated by Anthony Hobson in Great Libraries, London: Weidenfield and Nicolson, 1970.

Table of Contents

v

vii

Introduction*

The literature on the conservation of library materials is increasing at an astounding rate. Keeping informed on the mass of information coming from research laboratories, restoration centers and the technical data from other fields of conservation, equally applicable to libraries and archives, can only be done with the aid of bibliographies, of which this is only one.

Probably the first printed work on bookbinding and restoration was Capperonnier de Gauffecourt's now extremely rare Traité de la Reliure des Livres, La Motte, France, 1763 [315]. This is catalogued in Brunet's Manuel de Libraire, Paris, 1861, Volume II, page 1502, and described as a 72-page octavo volume of which only 25 copies were printed. No copies are recorded at the British Museum, Bibliothèque Nationale or the Library of Congress.

Since de Gauffecourt's time there has been a flood of books, pamphlets and magazine articles on the history of binding, binding techniques, binders, collectors and great collections. Wolfgang Mejer's 1925 list of 2691 titles in seven languages [4692] is considered to be the best bibliography on bookbinding up to that time. However, even the 2224 titles later added to Mejer's important catalogue by Herman Herbst [4693] did not make that reference all inclusive.

No research prior to 1920 on binding history and binding patrons should be taken for granted. Since then, however, there are reliable sources of historical and critical scholarship on bindings, binders and patrons, particularly the series by Howard Nixon in The Book Collector beginning in 1952 [720-771], and G. D. Hobson [412-418], Ernst Kyriss [689-691], Seymour de Ricci [597], E. G. Duff [460-465] and Charles Ramsden [503-508] to name only a few. In 1954

*Numbers in brackets refer to sequence numbers in this volume.

A. R. A. Hobson, Director in Charge of the Book Department
at Sotheby's, assembled for the National Book League a list
of references [4684] that he considered sufficient to provide
one with a first-rate knowledge of the history of binding. In
an appendix to the same pamphlet Hobson included what he
regarded as authentic texts in English on the binding craft
and industry.

✓   Bookbinding in America [52] containing three essays
by Hellmut Lehmann-Haupt, Joseph W. Rogers and Hannah
Dustin French gives an excellent description of binderies,
materials, and craftsmen to 1825 and the transition from an
ancient craft to a modern industry in the 1800's. The third
essay, Lehmann-Haupt's "On the Rebinding of Old Books,"
is an analysis of the ethics and aesthetics of rebinding and
warrants the attention of all librarians who must inevitably
make such decisions. Miss French's lengthy list of binders
appended to "Early American Bookbinding by Hand" should
be of great help in identifying colonial craftsmanship. Mr.
Rogers' discourse on "The Rise of American Edition Binding"
would be more properly titled if the word "American" were
not included and the dissertation were understood to be an
introduction to the mechanization of bookbinding on both sides
of the Atlantic.

     In regard to technique, in 1963 Max Hettler in Stutt-
gart published Anneliese Duehmert's Buchpflege [4682], a
bibliography of over 2000 titles in several languages on the
care and repair of bindings. The works of Douglas [3756-
3757] and Sidney Cockerell [3933] will for a long time to
come be the standard references on binding, although
Laurence Town's Bookbinding by Hand [3820] presents
Douglas Cockerell's information in a more comprehensible
✓ manner. Bernard Middleton's 1963 History of English Craft
Bookbinding [3947] is far wider in scope than the subject
suggests. This edifying volume was written by a master
craftsman reflecting his own experience plus over ten years
of exhaustive research. As a technical reference, it is un-
excelled and it is of particular importance to librarians who
in deciding whether to rebind or restore old books must be
able to recognize contemporary workmanship. Middleton
documents his sources in hundreds of footnotes.

     In the 20th century there has been a surprising num-
ber of technical papers on the various aspects of conservation as well as important contributions to our knowledge of
books. Leo Deuel's Testaments of Time [4622] is a scholarly account of what is being done to retrieve and restore

ancient records. This, a good point of departure for the study of the history of books in all the various forms, includes a lengthy bibliography. Douglas McMurtrie's The Book [4691] is unquestionably the best account of the development of the book in codex form. This, too, has fine bibliographies of technical as well as historical interest. All that librarians need to know about paper is available in Dard Hunter's Papermaking [916] and his Handmade Paper and Its Watermarks [4728], both of which include excellent bibliographies.

Between 1932 and 1942 the Fogg Art Museum published a quarterly journal, Technical Studies in the Field of Fine Arts [4823]. Long out of print, but now available on microfilm from the Intermuseum Conservation Association, Oberlin, Ohio, these journals are a gold mine of information on materials, craftsmanship and techniques, environmental control and general conservation, much of which is applicable to books. They were made doubly useful by the publication in 1964 of a subject index to the series done by Bertha E. Usilton, Librarian at the Freer Gallery of Art. In addition to more than 160 articles and notes and many reviews of technical books, Technical Studies contains 459 abstracts of articles that appeared in other journals. Later Mr. Rutherford Gettens of the Freer Gallery and Miss Usilton compiled Abstracts of Technical Studies in Art and Archeology 1943 to 1952 [4610], which was published by the Freer Gallery in 1955. Since that time the technical literature on art and archeology has been abstracted and published under the auspices of the International Institute for Conservation of Historical and Artistic Works (IIC) with headquarters in London. Known as the IIC Abstracts until 1966, they are now the Art and Archeology Technical Abstracts [4609], published by the Institute of Fine Arts, New York University.

In 1966 the New York State Historical Association released its Selective Reference Guide to Historical Preservation [4646]. Although primarily museum oriented, this important book must not be overlooked by librarians and archivists. In 1961 Dr. Santucci at the Institute of Book Pathology in Rome reviewed the literature to 1960 on "the application of chemical and physical methods to the conservation of archival materials" [3111]. There is no better way to commence the study of paper preservation than with this scholarly and constructive criticism in English of what Santucci then considered to be the 182 most important contributions to the problem of the preservation of paper and his subsequent survey in 1963 of the literature on paper stability [1608].

In August 1969 the University of Chicago's Graduate Library School's 34th Annual Conference was devoted to study of the deterioration and preservation of library materials. The proceedings, including important bibliographies, of this milestone in conservation, published in the Library Quarterly (January 1970) and by the University of Chicago Press [3125] should be required reading for all candidates for degrees in library science. The essay, "The Librarian as a Conservator" [2490] (in the "Chicago Blue Book," as it is getting to be called) by James W. Henderson and Robert G. Krupp, reviews the literature on conservation administration and offers excellent guidance with some thought provoking suggestions for senior administrators.

Three Russian publications are of much interest because of their detailed reporting on library conservation measures and restoration techniques in the U.S.S.R. Translations of these, A Collection of Materials on the Preservation of Library Resources [2425], New Methods for the Restoration and Preservation of Documents and Books [2537] and Preservation of Documents and Papers [2472], are available from the National Technical Information Service, 5285 Port Royal Road, Springfield, Virginia, 22151. N.G. Belan'Kaya's "Methods of Restoration of Books and Documents" [2537] in New Methods.... is an outstanding summary with much technical detail on the traditional as well as modern techniques for paper restoration in Russia, Europe, and America. Preservation of Documents and Paper, edited by D.M. Flyate, contains important bibliographies of the Russian literature on the aging of paper, materials and methods, and the examination of paper.

Restaurator, Restaurator Press, Copenhagen [4776], the first international journal devoted to the preservation of library and archival material, is a prime source of reliable technical and scientific guidance. Published three times annually since 1969 with an editorial board representing major preservation centers in East and West Europe and North America, it promises to be the long-needed medium for international cooperation in library conservation.

UNESCO's Museums and Monuments Series XI, The Conservation of Cultural Property [2453], edited by Harold Plenderleith and Paul Coremans, should be available to every librarian and archivist conscientiously concerned about the condition of the materials in their custody. Similarly the IIC's quarterly journal, Studies in Conservation [4777], should not be overlooked.

If we were asked to recommend a list of titles on the various aspects of preservation for everyday use by librarians and archivists, they would include:

1. McMurtrie, The Book [163]
2. Hunter, Papermaking [916]
3. Middleton, A History of English Craft Bookbinding [3947]
4. Lehmann-Haupt et al., Bookbinding in America [52]
5. Glaister, Glossary of the Book [140]
6. Labarre, Dictionary and Encyclopedia of Paper Making [925] and Loeber's 1967 Supplement to it [4597]
7. Ellis, The Principles of Archive Repair [3395]
8. Plenderleith and Werner, The Conservation of Antiquities and Works of Art [3437]
9. UNESCO, The Conservation of Cultural Property [2453]
10. Winger and Smith (eds.), Deterioration and Preservation of Library Materials [3125]
11. Archer et al., Rare Book Collections [2415]
12. Douglas Cockerell, Bookbinding [3756]
13. Sidney Cockerell, The Repairing of Books [3933]
14. Langwell, The Conservation of Books and Documents [3419]
15. Grant, Books and Documents: Dating, Permanence and Preservation [1196]
16. Horton, Cleaning and Preserving Bindings and Related Materials [3091]
17. Kane, A Guide to the Care and Repair of Manuscripts [3183]
18. Minogue, The Repair and Preservation of Records [3426]
19. Le Gear, Maps: Their Care, Repair and Preservation in Libraries [2892]
20. Handbook for Library Binding [3864]
21. ALA's Protecting the Library and its Resources [2797]
22. IIC's Museum Climatology [2656] in library
23. Pickett and Lemcoe, Preservation and Storage of Sound Recordings [3317]
24. Cunha, Conservation of Library Materials (Vols. I and II)

The bibliography that follows, to enhance its usefulness, is organized by subjects to correspond with the arrangement of the text in Volume I. When seeking titles by subject, reference to the table of contents will give page numbers. An author index arranged alphabetically is at the very end of the book. The many references to publications of museum origin or interest are included because of the close affinity of library conservation to certain aspects of museum science. Environment control as practiced in museums is equally applicable to libraries and archives. Measures developed in museums for the care and repair of paper, textiles, leather, parchment, and other materials are of utmost importance to librarians. The titles are primarily those available in English, but some entries in other languages are included because of their particular interest or importance.

Since no work of this sort could ever be complete or without human error, constructive criticism is welcomed.

G. M. C.
D. G. C.

CONSERVATION OF LIBRARY MATERIALS:
A BIBLIOGRAPHY

I. Historical Background

GENERAL

1. Abbott, T. K. Celtic Ornaments from The Book of Kells. Dublin: 1895. Fifty plates.
2. Allegro, John M. "The Copper Scroll from Qumran," Restaurator 1(1):13-19, 1969.
3. Andrews, W. L. Bibliopegy in the United States and Kindred Subjects. New York: Dodd, Mead, 1902. 128 p. Illus.
4. Arnett, J. A. [i. e. , J. Hannett]. An Inquiry into the Nature and Form of the Books of the Ancients: With a History of the Art of Bookbinding. London: R. Groombridge, 1837.
5. Barrow, John. Dictionarium Polygraphicum. London: C. Hitch and C. Davis (etc.), 1735. 2 vols.
6. Bennett, H. S. English Books and Readers: 1475-1557. Cambridge, England: University Press, 1952. Being a study of the history of the book trade from Caxton to the incorporation of the Stationers Company.
7. Binns, Norman E. "Bookbinding, Evolution and History," Introduction to Historical Bibliography. London: Association of Assistant Librarians, pp. 285-319, 1953.
8. Birss, J. H. "A Thought on Bookbinding," New England Quarterly No. 5, April 1932. Bibliographic proof of Herman Melville's authorship of an article in March 16, 1850, issue of The Literary World No. 6 under the same heading. See entry under Melville H. in this section in which Melville comments on the importance of bookcover design to suit the subject of the book.
9. Blades, W. Books in Chains. London: Stock, 1892.
10. Blagden, Cyprian. The Stationers' Company. Cambridge, Mass. : Harvard University Press, 1960.

11.   Blanck, Jacob. Bibliography in America. New Haven:
      Yale University Press, 1955. Includes the Biblio-
      graphical Society of America's Key to Identification
      of binder's cloths.

12.   "Books and Bookbinding in Syria and Palestine." Art
      Journal 20:41, 113.

13.   Briquet, C. M. Opuscula: The Complete Works of
      C. M. Briquet without Les Filigranes. Hilversum,
      The Netherlands: 1955.

14.   Brown, H. G. and Brown, M. O. A Directory of the
      Book Arts and Book Trade in Philadelphia to 1820.
      New York: New York Public Library, 1950.

15.   Brunet, Jacques-Charles. Manuel du Libraire et de
      l'Amateur de Livres. 5 vols. Paris: 1860-1864.
      Two supplementary volumes, 1878-1880. Despite
      its age, Brunet is still the best general reference
      book of international scope.

16.   Carter, John. Books and Book Collectors. New York:
      Knopf, 1957.

17.   _____. Taste and Technique in Book Collecting.
      New York: Knopf, 1948. (The Sanders Lectures
      for 1947.)

18.   Cennini. The Craftsman's Handbook. New York:
      Dover Publications, 1933. Modern translation by
      Daniel V. Thompson, Jr. of Cennini's 1437 Il
      Libro dell'Arte.

19.   Crabbe, George. The Library: A Poem. London:
      1781. Reprinted by G. K. Hall & Co., London, at
      Christmas, 1966.

20.   D'Ancona P. and Aeschlimann E. The Art of Illumina-
      tion. 1969. 126 plates, 23 in color.

21.   Deuel, Leo. Testaments of Time. New York: Knopf,
      1965.

22.   Dibdin, Thomas Frognall. The Bibliographical De-
      cameron. London: 1817. 3 vols. Illus. Dibdin
      must be used with caution because of the unrelia-
      bility of his facts.

√ 23.   Diderot, Denis. A Diderot Pictorial Encyclopedia of
      Trades and Industry. New York: Dover Publica-
      tions, 1959. 2 vols. Edited by Charles Coulston
      Gillispie. Includes bookbinding, papermaking,
      tanning.

√ 24.   Dimand, M. S. Handbook of Muhammadan Art. 2nd ed.
      New York: Rinehart, 1946. Includes chapters on
      bookmaking and decoration.

25.   Dioscorides, Pedanius, of Anazarbos. The Greek
      Herbal of Dioscorides. Edited by Robert T.

Gunther. Oxford: printed by J. Johnson for the author at the University Press, 1934.

✓ 26. Diringer, D. The Illuminated Book. London: Faber and Faber, 1967.

27. Du Halde, P. "Of Paper, Ink and Pencils; Also of the Printing and Binding of Chinese Books," The General History of China, Including an Exact and Particular Account of Their Customs, Manners, Ceremonies, Religion, Arts, and Sciences. London: 1736. 4 vols. In vol. 2, pp. 415-436.

28. Esdaile, Arundel. Manual of Bibliography. London: George Allen, 1931. See Stokes, Roy [88], for the latest revision of this important manual.

29. Farrer, J. A. Literary Forgeries. London: Longmans, Green, 1907.

30. Forbes, R. J. Studies in Ancient Technology. Vol. 5 (Leather). Leiden: E. J. Brill, 1957.

31. Gordon, Douglas. "Books in Pictures," The Book Collector 11(2):175-183, London: 1962. Illustrated essay on the use artists have made pictorially of books.

32. Greenwood, Thomas. Public Libraries. London: Cassell, 1890. A history of the movement and a manual for the organization and management of rate (tax) supported libraries.

33. Gruel, L. Manuel Historique et Bibliographique de l'Amateur de Reliures. Paris: Gruel and Engelmann, 1887. Contains much general information although some of the author's conclusions are open to question.

34. Gumuchian & Cie. Les Livres de l'Enfance du XVe au XIXe Siècle. Paris: 1930. Separate vol. of plates. (A 1967 reprint in one vol. includes all the text with a selection of the original illustrations.)

35. Hertzberger, Menno. Dictionary for the Antiquarian Booktrade. Paris: 1956. In French, English, German, Swedish, Danish, Italian, Spanish and Dutch.

36. Hessel, Alfred. A History of Libraries. Metuchen, N. J.: The Scarecrow Press, 1955.

37. Highet, Gilbert. "The Wondrous Survival of Records," Horizon 5(2), 1962.

✓ 38. Hind, Arthur M. A History of Engraving and Etching from the 15th Century to the Year 1914. New York: Dover Publications, 1963.

✓ 39. _____. An Introduction to the History of Woodcut. New York: Dover Publications, 1963. The origins

of woodcuts and wood engravings by a former Keeper of Prints at the British Museum.
40. [No entry.]
41. Hobson, Anthony. Great Libraries. London: Weidenfeld and Nicolson, 1970. An account of 32 great libraries in Western Europe and North America by the director of Sotheby's who was in charge of their book department for 30 years. Libraries range from the 4th-century Capitular Library of Verona to the 20th century's Texas University Library.
42. Hooke, Robert. Micrographia. London: J. Martin and J. Allestry, 1665. Description and illustration of the insect later identified as the silverfish. The illustration has been reproduced many times.
43. Horace. De Arte Poetica. In lines 331-332, Horace refers to the practice of smearing books with cedar oil and keeping them in boxes of cyprus as protection against insects.
44. Imberdis, Father (S. J.). Papyrus. Ambert: 1693. A Latin poem extolling the paper-maker's craft.
45. Jackson, Holbrook. The Anatomy of Bibliomania. New York: Charles Scribner's Sons, 1932.
46. Johnson, Elmer D. A History of Libraries in the Western World. 2nd ed. Metuchen, N. J.: The Scarecrow Press, 1971.
47. Kenyon, Frederick G. Ancient Books and Modern Discoveries. Chicago: The Caxton Club, 1927. History of lettering and illumination.
48. _____ . Books and Readers in Ancient Greece and Rome. Oxford: University Press, 1951. A short, scholarly, and interesting commentary.
49. Koops, Matthias. Historical Account of the Substances Which Have Been Used to Describe Events and Convey Ideas. London: Jaques & Co., 1801. Describes the use of all materials from clay tablets to paper. Sketchy and poorly documented.
50. Labarte, J. Histoire des Arts Industriels au Moyen Age. Paris: Morel & Cie, 1864-1866.
51. Leggett, William F. Ancient and Medieval Dyes. Brooklyn, N. Y.: Chemical Publishing Company, 1944.
√ 52. Lehmann-Haupt, Hellmut; Joseph W. Rogers, and Hannah Dustin French. Bookbinding in America. New York: Bowker, 1967. Three essays; a must for every librarian.
√ 53. Lehmann-Haupt, Hellmut. Gutenberg and the Master of the Playing Cards. New Haven: Yale University

Press, 1966.   Author proposes that Gutenberg pio-
neered in printed illustrations as well as movable
type.

54.   Li Shu-hua.   "The Early Development of Seals and
Rubbings," Tsing Hua Journal of Chinese Studies
N.S., 1(3):61-87, 1958.

55.   Lucas, Alfred.   Ancient Egyptian Materials and Industries.   3rd ed., rev.   London: Edward Arnold and
Co., 1948.

56.   Ludwig, Emil.   The Nile.   New York: Pyramid Books,
1963.

57.   Madan, Falconer.   Books in Manuscript.   London: K.
Paul, Trench, Trubner, 1893.   Reprinted 1920.

58.   Mansoor, Menahem.   The Dead Sea Scrolls.   Leiden:
E.S. Brill, 1964.

59.   Maskell, Alfred.   Ivories.   London: Methuen, 1905.

60.   Maskell, William.   Ivories, Ancient and Mediaeval.
London: Chapman and Hall, 1875.

61.   McKerrow, Ronald B.   An Introduction to Bibliography
for Literary Students.   Oxford: Clarendon Press,
1927.   Much important information on books, etc.,
in addition to bibliography.

62.   _____.   Introduction to Bibliography for Literary
Students.   Oxford: Clarendon Press, 1962.   This
reprint of the 1928 revised second impression is,
with Esdaile's Manual of Bibliography, an invaluable
reference on book construction, materials, binding,
etc., as they pertain to analytical bibliography.

63.   "Meander and the Mummy," Time 82:63-66, October
11, 1963.   Describes briefly the work of the Institut
de Papyrologie in the Sorbonne.   Recently a long
scroll of papyrus recovered from the wrappings of
a mummy was identified as part of an unknown play
of Meander's.

64.   Milik, J. T.   "Copper Document from Cave IV, Qumran," Bibl. Archaeology 19, September 1956.

65.   Munsell, Joel.   A Chronology of Paper and Paper-
Making.   Albany: J. Munsell, 1856.   An excellent
capsule review of the crafts of papyrus, parchment
and paper-making from 670 B.C. to the middle of
the 19th century.

66.   Newton, A. Edward.   This Book-Collecting Game.
Boston: Little, Brown & Co., 1928.   Hints to collectors and bibliophiles.

67.   Nixon, H. M.   "The Baltimore Binding Exhibition."
The Book Collector 7(4):419-426, 1958.   A
critical review of an important exhibition by a world-

       renowned authority.

68. Nordstrand, Ove K. Meddelelser om Konservering 1(6):18-22, 1968. In Danish. A list of the oldest Danish books about the technique of book-paintings, decorative and fine arts, arranged chronologically.

69. North Carolina, State Department of Archives and History. The North Carolina Historical Commission: Forty Years of Public Service, 1903-1943. Raleigh: North Carolina Historical Commission, 1943.

70. O'Conor, J. F. X. Facts About Bookworms. London: Suckling & Co., 1898. Their history in literature and work in libraries.

71. Orcutt, W. D. The Kingdom of Books. Boston: Little, Brown, 1927. Colored frontispiece with halftone and line illustrations of book design over the centuries.

72. Orne, Jerrold. Language of the Foreign Book Trade: Abbreviations, Terms, Phrases. 2nd ed. Chicago: American Library Association, 1962. 222 pp.

73. P'an Chi-hsing. "The Earliest Specimen of Paper Made of Plant Fiber," Wen Wu II, 1964. Describes paper unearthed in China in 1957 that was made in 206 B. C.

74. Pedley, Katherine G. The Library at Qumran. Berkeley: The Peacock Press, 1964. A librarian looks at the Dead Sea Scrolls.

75. Pinner, H. L. The World of Books in Classical Antiquity. New York: Humanities Press, 1958.

76. Pizzetta, Jules. Historia de un Pliego de Papel. Madrid: Biblioteca Cientifica Recreative (circa 1900). History of paper, paper making, writing and writing materials, books and printing, book making from the Spanish point of view.

77. Plant, Marjorie. The English Book Trade. London: George Allen & Unwin, 1965. An economic history of the making and sale of books including much information on bookbinding, paper, ink and other binding materials. Covers period from introduction of printing to modern times.

78. Pliny. Natural History. Cambridge, Mass.: Harvard University Press, 1952. vol. 8, ch. 11-12. Gives directions for making papyrus as it was done about A. D. 50; also, references to use of citrus leaves and juices of cedar as insect repellents.

79. [No entry.]

80. Plomer, H. R. "[Petition Regarding] The Makers of Embroidered Bindings," The Library 3rd Series, X,

1919. pp. 129-132.

81. Pollard, A. W. (ed.). Bibliographica. 3 vol. London:
     1895-97. Papers on books, their history and art.

82. Poole, J. B. and R. Reed. "The Preparation of Leather
     and Parchment by the Dead Sea Scrolls Community, "
     Technology and Culture 3(1):1-26, 1962.

83. Roberts, C. H. "Books in the Graeco-Roman World
     and in the New Testament, " The Cambridge History
     of the Bible. Cambridge, England: University
     Press, 1970. Vol. 1. A discussion of the emergence
     of the codex in lieu of scrolls as the preferred book
     form.

84. Ryder, M. L. "Parchment--Its History, Manufacture
     and Composition, " Journal of the Society of Archi-
     vists 3:391-399, 1964.

85. Schindler, B. "Preliminary Account of the Work of
     Henri Maspero Concerning the Chinese Documents
     on Wood and Paper Discovered by Sir Aurel Stein
     on His Third Expedition in Central Asia, " Asia Ma-
     jor N. S. 1:216-264, 1949.

86. Stark, L. M. "Branded Books from Mexican Li-
     braries, " Bulletin 46(8):738-741, 1942. New York
     Public Library.

87. Stein, Sir Mark Aurel. "Notes on Ancient Chinese
     Documents Discovered Along the Han Frontier Wall
     in the Desert of Tun-huang, " New China Review
     3:243-253, 1921.

✗ 88. Stokes, Roy (ed.). Esdaile's Manual of Bibliography.
     New York: Barnes and Noble, 1969. Fourth re-
     vised edition of this important manual which together
     with McKerrow offers much on book construction,
     materials, binding, etc. in their relation to analyti-
     cal bibliography.

✓89. Storm, Colton and Howard Peckham. Invitation to
     Book Collecting. New York: Bowker, 1947.

90. Streeter, Burnett Hillman. The Chained Library: A
     Survey of Four Centuries in the Evolution of the
     English Library. London: Macmillan and Co.,
     1931.

91. Stroupe, Henry S. "The North Carolina Department
     of Archives and History: the First Half Century, "
     North Carolina Historical Review 31(2):184-200,
     April 1954.

✓92. Sullivan, Sir Edward. The Book of Kells. London:
     Studio Publications, 1942. The story of a mediaeval
     book.

93.   Targ, William (ed). Bouillabaisse for Bibliophiles.
      Cleveland: World Publishing Co. , 1955. Reprinted
      1968 by The Scarecrow Press.

94.   Taylor, E. Fairfax. "Bibliography, " The Encyclopae-
      dia Britannica. 9th ed. Edinburgh: Adam and
      Charles Black, 1875. An excellent introduction to
      the science of the material as well as literary
      classification of books.

95.   Taylor, Isaac. History of the Transmission of An-
      cient Books to Modern Times. Liverpool: Ed-
      ward Howell, 1875.

96.   Thompson, James Westfall. Ancient Libraries.
      Berkeley: Univ. of California Press, 1940.

97.   _____. The Mediaeval Library. Chicago: Uni-
      versity of Chicago Press, 1939.

98.   Thompson, Lawrence S. , Bibliokleptomania. Berke-
      ley, Calif. : Peacock Press, 1968.

99.   _____. Bibliopegia Fantastica. New York: New
      York Public Library, 1947. A description of many
      unusual and "freak" bindings on books. Contains
      many references to other articles on bookbinding
      curiosities.

100. Tsien Tsuen-Hsuin [also, Ch'ien Ts'un-hsün]. Written
      on Bamboo and Silk. Chicago: University of Chi-
      cago Press, 1962. Thoroughly documented history
      of the beginnings of Chinese books and inscriptions
      including writings on stone and jade, metals and
      clay, and bones and shells, as well as bamboo and
      silk. Lengthy and excellent bibliography of Chinese
      literature on the subject.

101. Tweney, George H. "Bookbinding and the Collector, "
      American Book Collector 15(1):25, 1964.

102. Ure, Andrew. Dictionary of Arts, Manufactures and
      Mines. London: Longman, Brown, Green & Long-
      man, 1843.

103. Warren, S. R. & S. N. Clark (eds). Public Libraries
      in the United States of America. Washington:
      Dept. of Interior, 1876. Among many articles in
      part 1 is one on library buildings by J. S. Winsor.

104. Waterer, John W. "Irish Book-Satchels or Budgets, "
      Medieval Archaeology 12, 1968. A study of three
      surviving pieces including an analysis of the method
      of construction.

105. Wilder, Emily. "An Interesting Study, " The Book-
      Lover 4:205-206, 1903.

106. Wiseman, D. J. "Books in the Ancient Near East
      and the Old Testament, " The Cambridge History

of the Bible. vol. 1. Cambridge, England: University Press, 1970. Discusses the material form of books in the period of the Old Testament (papyrus clay tablets, writing boards).

107. Wroth, Lawrence. Some Reflections on the Book Arts in Mexico. Cambridge, Mass.: Harvard College Library, 1945.

108. Wu, K. T. "Libraries and Book Collecting in China before the Invention of Printing," T'ien Hsia Monthly 5:237-260, 1937.

109. _____. "Scholarship, Book Production and Libraries School," Unpublished Ph. D. Dissertation. Graduate School University of Chicago, 1944.

DEVELOPMENT OF THE BOOK

110. Ackroyd, P. R. (ed.). The Cambridge History of the Bible. Cambridge, Eng.: University Press, 1970. Includes an excellent discussion of books in the ancient world (as artifacts).

111. Arnold, Thomas W. (Sir) and Adolf Grohmann. The Islamic Book. London: Pegasus Press, 1929. pp. 37, 44, 57.

112. "Art and Skill Employed in Early Book-Making," The Book-Lover 3:393-395, 1902.

113. Audin, Marius. Le Livre; Son Architecture Sa Technique. Paris: Editions G. Crès et Cie, 1924.

114. Béraldi, Henri. La Reliure au XIXe Siècle. 4 vols. Paris: L. Conquet, 1895-97. The standard account, written most entertainingly.

115. Blumenthal, Joseph. "The Great Printed Book: From Gutenberg to the Oxford Lectern Bible," Journal American Institute of Graphic Arts 15:12-16, 1969; 16:8-10, 1970.

116. Bookbinding in Great Britain 16th to 20th Century. London: Maggs Brothers, 1964. (catalog #893.) Many photographs of fine bindings identified as to time and binder. Illustrates changes in bookbinding style over the years.

117. Bouchot, Henri. The Book: Its Printers, Illustrators and Binders. London: H. Grevel and Co., 1890.

√ 118. Bühler, Curt F. The Fifteenth Century Book: The Scribes, the Printers, the Decorators. Philadelphia:

University of Philadelphia Press, 1960.
119. Caille, Jean de la. Histoire de l'imprimerie et de
      librairie où l'ou voit son origine et son progress
      jusqu'à 1689. Paris: 1689. This early account
      of book making, etc. must be used with caution.
      Brunet in his Manuel du Libraire states that de la
      Caille is not a very exact writer.
120. Carter, Thomas F. The Invention of Printing in
      China. New York: Columbia University Press,
      1925. Much information on early oriental book
      building techniques as well as printing and illustra-
      tion.
✓ 121. Carter, John. ABC for Book-Collectors. 3rd ed.,
      rev. New York: Knopf, 1966. An extremely use-
      ful collection of definitions of terms used in book-
      making, binding, repair, restoration, etc.
122. _____. Binding Variants in English Publishing,
      1820-1900. London: Archibald Constable, 1923.
      A further development of Sadleir's first attempts
      at classification.
123. _____. More Binding Variants. London: Archi-
      bald Constable, 1938.
124. _____. "English Publisher's Bindings 1800-1900, "
      Bulletin 40(8):655-664, 1936. New York Public Li-
      brary. Description of an exhibition designed to
      show the changing forms in which books appeared
      in the 19th century.
125. _____. Publisher's Cloth. An Outline History.
      New York: R. R. Bowker, 1935. (London: Con-
      stable, 1935). A small pamphlet written and is-
      sued in connection with the New York Public Li-
      brary's 1935 exhibition of English publishers' bind-
      ings 1800-1900.
126. Carter, John and Brooke Crutchley. "Bookbinding, "
      The Printed Book. Chapter 9. Cambridge, Eng-
      land: Cambridge University Press, 1951.
127. Chapman, R. W. "Notes on Eighteenth-Century Book-
      binding, " Transactions of the Bibliographical Soci-
      ety, The Library December 1923.
128. Ch'ien Tsuen-Hsuin [also: Tsien Tsuen-hsuin]. Writ-
      ten on Bamboo and Silk: the Beginnings of Chinese
      Books and Inscriptions. Chicago: University of
      Chicago Press, 1962. The University of Chicago
      studies in library science. "Quasi-paper and paper
      manuscripts, " pp. 131-57.
✓ 129. Cobden-Sanderson, T. J. The Ideal Book or Book
      Beautiful. Hammersmith: The Doves Press, 1900.

130. Dahl, Svend. History of the Book. Metuchen, N. J. :
      The Scarecrow Press, 1958. The English edition
      of this book by a famous Danish librarian.
131. Dal, Erik. Scandinavian Bookmaking in the Twentieth
      Century. Urbana: University of Illinois Press,
      1969.
132. Davenport, Cyril James. The Book and Its History
      and Development. New York: Van Nostrand, 1908.
      All of Davenport's work, except his life of Payne,
      must be used with caution because of questionable
      research.
133. Degaast, Georges and Germaine Rigaud. Les Sup-
      ports de la Pensée Historique. Paris: 1942.
      Chiefly on the history of papermaking. Includes a
      bibliography.
134. The Dolphin No. 2, "A Journal of the Making of
      Books. " New York: Limited Editions Club, 1935.
135. Du Halde, P. "Of the Paper, Ink, and Pencils, Also
      of the Printing and Binding of Chinese Books, "
      The General History of China, Including an Exact
      and Particular Account of Their Customs, Manners,
      Ceremonies, Religion, Arts, and Sciences. 4
      vols. London: 1736.
136. Evelyn, John (ed.). Instructions Concerning Erecting
      of a Library. 1661. (See also Naude, G. [167].)
137. Ede, Charles (ed.). The Art of the Book: Some
      Record of Work Carried Out in Europe and the
      U. S. A. , (1939-1950). London: Studio Publications,
      1951. Mainly illustration.
138. Flacon, Albert. L'Univers des Livres. Paris: Her-
      mann, 1961. Study of the history of the book
      form, earliest times to the end of the 18th cen-
      tury. Bibliography.
139. Folmsbee, Beulah. A Little History of the Horn
      Book. Boston: The Horn Book, 1942.
140. Glaister, G. A. Glossary of the Book. London:
      George Allen and Unwin, 1960. Terms used in
      paper making, printing, bookbinding, and publish-
      ing.
141. The Golden Book. Chicago: Pascal Covici, 1927.
142. Goldschmidt, E. P. The Printed Book of the Ren-
      aissance. Amsterdam: Gérard Th. van Heusden,
      1966. Three lectures on type, illustrations and
      ornament; many illustrations.
143. Grycz, J. On the History and Techniques of the
      Book. Wrocław: 1951. In Polish, but of value
      because of 106 illustrations.

144. Hanson, T. W. Book Handbook. 1948.
145. Harper, Joseph Henry. The House of Harper. New
      York: Harper, 1912.
146. Harthan, John. Bookbindings. London: H. M. S. O. ,
      1950. This Victoria and Albert Museum illustrated
      booklet is a concise summary of the evolution of
      book decoration in the Near East and Europe.
147. Hobson, A. R. A. "Two Renaissance Bindings, "
      The Book Collector 7(3):265-268, 1958. Author
      deduces from evidence on two 15th-century bind-
      ings that gold tooling was introduced into Europe
      from the Near East through northeast Italy.
148. Holme, Charles (ed.). The Art of the Book: a Re-
      view of Some Recent European and American Work
      in Typography, Page Decoration and Binding. Lon-
      don: Le Studio, 1914. Quarto, mainly illustra-
      tion.
149. Hummel, Arthur, W. "The Development of the Book
      in China, " Journal of Oriental Studies 61:71-76,
      1941.
150. Ivins, W. M. , Jr. The Arts of the Book. New
      York: Metropolitan Museum of Art, 1924.
151. Jennett, Sean. The Making of Books. 3rd ed. Lon-
      don: Faber and Faber, 1964. General knowledge
      on the manufacture, structure and design of books.
152. Kepes, Gyorgy and others. Graphic Forms: The
      Arts as Related to the Book. Cambridge, Mass. :
      Harvard University Press, 1949.
153. Koops, Matthias. Historical Account of the Sub-
      stances Which Have Been Used to Describe Events,
      and to Convey Ideas, from the Earliest Date to the
      Invention of Paper. London: Jaques and Co. ,
      1801.
154. Lee, Marshall. Books for Our Time. New York:
      Oxford University Press, 1951.
155. _____ . Bookmaking: The Illustrated Guide to De-
      sign and Production. New York: R. R. Bowker,
      1965. Basic information on book construction.
156. Lehmann-Haupt, Hellmut; L. C. Wroth, and Rollo G.
      Silver. The Book in America. New York: R. R.
      Bowker Co. , 1952.
√ 157. Lejard, André (ed.). The Art of the French Book.
      London: P. Elek, 1947. Well illustrated history
      of French book production from early manuscripts
      to the present time.
158. Levarie, N. The Art and History of Books. New
      York: James H. Heineman, 1968. A source book

that gives in one volume a visual panorama of
books since the beginning of the written word. Excellent bibliography and index.

159. Levey, Martin. "Mediaeval Arabic Bookmaking, "
Transactions American Philosophical Society 52(4)
1962.

160. Lo Chin-Tang. The Evolution of Chinese Books. (In
English and Chinese.) Taipei: Natural History
Museum, 1959. Technical information on early
oriental book making.

161. Mansfield, Edgar. Modern Design in Bookbinding.
London: Peter Owen, 1966. Illustrations with
technical notes, of work by the foremost technical
designer of fine bindings. Includes essay on the
history of fine binding by the British Museum's
Howard Nixon.

162. Marius-Michel, H. La Reliure Française, Commerciale et Industrielle, Depuis l'Invention de l'Imprimerie jusqu'à nos jours. Paris: Morgand &
Fatout, 1881. Twenty-three plates of which two
show actual specimens of decorated cloth bindings.
Numerous illustrations in the text.

163. McMurtrie, Douglas C. The Golden Book. New
York: Pascal Covici, 1927. Traces the development of bookmaking from the beginning of written
records to the present time.

√ 164. _____. The Book. 3rd rev. ed. New York:
Oxford University Press, 1957. The story of
printing and bookmaking.

165. Middleton, Bernard C. A History of English Craft
Bookbinding Technique. New York: Hafner Publishing, 1963.

166. "Modern Book Production, " The Studio. London:
1928.

√ 167. Naude, G. Instructions Concerning Erecting of a
Library. Cambridge, Mass.: Houghton, Mifflin,
1903. A reprint of John Evelyn's 1661 edition of
Naude's 1627 book.

168. Orcutt, William Dana. Master Makers of the Book.
Garden City, N.Y.: Doubleday, Doran, 1928.

√ 169. _____. In Quest of the Perfect Book. Boston:
Little, Brown, 1926.

170. Plant, Marjorie. The English Book Trade. London:
George Allen and Unwin, 1965. An economic study
including materials, binding methods, etc., among
other problems. Fully documented.

171.   Power, John.   Handy Book about Books.   New York:
       Sabin & Sons, 1873.

172.   Putnam, George Haven.   Books and Their Makers
       During the Middle Ages.   2 vols.   New York: Hil-
       lary House, 1962.   A study of the conditions of the
       production and distribution of literature from the
       fall of the Roman Empire to the close of the 17th
       century.

173.   Quaritch, B.   A Collection from Examples of Historic
       or Artistic Binding.   London: Bernard Quaritch,
       1889.   103 colored plates illustrating the history of
       binding as a branch of the decorative arts.

174.   Rawlings, Gertrude Burford.   The Story of Books.
       New York: Appleton, 1902.

175.   Rico y Sinobas, Manuel.   El Arte de Libro en
       España.   Madrid: 1941.

176.   Roberts, C. H.   "The Codex," Proceedings of the
       British Academy 40:169-204, 1954.   The best mod-
       ern treatment of the development of the codex form
       of books.

177.   Rollins, Carl Purington.   "A Survey of Contemporary
       Bookmaking," The Dolphin no. 2, pp. 259-329,
       1935.

178.   Sadleir, Michael.   Evolution of Publishers' Binding
       Styles, 1770-1900.   London: Constable, 1930.

179.   _____.   "XIX Century Fiction," The Book Collector
       2(1), 1953.   Includes an expansion and refinement
       of the author's classification of 19th-century binding
       cloths.

180.   _____.   "The Nomenclature of Nineteenth Century
       Cloth Grains," The Book Collector 2(1):54-58.
       1953.   Photographs of 24 named cloth grains pre-
       sented as a potentially standard vocabulary.

181.   Sarre, F.   Islamic Bookbindings.   London: Kegan,
       Paul, Trench and Trubner, 1923.

182.   Schmieder, Eberhard and Ernst Kellner.   Schrift und
       Buch.   Leipzig: L. Staackman Verlag, 1939.   A
       delightful illustrated treatise on books and printing.
       Knowledge of German is not essential.

183.   (Trow Press).   Bibliopegistic, to which is appended a
       glossary of some terms used in the craft with il-
       lustrations of fine bindings.   New York: Trow
       Press, 1914.   32 p. illus.

184.   Taubert, Sigfred.   Bibliopola: Pictures and Texts
       about the Book Trade.   London: Penguin Press,
       1966.   2 vols. with English, French and German
       text profusely illustrated in color.   Includes a few

references to bookbinding.

185.   Taylor, E. Fairfax. "Books," Encyclopaedia Britan-
        nica 9th ed. Edinburgh: Adam and Charles Black,
        1876. Excellent essay on the material evolution of
        books and book materials from earliest times.
186.   Thuma, Max. Die Werkstoffe des Buchbinders: Ihre
        Herstellung und Verarbeitung. 4th ed. Stuttgart:
        Max Hettler, 1960. This training manual deals
        with all materials used in books.
✓ 187. Tsien Tsuen-hsuin [also, Ch'ien Tsuen-Hsuin] Written
        on Bamboo and Silk. Chicago: University of Chi-
        cago Press, 1962. The beginnings of Chinese
        books and inscriptions. Excellent technical and
        historical data on writing materials from bone,
        clay and shells to bamboo, silk and other prede-
        cessors of paper.
188.   Vachon, Marius. Les Artes et les Industries du
        Papier en France 1871-1894. Paris: Librairies
        Imprimeries Réunies, 1895. Illustrated descrip-
        tions include book, bookbinding, print and printmak-
        ing aspects of papermaking in France.
189.   Wedmore, Frederick. On Books and Arts. London:
        Redway 1898.
190.   Whitehouse, Howard, J. The Craftsmanship of Books.
        1929.
191.   Williamson, Hugh. Methods of Book Design. Lon-
        don: Oxford University Press, 1966. An examina-
        tion of the practices of an industrial craft includ-
        ing bookbinding and paper manufacture.
192.   Wroth, L. C. (ed.). A History of the Printed Book.
        No. 3 of The Dolphin. New York: The Limited
        Editions Club, 1938.
193.   _____. Some Reflections on the Book Arts of
        Mexico. Cambridge, Mass.: Harvard College Li-
        brary, 1945.

EARLY WRITING AND CALLIGRAPHY

194.   Abraham b. Judah Ibn Hayyim. Livro de como se
        fazen as côres. Loule, Portugal: 1262. Pub-
        lished by D. S. Blondheim: "An old Portuguese
        work on manuscript illumination," Jewish Quarterly
        Review 19(3):97-135.

195.   Alexander, J. J. G. and A. C. de la Mare.   The
        Italian Manuscripts in the Library of Major J. R.
        Abbey.   London: Faber and Faber, 1969.
196.   Alexander, Shirley M.   On the Origins and Develop-
        ment of the Luxury Manuscript.   New York: Con-
        servation Center, New York University, 1966.   A
        study of gold writing and purple parchment.
√ 197. Anderson, Donald M.   The Art of Written Forms:
        The Theory and Practice of Calligraphy.   New
        York: Holt, Rinehart and Winston, 1969.   A re-
        view of writing from before the development of the
        alphabet to contemporary calligraphy; historical
        and technical.   Profusely illustrated.   Exhaustive
        bibliography of historical and technical references.
198.   "The Art of Writing," The UNESCO Courier March,
        1964.   This brief history was later issued as The
        Art of Writing.   Paris: UNESCO, 1965.   An ex-
        cellent source book with fine notes and illustrations
        on all the important families of writing.
199.   Berger, P.   Histoire de l'Ecriture dans l'Antiquité.
        Paris: Imprimerie Nationale 1891.
200.   Couderc, C.   Les Enluminures des Manuscrits du
        Moyen Age, VIe au XVe Siècle.   Paris: Biblio-
        thèque Nationale, 1927.   119 pages of text and 80
        plates.
√ 201. Diringer, David.   The Illuminated Book.   London:
        Faber & Faber, 1967.   Contains much information
        and a wealth of illustrations.   Virtually an ency-
        clopedia on illumination.
202.   Evelyn, John.   Sculptura: or, The History and Art
        of Chalcography.   London: 1662.   A history of
        engraving on copper with a section on the "new
        manner of engraving; or mezzo tinto. "
203.   Falconer, Madan.   Books in Manuscript.   London:
        1893.
√ 204. Filby, P. William.   Calligraphy and Handwriting in
        America.   Caledonia, New York: Italimuse, Inc. ,
        1963.   An illustrated volume with 100 plates de-
        scribing the development of handwriting in America.
205.   Gelb, I. J.   A Study of Writing.   2nd rev. ed.   Chi-
        cago: University of Chicago Press-Phoenix Books,
        1963.
206.   The Gutenberg Documents.   New York: Oxford Uni-
        versity Press, 1941.
207.   Harrison, F. Canon F.   Treasures of Illumination:
        English Manuscripts of the 14th century (c. 1250
        to 1400).   London: 1937.

208. Heal, A. The English Writing Masters and Their
          Copy Books 1570-1800. Cambridge, England: Uni-
          versity Press, 1931. A bibliographical dictionary
          and a bibliography with an introduction on the de-
          velopment of handwriting.

209. Humphreys, Henry Noel. The Illuminated Books of
          the Middle Ages. London: Longman, Brown,
          Green and Longman, 1859. Account of the develop-
          ment and progress of the art of illumination from
          the 4th to the 17th centuries.

210. _____ . The Origin and Progress of the Art of
          Writing. London: Ingram Cooke & Co., 1853.

211. James, M. R. The Wanderings and Homes of Manu-
          scripts. New York: Macmillan, 1919.

212. Johnson, Elmer D. Communication. 3rd ed. Metuchen,
          N. J.: The Scarecrow Press, 1966. An introduction to
          the history of the alphabet, writing, printing, books
          and libraries.

✓ 213. Johnston, Edward. Writing and Illuminating and Let-
          tering. London: Pitman, 1945.

214. Kenyon, F. G. "The Papyrus Roll," Books and
          Readers in Ancient Greece and Rome. Oxford:
          University Press, 1951. Illustrated with facsimiles.

215. Ker, Neil Ripley. Fragments of Medieval Manuscripts
          Used as Paste-downs in Oxford Bindings with a
          Survey of Oxford Bindings, c. 1515-1620. Oxford:
          Oxford Bibliographical Society, 1954.

216. Lamb, C. M. (ed.). The Calligrapher's Handbook.
          London: Faber and Faber, 1956. Illus. Though
          designed for the practicing calligrapher of today,
          this contains historical material of interest to the
          preservationist. See also pp. 199-223, S. M.
          Cockerell's "The Binding of Manuscripts."

217. Mason, William A. A History of the Art of Classical
          and Mediaevil Writing. New York: Macmillan,
          1928.

218. Miner, Dorothy; Victor Carlson, and P. W. Filby.
          Two Thousand Years of Calligraphy. Baltimore:
          Walters Gallery of Art, 1965. An illustrated cata-
          log that is useful for dating calligraphic styles.

219. Ogg, Oscar. The 26 Letters. New York: Crowell,
          1948.

220. Pächt, Otto and J. J. G. Alexander. Illuminated
          Manuscripts in the Bodleian Library. Oxford: Uni-
          versity Press, 1966. vol. 1. German, Dutch,
          French and Spanish schools. Frontispiece in color
          and 66 plates. First of three projected volumes.

221.   Pierce, H. K. (trans.). The Instruments of Writing.
        Newport, R. I.: Berry Hill Press, 1953.   A
        translation from Palatino's writing book of 1540.
222.   Quaile, Ed. Illuminated Manuscripts: Their Origin,
        History and Characteristics.   A Sketch.   Liverpool:
        H. Young & Sons, 1897.
223.   Thompson, E. Maunde. "Palaeography, " Encyclo-
        paedia Britannica 9th ed.   Edinburgh: Adam &
        Charles Black, 1885.   An excellent introduction to
        the study of ancient handwriting by the then prin-
        cipal librarian at the British Museum.   Discussion
        includes early writing materials and book forms,
        writing styles, manuscripts as books, palimsests,
        and the restoration of erased or obliterated writ-
        ing.
√ 224. Valentine, Lucia N.   Ornament in Mediaeval Manu-
        scripts [a glossary].   London: Faber & Faber,
        1968.   An attempt to find a common language for
        manuscript ornament.   Well indexed.
225.   Van Hoesen, Henry Bartlett.   "History of Writing, "
        in Van Hoesen and Walters' Bibliography, Practical
        Enumerative, Historical, pp. 259-315.   New York:
        1928.

EARLY BOOKS

226.   Aga-Oglu, M.   Persian Bookbindings in the 15th Cen-
        tury.   Ann Arbor, Michigan: University of Michi-
        gan Press, 1935.
227.   "Ancient Books. " Art Journal 11:279, 1849.
228.   Arnett, J. A. [i. e., J. Hannett].   An Inquiry into
        the Nature and Form of the Books of the Ancients.
        London: Groombridge, 1837.
229.   Besterman, Theodore.   Early Printed Books to the
        End of the 16th Century.   Geneva: Societas Bib-
        liographica, 1961.   Contains bibliographies.
√ 230. Bühler, Curt F.   The Fifteenth Century Book: The
        Scribes, The Printers, The Decorators.   Phila-
        delphia: University of Philadelphia Press, 1960.
231.   Bushnell, George Herbert.   From Papyrus to Print:
        a Bibliographical Miscellany.   London: Grafton &
        Co., 1947.
232.   _____.   From Bricks to Books.   London: Grafton

        & Co., 1949.

233.   Carter, Thomas F. The Invention of Printing in China and its Spread Westward. New York: Columbia University Press, 1925. Includes descriptions of illustrating methods and details oriental book construction.

✓ 234.   Diringer, David. The Illuminated Book: Its History and Production. London: Faber & Faber, 1967.

235.   Flacon, Albert. L'Univers des Livres. Paris: Hermann, 1961. A history of the book since prehistoric times by a professor of history at Collège Technique Estienne.

236.   Grolier Club. A Description of Early Printed Books Owned by the Grolier Club. New York: 1894. Twenty-six facsimile plates of 15th-century books.

237.   Haebler, Konrad. The Story of Incunabula. New York: The Grolier Club, 1933.

238.   Hannett, John. An Enquiry into the Nature and Form of the Books of the Ancients: with a History of the Art of Bookbinding. 6th ed. London: Simpkin, Marshall, 1865.

239.   Kenyon, Frederick G. Ancient Books and Modern Discoveries. Chicago: The Caxton Club, 1927.

240.   . Books and Readers in Ancient Greece and Rome. Oxford: University Press, 1951.

241.   Klepikov, S. A. "Russian Bookbindings from the 11th to the 17th Century," The Book Collector 10(4):408-423. London: 1961.

242.   Kup, Karl. A Fifteenth-Century Girdle Book. New York: New York Public Library, 1939.

243.   Lamacraft, C. T. "Early Bookbindings from a Coptic Monastery," The Library 4th series, 20(2):214-233, September 1939.

244.   Levarie, N. The Art and History of Books. New York: James H. Heineman, 1968. Many illustrations of early books beginning with clay tablets and continuing through medieval manuscripts and early printed books to the present time.

245.   Madan, Falconer. Books in Manuscript. London: Kegan Paul, Trench & Trubner, 1920. Includes technical information on the making of early books.

246.   Sotheby, S. L. The Block Books Preserved in the Bibliothèque Imperiale, Paris. London: T. Richards, 1859.

247.   Turner, E. G. Athenian Books in the Fifth and Fourth Centuries B. C. London: H. K. Lewis & Co., 1952.

248.   Wilson, R. N. P. Books and Their History. London:
        T. C. and E. C. Jach, (n. d.). Juvenile but excel-
        lently done.

NON-CODEX BOOKS

249.   "Ancient Form and Material of Books, " Penny Maga-
        zine, 5:310, 1837.
250.   Arnett, J. A. [i. e. , J. Hannett]. An Inquiry into
        the Nature and Form of the Books of the Ancients,
        London: Groombridge, 1837, p. 212.
251.   Bedale, C. L. Sumerian Tablets from Umma. Man-
        chester: The University Press, 1915.
252.   Černý, Jaroslav. Paper and Books in Ancient Egypt.
        London: H. K. Lewis & Co. , 1952. 36 pp. with
        references. An inaugural lecture delivered at
        University College, London, May 29, 1947.
253.   Chiera, Edward. They Wrote on Clay. Chicago:
        University of Chicago Press, 1938. This descrip-
        tion of early Babylonian-Assyrian civilization con-
        tains much information on clay tablets.
254.   Locke, Leland. The Ancient Quipu or Knot Record.
        New York: American Museum of Natural History,
        1923.
255.   Tsien Tsuen-Hsuin [also, Ch'ien Ts'un-hsün]. Written
        on Bamboo and Silk; the Beginning of Chinese Books
        and Inscriptions. Chicago: University of Chicago
        Press, 1962.
256.   Tuer, A. History of the Horn Book. London: 1896.
        Reprinted, Amsterdam: S Emmching, 1971.

BOOKBINDING CRAFT

257.   Andrews, William Loring. Bibliopegy in the United
        States. New York: Dodd, Mead, 1902. The first
        book on American bookbinding by a charter mem-
        ber of the Grolier Club. 128 p.
258.   Arnett, J. A. [i. e. , J. Hannett]. Bibliopegia or The
        Art of Bookbinding in all its Branches. London:
        Groombridge, 1835.

259.   . The Bookbinders' School of Design as Applied to the Combination of Tools in the Art of
Finishing. London: Groombridge, 1837. 8 plates
engraved by Joseph Morris.

260. "A Short History of Bookbinding," Publishers Weekly
September 2, 1922, reprinted in The Library Binder 15(2), December, 1967.

261. Battershall, Fletcher. "Bookbinding for Bibliophiles,"
The Book-Lover III pp. 225-226, 1902-03.

262. The Bindery that Jill Built. London: Guild of Woman
Binders, 1901. An illustrated souvenir showing
women binders at work in London.

263. Binns, Norman E. "Bookbinding, its Evolution and
History," An Introduction to Historical Bibliography. London: The Association of Assistant Librarians, 1953. Chap. 20, pp. 285-318.

264. Blanc, Charles. "La Reliure," Gazette des Beaux
Arts, October and November, 1880.

265. Blanchon, H. L. Alphonse. L'Art et la Practique en
Reliure. Paris: J. Hetzel & Cie, 1898.

266. Bodleian Library. Gold-Tooled Bindings. Oxford:
Oxford University Press, 1951. A short history
of the technique of gold-tooled bookbinding, from
the first half of the 15th century when the Moors
were decorating books in Aragon, through the time
when gold-tooling was introduced into England during the reign of Henry VIII.

267. The Bookbinder's Manual. Containing a full description of leather and vellum binding, also instructions
for gilding of paper and book edges. Numerous
valuable recipes for sprinkling, coloring and marbling, together with a scale of bookbinder's charges.
5th ed. London: Cowie Printer (n. d., c. 1835).

268. The Bookbinders' Price Book. London: 1813. Mi-
nutely detailed prices established for their work
by the Associated Master-Bookbinders of London
and Westminster.

269. "Bookbinding from Craft to Industry," Publishers'
Weekly 196(22):56, 1969. Summary of an address
by James B. Blaine of the radical changes since
1945.

270. Bosch, G. K. "The Staff of the Scribes and Implements of the Discerning: an Excerpt," Ars
Orientalia 4:1-13, 1961. Translation of an A. D.
1100 Arab text on bookbinding.

271. Bosquet, E. La Reliure. Paris: Lahure, 1894.
The history and technology of binding and gold

tooling.

272.   Boudaroy, Fougeroux de.   "Art de Travailler les
        Cuirs Dorés,"   Descriptions des Arts et Metiers,
        etc. vol. 3, 1775.   Paris: Academie Royale des
        Sciences, 1771-1783 [1428].   Gilding as practiced
        in France, England and Holland in the 18th cen-
        tury.   Fold-out plates illustrating tools and equipment
        used in the elaborate decoration of leather for arti-
        facts other than books.

273.   Brassington, W. S.   History of the Art of Bookbind-
        ing, with Some Account of the Books of the An-
        cients.   London: Stock, 1894.

274.   Brassinne, Joseph.   La Reliure Mosane, 2 vols.
        Liege: DeCormaux, 1912-1932.   Supplemented by
        Verheyden's few published articles as in Le Livre
        en Brabant, 1935, and his catalog of the Antwerp
        Exhibition of 1930.   The last is a work of immense
        erudition, but its usefulness for the American
        reader is impaired by being written in Flemish and
        by its lack of illustrations.

275.   British Manufacturing Industry Series, 1877.   Volume
        on printing and bookbinding.

276.   British Museum.   Guide to the Exhibition in the King's
        Library, Illustrating the History of Printing, Mu-
        sic-printing, and Bookbinding.   London: British
        Museum, 1939.

277.   Browne, Sir Thomas.   Hydriotaphia.   London: H.
        Brome, 1658.

278.   Brunet, Gustave.   La Reliure Ancienne et Moderne.
        Paris: E. Rouveyre et G. Blond, 1884.

279.   Carter, John.   Binding Variants in English Publish-
        ing, 1820-1900.   London: Archibald Constable, 1923.

280.   _____ .   More Binding Variants.   London: Archi-
        bald Constable, 1938.

281.   _____ .   Publisher's Cloth: An Outline History of
        Publisher's Binding in England, 1820-1900.   New
        York: Bowker, 1935.

282.   _____ .   "The Origin of Publisher's Cloth Binding,"
        The Colophon Part 8, 1931.

283.   Clements, H. J. B.   "Check List of English Amorial
        Book-Stamps," The Book-Collector's Quarterly
        14:64-72, April-June, 1934.

284.   _____ .   "Check List of English Armorial Book-
        Stamps [cont.]," The Book-Collector's Quarterly
        15:68-78, July-September, 1934.

285.   _____ .   "Check List of English Armorial Book-
        Stamps [cont.]," The Book-Collector's Quarterly

16:64-72, October-December, 1934.

286. _____. "Check List of English Armorial Book-Stamps [cont.], " The Book-Collector's Quarterly 17:36-46, April-June, 1934.

287. _____. "Armorial Book-Stamps and their Owners, " The Library 4th series, 20:121-135, 1939-1940.

288. Clements, Jeff. Bookbinding. London: Aero Publications. 1968. 128 pages of basic instruction with 61 illustrations.

289. Cobden-Sanderson, T. J. "Craft Ideals, " Transactions of the National Association for the Advancement of Art and Its Applications to Industry. Liverpool: 1888.

√ 290. _____. The Ideal Book or Book Beautiful. Hammersmith: Dove Press, 1900.

291. _____. Bookbindings by T. J. Cobden-Sanderson. New York: Pierpont Morgan Library, 1969.

292. _____. The Journals of T. J. Cobden-Sanderson. 2 vols. London: R. Cobden-Sanderson, 1926.

293. Cockerell, Douglas. Bookbinding, 1905. A lecture by Douglas Cockerell delivered at Cambridge, May 16, 1902, with eight full-page illustrations of his bindings.

√ 294. _____. Bookbinding and the Care of Books. London: Pitman & Sons, 1925, Reprinted 1955. The best text on fine binding by an artist craftsman.

295. _____. "Development of Bookbinding Methods--Coptic Influence, " The Library 4th series, 13(1):1-19, June 1932.

296. _____. "Fine Bookbinding in England, " Art of the Book pp. 69-124. London: Studio Publications, 1914. Charles Holme, editor.

297. _____. "The Binding of the Codex Sinaiticus, " British Museum Quarterly 10:180-182, 1936.

√ 298. Comparato, Frank E. Books for the Millions. Harrisburg, Pa. : The Stackpole Company, 1971. This is the best book to date on commercial binding and book manufacture. Amply footnoted and excellent bibliography. A study of the men and machines.

299. Cundall, J. "Ancient and Modern Bookbinding, " Journal Franklin Institute 45:211, 1881.

300. Davenport, Cyril J. H. "The Decoration of Book-edges, " Bibliographica 2:385-407, London: 1896.

301. _____. "Bagford's Notes on Bookbindings, " Transactions of the Bibliographical Society 7:123-159, 1904. A presentation of Bagford's notes on bookbindings, preserved from two of his scrap books

written before 1716. The first is "Of Booke Binding Ancient" and gives an account of vellum rolls
and waxen diptychs. He treats boards, paste-
boards, and boards made of "oulde ropes," the
sewing and headbandings, and describes a few old
bindings which he had been able to collect. The
second paper is "Of Booke Binding Modourne" in
which he explains the various processes of collat-
ing, folding and beating the leaves and ruling the
books with red. Gilding is mentioned but not ex-
plained. The various specimens of bindings that
were included in "Booke Binding Modourne" are
described.

302.   Davis, Hassoldt. "Book Binding in the South Seas,"
        Scribner's Magazine 99:120-121, 1936. Interesting
        account of Mrs. Davis' use of local material for
        book covers.

303.   Derôme, L. La Reliure Deluxe. Paris: Edouard
        Rouveyre, 1888. A well illustrated discussion of
        the refinements of deluxe binding practices in
        France.

304.   Devauchelle, Roger. La Reliure en France; De Ces
        Origines à Nos Jours. Paris: Rousseau-Girard,
        1959.

√ 305. Diehl, Edith. Bookbinding. Its Background and
        Technique. 2 vols. New York: Rinehart & Co.,
        1946. Vol. 1: History, etc.; has a lengthy bibli-
        ography.

√ 306. Diringer, David. The Hand Produced Book. London:
        Hutchinson & Co., 1953.

307.   duBois, H. P. Historical Essay on the Art of Book-
        binding. New York: Bradstreet Press, 1883.

308.   Dudin, René Martin. "L'Art du Reliure et Doreur de
        Livres," Descriptions Des Artes et Metiers, etc.,
        vol. 8, 1777 [1418]. Paris: Academie Royale des
        Sciences, 1771-1783. This issue of Dudin's
        treatise on binding and gold tooling books has only
        two illustrative plates.

309.   Dutton, M. K. Historical Sketch of Bookbinding as
        an Art. Norwood, Mass.: Holliston Mills, 1926.
        Beginnings in Italy, France, England and America.

310.   Ede, Charles (ed.). "Hand Binding," The Art of the
        Book. London: Studio Publications, 1951.

311.   _____. "Commercial Binding," The Art of the
        Book. London: Studio Publications, 1951.

312.   Fair, Anthony. "English Bookbinding Today," Auction.
        New York: Parke-Bernet Galleries, June 1968.

313. Fletcher, W. Y. Bookbinding in France. London: Seeley & Co., 1894. A short but good history of French binding by a former Assistant Keeper of Printed Books in the British Museum.

√ 314. French, Hannah D.; Rogers, Joseph W.; and Lehmann-Haupt, Hellmut. Bookbinding in America. Portland, Me.: The Southworth Anthoensen Press, 1941. Reprinted New York: Bowker, 1967.

315. Gauffecourt, Capperonnier de. Traité de la Reliure des Livres. La Motte, France: 1763. Only 25 copies of this first book on bookbinding were printed.

316. "Gauffered Edges 16th Century, Method or Technique," Stone's Impressions vol. 4, 1934-1935.

317. Gottlieb, T. K. K. Hofbibliothek, Bucheinbände. Vienna: Anton Schroll, 1910.

318. Gratzl, E. Islamische Bucheinbände. Leipzig: Hiersemann, 1924.

319. Haebler, Konrad. Rollen-und Platten-Stempel des XVI-ten jahrhunderts, 2 vols. Leipzig: 1928-1929. Data on early German book decoration tools by the great authority in this field.

320. Hamanova, P. A History of Bookbinding from the Beginning to the End of the 19th Century. Prague: Orbis, 1959. 161 illustrations.

321. Hannigan, M. V. et al. "Evolution of the Relative Serviceability of Vegetable and Chrome Tanned Leathers for Bookbinding," Journal American Leather Chemists Association 60 (9) 1965.

322. Harrison, T. The Bookbinding Craft and Industry: An Outline of its History, Development and Technique, Illustrated, 2nd ed. London: Pitman, 1930.

323. Helwig, H. Das Deutsche Buchbinder Handwerk. 352 pp. Stuttgart: Hiersemann, 1962. Discusses German bookbinding since the Middle Ages.

√ 324. The History of Bookbinding, 525-1950. An exhibition held at the Baltimore Museum of Art, November 12, 1957, to January 12, 1958. Baltimore: Walters Art Gallery, 1957.

√ 325. Hobson, A. R. A. The Literature of Bookbinding. London: Cambridge University Press, 1954. Xerox

326. Hobson, G. D. "Further Notes on Romanesque Bindings," The Library 4th series, 15(2):161-211, 1934.

327. _____. "Some Early Bindings and Binders' Tools," The Library 4th series, 19:202-246, 1938.

328. Hoe, Robert. A Lecture on Bookbinding as a Fine Art. New York: The Grolier Club, 1886.

Delivered before the Grolier Club, February 26, 1885. Sixty-three illustrations.

329. Horne, Herbert Percy. The Binding of Books. London: Kegan Paul, Trench, and Trubner, 1894.

330. _____. The Binding of Books, 2nd ed. London: Kegan Paul, Trench and Trubner, 1915. An essay in the history of good-tooled bindings.

331. Husung, Maximilian Joseph. Bucheinbände aus der Preussischen Staatsbibliothek zu Berlin in historischer Folge erläutert. Leipzig: 1925.

332. _____. "Geschichte des Bucheinbändes," Handbuch der Bibliothekswissenschafts herausgegeben von Fritz Milkau 1:666-716, Leipzig: 1931.

333. _____. "Neues Materiell zur Frage des Stempeldrucks von Gutenberg," Gutenberg Festschrift pp. 66-72. Mainz: 1925. Description of binder's stamps in use before the invention of printing.

334. Hutner, J. C. Englische Miscellen Band 6. Tübingen: 1802.

335. Jackson, William A. "Our Ingenious Ancestors," Walpole Society Notebook 1963, pp. 3-6. Discusses binders' labels.

336. Kent, Henry Watson. "Some Notes on Mosaic Bookbinding," The Bibliographer 1:169-180, 1902.

337. Ker, Neil R. Paste-downs in Oxford Bindings. Oxford: Oxford Bibliographical Society, 1954. Describes fragments of medieval manuscripts used as pastedowns. Also includes a survey of bookbinding at Oxford in the 16th century.

338. Kersten, Paul. Der Exakte Bucheinbände. Halle, Germany: A. D. Saale Wilhelm Knapp, 1929.

339. Kiel, Gustav. Neue Bucheinbände. Leipzig: 1901. A well-illustrated monograph on late 19th-century elaborately decorated cloth book covers in Germany.

340. Klepikov, S. A. "Historical Notes on Ukrainian Bookbinding," The Book Collector 15(2):135-142, 1966. Technical details discussed fully.

341. _____. "Iz Istorii Russkogo Khudozhestvenhogo Pereplata," Kniga Moscow: 1959. The history of Russian craft bookbinding.

342. _____. "Russian Bookbinding from the Middle of the 17th to the End of the 19th Century," The Book Collector 11(4):437-447, 1962.

343. Lamb, Lynton. "The Binding of the Coronation Bible," The Book Collector 2(1):139, 1953. Photographs and description of the binding on the bible used at the coronation of Elizabeth II.

344. Lecky, Margaret. "Of Books and Bindings," Creative Crafts June/July, 1960. An introduction to fine binding by one of the foremost binders in America and a lecturer in Art at UCLA.

✓ 345. Lehmann-Haupt, Hellmut (ed.). Bookbinding in America. Portland, Me.: Southworth-Anthoensen Press, 1941, 293 pp. illus. Three essays: "Early American Bookbinding by Hand," by H. D. French; "The Rise of American Edition Binding," by J. W. Rogers; and "On the Rebinding of Old Books," by Hellmut Lehmann-Haupt. Reprinted New York: Bowker, 1967.

346. Leighton, Douglas. Modern Bookbinding, a Survey and a Prospect. London: London School of Printing, 1935. The technical challenge as presented in the fifth annual J. M. Dent Memorial Lecture, 1935.

347. Lesné. Poème Didactique en Six Chants. Paris: 1820. A poem about bookbinding by a bookbinder.

348. Levey, Martin; Krek Miroslav; and Husni Haddad. "Some Notes on the Chemical Technology in an Eleventh Century Arabic Work on Bookbinding," ISIS 47, 1956.

349. Lima, Matias. A Encadernação em Portugal. Gaia: 1933. Portuguese bookbinding.

350. Louisy, M. P. Le Livre et les Arts Qui S'y Rattachent. Paris: Librairie de Fermin-Didot et Cie, 1887. Includes chapters on history of paper, parchment and bookbinding in France to the end of the 18th century.

351. Marius-Michel, H. La Reliure Française Commerciale et Industrielle Depuis l'Invention de l'Imprimerie. Paris: Morgand & Fatout, 1881.

352. Martin, G. The Bookbinder's Complete Instructor in All Branches of Fine Binding: Particularly Marbling, Staining and Gilding the Covers and Edges of Books: With All the Late Improvements and Discoveries in That Useful Art. By a Practical Bookbinder. Peterhead, England: P. Buchan, 1823. 40 pp.

353. Matthews, Brander. Bookbindings Old and New. London: George Bell & Sons, 1896. Discusses early binding, the late 19th-century binders and 19th-century commercial binding, including a lengthy section on printed paper covers.

354. Matthews, William. Modern Bookbinding Practically Considered. New York: The Grolier Club, 1889.

A lecture delivered before the Grolier Club, March 25, 1885.

355. McCarthy, W. H. , Jr. "Outline of the History of Bookbinding, " The Dolphin 3:447-468, 1938.

356. Melville, Herman. A Thought on Bookbinding. Boston: Boston Bookbuilders' Workshop, 1948. Reprint of an unsigned H. Melville review of James Fenimore Cooper's The Red Rover in The Literary World, March 16, 1850, in which Melville comments on the importance of the design of book cover decoration to suit the subject of the book.   (See Birss, J. H. [8].)

357. Michon, Marie-Louise, La Reliure Française: Artes, Styles et Techniques. Paris: 1951.

358. Middleton, Bernard C. A History of English Craft Bookbinding Techniques. London: Hafner Publishing Co. , 1963. An excellent history plus much technical information.

✓ 359. Miner, Dorothy (ed.). The History of Bookbinding 525 AD to 1950 AD. Baltimore: Walters Art Gallery, 1950. Illustrated catalog.

360. Mitchell, William S. A History of Scottish Bookbinding. Edinburgh: Oliver & Boyd, 1955.

361. Mitius, O. "Frankische Lederschnittbände des XV. Jahrhunderts: ein burgeschicchtlicher Versuch, " Sammlung bibliothekswissenschaftlicher Arbeiten Heft 28 (2te ser. Heft 11) Leipzig: 1909.

362. "Modern Book Production, " The Studio 1928. Illustrations.

363. Morison, David. Bookbinding: Its History and Improvement. London: Simpkin Marshall Co. , 1841.

364. Moutard-Uldry, R. "L'Art de la Reliure en France, " Jardin des Artes 169, 1968. A condensed history of bookbinding in France from the 5th century.

365. [No entry.]

366. Nelson, Charles Alexander. Catalogue Raisonnee: Works on Bookbinding from the collection of Samuel Putnam Avery. Columbia University Library. New York: Privately printed, 1903.

367. "Oxford University Press Binding House, " The Periodical. London: March, 1970. Illustrated description of the binding processes applied to Oxford University Press books in the early 20th century.

368. Peignot, Gabriel. La Reliure des Livres. Paris: Jules Renouard, 1834. Essay on history of bookbinding.

369. Penny, Clara L. An Album of Selected Bookbindings.
New York: Hispanic Society of America, 1967.
Sixty photographs illustrating Spanish binding styles
since the 15th century. Excellent glossary of
Spanish bookbinding terms and excellent bibliography
of Spanish references to bookbindings and binding
techniques.

370. Pollard, Graham. "Changes in the Style of Bookbinding, 1550-1830," The Library 5th Series 11(2):71-
94, 1956.

371. _____. "The Construction of English Twelfth Century Bindings," The Library 5th Series, 17:1-22,
1962.

372. Pope, A. Upham (ed.). A Survey of Persian Art.
6 vols. London: 1938-1939. The best known account of Persian binding is an article by E. Gratzl
in vol. 3 of this work.

373. Powell, Roger. "The Lichfield St. Chad's Gospels:
Repair and Rebinding, 1961-1962," Transactions of
the Bibliographical Society pp. 259-276, with 9
plates.

374. Prideaux, Sarah Treverbian. An Historical Sketch of
Bookbinding. London: Lawrence and Bullen, 1893.

375. _____. A Catalog of Books Bound by S. T. Prideaux. London: Prideaux, 1900.

376. _____. Bookbinders and Their Craft. London:
Zaehnsdorf, 1903.

377. _____. Modern Bookbindings: Their Design and
Decoration. London: Archibald Constable, 1906.

378. _____. Notes on Printing and Bookbinding. London: South Kensington Museum, 1921.

379. Quaritch, Bernard. Facsimiles of Choice Examples
of Historical and Artistic Bookbinding in the 15th
and 16th Centuries. London: Quaritch, 1889.
103 plates printed in gold and colors.

380. Regemorter, Berthe Van. "The Binding of the Archangel Gospels," The Book Collector 13(4), 1964.
Describes technical details of a Byzantine binding.

381. Rogers, Joseph W. "The Rise of American Edition
Binding," Bookbinding in America New York:
Bowker, 1967.

382. Sadleir, Michael. Evolution of Publishers' Binding
Styles, 1770-1900. London: Constable, 1930. Includes the first systematic attempt to classify the
basic fabrics used in publisher's bindings.

383. Samford, C. Clement and John M. Hemphill. Bookbinding in Colonial Virginia. Charlottesville: The

University of Virginia Press, 1966.

Rare BF cole 384. Sarre, F. Islamic Bookbindings. London: Kegan
Paul, Trench and Trubner, 1923. With 36 colored
plates reproducing bindings.

385. Schmidt, A. Beiträge zum Rollen-und Platten-Einband
im XVI ten Jahrhundert. Leipzig: 1937. Data on
early German binding, etc.

386. Thoinan, E. Les Reliures Française (1500-1800).
Biographie Critique et Anecdotique, precedee de l'
Histoire de la Communaute ... et d'une Etude sur
les Styles de Reliure. Paris: Paul, Huard &
Guillemin, 1893.

387. Thompson, Elbert A., and L. S. Fine Binding in
America. Urbana, Ill., Beta Phi Mu, 1956.

388. Thompson, Lawrence S. "Some Notes on the History
of Bookbinding in the United States," American
Book Collector 7(5):24-27; (6):22-26; (7):24-30,
January-March, 1957.

389. _____. "Fritz Eberhardt: American Binder,"
American Book Collector 8(10):10-14, June, 1958.

390. _____. "George Baer of the Cuneo Press," American Book Collector 12(10):43-44, June, 1962.

391. Toldo, Vittorio de. The Italian Art of Bookbinding.
London: B. T. Batsford, 1925. Twenty-seven
plates, some in color.

392. Tooke, Mary A. "History of the Art of Bookbinding,"
The Art Journal. London: 1876.

393. _____. "History of Bookbinding," American Bibli-
opegist. 2:176, 220, 316, 1870.

394. Uzanne, Octave. La Reliure Moderne: Artistique et
Fantaisiste. Paris: Edouard Rouveyre, 1887.
Well illustrated treatise on fine binding as practiced
in France in latter part of 19th century.

395. Walker, E. The Art of Bookbinding: Its Rise and
Progress. New York: E. Walker & Sons, 1850.
Includes description of a mid-19th century book-
bindery.

396. Wallis, Alfred. "Bookbinding in the Sixteenth and
Seventeenth Centuries," The Library 1(3):181-184,
1891.

√ 397. Walters Art Gallery. The History of Bookbinding,
525-1950 A.D. Baltimore: Walters Art Gallery,
1958.

398. Westwood, John. "Renaissance Bookbinding," Folio
Jan-Mar 1971: 15-21. London: The Folio Society, 1971.

399.   Wheatley, H. B. Bookbinding Considered as a Fine
        Art, Mechanical Art, and Manufacture.   London:
        Elliot Stock, 1882.
400.   .   "Bookbinding Considered as a Fine Art,
        Mechanical Art and Manufacture," Journal of the
        Society of Arts. London: 1880.
401.   Wiemeler, Ignatz. "Bookbinding, Old and New,"
        The Dolphin 1933.
402.   Zaehnsdorf, Joseph M. A Short History of Bookbind-
        ing. London: Chiswick Press, 1895. A brief ac-
        count of celebrated binders and their patrons.   Also
        a glossary of styles and terms used in binding.

BOOKBINDING PATRONS

403.   Beatty, Sir Alfred Chester. Some Oriental Bindings
        in the Chester Beatty Library. Dublin: Hodges,
        Figgis, 1961.
404.   Brunet, Gustave. Etudes sur la Reliure des Livres.
        Bordeaux: Moquet, 1891. Also includes notes on
        collections of famous bibliophiles.
405.   Crawford, James Ludovic Lindsay, 26th Earl of.
        Bibliotheca Lindesiana. Aberdeen: Aberdeen Uni-
        versity Press, 1898.
406.   duBois, H. P. American Bookbindings in the Library
        of Henry William Poor. Jamaica, New York:
        Marion Press, 1903. Illustrated in goldleaf and
        colors by Edward Bierstadt. 8 vols.
407.   Forman, Harry. The Books of William Morris.   Lon-
        don: F. Hollings, 1897.
408.   Goldschmidt, E. P. H. Seventy-Five Books from a
        Library Formed by E. P. H. Goldschmidt of
        Trinity College, Cambridge, 1905-1909. Cam-
        bridge, England: Cambridge University Press,
        1909.
409.   Gray, George J. "Queen Elizabeth and Bookbinding,"
        The Library 3(7):66-69, 1916.
410.   Hobson, A. R. A. (ed.). French and Italian Collec-
        tors and Their Bindings. Oxford: Roxburghe Club,
        1953.
411.   .   The Literature of Bookbinding.   Cam-
        bridge, England: Cambridge University Press,
        1954.

412.   Hobson, Geoffrey Dudley. Short Title List of Books
        Bound for Thomas Maioli. London: J. Davy &
        Sons, c. 1920.

413.   _____ . Maioli, Carnevari, and Others. London:
        Ernest Benn, 1926.

414.   _____ . Bindings in Cambridge Libraries. Cam-
        bridge, England: Cambridge University Press,
        1929.

415.   _____ . English Binding Before 1500. Cambridge,
        England: Cambridge University Press, 1929.

416.   _____ . Notes on Grolier, with an Eulogy of the
        Late Dr. Theodor Gottlieb. London: Waterlow &
        Sons, 1929.

417.   _____ (ed.). English Bindings 1490-1940 in the
        Library of J. R. Abbey. London: Chiswick Press,
        1940.

418.   _____ . "German Renaissance Patrons of Bookbind-
        ing," The Book Collector 3:171-190, 251-271, 1954.

419.   Hevesy, André de. La Bibliothèque du Roi Matthias
        Corvin. Paris: Société Française pour la Repro-
        duction de Manuscrits à Peintures, 1923.

420.   Lane, A. Elbert Hubbard and His Work. Worcester,
        Mass.: Blanchard Press, 1901. Photographs and
        textual explanation on the distinguished American
        binder and printer who established the Roycroft
        Shop.

421.   Ledieu, Alcius. Les Reliures Artistiques. Paris:
        Gruel-Engelman, 1891. Many illustrations of fine
        bindings in the library of Abbeville.

422.   Le Roux de Liney, A. J. V. Researches Concerning
        Jean Grolier, His Life and His Library. (C. Ship-
        man trans) New York: Grolier Club, 1907.

423.   _____ . Recherches sur Jean Grolier sur sa Vie
        et sa Bibliotheque. Paris: L. Portier, 1866. 2
        vols. Includes catalog of Grolier books and six
        plates, one in color.

424.   Moss, W. E. Bindings from the Library of Robert
        Dudley, Earl of Leicester, 1533-1588. Sussex,
        England: Moss, 1939.

425.   Nichols, Charles N. The Library of Rameses the
        Great. Berkeley: The Peacock Press, 1964. A
        48-page illustrated essay.

426.   Nixon, Howard Millar. Twelve Books in Fine Bind-
        ings from the Library of J. W. Hely-Hutchinson.
        Oxford: Roxburghe Club, 1953.

427.   _____ . Broxbourne Library Styles and Designs of
        Bookbindings from the Twelfth to the Twentieth

Century. London: Maggs Bros., 1956.

428. Pearson, J. & Co. Les Femmes Bibliophiles. London: J. Pearson & Co., 1919. Catalog of a collection of books bound by famous binders for distinguished ladies.

429. Poor, H. W. American Bookbindings in the Library of Henry William Poor, Described by Henri Pène du Bois. New York: G. D. Smith, 1903. 77 pp. illus.

430. Ran, Arthur. "Contemporary Collectors - André Langlois," The Book Collector 6(2):129-142, 1957. Illustrated essay on a 20th century collection of rare and valuable books and bindings.

431. Regemorter, Berthe V. Some Early Bindings from Egypt in the Chester Beatty Library. (Chester Beatty Monographs, No. 7) Dublin: Hodges, Figgis, 1958.

432. _____. Some Oriental Bindings in the Chester Beatty Library. Dublin: Hodges, Figgis, 1961.

433. Researches Concerning Jean Grolier, His Life and His Library. Edited by Baron Roger Portalis. Translated and revised by Carolyn Shipman. New York: The Grolier Club, 1907.

434. Richardson, E. C. Some Old Egyptian Librarians. Berkeley: The Peacock Press, 1964. A 95-page essay indexed.

BINDERIES

435. A Modern Library Binder, a Description of the Work of the Firm - B. Riley & Co. Ltd. 1909-1949. Huddersfield, England: Riley, 1949.

436. Brainard, Newton C. The Andrus Bindery, A History of the Shop 1831-1938. Hartford: Andrus Bindery, 1940. Report of working conditions and management by the shop's employees.

437. Darly, Lionel. Bookbinding Then and Now. London: Faber & Faber, 1959. The story of one bindery from its beginning in the 18th century to the present.

438. Dodd, George. "A Day at a Bookbinder's," Days at the Factories, Ser. I, pp. 363-384. London:

Knight, 1843.
439.   Guild of Women-Binders.   The Bindery that Jill Built.
London: Hampstead Bindery, 1901.   Illustrated
pamphlet of verse describing the work of the members of the guild of women bookbinders.
440.   Nixon, Howard M.   Roger Powell and Peter Waters.
Privately published, Peterborough, Hants, England:
1966.   Describes the work of these two master
craftsmen.
441.   Nordhoff, Evelyn H.   "The Doves Bindery," Chap-
Book 4:353-370, March 1, 1896.   A short illustrated account of one of the finer binderies.
442.   The Rose Bindery: Your Library and Our Work.
Boston: The Rose Bindery, 1925.   Describes fine
binding as it can be done by a commercial firm.
443.   Spawn, Wilman and Carol.   "The Aitkin Shop: Identification of an 18th Century Bindery and Its Tools,"
Bibliographical Society of America Papers 57:422-
437, 1963.
444.   Westley and Clarke.   "A Day at the Bookbinders,"
Penny Magazine, 1842.   (Supplement.)

BINDERS

445.   Adams, John.   The House of Kitcat, a Story of Bookbinding, 1798-1948.   London: Kitcat, 1948.
446.   Andrews, William Loring.   Jean Grolier de Servier,
Viscount d'Aguisy.   New York: Grolier Club, 1892.
8 vols.   Account of his life and of his famous library.   6 plates of bindings.
447.   _____.   Roger Payne and His Art.   New York:
DeVinne Press, 1892.   120 copies printed on Holland paper and 10 on Japanese paper.
448.   Bendikson, Lodewyk.   "The House of Magnus, Famous
Bookbinders of the Seventeenth Century," Pacific
Bindery Talk 8(6):94-100, February, 1936.
449.   Birley, Robert.   "Roger and Thomas Payne: With
Some Account of their Earlier Bindings," The Library 5(15):33-41, 1960.
450.   _____.   "The Library of Louis-Henri de Lonéuie,
Comte de Brienne, and the Bindings of the Abbé
Du Sevil," The Library 5(17):105-131, 1962.

451.   The Bookbinder in Eighteenth Century Williamsburg.
        Williamsburg, Va.:   Colonial Williamsburg, Inc.,
        1959.
452.   "Bookbinders' Historian," Times Literary Supplement
        p. 64, January 22, 1949.
453.   Bowtell, J. and A. B. Gray.   John Bowtell: Book-
        binders of Cambridge (1753-1813).   Cambridge,
        England: Cambridge University Press, 1907.
        Bibliographical notes with plates.
454.   Child, John and Ellic Howe.   The Society of London
        Bookbinders 1780-1951.   London: Sylvan Press,
        1952.
455.   Davenport, C. J. H.   "The Bindings of Samuel
        Mearne and His School," Bibliographica 3:137-139,
        1897.
456.   _____ . Life of Samuel Mearne.   Chicago: Caxton
        Club, 1907.   Howard Nixon at the British Museum
        has proved that only 11 of the 20 books selected
        for illustration of Mearne's work are his.
457.   _____ . Roger Payne.   Chicago: Caxton Club,
        1929.   One of the most famous 18th century bind-
        ers.   This is the only biography by Davenport that
        is considered to be reliable.
458.   _____ . Thomas Berthelet, Royal Printer and Book-
        binder to Henry VIII, King of England, with Special
        Reference to his Bookbindings.   Chicago: The Cax-
        ton Club, 1901.
459.   Dreppard, C. W   American Pioneer Arts & Artists.
        Springfield, Mass.:   1942.   Includes book workers.
460.   Duff, E. Gordon.   "The Bindings of Thomas Wotton,"
        The Library 3(1):337-347, 1910.
461.   _____ . The English Provincial Printers, Station-
        ers, and Bookbinders to 1557.   Cambridge, Eng-
        land: Cambridge University Press, 1912.   (The
        Sandars Lectures.)
462.   _____ . The Printers, Stationers, Bookbinders of
        London and Westminster in the Fifteenth Century.
        Aberdeen: Aberdeen University Press, 1899.
463.   _____ . The Printers, Stationers, and Bookbinders
        of Westminster and London from 1476-1535.   Cam-
        bridge, England: Cambridge University Press,
        1906.
464.   _____ . Catalogue of the Library of the Late Ed-
        ward Gordon Duff, Esq.   London: J. Davy &
        Sons, 1925.
465.   _____ . "The Printers, Stationers, and Bookbind-
        ers of York up to 1600," Transactions of the

Bibliographical Society 5:87-107, 1898-1899.

466. Farleigh, John. "Sydney Cockerell-Bookbinder," The Creative Craftsman London: G. Bell, 1950.

467. Fletcher, William Younger. "Florimond Badier (Bookbinder)," Bibliographica 1:257-261, 1895.

468. _____. "English Armorial Book-Stamps and their Owners," Bibliographica 3:309-343, 1897.

469. _____. "The Library of Grolier," The Book-Lover 4:10-14, 1903.

470. French, Hannah D. "The Amazing Career of Andrew Barclay, Scottish Bookbinder, of Boston," Studies in Bibliography 14:145-162, 1961.

471. _____. "Bound in Boston by Henry B. Legg," Studies in Bibliography 17:135-139, 1964. The author relates the presentation of the Town Bible of Salisbury, Connecticut, to the Selectmen on May 19, 1800.

472. Gibson, Strickland. Abstracts from the Wills and Testamentary Documents of Printers, Binders, and Stationers of Oxford 1493-1638. London: Oxford University Press, 1903.

473. Gray, A. B. and John Bowtell. "John Bowtell, Bookbinder of Cambridge (1753-1813)," Proceedings Cambridge Antiquarian Society 11, 1907.

474. Gray, G. J. The Earlier Cambridge Stationers and Bookbinders and the First Cambridge Printer. London: Bibliographical Society, 1904.

475. _____. A Note Upon Early Cambridge Binders of the Sixteenth Century. Cambridge, England: Cambridge University Press, 1900.

476. Gray, G. J. and Palmer, W. M. Abstracts from the Wills and Testamentary Documents of Printers, Binders and Stationers of Cambridge from 1564 to 1699. Cambridge, England: Cambridge University Press, 1915.

477. Guild of Women-Binders. The Bindings of Tomorrow. London: Hampstead Bindery, 1902. A record of the work of the Guild and the Hampstead Bindery. Critical introduction by G. Elliott Anstruther.

478. Hamilton, Doris. "Roger Payne Submits His Bill," American Book Collector 8(9):12-15, May, 1958.

479. Hartig, O. Die Gründung der Münchener Hofbibliothek. Munchen: Bayerische Staatsbibliothek, 1917. German binders and bindings.

480. Hobson, G. D. "The Great Mearne Myth," Papers of the Edinburgh Bibliographical Society, 1918. An attempt to discredit the greatest English binder of

the Restoration which was later corrected by H.
M. Nixon in his Broxbourne Library, pp. 150-151,
[427].

481. _____ . Maioli, Carnevari and Others. London:
Ernest Benn, 1926. The author shows that "Carnevari" bindings were executed for the Italian collector Pierluigi Franesi (1503-1547).

482. Holmes, Thomas James. "The Bookbindings of John
Ratcliff and Edmund Ranger, Seventeenth Century
Boston Bookbinders," Proceedings of the American
Antiquarian Society 38:31-50, 1928.

483. _____ . "Additional Notes on Ratcliff and Ranger
Bindings," Proceedings of the American Antiquarian
Society 39:291-302, 1929.

484. Holt, Penelope. Roger Payne: Bookbinder. London:
Brewhouse Press, 1969. A brief summary of the
life of this important 18th century binder.

485. Horman, William. "The Virgin and Child Binder,
LVL, and William Horman," The Library 5(17):77-
85, 1962.

486. Howe, Ellic. List of London Bookbinders, 1648-1815.
London: Bibliographical Society, 1950.

487. _____ . London Bookbinders, 1780-1806. London:
Dropmore Press, 1950.

488. _____ . "London Bookbinders: Masters and Men,
1780-1840," The Library 5(1):28-38, 1946-1947.

489. Howe, Ellic and Child, John. The Society of London
Bookbinders, 1780-1951. London: Sylvan Press,
1952.

490. Jackson, William. "Our Ingenious Ancestors," Walpole Society Notebook 1963, pp. 3-6. Discusses
binder's labels.

491. Land, William G. "Further Notes on Ratcliff and
Ranger Bindings," Proceedings of the American
Antiquarian Society 39:302-306, 1929.

492. McMurtrie, Douglas C. "The First American Bookbinder," Bookbinding Magazine 6(6):22, June, 1927.
McMurtrie credits Edmund Ranger of Boston, 1673,
with this distinction.

493. Mitchell, William S. A History of Scottish Bookbinding, 1432-1650. Edinburgh (and London): Oliver
& Boyd, 1955. A list of Scottish binders and a
bibliography are appended.

494. Moss, W. E. "Elkanah Settle: The Armorial Binding Expert," The Book-Collector's Quarterly 13:7-
22, January-March, 1934.

495. Nixon, Howard M.   "Binding and Binders, " Talks on
     Book Collecting.   P. H. Muir (ed.).   London:
     Cassell and Company, Ltd. , 1952.

496. _____ .   "Grolier's Binders, " The Book Collector
     pp. 45-51, 165-170, 1960.

497. _____ .   "Grolier's 'Chrysostom', " The Book Col-
     lector pp. 64-70, 1962.

498. Pantazzi, Sybille.   "Four Designers of English Pub-
     lishers' Bindings, 1850-1880, and Their Signa-
     tures, " The Papers of the Bibliographical Society
     of America 55:88-99, 1961.

499. Payne, Roger.   Two Bindings by Roger Payne, Master
     Bookbinder and Gilder, in the Library of Lord
     Rothschild.   Privately printed for Lord Rothschild,
     1947.   Two colored plates.

500. Philip, I. G.   "Roger Bartlett, Bookbinder, " The Li-
     brary 5(10):233-243, 1955.

501. Prideaux, S. T.   Bookbinders and Their Craft.   Lon-
     don: Zaehnsdorf, 1903.

502. _____ .   "Characteristics and Peculiarities of Roger
     Payne, Binder, " Magazine of Art pp. 607-613,
     September 1898.

503. Ramsden, Charles Frederick Ingram.   "Bookbinders
     to George III and His Immediate Descendants and
     Collaterals, " The Library 5(13):186-193, 1958.

504. _____ .   "The Collection of Hollis Bindings at
     Berne, " The Book Collector 7(2):165-170, Summer,
     1958.

505. _____ .   French Bookbinders, 1789-1848.   London:
     L. Humphries, 1950.

506. _____ .   Bookbinders of the United Kingdom (Out-
     side London) 1780-1840.   London: Queen Anne
     Press, 1954.

507. _____ .   London Bookbinders, 1780-1840.   London:
     Batsford, 1956.

508. _____ .   "Richard Weir and Count MacCarthy-
     Reagh, " The Book Collector 2(4), 1953.   Identifies
     Weir as the creator of a series of beautiful 18th
     century bindings.

509. Ritchie, Ward.   "The Man Who Became a Bookbind-
     er, " The Dolphin 4(3):235-242, Spring, 1941.   The
     Story of Cobden-Sanderson.

510. Rogers, David.   "A Portrait of John-George of
     Brandenburg on Presentation Bindings: A Footnote
     to Haebler, " The Library 5(17):88-93, 1962.

511. Roquet, Antoine Ernest.   Les Relieurs Français (1500-
     1800).   Biographic critique et anecdotique, précédée

de l'histoire de la communauté des relieurs et doreurs de la ville de Paris et d'une étude sur les styles de reliure, par Ernest Thoinan (Pseud.). Paris: Paul, Huard & Guillemin, 1893.

✓ 512. Sanford, C. Clement. The Bookbinder in Eighteenth-Century Williamsburg. Williamsburg: Colonial Williamsburg, 1964.

513. Schmidt-Künsemüller, E. A. T. J. Cobden-Sanderson as Bookbinder. Esher, England: The Tobard Press, 1966. Translated by I. Grafe. A short biography of the troubled artist, his Dove Bindery and its relation to the Kelmscott Press.

514. Schunke, Ilse. "Bindings by Krause and His School in English Collections," The Book Collector 8(1):25-30, Spring, 1959.

515. _____. Leben und Werke Jacob Krause. Leipzig: Insel-Verlag, 1943. Data on early German bindings and binders.

✓ 516. Spawn, Wilman & Carol. "Francis Skinner, Book-binder of Newport - An 18th Century Craftsman Identified by His Tools," Winterthur Portfolio II 1965.

517. Valéry, Paul and others. Paul Bonet. Paris: Librairie Auguste Bleizot, 1945.

518. Weiss, Harry B. "The Growth of the Graphic Arts in Philadelphia," Bulletin 56:76-83; 139-145, 1952. New York Public Library. Includes information on bookbinders, paper and parchment makers, ink makers, paper stainers and book folders.

BOOKBINDINGS

519. Abbey, John Roland. English Bindings 1490-1940 in the Library of J. R. Abbey. London: Chiswick Press, 1940.

520. _____. An Exhibition of Modern English and French Bindings from the Collection Of Major J.R. Abbey. London: Arts Council, 1949.

521. Adams, Charles M. "Illustrated Publishers' Bind-ings," Bulletin 41:607-611, 1937. New York Public Library.

522. Adams, Frederick B. Jr. Bookbindings by T. J. Cobden-Sanderson. New York: J. P. Morgan

Library, 1969.
523. _____. "Fine Bindings," Fifteenth Report to the
Fellows of the Pierpont Morgan Library - 1967-
1968. New York: J. P. Morgan Library, 1969.
Chapter on bindings describes in detail the history,
design and personalities involved in the binding of
11 books acquired during the period of the report.
524. Adams, P. "Turkish, Arabic and Persian Bookbindings," Archiv fur Buchbinderei 1904.
X 525. Aga-Oglu, M. Persian Bookbindings of the Fifteenth
Century. Ann Arbor: University of Michigan,
1935.
526. An Exhibition of Hand Bookbinding, Casemaking, Restoration, Calligraphy and Illumination and Hand-
decorated Paper. New York: The Guild of Book-
workers, 1959. Examples of fine bookbinding by
some of today's professionals and amateurs.
527. Andrews, William Loring. Roger Payne and His Art.
New York: DeVinne Press, 1892.
528. Arts Council. An exhibition of modern English and
French bindings from the collection of Major J. R.
Abbey. London: Arts Council, 1949.
529. (Bachelin). Album de Reliures Artistiques & Historiques. Paris: Libraire Bachelin-Deflorerine,
1869. Photographic catalog of fine French binding.
530. Bailey, H. Short Notes on the Bookbindings of Salisbury Cathedral Library. Salisbury, England: 1950.
531. Barber, Giles. "Notes on Some English Centre and
Corner Piece Bindings c.1600," The Library
5(17):93-95, 1962.
532. Barwick, F. G. A Book Bound for Mary, Queen of
Scots: being a description of the binding of a copy
of the Geographia of Ptolemy printed in Rome 1490,
with notes on other books bearing Queen Mary's
insignia. London: Bibliographical Society, 1901.
533. Bauer, Hans (ed.). L. Brades Illustriertes Buch-
binderbuch. Halle: A. D. Saale, 1904. Reprint
of Brades 1868 work.
534. (Belin). Livres Anciens de Provenances Historiques.
Paris: Librairie Theophile Belin, 1910. Many illustrations of armorial bindings.
535. Bendikson, Lodewyk. "The House of Magnus, Famous
Bookbinders of the Seventeenth Century," Pacific
Bindery Talk 8:94-100, February, 1936.
536. Bickell, Dr. L. Bookbindings from The Hessian Historical Exhibition. Leipzig: Karl Hiersman, 1893.

537.   Birley, Robert. "Roger and Thomas Payne: With
        Some Account of Their Earlier Bindings," The Li-
        brary 15(1), 1960.
538.   Bodleian Library. Gold Tooled Bookbindings. Ox-
        ford: Bodleian Library, 1951. Bodleian Picture
        Book No. 2.
539.   Bookbindings from the Library of Jean Grolier. Ox-
        ford: The Alden Press, 1965.
540.   Bookbinding in Great Britain 16th to 20th Century.
        London: Maggs Brothers, Ltd., 1964. Booksel-
        lers catalog, includes many photographs of fine
        bindings.
541.   Bouchot, H. De la Reliure. Paris: Edouard
        Rouveyre, 1891.
542.   . Les Reliures d'Art a la Bibliothèque
        Nationale. Paris: Edouard Rouveyre, 1888.
        Many black and white illustrations.
543.   Bowdoin, W. G. "Bookbinding: Progress of the Art
        During the Past Year - Exhibitions of Bookbindings,"
        New York Times Saturday Review of Books, Janu-
        ary 9, 1904. Reprinted in the Guild of Book Work-
        ers Journal 7(3):23-26, 1969.
544.   Brassington, William Salt. Historical Bindings in the
        Bodleian Library, Oxford. London: S. Low,
        Marston, 1891.
545.   Briggs, Victor H. & L. Ernest. Twentieth-century
        Cover Designs. Plymouth, Mass.: 1902.
546.   British Museum. Royal English Bookbindings in the
        British Museum. London: British Museum, 1957.
547.   Brun, Robert. "Bindings," The Art of the French
        Book. Paris: P. Elak, 1947, pp. 141-164. A.
        Léjard, editor.
548.   Brunet, Gustave. Etudes sur la Reliure des Livres.
        Bordeaux: Moquet, 1891. Mostly on collections
        of bindings.
549.   Burlington Fine Arts Club. "The Exhibition of Book
        bindings at the Burlington Fine Arts Club," The
        Library 1(3):251-255; 287-291, 1891.
550.   "Cambridge Bindings," Times Literary Supplement,
        p. 780, November 25, 1949.
551.   Carter, John. Binding Variants in English Publish-
        ing, 1820-1900. London: Constable, 1923. A
        further development of Sadlier's attempts to classi-
        fy publishers' binding cloth. [180].
552.   . More Binding Variants. London: Con-
        stable, 1938.

553. _____. "English Publishers' Bindings 1800-1900,"
     Bulletin 40(8):655-664, 1936. New York Public Li-
     brary.

554. _____. "The Origin of Publishers' Cloth Binding,"
     The Colophon. Part 8, 1931.

555. _____. Publishers' Cloth. London: Constable,
     1935; and New York: Bowker, 1935. An outline
     history of publisher's bindings in England 1820-
     1900.

556. Cockerell, S. C. The Gorleston Psalter. London:
     Chiswick Press, 1967. Description of the binding
     on a fourteenth-century manuscript.

557. (Columbia University Libraries). Modern bookbinding;
     new design in an old craft. An international ex-
     hibition. New York: Columbia University Library,
     1935. 16pp.

558. [No entry.]

559. Contemporary Books, 1950. New York: E. I. du-
     Pont de Nemours & Co., 1950.

560. Cook, Davidson. "Illustrations on Bindings," Times
     Literary Supplement, p. 296, April 17, 1937.

561. Craig, Maurice. Irish Bookbindings, 1600-1800.
     London: Cassell & Co., 1954.

562. _____. "Irish Parlimentary Bindings," The Book
     Collector 2(1):24-36, 1953. Describes the bindings
     of the 149 Parliamentary Journals destroyed by
     fire in 1922.

563. Crawford, James Ludovic Lindsay. "List of Manu-
     scripts and Examples of Metal and Ivory Bindings
     from Bibliotheca Lindesiana," Transactions of the
     Bibliographical Society 4:213-232, 1898.

564. Cundall, Joseph. Bookbindings, Ancient and Modern.
     London: George Bell & Sons, 1881.

565. _____. On Ornamental Art Applied to Ancient and
     Modern Bookbinding. London: Society of Arts,
     1848.

566. Davenport, Cyril J. H. Early London Bookbindings.
     London: The Queen, 1891.

567. _____. Royal English Bookbindings. London:
     Seeley & Co., 1896.

568. _____. Cantor Lectures on Decorative Bookbind-
     ing. London: Society of Arts, 1898.

569. _____. English Embroidered Bookbindings. Lon-
     don: Kegan Paul, Trench, Trubner, 1899.

570. _____. Cameos. London: Seeley, 1900.

571. _____. Thomas Berthelet, Royal Printer and
     Bookbinder to Henry VIII, King of England, with

Special Reference to his Bookbindings. Chicago: The Caxton Club, 1901.

572. ———. Samuel Mearne, Binder to King Charles II. Chicago: The Caxton Club, 1906.

573. ———. English Heraldic Bookstamps. London: Archibald Constable, 1909.

574. ———. Cameo Book-Stamps. London: Edward Arnold, 1911.

575. ———. Beautiful Books. London: Methuen, 1929.

576. ———. Roger Payne, English Bookbinder of the Eighteenth Century. Chicago: The Caxton Club, 1929.

577. ———. "Notes on Bookbinding," The Library First Series 5:217-225, 1893.

578. ———. "Bookbindings at the British Museum, Summary," Transactions of the Bibliographical Society 2:93-96, 1894.

579. ———. "Little, Gidding, Bindings," Bibliographica 2:129-149, 1896.

580. ———. "The Bindings of Samuel Mearne and His School," Bibliographica 3:129-141, 1897.

581. ———. "Roger Payne and His Indebtedness to Mearne," Bibliographica 3:371-377, 1897.

582. ———. "English Embroidered Bindings Summary," Transactions of the Bibliographical Society 4:144-148, 1898.

583. ———. "Leather as Used in Bookbinding," The Library First Series 10:15-19, 1898.

584. ———. "Leathers Used in Bookbinding," Transactions of the Bibliographical Society 5:161-162, 1899.

585. ———. "King Charles I's Embroidered Bible," The Library 2nd Series 1:373-377, 1900.

586. ———. "Three Recently Discovered Bindings with Little Gidding Stamps," The Library 2nd Series 1:205-212, 1900.

587. ———. "Forgeries in Bookbinding," The Library 2nd Series 2:389-395, 1901.

588. ——— and others. "The Report of the Committee on Leather for Bookbinding," The Transactions of the Bibliographical Society 6:143-145, 1901.

589. ———. "Some Popular Errors as to Old Bindings," The Library 2nd Series 2:231-237, 1901.

590. ———. "Library Bookbinding," The Library Association Record 5:5-15; 50-53, 1903.

591. ———. "Some Popular Errors as to Old Bindings," The Book-Lover 4:509-511, 1903.

592.   _____. "Bookbinding and Book-Production," The
          Library Association Record 7:553-555, 1905.
593.   _____. "Bookbinding in England. Early Work and
          Sixteenth Century," The Library Association Re-
          cord 9:19-23, 1907.
594.   _____. "The Heraldry of English Royal Bindings,"
          Transactions of the Bibliographical Society 8:73-76,
          1907.
595.   _____. "Bookbinding in Germany," The Library
          Association Record 12:49-51, 1910.
596.   _____. "Bookbinding in France," The Library
          Association Record 13:93-104, 1911.
597.   De Ricci, Seymour. Signed Bindings in the Mortimer
          L. Schiff Collection. 4 vols. New York: Schiff,
          1935. In Volume 1-3 (French Binding) and Volume
          4 (English Binding) there are 315 plates and many
          reproductions of binders' tickets. 413 bindings in
          chronological order. 300 specimens of binders'
          stamps and binders' tickers.
598.   Derôme, L. La Reliure de Luxe: Le Livre et
          l'Amateur. Paris: Edouard Rouveyre, 1888.
          Text and full-page illustrations describing typical
          19th century French luxury binding.
599.   Design in Bookbinding: As Represented in Exhibits
          at the Sixth Triennial Exposition of Graphic Arts
          at Milan, Italy, in 1936, with Illustrations of
          Eighteen Bookbindings There Exhibited. Chicago:
          privately printed, 1938.
600.   Dreis, Hazel. "Lancaster, Pennsylvania, Bookbind-
          ings: An Historical Study," Papers of the Biblio-
          graphical Society of America 42:119-128, 1948.
601.   Du Bois, H. P. American Bookbindings in the Li-
          brary of Henry William Poor. Jamaica, N.Y.:
          Marion Press, 1903.
602.   Duff, E. G. "Early Stamped Bindings," in Prideaux's
          Historical Sketch of Bookbinding. London: Law-
          rence & Bullen, 1893.
603.   _____. "The Trinity Bindings," Bibliographica
          1:189-191, 1895.
604.   _____. "Scottish Bookbinding, Armorial and Ar-
          tistic," Transactions of the Bibliographical Society
          15:95-113, 1917-1919.
605.   Durel, A. Catalogue de la Bibliotheque de M. E.
          Massicot. Paris: A. Durel, Libraire, 1903.
          Modern (1903) luxury bindings.
606.   Edmunds, W. H. "The Nineteenth Century Renais-
          sance in Bookbinding Art," The Book-Lover

4:137-144, 1903.

607. Ehrman, Albert. "The Origin of English Panel Stamps," The Library 4(11):104, 1931.

608. _____. "A Short Introduction to Armorial Bindings," The Book-Collector's Quarterly 13:42-44, January-March, 1934.

609. _____. "Early American Bookbinders," Bibliographical Society of America 35:210-212, 1941.

610. _____. "Les Reliures Vernis sans Odeur," The Book Collector 14(4):523-527, 1965. Illustrated essay on late 18th and early 19th century French "Varnished" bindings.

611. "English Blind Stamped Bindings," Times Literary Supplement, p. 364, December 30, 1949.

612. Falk, Franz. "Der Stempeldruck von Gutenberg," Zentralblatt für Bibliothekswesen. Leipzig: Beihefte, 1900. vol. 8, pp. 73-79. Describes binder's stamps in use before the invention of printing.

613. "Fine Bindings," The Book-Lover 4:195-198; 417-422, 1903.

614. Fine Bindings 1500-1700 from Oxford Libraries. Oxford: Bodleian Library, 1968. An illustrated and profusely annotated exhibition catalog.

615. Fletcher, William Younger. Bookbinding in France. London: Seeley, 1894.

616. _____. English Bookbinding in the British Museum. London: K. Paul, Trench, Trubner, 1895.

617. _____. English Bookbindings. London: Seeley, 1896.

618. _____. Foreign Bookbindings in the British Museum. London: K. Paul, Trench, Trubner, 1896.

619. _____. Bookbinding in England and France. London: Seeley, 1897.

620. Flower, Desmond. "Some French Contributions to the Art of the Book," Signature 7:7-16, 1948.

621. Fournier, Edouard. L'Art de la Reliure en France. Paris: Gay, 1864.

622. French, Hannah D. "Scottish-American Bookbindings," The Book Collector 6(2):150-159, 1957. Describes six examples by Colonial North American binders trained in Scotland.

623. Gibson, Strickland. "Early Oxford Bindings," Illustrated Monographs of the Bibliographical Society 10, 1903.

624. _____. "The Localization of Books by Their Bindings," Transactions of the Bibliographical Society

8:25-38, 1907.

625. _____. "Recent Books on Binding, " The Library
4(3):137-140, 1923.

626. _____. "Fragments from Bindings at the Queen's
College, Oxford, " The Library 4(12):429-433, 1932.

627. _____. Some Notable Bodleian Bindings, XII to
XVIII Centuries. Oxford: Oxford University
Press, 1901-1904.

628. Goldschmidt, E. P. H. Gothic and Renaissance Bookbindings. Amsterdam, N. Israel, 1969. Two
volume reprint (with all plates and photographs)
of the original two volume deluxe edition, London,
1928.

629. _____. "Theodore Gottlieb: A Reformer of the
History of Bookbinding, " The Library 4(10):274-
281, 1930.

630. _____. "Some Cuir-Ciselé Bookbindings in English
Librairies, " The Library 4(13):337-365, 1932-1933.

631. _____. "The Study of Early Bookbinding, " Studies
in Retrospect. pp. 175-184, 1945.

632. Gold-Tooled Bindings. Oxford: Bodleian Library,
1951.

633. Gottlieb, Theodor. K. K. Hofbibliothek. Bucheinbände. Vienna: Anton Schroll, 1910. Viennese
bindings.

634. Gratzl, E. Islamische Bucheinbände. Leipzig:
Hiersemann, 1924.

635. Grolier Club. Catalogue of Decorated Early English
Bookbindings. New York: The Grolier Club, 1899.

636. _____. A Catalogue of an Exhibit of Mosaic Bookbindings. New York: The Grolier Club, 1902.

637. _____. Catalogue of an Exhibit of Silver Embroidered and Curious Bookbindings. New York:
The Grolier Club, 1903.

638. _____. Catalogue of Some of the Latest Artistic
Bindings Done at the Club Bindery. New York:
The Grolier Club, 1906.

639. _____. Catalogue of Ornamental Leather Bookbindings. New York: The Grolier Club, 1907.

640. _____. Catalog of an Exhibition of Renaissance
Bookbindings. New York: The Grolier Club,
1937. Sixteen black and white plates of 16th century gold-tooled bindings, identified by binder and
owner, together with an address on 16th century
binders and binding practices by Lucius Wilmerd-
ing.

641. _____ . Italian Books. New York: The Grolier
Club, 1902. Catalog of an exhibition.

642. _____ . Commercial Bookbindings. New York:
The Grolier Club, 1894. An historical sketch of
commercial binding in the 19th century.

643. Guigard, Joannis. Nouvel Armorial du Bibliophile.
Paris: Rondeau, 1890. Guide to armorial bindings with hundreds of facsimiles in two volumes.

644. Guigard, J. and Brin, T. Exposition de la Société
de la Reliure Originale, accompagnée d'une
présentation de reliures ayant appartenu à Jean
Grolier. Paris, Bibliotheque Nationale, 1959.

645. Gumuchian & Cie. Les Livres de l'Enfance du XVe au
XIXe Siècle. Paris: 1967. A reprint of the 1930
edition.

646. Haebler, Konrad. Deutsche Bibliophilen. Leipzig:
Hiersemann, 1923. Many illustrations of early
luxury bindings in Germany.

647. Hannover, E. Kunstfaerdige eamle Bogbind. Copenhagen: Lehmann & Stage, 1907. Illustrated text
on historic Danish bindings.

648. Harrison, Thomas. "Contemporary Bindings: a
Commentary," The Penrose Annual 44:71-74, 1950.

649. Harthan, John P. Bookbindings. London: Her Majesty's Stationery Office, 1961. Traces the development of book decoration in the Near East and
Europe.

650. Hayward, J. F. Silver Bindings from the J. R. Abbey Collection. 1955. With numerous illustrations
of bindings.

651. Hedberg, Arvid. Stockholms Bokbindare 1460-1880.
2 vols. Stockholm, 1949-1960, A 751-page history of Swedish binding, illustrated by 165 plates
and many photographs and drawings in the text.

652. Helwig, Hellmuth. Das Deutsche Buchbinder-Hand-
werk. Stuttgart: Anton Hiersemann, 1962. Two-
volume history of German handbinding.

653. _____ . Handbüch der Einbandkunde, 3 vols. Ham-
burg: Maximilian-Gesellschaft, 1953. Bookbinders
and binding--a study of styles, etc.

654. Hermann, H. J. Die Illuminierten Handschriften und
Inkunabeln der National-bibliothek in Wein. Leipzig, 1930. 248 facsimile reproductions.

655. Historic and Artistic Bookbindings. London: Maggs
Bros., 1914. Illustrated catalog of fine bindings
dating from the 14th century to the 20th.

656. "Historical Bindings," The Book-Lover 4:513-520, 1903.

657.   Hobson, A. R. A.   "The Pillone Library," The Book
        Collector 7(1):28-37, Spring, 1958.
658.   _____.   "Two Renaissance Bindings," The Book
        Collector 7(3):265-268, Autumn, 1958.
659.   _____.   "Waddesdon Manor," The Book Collector
        8(2):131-139, Summer, 1959.
660.   _____.   French and Italian Collectors and Their
        Bindings.   Oxford: Roxburghe Club, 1953.   Illus-
        trated from examples in the library of J. R. Ab-
        bey.
661.   Hobson, Geoffrey Dudley.   "On a Group of Bindings
        with Painted Plaquettes," The Library 4(5):47-58,
        1925.
662.   _____.   "Short Title List of Books Bound for
        Thomas Maioli," The Library 4(5):259-263, 1925.
663.   _____.   "Parisian Binding, 1500-1525," The Li-
        brary 4(2):393-434, 1931.
664.   _____.   "Books on Bookbinding," The Book-Col-
        lector's Quarterly 7:70-84, July-September, 1932.
665.   _____.   "Further Notes on Romanesque Bindings,"
        The Library 4(15):161-211, 1934-1935.
666.   _____.   "Some Early Bindings and Binder's Tools,"
        The Library 4(19):202-249, 1938-1939.
667.   _____.   "Blind-Stamped Panels in the English Book
        Trade, c. 1485-1555," Supplement to the Transac-
        tions of the Bibliographical Society 17, 1944.
668.   _____.   "'Et Amicorum'," The Library 5(4):87-99,
        1949-1950.
669.   _____.   Les Reliures a la Fanfare: Le Probleme
        de L'S Fermé.   London: Chiswick Press, 1935.
670.   _____.   Les Reliures a la Fanfare.   Amsterdam:
        1969.   Reprint of 1935 edition with 37 plates, 82
        text illustrations.
671.   _____.   English Bindings 1490-1940 in the Library
        of J. R. Abbey.   London: Chiswick Press, 1940.
672.   _____.   English Binding Before 1500.   Cambridge,
        England: Cambridge University Press, 1929.
        (Sanders lectures, 1927.)
673.   _____.   Bindings in Cambridge Libraries.   Cam-
        bridge, England: Cambridge University Press,
        1929.
√ 674.   _____.   Thirty Bindings.   London: The First Edi-
        tion Club, 1926.   Photographs and descriptions of
        thirty 15th-18th century European bindings selected
        from The First Edition Club's Seventh Exhibition.
675.   Hoe, Robert.   One Hundred and Seventy-Six Historic
        and Artistic Bookbindings.   2 vols.   New York:

Dodd, Mead and Company, 1895. Etchings and
lithographs of fine bindings dating from the 15th
century.

676. Holmes, Richard Rivington. Specimens of Royal,
Fine, and Historical Bookbindings Selected from
the Royal Library Windsor Castle. London: W.
Greggs & Sons, 1893.

677. Holmes, Thomas James. The Bookbindings of John
Ratcliff and Edmund Ranger, Seventeenth Century
Boston Bookbinders. Worcester, Mass: American
Antiquarian Society, 1929. 22 pages of illustra-
tions.

678. _____ . "Additional notes on Ratcliff and Ranger
bindings," Proceedings of the American Antiquarian
Society pp. 291-306, October, 1929.

679. (Jahrbuch der Einbandkunst). Herausgegeben von
Hans Loubier und Erhard Klette. Dritter und
Vierter Jahrgang 1929-30. Leipzig: Poeschel &
Trepte, 1931. 167 pages, 64 full page plates of
old and modern bindings.

680. Julien, le Bibliophile. Album de Reliures Artistiques
& Historiques. Paris: 1869.

681. Kent, H. W. "Some Notes on Mosaic Bookbindings,"
The Bibliographer 1(5):169-181, May, 1902. A
journal of bibliography and rare book news.

682. Kiel, Gustav. Neue Bücheinbände. Leipzig: 1901.
Well illustrated monograph on late 19th century
elaborately decorated cloth book covers in Germany.

683. Klepikov, S. A. "Russian Bookbindings from the 11th
to the 17th Century," The Book Collector 10(4):408-
422, Winter, 1961.

684. _____ . "Russian Bookbinding from the Middle of
the 17th to the end of the 19th Century," The Book
Collector 11(4):437-447, Winter, 1962.

685. Kristeller, Paul. "Woodcuts as Bindings," Bibliographica 1:249-251, 1895.

686. [No entry.]

687. Kühnert, E. Geschichte der --- Bibliothek Zu
Konegsberg. 1926. Early German luxury bindings.

688. Kurz, Otto. Fakes: A Handbook for Collectors &
Students. London: Faber & Faber, 1948. Pages
294-300 deal with fraudulent bindings.

689. Kyriss, Ernst. "Bookbindings in the Libraries of
Prague," Studies in Bibliography 3:105-130, 1950-
1951.

690.   _____. "Notes on Bindings from English Collec-
            tions at Stuttgart," The Book Collector 5(2):158-
            161, Summer, 1956.
691.   _____. "Parisian Panel Stamps Between 1480 and
            1530," Studies in Bibliography 7:113-124, 1955.
692.   Kyster, Ankar. Bookbindings in the Public Collec-
            tions of Denmark, vol. 1. Copenhagen: The Royal
            Library, 1938.
693.   Lamacraft, C. T. "Early Bookbindings from a Coptic
            Monastery," The Library 4(20):214-233, 1939-1940.
694.   Land, William G. "Further notes on Ratcliff and
            Ranger bindings," Proceedings of the American
            Antiquarian Society 39:302-306, 1929.
695.   "La Reliure Romantique," Connaissance des Artes.
            19, 1953. Description and illustration of elaborate
            bindings of the 18th and 19th centuries.
696.   Larsen, Sofus and Ankar Kyster. Danish Eighteenth
            Century Bindings, 1730-1780. London: Oxford
            University Press, 1930.
697.   Ledieu, Alcius. Les Reliures Artistiques. Paris:
            Gruel-Engelmann, 1891.
✓ 698. Lehmann-Haupt, Hellmut (ed.). Bookbinding in
            America: three essays: Early American Book-
            binding by Hand, by H. D. French; The Rise of
            American Edition Bookbinding, by J. W. Rogers;
            On the Rebinding of Old Books, by Hellmut Leh-
            mann-Haupt. Portland, Maine: Southworth-
            Anthoensen Press, 1941. 293 pp. illus.
✓ 699. Léjard, André. The Art of the French Book from
            Early Manuscript to the Present Time. London:
            P. Elek, 1947.
700.   Levey, Martin et. al. "An Eleventh Century Arabic
            Work on Bookbinding," ISIS 47, 1956.
701.   Lindsay, James Ludovic. Bibliotheca Lindesiana,
            List of Manuscripts and Examples of Metal and
            Ivory Bindings Exhibited by the Bibliographical So-
            ciety. Aberdeen: Privately Printed, 1898.
702.   Livres dans de Riches Reliures des 16e, 17e, 18e,
            et 19e Siecles. Paris: Libraire O. Morgand,
            1910. Fifty plates.
703.   Loubier, Hans. Der Bucheinband. Leipzig: 1926.
            Early German luxury bindings including metal
            decorations.
704.   Mansfield, Edgar. Modern Design in Bookbinding.
            London: Peter Owens, 1966. Seventy-six illustra-
            tions and essay on modern fine binding design.
            Introduction by Howard Nixon.

705. Marinis, T. de. Appunti e Ricerche Bibliografiche.
      Florence: T. de Marinis & Co., 1940. Italian
      and Viennese Renaissance bindings.
706. Marius-Michel, H. Essai sur la Decoration Exteri-
      eure des Livres. Paris: Morgand, 1880.
707. Masterpieces of French Modern Bindings. New York:
      Services Culturels Français, 1947.
708. Matthews, Brander. Bookbindings, Old and New.
      London: George Bell & Sons, 1896.
709. McLean, R. Victorian Book Design. London: 1963.
      Numerous illustrations with some in color.
710. Melville, Herman. A Thought on Bookbinding. Bos-
      ton: Bookbuilders of Boston, 1948. A reprint of
      the original unsigned review in The Literary World,
      6, March 16, 1850. Melville's views on the
      propriety of the binding on J. Fenimore Cooper's
      Red Rover (revised ed.).
711. Michon, Marie-Louis. Les Reliures Mosäiquées du
      18e Siècle. Paris: Société de la Reliure Origin-
      ale, 1956.
712. Miner, Dorothy (ed.). The History of Bookbinding
      525 AD to 1950 AD. Baltimore: Walters Gallery
      of Art, 1950. A profusely illustrated catalog which
      records many unknown or long lost bindings. See
      also Nixon, H. M. "The Baltimore Binding Ex-
      hibition," The Book Collector 7:419-426, 1958.
713. Mitchell, William S. A History of Scottish Bookbind-
      ing, 1432-1650. Edinburgh: University of Aber-
      deen, 1955. Well illustrated and extremely well
      documented.
714. _____. British Signed Bindings in the Library of
      King's College, Newcastle-upon-Tyne. Newcastle:
      King's College Library, 1954. Publication No. 1.
715. _____. "German Bindings in Aberdeen University
      Library: Iconographic Index, and Indices of Ini-
      tials, Binders, and Dates," The Library 5(17):46-
      55, 1962.
716. "Modern Bookbindings and Their Designers," The
      Studio Special Winter Number, 1899-1900. Entire
      issue is a profusely illustrated essay on turn of
      the century binding design.
717. Modern French Bookbindings. London: The Arts
      Council of Great Britain, 1961. Illustrated catalog
      of an exhibition of work by members of the Société
      de la Reliure Originale.
718. Mosaic Bookbindings, a Catalogue of an Exhibition.
      New York: The Grolier Club, January 23 -

February 22, 1902.   Bibliography on pp. 46-48.

719.   Munby, A. N. L.   "Collecting English Signed Bind-
        ings," The Book Collector 2(3):177-193, 1953.
720.   [No entry.]
721.   Nixon, Howard M.   Broxbourne Library Styles and
        Designs of Bookbindings from the Twelfth to the
        Twentieth Century.   London: Maggs Bros., 1956.
        118 illustrations of bindings in the text, many full-
        page.
722.   _____ .   Royal English Bookbindings in the British
        Museum.   London: British Museum, 1957.
723.   _____ .   "English Bookbindings," The Book Collec-
        tor 1(1) and continuing.   A series of interesting
        monographs (now numbering in the seventies) on
        early English bindings by the foremost authority
        on the subject.
724.   _____ .   "An Irish Bookbinding," The Book Collec-
        tor 3(3):216-217, 1954.
725.   _____ .   Twelve Books in Fine Bindings from the
        Library of J. W. Hely-Hutchinson.   Oxford: The
        Roxburghe Club, 1953.
726.   _____ .   "A Binding by the Naval Binder, c. 1675,"
        The Book Collector 4(1):45-46, Spring, 1955.
727.   _____ .   "A London Binding by Richard Balley,
        1700," The Book Collector 4(2):144, 1955.
728.   _____ .   "A Binding for King Henry VIII, c. 1540,"
        The Book Collector 4(3):236, 1955.
729.   _____ .   "A George III Binding, c. 1810-20," The
        Book Collector 4(4):308, 1955.
730.   _____ .   "A London Binding by Fletcher, 1660,"
        The Book Collector 5(1):53-54, 1956.
731.   _____ .   "A London Binding by Fletcher, 1662,"
        The Book Collector 5(2):150, 1956.
732.   _____ .   "A Mosaic Binding by A. De Sauty, c.
        1904," The Book Collector 5(3):248, 1956.
733.   _____ .   "A Binding for John Carteret, 2nd Earl
        Granville, 1741," The Book Collector 5(4):368,
        1956.
734.   _____ .   "A Mosaic Binding for Lord Kingsale,
        1720," The Book Collector 6(1):60, 1957.
735.   _____ .   "An Angling Binding by Thomas Gosden,
        c. 1825," The Book Collector 6(2):170, 1957.
736.   _____ .   "A Binding by the Morocco Binder, c.
        1563," The Book Collector 6(3):278, 1957.
737.   _____ .   "A Binding for Archbishop Parker, c.
        1574," The Book Collector 6(4):386, 1957.

738.   . "A Binding by James Hayday, c. 1845,"
      The Book Collector 7(1):62, 1958.

739.   . "A Binding by the Settle Bindery, 1704,"
      The Book Collector 7(2):180, 1958.

740.   . "An Illuminated Vellum Binding for the
      Prince Consort, 1843," The Book Collector 7(3):
      284, 1958.

741.   . "A Cambridge Binding by Titus Tillet,
      1677," The Book Collector 7(4):396, 1958.

742.   . "A London Binding by Queen's Binder B,
      c. 1675," The Book Collector 8(1):50, 1959.

743.   . "A Binding by Lewis for Oliver Cromwell,
      1656," The Book Collector 8(2):168, 1959.

744.   . "A Binding by the Dudley Binder, c.
      1558," The Book Collector 8(3):282, 1959.

745.   . "A Newcastle Binding by Lubbock, c.
      1820," The Book Collector 8(4):416, 1959.

746.   . "Grolier's Bindings," The Book Collector
      9(1):45-51, 1960.

747.   . "A Binding from the Mearne Shop, c.
      1680," The Book Collector 9(1):52, 1960.

748.   . "A Binding for William Bullein by the
      Initial Binder, 1562," The Book Collector 10(2):
      184, 1961.

749.   . "A Binding from Charles Mearne's Shop,
      1685," The Book Collector 10(3):320, 1961.

750.   . "A Binding from the Samuel Mearne Bind-
      ery, c. 1669," The Book Collector 10(4):440, 1961.

751.   . "A Binding Supplied by John Bill to James
      I, c. 1621," The Book Collector 11(1):62, 1962.

752.   . "Grolier's Chrysostom," The Book Collec-
      tor 11(1):64-70, 1962.

753.   . "A Gift from the Maidens of the United
      Kingdom, 1874," The Book Collector 11(2):204,
      1962.

754.   . "A Little Gidding Binding, c. 1635-40,"
      The Book Collector 11(3):330, 1962.

755.   . "A Binding by John Brindley, 1743," The
      Book Collector 11(4):466, 1962.

756.   . "Roger Bartlett's Bookbindings," The Li-
      brary 5th Series, 17:56-65, 1962.

757.   . "A London Binding by the Medallion Bind-
      er, c. 1545," The Book Collector 12(1):60, 1963.

758.   . "An Eton Binding by Roger Payne, 1764,"
      The Book Collector 12(2):194, 1963.

759.   . "A Pyramus and Thisbe Binding, c. 1616,"
      The Book Collector 12(3):338, 1963.

760.   . "A London Binding by Queens' Binder A, c. 1670, " The Book Collector 12(4):488, 1963.

761.   . "A Binding from the Caxton Bindery, c. 1490, " The Book Collector 13(1):52, 1964.

762.   . "A Harleian Binding by Thomas Elliot, 1721, " The Book Collector 13(2):194, 1964.

763.   . "A Binding Attributed to John de Planche, c. 1572, " The Book Collector 13(3):340, 1964.

764.   . "A London Binding by John MacKinlay, c. 1810, " The Book Collector 13(4):486, 1964.

765.   . "A Binding by Lord Herbert's Binder, c. 1633, " The Book Collector 14(1):60, 1965.

766.   . "A Binding by the Flamboyant Binder, c. 1540-45, " The Book Collector 14(2):200, 1965.

767.   . "A Binding by Alexander Cleeve, c. 1690, " The Book Collector 14(3):348, 1965.

768.   . "A Binding Designed by James Stuart, 1762, " The Book Collector 14(4):538, 1965.

769.   . "An Adam Binding, 1764, " The Book Collector 15(2):184, 1966.

770.   . "Harleian Bindings by Chapman, 1721, " The Book Collector 15(3):321-322, 1966.

771.   . "A London Panel-Stamped Binding, c. 1530. Rebacked for James West, c. 1755, " The Book Collector 15(4):460, 1966.

772. Oldham, J. B. English Blind Stamped Bindings. Cambridge, England: Cambridge University Press, 1952. The only satisfactory classification of these bindings.

773.   . Schrewsbury School Library Bindings, Catalogue Raisonné. Oxford: Oxford University Press, 1943.

774.   . Blind Panels of English Binders. Cambridge, England: Cambridge University Press, 1958.

775. Oliver, Eugène; George Hermal; & Capitaine R. de. Roton. Manuel de l'Amateur de Reliures Armoriées Français. Paris: Ch. Bosse, Libraire, 1924-1938. Twenty-nine volume catalog with hundreds of illustrations of French armorial bindings, together with historical backgrounds. Excellent for identifications--2, 685 plates.

776. Olschki, Leo S. Riche et Précieuse Collection des Livres de XVe et XVIe Siecles. Florence: L. S. Olschki, 1900. A Booksellers catalog with 166 facsimiles.

777. Paton, Lucy A. Selective Bindings from the Gen-
      nadius Library. Cambridge, Mass.: Harvard
      University Press, 1924.

778. Penney, Clara L. An Album of Selected Bindings.
      New York: The Hispanic Society of America, 1968.
      Sixty-one plates offer examples of binder's craft in
      Spain since 1400. 93 pages.

779. "Persian Bookbinding of the Sixteenth Century,"
      British Museum Quarterly 30:10-100, 1964-1965.

780. Podlaha, A. Die Bibliothek des Metropolitan-Kapitels.
      Prague: 1904. Renaissance bindings.

781. Pollard, Alfred W. "The Franks Collection of Ar-
      morial Book-Stamps," The Book-Lover 4:423-429,
      1903.

782. _____. "An English Bookbinder's Ticket, c. 1610.
      'Facsimile'," The Library 4(12):332-335, 1932.

783. Pollard, Graham. "Changes in the Style of Bookbind-
      ing. 1550-1830," The Library 11(2), 1956. 24 pp,
      2 plates.

784. _____. "Changes in the Style of Bookbinding,
      1580-1830," Transactions of the Bibliographical
      Society, 1956.

785. _____. "The Construction of English Twelfth-Cen-
      tury Bindings," The Library 17:1-22, 1962.

786. (Poor, H. W.). American Bookbindings in the Li-
      brary of Henry William Poor. Described by Henri
      Pène du Bois. New York: G. D. Smith, 1903.
      77 pp. illus.

787. Prideaux, S. T. An Historical Sketch of Bookbinding,
      with a chapter on Early Stamped Bindings by E.
      Gordon Duff. London: Lawrence & Bullen, 1893.

788. _____. Modern Bookbindings. Their Design and
      Decoration. London: Constable, 1906. Modern
      English and French bindings.

789. _____. Notes on Printing and Bookbinding. Lon-
      don: South Kensington Museum, 1921. 40 pp. plus
      16 plates.

790. _____. "Some Scottish Bindings of the Last Cen-
      tury," Magazine of Art pp. 10-14, January, 1895.

791. Quaritch, Bernard. A Collection of Facsimiles from
      Examples of Historic or Artistic Bookbinding.
      London: Bernard Quaritch, 1889.

792. _____. Catalogue of the Special Exhibition of Art
      Bookbindings. Nottingham: Museum of Art Gal-
      lery, 1891.

793. _____. A Catalogue of English and Foreign Book-
      bindings for Sale. London: Bernard Quaritch, 1921.

794.   _____. A Catalogue of Fifteen Hundred Books.
            Remarkable for the Beauty or Age of Their Bind-
            ings. London: Bernard Quaritch, 1889. Catalogs
            by booksellers such as Quaritch are excellent
            sources for illustrations of fine bindings. They
            are always carefully identified.
795.   Ramsden, Charles. "The Collection of Hollis Bind-
            ings at Berne, " The Book Collector 7(2):165-170,
            1958. Describes 18th century binding decorations
            on an important collection of books.
796.   Regemorter, Berthe v. "Ethiopian Bookbindings, "
            The Library 5(17):85-88, 1962.
797.   _____. "The Binding of the Archangel Gospels, "
            The Book Collector 13(4):481-485, Winter, 1964.
798.   _____. Some Oriental Bindings in the Chester
            Beatty Library. Dublin: Hodges, Figgis, 1961.
            With 71 plates, 21 in color.
799.   _____. Some Early Bindings from Egypt in the
            Chester Beatty Library. Dublin: Hodges, Figgis,
            1958.
800.   Ricci, Seymour de. Catalogue of the British Signed
            Bindings in the M. L. Schiff Collection, 1935.
801.   Richardson, H. S. Examples of Ancient Bookbindings.
            London: South Kensington Museum, 1860. A
            portfolio of rubbings in the possession of the Art
            Library of South Kensington Museum.
802.   Rolland, Francisco Hueso. Exposicion de Encuader-
            naciones Españolas. Madrid: Sociedad Española
            de Amigos del Arte, 1954. A catalog of 534 12th
            to 19th century Spanish artistic bindings. 61 large
            plates, many in color. Extensive bibliography.
            Much information on various aspects of the develop-
            ment of artistic bindings in Spain. An important
            book.
803.   [No entry.]
804.   Rudbeck, Johannes. Svenska Bokband Under Nyare
            Tiden. Stockholm: Foreningen for Bok Handtverk,
            1912-1914. 3 vols: 1521-1718; 1718-1809; 1809-
            1880; 158 monochrome and 8 colored reproductions
            of bindings and illus. in the text.
805.   Rye, Reginnald Arthur and Muriel Sinton Quinn. His-
            torical and Armorial Bookbindings. Exhibited in
            the University Library; a descriptive catalogue.
            London: University of London, 1937.
806.   Sadleir, Michael. Evolution of Publishers' Binding
            Styles, 1770-1900. London: Archibald Constable,
            1930.

807. _____. "XIX Century Fiction, " The Book Collector 2(1), 1953. Includes an expansion of the author's earlier classification of binder's cloth.
808. Samford, C. Clement & John M. Hemphill. Bookbinding in Colonial Virginia. Charlottsville, Virginia:
The University of Virginia Press, 1966.
809. Sarre, F. Islamic Bookbindings. London: K. Paul,
Trench, Trubner, 1923.
810. Schjoldager, A. Bokbind ag Bokbindere I Norge inntil
1850. Oslo: 1927. Norwegian bookbinding.
811. Schmidt, A. Bucheinbände aus dem XIV-XIX.
Jahrhundert in der Landesbibliothek zu Darmstadt.
Leipzig: Hiersemann, 1921. The author pays
particular attention to German 16th century bookbindings.
812. Schunke, Ilse. Archiv für Buchbinderei. Leipzig:
1928. Heraldic binding identifications, etc.
813. _____. "Bindings by Krause and his School in
English Collections, " The Book Collector 8(1):25-
30, 1959.
814. _____. "Foreign Bookbindings II, " The Book Collector 18(2):201, 1969. Describes a 1519 binding
done in Bologna.
815. _____. Krause-Studien. Leipzig: 1932. German
decorative motives for bindings.
816. _____. Leben und Werke. Jacob Krause. Leipzig: 1943. Early German binder and his associates.
817. Sjogren, Arthur. Svenska Kunkliga och furstliga
Bokagaremarken. Stockholm: 1915. Many plates
of Swedish Royal bindings.
818. Smith, Simon Nowell. "Binding Variants, " The Book
Collector's Quarterly 10:84-87, April-June, 1933.
819. Sommerlad, M. J. Scottish "Wheel" and "Herring-
bone" Bindings in the Bodleian Library. Oxford:
Bibliographical Society, 1967. An illustrated hand
list of two distinctive decorative styles that were
popular in the 18th century.
820. Sotheran & Co. Beautiful Cosway Bindings. London:
Henry Sotheran & Co. , 1913. Illustrated catalog
of fine bindings in which are inlaid miniature
paintings.
821. Stark, Lewis. "Branded Books from Mexico, " Bulletin 4(8):738-741, 1942. New York Public Library.
822. Stevenson, J. H. "The Fifteenth-Century Scots Binding of the Haye Manuscript, " Endinburgh Bibliographical Society, Journal 6:77-82, 1901-1904.

823.   Stonehouse, J. S.   The Story of the Great Omar.
        London: Piccadilly Fountain Press, 1933.
824.   Strange, E. F.   "Modern Bookbindings & Their De-
        signers, " The Studio Winter, 1899-1900. Ameri-
        can bookbindings.
825.   Symons, A. F. A.   "Postwar English Bookbinding, "
        The Book-Collector's Quarterly 13:1-6, January-
        March, 1934.
826.   _____.   "Modern English Bindings at the First Edi-
        tions Club, " The Book Collector's Quarterly 13:81-
        86, January-March, 1934.
827.   Techner, J. J.   Reliures.   Paris: 1861.   (Accom-
        pagnée de Planches a l'eau-forte par Jules Jacque-
        mart - Folio).
828.   Thoinan, E.   Les Reliures Français, 1500-1800.
        Paris: Paul, Huard & Guillemin, 1893.
829.   Thomas, Henry.   Early Spanish Bookbindings.   Lon-
        don: The Bibliographical Society, 1939.   Devoted
        to the 11th to 15th century Madejar bindings deco-
        rated in blind.
830.   Thompson, Elbert A.   Fine Binding in America.
        Urbana, Illinois: Beta Phi Mu, 1956.
831.   Toldo, Vittorio de.   L'art Italien de la Reliure du
        Livre.   Milan: 1924.   Thirty-seven illustrations
        of the development of binding styles in Italy from
        the 15th to the 20th century.
832.   (Trow Press).   Bibliopegistic, to which is appended
        a glossary of some terms, used in the craft with
        illustrations of fine bindings.   New York: Trow
        Press, 191-.   32 p. illus.
833.   Tuckett, C. , Jr.   Specimens of Ancient and Modern
        Bookbinding.   London: 1846.   4 to.   Eight plates
        selected chiefly from the Library of the British
        Museum.
834.   Uzanne, Octave.   La Reliure Moderne Artistique et
        Fantaisiste.   Paris: Edouard Rouveyre, 1887.
        Fully illustrated descriptions in color of elaborate
        French bookbindings of the late 19th century.
835.   _____.   L'Art dans la Decoration Extérieure des
        Livres en France.   Paris: Henry May, 1898.
836.   Valuable Printed Books and Fine Bindings.   London:
        Sotheby, 1965.   Illustrated sale catalog of books
        from the collection of Major J. R. Abbey.
837.   (Victoria and Albert Museum).   A Picture Book of
        Bookbinding.   Part I: Before 1550; Part II: 1550-
        1800.   London: Victoria & Albert Museum, 1938.

838. _____. A Picture Book of Bookbindings. London: Victoria & Albert Museum, 1927.

✓839. _____. Bookbindings. London: Victoria & Albert Museum, 1950.

840. Wead, Eunice. "Early Binding Stamps of Religious Significance," The Colophon Part 20, 1935.

841. _____. "Early Binding Stamps of Religious Significance in Certain American Libraries: A Supplementary Report," Studies in Bibliography 2:63-77, 1949-1950.

842. Weale, W. H. L. Bookbindings and Rubbings of Bindings in the National Art Library, South Kensington Museum. London: Eyre and Spottiswoode, 1894-1898.

843. _____. "English Bookbinding in the Reign of Henry VII and Henry VIII," Journal of the Royal Society of Arts 37(1893):309-317, March 1, 1889.

844. Weill-Quillardet, Pierre-André and Lucie. Exhibition of Contemporary French Bookbindings and Illustrations. London: Ambassade de France, 1956.

845. Westendorp, Dr. K. Die Kunst Der Alten Buchbinder. Halle: A. D. Saale, Wilhelm Knapp, 1909. Descriptive text and 133 illustrations of 15th to 18th century European bindings.

846. Wheatley, H. B. Remarkable Bindings in the British Museum. London: S. Low, Marston, 1889.

847. _____. Catalogue of the Magnificent Library Formed by the Late H. B. Wheatley. London: Dryden Press, 1918.

848. _____. "The History and Art of Bookbinding," Journal of the Society of Arts 28:449-466, 1880.

849. _____. Bookbinding, Considered as a Fine Art, Mechanical Art and Manufacture. London: Elliot Stock, 1882.

850. Wilson, D. M. "An Anglo-Saxon Binding at Fulda," Antiquarian Journal July-October, 1901. (Codex Bonifalianus.)

851. Wilson, Edward. "The Book Stamps of the Tollemache Family of Helmingham and Ham," The Book Collector 16(2):178-186, 1967. A description of armorial stamps on book covers.

852. Woodward, G. M. Irish Binding. London: 1812.

FORE-EDGE PAINTING

853.   Davenport, Cyril James Humphries. "The Decoration
       of Book-Edges, " Bibliographica 2:385-406, 1896.
854.   Hamel, Frank. "The Art of Book-Edge Decoration, "
       The Book-Lover's Magazine 6:214-223, 1907.
855.   Hanson, T. W. "Edwards of Halifax, " Transactions
       of the Halifax Antiquarian Society pp. 141-200,
       November 1912.   Partial biography of a distin-
       guished fore-edge painter.
856.   Kellaway, C. William. "The Fore-Edge Paintings of
       Stephen and Thomas Lewis, " The Guildhall Miscel-
       lany 8:27-32, 1957.
857.   Raymond, Eugenia. "Fore-Edge Painting, " Bulletin
       of the Cincinnati Art Museum 3:131, 1932.
858.   Weber, Carl J. A Thousand and One Fore-Edge
       Paintings.   Waterville, Maine: Colby College
       Press, 1949.   Includes notes on the artists, book-
       binders, publishers and others connected with the
       art.   Reprinted 1966 [859].
859.   _____ . Fore-Edge Painting.   Irvington-on-Hudson:
       Harvey House, Inc., 1966.   Essentially a rewriting
       and updating of the author's 1949 A Thousand and
       One Fore-Edge Paintings.
860.   Zaehnsdorf, J. W. The Art of Bookbinding.   London:
       George Bell & Sons, 1890.   Chapter 17 describes
       various treatments for book edges including gilding
       over painted scenes.

BOOKPLATES

861.   Almack, Edward. Book-Plates.   London: Methuen,
       1904.   Well illustrated, descriptive history of
       bookplates.
862.   Carver, Clifford N.   Book-plates of Well Known
       Americans.   Princeton: Princeton University
       Press, 1911.
863.   Fletcher, R. K. Selected Book-Plates.   Boston:
       Smithsonian Press, 1947.
864.   Fowler, H. A. The Book-Plate Booklet.   Kansas
       City: 1908 to 1911 (?).   A quarterly magazine de-
       voted to book plates.

865. Fuller, George W. A Bibliography of Book-Plate
      Literature. Spokane, Wash.: Public Library,
      1926. A well indexed list of about nine hundred
      books and articles on book plates. American and
      European sources.
866. Vinycomb, John. On the Processes for the Produc-
      tion of Ex Libris (Book-Plates). London: A & C
      Black, 1894. Technical data with bound in samples
      for book plates in general use around the turn of
      the century.

PAPER AND PAPERMAKING

      PAPER (The Substance)

867. Ainsworth, J. H. Paper the Fifth Wonder. Kaukana,
      Wisconsin: Thomas Printing Co., 1967. A simpli-
      fied, well illustrated description of modern paper
      making.
868. Amman, Jost. Panoplia Omnium Illiberalium Me-
      chanicarum aut Sedentiarem Artium Genera Con-
      tinens. Frankfurt am Main: Sigismund Feyera-
      bend, 1568. This early book of trades, with Latin
      verses by Hartman Schopper, is dated January
      1958. The illustration of a papermaker is, ac-
      cording to Dard Hunter, the first in Western liter-
      ature. This book has always had great graphic
      arts interest because of its portrayals of type-
      founder (schriftgiesser), printer (buchdrucker),
      binder (buchbinder) and woodcut artist (form-
      schneider) as well as vellum maker (pergamenter)
      and papermaker.
869. Art of Paper-making. London: 1874. By Editor of
      The Paper Mills Dictionary.
870. The Art of Paper Making: a Guide to the Theory and
      Practice of the Manufacture of Paper. 2nd ed.
      London: 1876. A compilation from the best-
      known French, German, and American writers.
871. Barrow, W. J. "History of the Barrow Lab., or,
      the thirty years that revolutionized paper," Pub-
      lishers' Weekly 189(14):72-80, April 4, 1966.
872. Bayldon, Oliver. The Paper Makers Craft. Lei-
      cester: The Twelve by Eight Press, 1965. Oliver

Bayldon's translation of Imberdis' 17th century
Latin poem, Papyrus, is illustrated by Rigby Graham.

873.   Blanchet, A.   Essai sur l'Histoire du Papier et de
        sa Fabrication.   Paris: E. Leroux, 1900.

874.   Blum, André.   La Route du Papier.   Grenoble: Edi-
        tions de l'Industrie Papetière, 1946.   With seven
        plates.

875.   _____. On the Origin of Paper.   New York:
        Bowker, 1934.   Seventy-nine pages of which three
        or four are devoted to Asiatic paper.   Translated
        from the French by Harry Miller Lydenberg.

876.   The Book of English Trades and Library of the Useful
        Arts.   10th edition.   London: n. d. (c. 1821).   This
        popular little juvenile contains a seven-page article
        on papermaking and a rather crude illustration of
        a papermaker.   The article mentions the Four-
        drinier brothers' patent for paper machines and that
        a "great number" have been erected, as well as
        making passing reference to Mr. Koop (sic) and
        his lack of success with straw paper.

877.   Breitkopf, J. G. I.   Versuch den Ursprung der
        Spielkarten, die Einführung des Leinenpapiers, und
        den Anfang der Holzschneiderkunst in Europa zu
        Erforschen.   Leipzig: Breitkopf, 1784. 2 vols.,
        quarto.   The first volume of this work deals ex-
        tensively with the history of paper, and contains
        fourteen plates, of which seven illustrate paper-
        making, both Oriental and Western.

878.   Briquet, C. M.   Recherches sur les Premiers Papiers
        en Occident et en Orient du Xe au XIVe Siècle.
        Paris: 1886.

879.   Brown, T.   Introducing Paper.   London: J. Whitaker
        & Sons, 1939.

880.   Carter, Thomas F.   The Invention of Printing in
        China and Its Spread Westward.   New York: Co-
        lumbia University Press, 1925.   Pages 1-6 de-
        scribe the invention of paper in China.   Three il-
        lustrations.

881.   Černy, Jaroslav.   Paper and Books in Ancient Egypt.
        London: H. K. Lewis, 1952.

882.   Chapman, R. W.   "An Inventory of Paper, 1674, "
        The Library 1926-1927.

883.   Churchyard, Thos.   A Description and Playne Dis-
        course of Paper.   London: 1588.   Reprinted in
        the Progress and Public Processions of Queen
        Elizabeth ed. by John Nicols, 2:592-602, 1823,

(London); and in R. H. Clapperton, A Historical
Account, etc. Oxford: 1934. [884]

884. Clapperton, R. H. Paper. An historical account of
its making by hand from the earliest times down
to the present day. Oxford: Shakespeare Head
Press, 1934. Includes a facsimile reproduction of
text and illustrations of Kamisuki Chohoki (a handy
guide for paper makers) published in Japan in
1798, [1514].

885. _____. "The History of Papermaking in England,"
Paper Maker 22:9-22, September, 1953.

886. _____. The Papermaking Machine. Oxford:
Pergamon Press, 1967. Eighteen folding plates
and 200 other illustrations. Covers invention and
development over the years.

887. Coleman, D. C. The British Paper Industry 1495-
1860. London: 1958. A study of the economic
development of the book trade.

888. Contribution à l'Histoire de la Papetèrie en France.
Grenoble: 1934-1945. vols 1 to 11, containing
numerous important articles by various French
writers, chiefly on the local history of paper-making in France, with many of the watermarks of
the mills.

889. Curzon, Robert. "Printing in China and Europe,"
Miscellanies of the Philobiblon Society 6:1-33,
1860. Description of invention of paper in China
and spread of the knowledge into Europe.

890. Degaast, Georges & Germaine Rigaud. Les Supports
de la Pensée: Historique. Paris: circa 1942.
Chiefly on the history of papermaking; includes a
bibliography.

891. de Villette, Charles Marquis. Oeuvres. Londres
(Paris): 1786. This is the first European book
printed on paper made from vegetable material
without the use of any rag fiber.

892. Dureau De La Malle, D. J. C. A. Le Papyrus et
Fabrication du Papier Chez les Anciens. Paris:
Institute Academie de Science 19(1), 1851.

893. Edkins, Joseph. "On the Origin of Paper Making in
China," Notes and Queries on China and Japan
1(6):67-68, June, 1867.

894. Egger, E. Le Papier dans l'Antiquité et dans les
Temps Modernes. Paris: L. Hachette, 1866.

895. Erfurt, Julius. The Dyeing of Paper Pulp. London:
Scott, Greenwood & Co., 1901. An English translation of the only book of its time devoted to the

dyeing of paper pulp. Discusses extensively the
use of aniline colors, and contains 157 colored
specimens.

896. Evans, Joan. The Endless Web: John Dickinson &
      Co. Ltd. , 1804-1954. London: Jonathan Cape,
      1955. A company history.

897. Evans, L. Ancient Paper Making. London: 1896.

898. Evelyn, John, The Diary of. Oxford: Claredon
      Press, 1958. On 24 August, 1678, Evelyn's diary
      describes a visit to a papermill in London where
      he saw the material being made. Reports that the
      finished sheets were dipped in allume (sic) water
      then polished.

899. Ewald, A. C. Paper and Parchment: Historical
      Sketches. London: Ward & Downey, 1890.

900. Garnett, R. Essays in Librarianship. London:
      George Allen, 1899. The manufacture of fine pa-
      per in England in the 18th century.

901. Garzoni, Tomasso. Piazzi Universale: Das ist
      Allgemeine Schawplatz. Frankfurt am Main:
      Venezia: Alberti, 1616. This German reprint of
      the original Venetian work of 1586 is illustrated
      with the Jost Amman woodcuts of trades from the
      illustrator's books of 1568. The volume is in the
      form of 153 discourses on various trades and pro-
      fessions of which the one concerning paper and
      other writing materials is the 28th. With its 1084
      pages of text, including ten on paper, the book
      gives a broad picture of commercial life of the
      time.

902. Gaskell, P. "Notes on 18th Century British Paper, "
      The Library 5th series, vol 12, March 1957.

903. Goodrich, L. Carrington. "Paper: A Note on its
      Origin, " ISIS 42(2):128-145, June 1951.

904. Grand-Carteret, John. Papeterie et Papetiers de
      l'Ancien Temps. Paris: 1913.

905. Guettard, J. E. "Inquiry concerning the Materials
      that may be Used in Making Paper, by Mr. Guet-
      tard, of the Royal Academy of Sciences, and
      Physician to His Serene Highness, the Duke of
      Orleans, " Select Essays on Commerce, Agricul-
      ture, Mines, Fisheries, and Other Useful Subjects.
      Paris: Durand, 1747.

906. Guilmain, Réné. Technologie du Papier, La fabr. du
      Papier de ses origines au 19ème Siècle. n. d.
      First and only section published.

907. Happelius, E. G. Mundus Mirabilis. Von der Papiermacher-Kunst (1689). Berlin: Officina Serpentis, 1930.

908. Hartmann, Carl. Handbuch der Papierfabrikation. Berlin: 1842. The eight lithographed plates in this early technical handbook show equipment both for hand and machine papermaking, as well as for stock preparation and finishing.

909. Herring, R. Paper and Paper Making, Ancient and Modern. London: Longman, Brown, Green & Longmans, 1856. A good account of early 19th century papermaking by machine.

910. Hoernle, A. F. R. "Who Was the Inventor of Rag Paper?" Journal Royal Asiatic Society pp. 663-684, 1903.

911. Hofmann, Carl. A Practical Treatise on the Manufacture of Paper. Philadelphia: Henry Carey Baird Co., 1873. Paper making in all its branches as it was known and practiced in the latter half of the 19th century.

912. Hou Han Shu (Book of the Second Han Dynasty) AD 990-994. This official history of the second Han dynasty includes Fan Yeh's biographical sketch of Ts'ai Lun and the invention of paper.

913. Hunter, Dard. "Fifteenth Century Papermaking," Ars Typographica 3(1):37-51, 1926.

914. _____. The Literature of Papermaking 1390-1800. Chillicothe, Ohio: The Mountain House Press, 1925. 48 pages, 20 illustrations, 23 facsimile title pages.

915. _____. Papermaking by Hand in America. Chillicothe, Ohio: The Mountain House Press, 1950. Large folio. The last work of the Mountain House Press and the author's magnum opus, this book provides a history of American papermaking by listing and describing the first paper mill in each State from 1690 until 1811, six years prior to the introduction of the first paper machine into the United States. 123 facsimiles of documents and watermarks and 42 reproductions of labels used by these early paper manufacturers. The thick folio volume was to have been issued in an edition of 210 copies, but the author's own bibliography says that only 180 were completed. The book is printed on Dard Hunter's paper.

916. _____. Paper Making: The History and Technique of an Ancient Craft. 2nd ed. New York: Knopf,

1947.   611 p. illus. (reprinted 1967). *1957*
917.   [No entry.]
918.   _____.   Paper Making Through Eighteen Centuries.
New York: W. E. Rudge, 1930.   This is a more
comprehensive treatment of the material in the author's Old Papermaking, (1923).   Excellent information on early paper; early papermakers and their
products.   Good introduction to the study of watermarks.
919.   Imberdis, Le P. Jean, (S. J.).   Papyrus, Sive Ars
Conficiendae Papyri ... Le Papier, ou l'Art de
Fabriquer le Papier.   1693 Traduction par Augustin Blanchet.   Paris: C. Beranger, 1899.   One
of the earliest works on papermaking.
920.   Jenkins, Rhys.   "Early Papermaking in England,
1495-1788, " The Library Association Record 2:9-
11;   3:5;   4:3-4, 1900-1902.
921.   Kaempfer, Engelbertus.   The History of Japan.   2
vols.   London: 1727.   This work, translated from
Kaempfer's unpublished manuscript by J. G.
Scheuchzer, contains the earliest reference known
in the West to Japanese papermaking.   In Appendix
contained in vol. 2 there is a seven-page reference
to the methods and materials used by the Japanese
for making paper, as well as three plates illustrating the plants used in the process.   This reference
to the use of wood for papermaking long precedes
any European experimentation along the same lines.
922.   Kameso, Asakura.   History of Early Printing in
Japan.   Tokyo: 1909.   Includes early Japanese
papermaking.
923.   Karabacek, Josef von.   Das Arabische Papier.   Vienna: 1887.
924.   Koops, Matthias.   Historical Account of the Substances Which Have Been Used to Describe Events
and Convey Ideas.   London: Jaques & Co. , 1801.
A sketchy history of writing materials, but interesting because the book is printed on paper made
from straw and an appendix is printed on paper
made from wood in 1801.
925.   Labarre, E. J.   Dictionary and Encyclopedia of Paper and Paper Making.   Amsterdam: Swets and
Zeitlinger, 1952.   Indexed in English, French,
German, Dutch, Spanish, Swedish and Italian.   See
also [938.]
926.   Lalande, J. J. L. F. de.   "Art de Faire le Papier, "
Déscriptions des arts et metiers faites ou

approuvees par messieurs de l'Academie royal des
sciences. vol. 1, sec. 5. Paris: Chez Dessaint
& Saillant, 1761.

927.   . "Art de Faire le Papier, " Déscriptions
des arts et metiers, faites ou approuvees par
messieurs de l'Academie des sciences de Paris.
vol. 4 (nouvelle edition). Neuchatel: De l'Imprimerie de la Society typographique, 1776.

928.   . Art de Faire le Papier. Paris, Saillant
et Nyon, 1761. Technical treatise with fold-out
plates on papermaking as practiced in France,
Holland, China and Japan. Plates are those engraved by M. Desbillets in 1698 for the Academy
of Sciences. Also in Déscriptions des arts et
metiers etc. Paris: l'Academie Royale des Sciences, 1771-1783, (vol. 4 1776).

929.   . Art de Faire le Papier. Paris: J.
Moronval, 1820. Revised edition of 1761 edition
includes in addition to the original text, "all that
had been written" (to 1820) on the subject of papermaking in Germany, England, Switzerland and
Italy.

930.   Lemoine, H. Typographical Antiquities. London: •
S. Fisher, 1797. Includes dissertation on the origin and uses of paper.

931.   Lenz, Hans. Mexican Indian Paper: Its History and
Survival. Mexico: Editorial Cultura, 1961. Translated from the Spanish by H. M. Campbell.

932.   Letter on the Origin of the Natural Paper of Cortona,
with Other Observations Relative to the Uses and
Excellent Qualities of the Conferva of Pliny. Pisa:
1764.

933.   Li Shu-Hua. The Spread of the Art of Paper Making.
Taipei, Taiwan: National Historical Museum, 1960.
Text in English and Chinese.

934.   Lenormand, Louis Seb. Manuel du Fabricant de
Papiers. Paris: Encyclopédie-Roret, 1833-1834.
2 vols., small octavo. This technical book contains, in its second volume, a brief note of improvements in the industry since 1800. The industrial, rather than craft, approach is evident
throughout. An appendix and plates deal with the
paper machine, still comparatively new in use on
the continent.

935.   Lloyd, E. "Account of a Sort of Paper Made of
Linum Asbestinum Found in Wales, " Philosophical
Transactions 3:105, 1684.

936. Lloyd, L. C. "Paper-making in Shropshire, 1656-
      1912, " Transactions Shropshire Archaeology Soci-
      ety 1930.
937. Lockwood Trade Journal Co. 1690-1940. New York:
      Lockwood Trade Journal Co., 1940. 250 years of
      papermaking in America. 180 p. illus.
√ 938. Loeber, E. G. Supplement to Labarre's Dictionary
      and Encyclopedia of Paper and Paper Making.
      Amsterdam: Swetz and Zeitlinger, 1967. See also
      925.
939. Maddox, H. A. Paper, Its History, Sources and
      Manufacture. London: Pitman & Sons, 1933.
      Reprinted 1945.
940. Mason, J. The Paper Makers Craft. Leicester:
      Twelve by Eight Press, 1965. Verse translation
      from a 17th century Latin poem, "Papyrus"(Father
      Imberdis) [919] printed on various handmade pa-
      pers from English mills.
941. Means, P. A. "Ancient American Papermaking, "
      ISIS 35(99), Winter, 1944.
942. Mitford, A. B. F. The History of Paper, 1912.
      An address to the Royal Photographic Society.
943. Monumenta Chartae Papyraceae Historiam Illustrantia.
      Hilversum: Paper Publications Society, 1950-1965.
      vols. 1-5 watermarks; vol. 6 English papermills;
      vol. 7 ancient Basle papermills; vol. 8 Austro-
      Hungarian mills; vol. 9 paper mills of Berne; vol.
      11 Tromanin's watermark album.
944. Morris, Henry. Omnibus. North Hills, Penn. :
      The Bird & Bull Press, 1967. The text of this
      book recites Morris' experiences with hand paper-
      making, and offers "instructions for amateur pa-
      permakers. " There are seven specimens of Mor-
      ris' paper, one of Dard Hunter's, one of paper
      made at De Schoolmeester mill in the Netherlands,
      and one of paper by Roger Daniels. 500 copies
      were issued.
945. Murray, John. Practical Remarks on Modern Paper,
      with an Introductory Account of its Former Sub-
      stitutes; Also Observations on Writing Inks, the
      Restoration of Illegible Manuscripts, and the Pre-
      servation of Important Deeds from the ... Effects
      of Damp. London: T. Cadell, 1829.
946. _____. An Account of the Phormium Tenax; or
      New Zealand Flax. London: Henry Renshaw,
      1836. Printed on paper made from leaves of the
      flax with a postscript on paper.

947.   _____. A Descriptive Account of the Palo de Vaca,
        or Cow-Tree of the Caracas, etc. 2nd ed. Lon-
        don: Relfe & Fletcher, 1838.
948.   _____. Observations and Experiments on the Bad
        Composition of Modern Paper. London: Whittaker,
        1824.
949.   Narita, Kiyofusa. A Life of Ts'ai Lun and Japanese
        Paper-Making. Tokyo: The Dainihon Press, 1966.
        A short account of the life of the "inventor" of
        paper in China, and a brief historical account of
        the development of paper making in Japan. The
        author is Director of the Paper Museum in Tokyo.
950.   _____. Japanese Paper-Making. Tokyo: Hoku-
        seido Press, 1954. A short concise account of
        history and technique of Japanese papermaking in-
        tended for tourist information but of value in lieu
        of earlier but now out of print books on the sub-
        ject.
951.   The Paper-Maker and Stationer's Assistant. London:
        1794.
✓ 952. Papermaking, Art and Craft. Washington: Library
        of Congress, 1968. 96-page account of the history
        of papermaking from earliest times. Well illus-
        trated.
953.   Parkes, Harry S. Report on the Manufacture of Pa-
        per in Japan. London: House of Commons, 1871.
        Includes facsimile reproduction of Kamisuki Choho-
        ki (Handbook of paper making). Osaka: 1798.
954.   Perkins, P. D. The Paper Industry and Printing in
        Japan. New York: Japan Reference Library, 1940.
955.   Pizzetta, Jules. Historia de un Pliego de Papel
        traducida for DJVYC. Madrid: Biblioteca Cienti-
        fica Recreative (ca. 1900).
956.   Planche, Gabriel. De l'Industrie de la Papeterie.
        Paris: Didot, 1853. A midnineteenth century
        manual by Didot's chief papermaker.
957.   Principia Typographica, 3 vols. London: Samuel
        Leigh Sotheby, 1858. Block Books, Origin of
        Printing, Paper-marks.
958.   Prouteaux, A. (ed.). Practical Guide for the Manu-
        facture of Paper and Boards. Philadelphia: 1866.
        This is the first practical treatise on papermaking
        published in the United States. In a chapter by
        Henry T. Brown, there are recorded the earliest
        commercial efforts at manufacture of wood pulp
        paper in the United States. The chapter, five
        pages long, describes the manufacture of woodpulp

         by this process in Pennsylvania.
959. Puget, P. La Fabrication du Papier. Paris: J. B.
         Baillière, 1911.
960. Rein, J. J. The Industries of Japan, with an Account
         of its Agriculture, Forestry, Arts, and Commerce.
         London: Hodder & Stoughton, 1889. 30 pages of
         text, 5 illustrations and one specimen devoted to
         Japanese papermaking.
961. Reko, Victor A. "Altmexikanisches Papiers, "
         Faserforschung 10(2), 1933. An essay on ancient
         Mexican papers.
962. Renker, Armin. Das Buch vom Papier. Leipzig:
         Insel-Verlag, 1934. This is the first of several
         editions of the book written by the German paper-
         maker and paper historian. Reprinted Leipzig:
         Ensel, 1935.
963. Report of the Federal Trade Commission on the News-
         print Paper Industry. Washington: Federal Trade
         Commission, 1917.
964. Reports on the Manufacture of Paper in Japan. Lon-
         don: House of Commons, 1871. Harry S. Parkes'
         Report to the Parliament [953].
965. Sayce, R. Primitive Arts and Crafts. New York:
         Biblo & Tannen, 1963. Includes articles on early
         paper making.
966. Schäffer, Jacob Christian. Versuche und Muster ohne
         alle Lumpen oder dock mit einem geringen Zusatze
         derselben Papier zu Machen. Regensburg: 1765-
         1771, 6 vol. small quarto. Issued in six volumes
         over a six-year period, this work is the first
         carefully documented research into the use of
         materials other than rags for the manufacture of
         paper in the West. In all, the six volumes con-
         tain 176 pages of text and 87 specimens.
967. _____ . Sämtliche Papierversuche. Regensburg:
         1772, small quarto. This is a collected version
         of Schäffer's earlier six-volume work and contains
         81 specimens in all.
√ 968. Schlosser, Leonard B. "Books on the history of pa-
         permaking, " Guild of Book Workers Journal 8(1)
         1969. pp. 20-23. Author emphasizes and demon-
         strates that all handmade papers from 16th-19th
         century were not of high quality.
969. Smith, J. E. A. A History of Paper its Genesis and
         its Revelations. Holyoke, Mass. : Clarke W.
         Bryan & Co. , 1882.

970.   The Spread of the Art of Paper-making and the Dis-
        coveries of Old Paper. Taipei: National Histori-
        cal Museum, 1958.
971.   Starr, Frederick. "Mexican Paper," American Anti-
        quarian 22(11), 1900.
972.   Stedman, E. H. Bluegrass Craftsman. Lexington:
        University of Kentucky Press, 1959. Reminiscences
        of an early 19th century paper maker.
973.   Stein, Sir Mark Aurel. Serindia. Oxford: Clarendon
        Press, 1921. On page 674 Stein describes his dis-
        covery in Western China of one of the oldest pieces
        of paper (mulberry) in the world (AD 137).
974.   Stevens, Richard T. The Art of Papermaking in
        Japan. New York: privately printed, 1909. Re-
        printed by the Japanese in facsimile in 1943.
975.   Stevenson, L. T. The Background and Economics of
        American Papermaking. New York: Harper, 1940.
976.   The Story of Paper-making. Chicago: J. W. Butler
        Paper Co., 1901.
977.   Stromer, Ulman. Püchl von Meim Geslecht und von
        Abentewr. Nürnberg: 1390. This is the earliest
        known European document regarding papermaking.
978.   Suarez Y Nuñez, Don Miguel Geronymo (trans.).
        Arte de Hacer el Papel. Madrid: D. Pedro Mar-
        in, 1778. Spanish edition of De Lalande's Arte de
        Faire le Papier. Paris, 1761, [926].
979.   Subira, O. V. "Three Hundred Years of Paper in
        Spain," The Paper Maker 34, 1965.
980.   Sung Ying-Hsing. T'ien Kung K'ai Wu, 1634. The
        earliest Chinese book to deal with paper making.
        Four wood block illustrations.
981.   Tindale, Thomas K. & Harriett R. The Handmade
        Papers of Japan. Rutland, Vermont (and Tokyo):
        Charles E. Tuttle Co., 1952, large quarto., 4
        vols. This monumental study of the subject has
        a foreword by Dard Hunter and consists of four
        parts. Vol. 1, The Handmade Papers of Japan,
        contains photographs of the process, as well as the
        prefatory material, and a color reproduction of
        Kamisuki Taigai (General Outlining of Papermak-
        ing) and a bibliography by Bunsho Jugaku. Vol. 2
        contains 187 specimens of paper from the Nara
        period (710-793) to the present day. Vol. 3 con-
        tains the Contemporary Collection: 139 specimens
        of modern paper from the various prefectures of
        Japan. Vol. 4, The Watermark Collection, has in
        it five specimens of fiber and twenty large samples

of the finest of Japanese light-and-shade watermarks.
982. Tschudin, Walter F. "Oldest Methods of Papermaking in the Far East," Chemical Abstracts 53: 1959.
983. Vachon, Marius. Les Artes et les Industries du
Papier en France, 1871-1894. Paris: Librairies
Imprimeries Réunies, 1895.
984. Valentine, J. J. "Mexican Paper," Proceedings,
American Antiquarian Society 1, 1881.
985. Van Gelder-Zonen. The Poetry of the Paper Industry.
Amsterdam: Van Gelder-Zonen, n. d.
986. Von Hagen, Victor Wolfgang. Aztec and Mayan Paper
Makers. New York: J. J. Augustin, Limited Edition, 1943, Trade Edition, 1944. 115 pp. 32
plates. A scholarly study of the history and technique of ancient paper making in America. (Samples bound in 1943 edition.)
987. Voorn, H. The Paper Mills of Denmark and Norway
and Their Watermarks. Hilversum: Paper Publications Society, 1959.
988. _____. "Papermaking in the Moslem World,"
Paper Maker 28, 1959.
989. Weeks, L. H. A History of Paper-manufacturing in
the United States, 1690-1916. New York: Lockwood Trade Journal Co., 1916.
990. Wehrs, Georg Fr. Vom Papier, den vor der Erfin-
dung desselben üblich gewesenen Schreibmassen und
Sonstigen Schreibmaterialen. Halle: 1789.
This is the earliest major bibliographical and historical effort on papermaking, and remains important today although scarce and never translated into
English.
991. White, Oswald. Japanese Paper Making. London:
H. M. Foreign Office, 1905.
992. Williamson, Hugh. Methods of Book Design. London:
Oxford University Press, 1966. Includes chapters
on paper and bookbinding.
993. (Wood Pulp). "America's Pioneer in Wood Pulp,"
The Paper Mill and Wood Pulp News 50(9), 1927.
A brief account of the work of Albrecht Pagenstecher who introduced the ground wood pulp industry into the United States and later both the
sulfite and sulfate processes.
994. Zonghi, Aurelio. Le marche principali delle carte
fabrianesi dal 1293 al 1599. Fano: Tipographia
Sonciniana, 1881.

995.   _____.   Le antiche carte fabrianesi alla Esposi-
       zione generale Italiana di Torino.   Fano: Tipo-
       graphia Sonciniana, 1884.

Paper Mills

996.   Alibaux, Henri.   Les Premieres Papeteries Fran-
       çaises.   Paris: 1926.
997.   Balston, T.   James Whatman Father and Son.   Lon-
       don: Methuen & Co., 1957.   Appendices contain
       much information on Whatman watermarks.
998.   _____.   William Balston Paper Maker.   London:
       Methuen & Co., 1954.   Considerable technical in-
       formation on Turkey Mill paper.
999.   Barker, Charles, R.   "Old Mills of Mill Creek,
       Lower Merion, Pennsylvania, " The Pennsylvania
       Magazine of History and Biography 50(1), 1926.
1000. Blake, Moffitt & Towne.   Pioneers in Paper; the
       Story of Blake, Moffitt & Towne.   San Francisco:
       Blake, Moffitt & Towne, 1930.
1001. Blum, Andre.   "Les Premieres Fabriques de Papier
       en Occident, " Comptesrendes des Seances de
       l'Académie des Inscriptions et Belles-Lettres.
       Paris: 1932.
1002. Canfield, R. E.   "The Paper Industry," Think.   May,
       1947.
1003. Carter, Harry.   Wolvercote Mill: A Study of Paper-
       Making at Oxford.   Oxford: Bibliographical Soci-
       ety, 1957.   Illustrated.
1004. Crane, Ellery B.   Early Paper Mills in Massachu-
       setts, Especially Worcester County.   Worcester,
       Mass.:   F. P. Price, 1887.
1005. Designs and Typography for Cover Paper.   Washing-
       ton: The District of Columbia Paper Manufactur-
       ing Company, 1924.   This sample book contains
       work by a number of distinguished American graph-
       ic designers, among them W. S. Dwigins and
       Walter Dorwin Teague.
1006. Directory of Paper Makers.   London: Marchant
       Singer and Co., 1885.
1007. Eineder, G.   The Ancient Paper Mills of the Former
       Austro-Hungarian Empire and Their Watermarks.
       Hilversum: Paper Publications Society, 1960.
1008. Evans, Joan.   The Endless Web.   London: Jonathan
       Cape, 1955.   The history of papermakers John
       Dickinson & Co., Ltd. 1804-1954.

1009. Geyer's American Paper Trade Directory, Containing
       a complete list of all paper, fiber and wood pulp
       mills in the United States and Canada.   v. 1, New
       York, 18-?.   Title changed: 1885, Geyer's Di-
       rectory of the American Paper Trade.   1886-1891,
       Geyer's Reference Directory of the Booksellers and
       Stationers of the United States and Canada.   1893,
       Geyer's Directory of the American Paper Trade.
       1894, Geyer's American Paper Trade Directory.

1010. Goodwin, Rutherford.   The William Parks Paper Mill
       at Williamsburg.   Lexington, Va.:   Washington &
       Lee University Press, 1939.

1011. Goold, William.   Early Papermills of New England.
       Boston: Maine Historical Society, 1875.

1012. Hurlbut's Papermaker Gentleman   1(3), January, 1933-
       1935.   South Lee, Mass.:   Hurlbut Paper Co.,
       1933-1935.

1013. Isnard, Emile.   Les Papeteries de Provence ou 18me
       Siècle.   Paris: 1916.

1014. Jones, Horatio Gates.   "Historical Sketch of the Rit-
       tenhouse Paper Mill; the First Erected in America,
       AD 1690, " The Pennsylvania Magazine of History
       and Biography 20(3), 1896.

1015. [No entry.]

1016. Lihdt, J.   The Paper-Mills of Berne and their Water-
       marks.   Hilversum: Paper Publications Society, 1964.

1017. Melville, Herman.   "The Paradise of Bachelors and
       the Tartarus of Maids, " (Paper factory Devils
       Dungeon) Billy Budd.   London: John Lehmann, 1946.

1018. Nicolai, A.   Histoire des Moulins a Papier du Sud-
       ouest de la France, 1300-1800.   Bordeaux: G.
       Delmas, 1935.

1019. Onfroy, Henri.   Papermaking as Conducted in Western
       Mass. , with a Brief History from the Earliest
       Ages.   Springfield, Mass.:   1874.

1020. Paper Manufacturers.   New York: 1842.   A memo-
       rial.

1021. (Paper Manufacturers).   Census of Manufacturers
       1905: Paper and Wood Pulp.   Washington: United
       States Census Office, 1907.

1022. Perrin, A.   Les Caproni, fabricants de papier aux
       XVIIe et XVIIIe Siècles, Leurs Marques et Fili-
       granes.   Chambery: 1892.

1023. Planche, G.   De l'Industrie de la Papeterie.   Paris:
       Didot, 1853.

1024. Riddle, E. C.   Whatman Paper Mill.   Maidstone,
       Kent: 1907.

1025. Roger, Daniel. Rapid, a Private Paper Mill. Mel-
      bourne: Privately Printed, 1963. Small folio
      (5" x 7 1/2"). Contained in the book are eleven
      specimens of experimental paper made by the au-
      thor from various materials along with photographs
      of his equipment. 15 copies.
1026. Schedel, Hartmann. Liber Chronicarum. Nürnberg:
      Anton Koberger, 1493. The woodcut of the city of
      Nürnburg contains what has traditionally been con-
      sidered the first illustration of a paper mill.
1027. Shears, W. S. William Nash of St. Paul's Cray,
      Papermakers. London: Batchworth Press, 1950.
1028. Shorter, A. H. Paper Mills and Paper Makers in
      England 1495-1800. Hilversum: Paper Publications
      Society, 1957.
1029. Smith, J. E. A. Pioneer Papermaking in Berkshire.
      Holyoke, Mass.: Clarke W. Bryan & Co., n. d.
1030. Stevenson, L. T. The background and Economics of
      American Papermaking. New York: Harper, 1940.
1031. Tschudin, Walter F. The Ancient Paper-Mills of
      Basle and Their Marks. Hilversum: Paper Pub-
      lications Society, 1958. Edited and translated by
      E. J. Labarre.
1 032. Turgan, J. "Papeterie de'Essonne," Les Grandes
      Usines de France 1861.
1033. Twerdy, E. "Papier Industrie," Austria. Gen. Direc.
      der Weltausstil 1873. (Offic. Bericht, No. 38.)
1034. Uchastkina, Z. V'E. A History of Russian Hand Pa-
      per Mills and Their Watermarks. Hilversum:
      Paper Publications Society, 1962.
1035. Vallette de Veriville, A. 'Notes pour servir a l'His-
      toire du Papier," Gazette des Beaux-artes 2(4),
      1859. (To 1510.)
1036. Valls I Subira, Oriel. "El Papel Catalan y el
      Museo-Molino Papelero de Capellades," Bolletino
      dell Istituto di Patologia del Libro 22, 1963. Il-
      lustrated article on a paper museum in a town
      where paper has been made by hand since 1238.
1037. von Murr, C. G. Beschreibung der vornehmsten
      Merkwurdigkeiten in ... Nürnberg und ... Altdorf.
      Nürnburg: 1778. This guidebook contains a
      reference in its chronological section to the Ulman
      Stromer [977] Mill and to his diary as well as to
      von Murr's earlier journals in which he discussed
      Germany's first papermaker at greater length.
1038. Voorn, H. The Paper Mills of Denmark and Norway
      and Their Watermarks. Hilversum: Paper

Publications Society, 1959.
1039. Wardrop, James. "Mr. Whatman, Papermaker, 1702-
       1750, and his son, James Whatman, 1741-1798, "
       Signature 9, 1938.
1040. (Warren). A History of the S. D. Warren Company
       1854-1954. Westbrook, Maine: S. D. Warren
       Co., 1955. Much technical data on papermaking
       and an interesting exposition of the transition from
       rags to wood pulp as the principle raw material in
       this company's operations.
1041. Weckbach, H. "On the History of Heilbroun Paper
       Mills, " Papiergeschichte 15(5-6):53-59, 1965.
1042. Weeks, L. H. A History of Paper-Manufacturing in
       the United States, 1690-1916. New York: Lock-
       wood Trade Journal Co., 1916.
1043. Wilcox, Joseph. Ivy Mills 1729-1866: Wilcox and
       Allied Families. Baltimore: 1911.
1044. Wiswall, Clarence A. & E. B. Crafts. One Hundred
       Years of Papermaking: A History of the Industry
       on the Charles River at Newton Lower Falls, Mas-
       sachusetts. Reading, Massachusetts: Reading
       Chronical, 1938.
1045. Zonca, Vittorio. Novo Teatro Di Machine Et Edi-
       ficii. Padova: 1621. The stamping-mill for the
       preparation of paper pulp, is one of 39 mechanical
       devices of various kinds. The illustration is one
       of the earliest known.

Watermarks

1046. Bayley, H. A New Light on the Renaissance: Dis-
       played in Contemporary Emblems. London: J. M.
       Dent, 1909. Over 400 illustrations of emblems
       used in watermarks, etc.
1047. Beans, G. H. Some Sixteenth Century Watermarks
       Found in Maps Prevalent in Italian-assembled-to-
       order (IATO) Atlases. Jenkintown: George H.
       Beans Library, 1938.
1048. Blum, Andre. On the Origin of Paper. New York:
       R. R. Bowker, 1934. Translated from the French
       by Harry M. Lydenberg. Includes chapter on the
       dating of paper by watermarks.
1049. Bojarull y Sans, F. de. Animals in Watermarks.
       Hilversum: Paper Publications Society, 1959.
1050. Briquet, Charles M. Les Filigranes Dictionnaire
       Historique des Marques du Papier des Leur

Apparition vers 1282 Jusqu'en 1600, 4 vols. Paris:
A. Picard & fils, 1907.

1051. _____. Les Filigranes ont-ils un sens caché?
Besancon: Typographie et Lithographie Jacquin,
1910.

1052. _____. Papiers et Filigranes des Archives de
Genes, 1154 a 1700. Geneva: H. Georg, 1888.
Identifies hundreds of early watermarks.

1053. _____. Les Filigranes. 2nd ed. Leipzig: 1923.
Four illustrated volumes of watermarks from 13th
thru 16th centuries.

1054. _____. The Briquet Album. Hilversum: Paper
Publications Society, 1952. A miscellany on watermarks supplementing Dr. Briquet's Les Filigranes
[1050] by various paper scholars.

1055. Churchill, W. A. Watermarks in Paper. Amsterdam: Menno Hertzberger, 1935. Illustrated text
on 17th and 18th century watermarks.

1056. _____. Watermarks in Paper. Amsterdam: Menno Hertzberger & Co., 1967. This is the third
impression of the 1935 edition of nearly 600 full-
size reproductions of 17th and 18th century European watermarks together with additional information on papermakers, their mills, etc.

1057. Denne, Samuel. "Observations on Paper-Marks,"
Archaeologia 12, 1796.

1058. Gruel, Leon. Recherches sur les origines des mar-
ques anciennes, par rapport au chiffre quatre.
Paris: 1926.

1059. Heawood, Edward M. A. Monumenta Charte Papyraceae - I, Watermarks. Hilversum: The Paper
Publications Society, 1950. Rather than a general
survey, this is a collection (4060 items) of mainly
17th and 18th century watermarks many not pre-
viously recorded.

1060. _____. Watermarks Mainly of the 17th and 18th
Centuries. Hilversum: Paper Publications Society, 1957. An offset reprint, corrected but not
revised, of the original of 1950.

1061. _____. Historical Review of Watermarks. Amsterdam: Swets & Zietlinger, 1950. Includes 16
leaves with watermarks.

1062. Heitz, Paul. Les Filigranes des Papiers contenus
dans les archives de la ville de Strasbourg. Strasbourg: J. H. E. Heitz, 1902.

1063. _____. Les Filigranes des Papiers contenus dans
les incunables Strasbourgeois de la Bibliothèque

Impériale de Strasbourg. Strasbourg: J. H. E.
Heitz, 1903.

1064. _____. Les Filigranes avec la crosse de Bâle.
Strasbourg: J. H. E. Heitz, 1904.

1065. Heraldic Watermarks. Hilversum: Paper Publications Society, 1956. From the Spanish essay "La
Heraldica en la Filigrana del Papel."

1066. Hilton, John A. Notes on 17th Century Paper and its
Watermarks. N. Staffs Field Club, 1944-1945.

1067. Hunter, Dard. Romance of Water-Marks by Dard
Hunter, and a biographical sketch of the author.
Cincinnati: Stratford Press, 1939.

1068. Hunter, J. "Paper Marks in Public Archives in England," Archaeologia 37, 1858.

1069. LeClert, L. LePapier: Recherches et Notes pour
Servir à l'Histoire du Papier à Troyes et aux
Environs depuis le 14e Siècle. Paris: du Pégase,
1926. Two folio volumes with many plates of
watermarks.

1070. Lemon, R. "A Collection of Watermarks," Scott &
Davey's Guide to the Collector of Historical Documents. London: 1891.

1071. Lister, Raymond. How to Identify Old Maps and
Globes. Hamden, Conn.: Archon Books, 1965.
Contains much information on history of maps and
map making, and a useful appendix on the use of
watermarks in dating old maps and documents.

1072. Marmol, Le Baron F. Del. Dictionaire des Filigranes. 2 vols. Namur, France: 1900.

1073. Midoux, E. et A. Matton. Etude sur les Filigranes
des papiers employés en France aux XIVe et XVe
Siècles. Paris: Dumoulin, 1868.

1074. Nicolai, Alex. "Le Symbolisme Chrétien dans les
Filigranes du Papier," Contribution a l'Histoire de
la Papeterie en France vol. 3, Grenoble: 1936.

1075. Nostitz Papers. Hilversum: Paper Publications Society, 1956. Notes on watermarks found in German
Imperial archives of the 17th and 18th centuries.

1076. Simmons, J. S. G. Tromonin's Watermark Album.
Hilversum: Paper Publications Society, 1965. A
facsimile of the Moscow 1855 edition.

1077. A Short Guide to Books on Watermarks. Hilversum:
Paper Publications Society, 1955.

1078. Valls I Subira, O. Paper and Watermarks in Cata-
lonia. 2 vols. Hilversum: Paper Publications
Society, 1965. This is vol. 12 of the Monumenta
Chartae Papyraceae Historiam Illustrantia, [943].

1079. Wiener, Lucien. Etude sur les Filigranes des
       Papiers Lorrains. Nancy: 1893.

Decorative Paper

1080. Adams, Charles M.   "Some Notes on the Art of Mar-
       bling in the Seventeenth Century, " Bulletin 51(7):411-
       422, 1947. New York Public Library.
1081. Bacon, Sir Francis. Sylva Sylvarum. London: Wm.
       Lee, 1627. Mentions the decorating of paper as
       practiced by the Turks (i. e. marbling).
1082. Combed Pattern Papers. Leicester: Dryad Press,
       n. d. Leaflet No. 107. Twelve pages with color
       illustrations on making patterned papers with paste
       colors or printers ink.
1083. Guegan, Bertrand.   "History and Manufacture of End
       Papers, " Publisher's Weekly October 5, 1929, pp.
       1755-1759. Translated by Katherine Knight from
       Arts et Mitiers Graphiques.
1084. Halfer, Joseph. The Progress of the Marbling Art
       from Technical Scientific Principles. Buffalo:
       American Bookbinder Co. , 1893. Translated by
       Herman Dieck. 224 pages text; 35 specimens of
       marbled papers.
1085. _____. The Art of Marbling and the Treatment of
       New Bronze Colours. London: 1904.
1086. Hirsch, Olga. "Decorated Papers, " The Penrose An-
       nual 51:48-53, 1957. Illustrated description of
       marbled, wood block, paste and embossed papers.
1087. Hunter, Dard. "A Bibliography of Marbled Paper, "
       The Paper Trade Journal April 28, 1921. 69
       entries.
1088. Ingpen, Roger. "Decorated Papers, " The Fleuron
       No. 2, 1924. 8 pages, paper samples.
1089. Jennett, Sean. "Endpapers, " The Making of Books
       2nd ed. London: Faber and Faber, 1966.
1090. Kantrowitz, M. and E. W. Spencer. The Process of
       Marbling Paper. Washington: USGPO, 1953. His-
       tory plus good technical instructions and a lengthy
       bibliography by Dard Hunter.
1091. Loring, Rosamond B. Marbled Papers, an address
       delivered before the members of the Club of Odd
       Volumes, November 16, 1932. Boston: Club of
       Odd Volumes, 1933.
1092. _____. Decorated Book Paper. Cambridge,
       Mass. : Harvard University Press, 1942. A

classic description of all types of decorated paper
with appendices of instructions for making these
papers in the traditional manner.   Illustrated with
actual examples of paper described.

√1093.   . Decorated Book Papers.   Cambridge,
Mass.: Harvard University Press, 1952.   An excellent reprint of 1942 edition with additional biographical material by Walter Muir Whitehill, Dard
Hunter and Veronica Ruzicka but lacks the tipped
in samples of papers which are in the original edition.

1094. Löwenstjern, Kunckel V.   Ars Vitraria Experiment-
alis.   Leipzig: 1674.   Part 1 of two volumes contains what is purported to be the first technical
account of the marbling of paper and the utensils
for it.

1095.   . "Marbreur du Papier," Encyclopaedie
Diderot.   Paris: 1751.

1096. Martin, Thomas.   Circle of the Mechanical Arts:
containing practical treatises on the various manual
arts, trades, and manufacturing.   Bookbinding,
papermaking, printing and surface colouring of
papers.   London: R. Rees, 1813.

1097. Narita, Kyofusa.   "Sumi-nagashi," Paper Maker 24,
1955.   History and production of a "marbled" type
paper.

1098. Nash, Paul.   A Specimen Book of Pattern Papers Designed for and in Use by the Curwin Press.   London: Curwin Press, 1928.   Thirty plates in color.

1099. "Paper, Marbled," American Archivist 1:15, 1938.

1100. Peach, Geoffry.   Hand Decorated Pattern Papers for
Bookcraft.   London: Dryad Press, 1931.   A guide
to the various methods of decorating paper.

1101. Peignot, E. G.   "Parchemin, papier," in Lacroix P.
Le Moyen Age, vol. 2, 1849.

1102. Portfolio: The Annual of the Graphic Arts.   Cincinnati: Zebra Press, 1951.   Article on "French
Marble Papers" shows methods of making the papers and includes an actual example.

1103. Rushmore, Arthur.   Ceremonial Papers of America,
by Theodore Bachaus, D. S. E.   (The Golden Hind
Press) 1938.   This spoof on a book of similar title
was done for members of the Columbian Club and
contains 13 specimens and one drawing of "ceremonial" papers.   Fewer than thirty-five copies
were issued.

1104.   Woolnough, C. W.   The Art of Marbling as Applied
        to Book Edges.   London: A. Heylin, 1853.
1105.   _____ .   The Whole Art of Marbling as Applied to
        Paper and Book Edges, Containing a Full Descrip-
        tion of the Nature and Properties of Materials Used
        and the Method of Preparing Them.   London:
        George Bell & Sons, 1881.   Eighty-two pages of
        text and thirty-eight examples of surface decorated
        paper.

        my german Buntpapier

INK

1106.   Barrow, William J.   "New Non-acid Permanent Iron
        Ink, " American Archivist 10:338, 1947.
1107.   _____ .   "Black Writing Ink of the Colonial Period, "
        American Archivist 11:291-307, 1948.
1108.   Bloy, Colin H.   A History of Printing Ink, Rolls and
        Rollers, 1440-1850.   London: Wynken de Worde
        Society, 1967.
1109.   Canepario, Petro Maria.   De Areamentis Cujuscunque
        Generis.   Opus sane novum.   Hactenus a nemine
        promulgatun.   In sex Descriptiones digestum.
        Venice: 1619; London: 1660.   A scientific treatise
        including information on writing and printing inks,
        writing materials, erasing written letters.
1110.   Carvalho, David N.   Forty Centuries of Ink.   New
        York: Banks Law Publishing Co. , 1904.
1111.   Davids, T.   The History of Ink.   New York: Thaddeus
        Davids & Co. , 1860.
1112.   Gode, P. K.   "Recipes for Hair-Dyes in the Narani-
        taka (c. 2nd century A. D.) and Their Close Affin-
        ity with the Recipes for Ink Manufacture after A. D.
        1000, " Bharatiya Vidya 11, 1950.
1113.   _____ .   "Studies in the History of Indian Palaeog-
        raphy - Some notes on the History of Ink Manu-
        facture in Ancient and Medieval India and Other
        Countries, " Praeyavani 3, October 1946.
1114.   [No entry.]
1115.   Jametel, Maurice.   L'Encre de Chine.   Paris: Ern-
        est Leroux, 1882.   History of Chinese ink from
        the earliest times.
1116.   Paltsits, V. H.   "The Use of Invisible Ink for Secret
        Writing during the American Revolution, " Bulletin

1117. Steckoll, Soloman H. "Investigations of the Inks Used
       in Writing the Dead Sea Scrolls," Nature 220(5162):
       91-92, 1968.
1118. Vaultier, R. "The History of China Ink," Papetier
       2(7), Special Fall Issue, 1957.
1119. Wang Chi-chen. "Notes on Chinese Ink," Metropolitan
       Museum Studies 3, Part I, pp. 114-133, 1930.
1120. Weiss, Harry B. "The Writing Masters and Ink
       Manufacturers of New York City," Bulletin 56:383-
       394, 1952. New York Public Library.
1121. Zimmerman, Elmer W. "Iron Gallate Inks - Liquid
       and Powder," Journal of Research 15:35-40, 1935.
       Washington, National Bureau of Standards.

39:361-364, 1935. New York Public Library.

LEATHER, VELLUM, AND OTHER SKINS

1122. Anon. "Dead Sea Scrolls Set a Problem for Leather
       Scientists," The Journal of the Leather Chemists
       Association 51(6):322, 1956.
1123. Clarkson, L. A. "The Leather Crafts in Tudor and
       Stuart England," Agriculture History Review
       14(1):25-39, 1966. A historical discussion.
1124. Forbes, R. J. "Leather in Antiquity," Studies in
       Ancient Technology Vol. 5 (Leather). Leiden:
       E. J. Brill, 1957.
1125. Gansser-Burckhardt, A. "The Early History of Tan-
       ning," Ciba Review 81:2938-2962, 1950.
1126. _____. "Leather Making in Antiquity and its
       Preservation," Journal American Leather Trades
       Chemists Association 49, 1954.
1127. Hemmerling, K. "The History of Leather," Dyestuff
       41(9):180-183, 1956.
1128. Lalande, Jérome Le Francais de. "Art du Tanneur,"
       Descriptions des arts et Metiers etc., vol. 38.
       Paris: Academie Royale des Sciences, 1764.
       [1428.]
1129. _____. L'Art de Faire le Moroquin. Paris:
       Saillant et Nyon, 1761. Also in Descriptions des
       Artes et Metiers. Paris: l'Academie Royale des
       Sciences, 1771-1783. [1428.]
1130. The Leather Worker in 18th Century Williamsburg.
       Williamsburg: Williamsburg, Virginia, Inc., 1967.

1131. Levey, Martin. "Chemistry of Tanning in Ancient
Mesopotamia, " Journal of Chemistry 34:3, 1957.
1132. Peignot, E. G. Essai sur l'Histoire du Parchemin
et du velin. Paris: A. A. Renouard, 1812.
1133. Poole, J. B. and R. Reed. "The Preparation of
Leather and Parchment by the Dead Sea Scrolls
Community, " Technology and Culture 3(1):1-26,
1962.
1134. _____. "A Study of Some Dead Sea Scrolls and
Leather Fragments from Cave 4 at Qumran, Part
I -- Physical Examination, " Proceedings of the
Leeds Philosophical Literary Society, Scientific
Section 9(1). (n. d.)
1135. _____. "A Study of Some Dead Sea Scrolls and
Leather Fragments from Cave 4 at Qumran, Part
II -- Chemical Examination, " Proceedings of the
Leeds Philosophical and Literary Society, Scientific
Section 9(6). (n. d.)
1136. Ryder, M. S. "Parchment: Its History Manufacture
and Composition, " Journal of the Society of Archivists 3:391-399, 1964.
1137. Stambolov, T. Manufacture, Deterioration and Preservation of Leather. Amsterdam: Central Research Laboratory for objects of art and science,
1969. Paper presented at 1969 plenary meeting of
the ICOM Committee on Conservation in Amster-   X
dam. Photostat copies available from Rome
Centre, 256 Via Cavour, Rome. Includes history
of leather, parchment, tanned skins, etc.
1138. Waldram of St. Gall. c. 890-920 (?) The poet, talk-
ing to the Muse Euterpe, expresses the desire to
prepare parchment leaves with a knife, to smooth
them with pumice, to rule them for writing, and
to correct the text.
1139. Waterer, J. W. Leather in Life, Art and Industry.
London: Faber & Faber, 1943.
1140. _____. "Leather, " A History of Technology Vol.
2. London: Oxford University Press, 1957.
1141. Welsh, Peter C. Tanning in the United States to
1850. Washington, D. C.: Smithsonian Institution,
1964.

GRAPHIC ARTS AND PRINTING

1142. Berjeau, J. , Ph.   Early Dutch, German and English
       Printers' Marks.   London: E. Rascol, 1866.
√1143. Bennett, Paul A. (ed.).   Books and Printing.   New
       York: The World Publishing Co. , 1963.   A
       treasury for typophiles but of general interest to
       librarians and conservators.
1144. Beraldi, H.   Estampes et Livres - 1872-1892.   Paris:
       L. Danel, 1892.
√1145. Bland, David.   A History of Book Illustration.   Berke-
       ley: University of California Press, 1958.   A
       basic guide to all forms of picture making for
       books.
1146. _____. The Illustration of Books.   2nd revised
       edition, 1969.
1147. British Museum.   A Guide to the Processes and
       Schools of Engraving.   4th ed. , London: British
       Museum, 1952.
1148. Brown, H. G. and M. O. Brown.   "A Directory of
       the Book-Arts and Book Trade in Philadelphia to
       1820 including Painters and Engravers, " Bulletin
       53, 1949 and 54, 1950.   New York Public Library.
1149. Brunner, Felix.   A Handbook of Graphic Reproduction
       Processes.   New York: Visual Communication
       Books, 1968.   Useful information on techniques
       and identification of the same.
1150. Carter, Thomas F.   The Invention of Printing in
       China and Its Spread Westward.   New York: Co-
       lumbia University Press, 1925.
1151. _____. The Invention of Printing in China and Its
       Spread Westward.   Rev. by L. Carrington Good-
       rich, 2nd ed.   New York: Ronald Press Co. ,
       1955.   "The Invention of Paper, " pp. 3-10; "Pa-
       per's Thousand-Year Journey from China to Eu-
       rope, " pp. 132-139.
1152. Cohen, Henry.   Guide de l'Amateur de Livres a
       Gravures du XVIIIe Siècle.   Paris: A. Rouquette,
       1912.   The best reference work on 18th century
       book illustration techniques.
1153. Cundall, Joseph.   A Brief Description of Wood En-
       graving.   London: S. Low, Marston & Co. , 1895.
1154. Curwen, Harold.   Processes of Graphic Reproduction
       in Printing.   New York: Dover, 1958.   Excellent
       for technical details on illustration processes.

1155. Delaborde, Henri. "Notice sur deux Estampes de
      1406 et sur les Commencements de la Gravure, "
      Gazette des Beaux Arts 2(1), 1869. On the origin
      of engraving.
1156. Frankenberg, C. G. Picture Sources. New York:
      Special Libraries Asso., 1964.
1157. Guide to the Processes and Schools of Engraving.
      4th ed. London: British Museum, 1952.
1158. Harris, Elizabeth M. Methods of Reproducing Prints
      and Their Detection. Paper presented at the Octo-
      ber 1970 meeting of the Washington Region Con-
      servation Guild.
1159. _____. "Sir William Congreve and His Compound-
      plate Printing, " U. S. National Museum Bulletin
      252:71-87, 1967.
1160. Hind, A. M. A Short History of Engraving and Etch-
      ing. London: Constable & Co., 1927. An intro-
      duction to illustration processes.
1161. _____. A History of Engraving and Etching from
      the 15th Century to the Year 1914. New York:
      Dover Publications, 1963.
1162. _____. An Introduction to the History of Woodcut.
      2 vols. New York: Dover Publications, 1963.
      Includes a detailed survey of the work done in the
      15th century.
1163. Kruiningen, H. The Techniques of Graphic Art. New
      York: Praeger, 1969. Brief guide on printmaking
      techniques together with short historical sketches
      on origins of etching, aquatints, woodcuts, litho-
      graphs and line engravings. Translated from the
      Dutch by B. K. Bowles.
1164. Lumsden, E. S. The Art of Etching. Philadelphia:
      Lippincott, 1925. Complete and detailed English
      manual of practical etching; illustrated. Includes
      variations such as dry point and aquatint.
1165. Majewski, Lawrence. "Classifying Paintings, Draw-
      ings, and Prints by Media, " Museum Registration
      Methods. Washington: 1968.
1166. Morrow, B. F. Aquatint. New York: Putnam, 1935.
      Describes the technique of aquatint and all its
      variations, with reproductions of contemporary
      American work.
1167. Poortenaar, Jan. The Techniques of Prints and Art
      Reproduction Processes, 1933. A study of technical
      processes with 45 specimens and 90 illustrations.
1168. (Print Council of America). List of Films on Prints
      and Print-Making. New York: Print Council of

America, n. d.
1169. Richmond, W. D. The Grammar of Lithography.
London: Meyers & Co., 1912. This English manual, a complete work on the subject, is largely
concerned with industrial methods.
1170. Ruhman, Helmut. "The Masters' Methods and Colour
Reproduction, " The British and Colonial Printer
542, 543, 546, 1951. An assessment of the capabilities and limitations of color printing.
1171. Satow, Sir Ernest. "On the Early History of Printing
in Japan, " Transactions of the Asiatic Society of
Japan 10, 1882. Early Japanese printmaking described on pp. 48-83 and 252-259.
1172. Schreiber, W. L. Manuel de l'Amateur de la Gravure
sur Bois et sur Metal au XVe Siècle. New York:
Burt Franklin, 1970. 8 vols in 7. Reprint of
1891-1911. Berlin-Leipzig edition. 116 plates
with 3 in color.
1173. Schullian, Dorothy M. "Early Print Transfer, " Journal of the History of Medicine and Allied Sciences
7:86-88, 1952.
1174. Senefelder, A. A Complete Course in Lithography.
London: R. Ackerman, 1819. The original work
of the inventor of the process.
1175. Shokler, Harry. Artists' Manual for Silk Screen
Print Making. New York: American Artists
Group, 1946. A practical, efficient, and lucid
account of the serigraph for creative artists.
1176. Strange, E. F. Tools and Materials Illustrating the
Japanese Methods of Colour Printing. London:
1924.
1177. Sullivan, Michael. "Pictorial Art and the Attitude
Toward Nature in Ancient China, " Bulletin of College Art Association of America 36(1), 1954.
1178. Turk, Frank A. The Prints of Japan. London:
Arco Publications, 1966. First chapter includes
technical data on the development of bookmaking
in China, circa 500-800 A. D. Chapter 2 contains
information on early papers used for book and
print making in Japan. Chapter 3 is an introduction to the techniques of Japanese print production
from the earliest times to the present, including
lists of printers, engravers, publishers, etc., and
their marks. Extensive bibliography.
1179. Vachon, Marius. Les Arts et les Industries du
Papier en France 1871-1894. Paris: Librairies
Imprimeries Réunies, 1895. Sections on paper,

       printing, engraving, books, prints, binding, etc.
1180. Weiss, H. B. The Number of Persons and Firms
       Connected with the Graphic Arts in New York City
       1633-1820. New York: The New York Public Li-
       brary, 1946. Includes book workers.
1181. _____. "The Growth of the Graphic Arts in Phila-
       delphia 1663-1820, " Bulletin 56(1):76-83, 1952 and
       56(2):139-145, 1952. New York Public Library.
       Includes bookbinding, paper and parchment making,
       paper staining, ink making.
1182. Weitenkamp, Frank. "List of Works in the New York
       Public Library Relating to Prints and Their Pro-
       duction, " Bulletin 19:847-935; 959-1002, 1915.
       New York Public Library. A bibliography of about
       2400 items on the literature of the print making
       processes (including photomechanical techniques)
       and the applications of the reproductive graphic
       arts to bookmaking, portraits, posters, etc. In-
       cludes section on the care of prints.
1183. _____. American Graphic Art. New York: Mac-
       Millan, 1924. A history and critical review of all
       artistic reproductive, illustrative, journalistic and
       industrial graphic arts media in the United States.
       Illustrated. Bibliography.
1184. Wilder, F. L. How to Identify Old Prints. London:
       G. Bell & Sons, 1969. This distinguished and well
       known expert presents a wealth of information
       gleaned from his 55 years of experience at Sothe-
       by's.
1185. Wroth, Lawrence C. The Colonial Printer. Char-
       lottsville: The University of Virginia Press, 1964.
       A recent reprinting of the 1938 revised and en-
       larged second edition.
1186. Yoshida, Toshi & Rei Yuki. Japanese Print Making:
       a handbook of traditional and modern techniques.
       Tokyo (& Rutland, Vt.): Charles E. Tuttle Co. ,
       1966. A definitive guide to the Japanese wood
       block print by practicing artists and craftsmen.

EARLY CONSERVATION

1187. Jones, Louis C. "Primer for Preservation: A Look
       at Historic Preservation," History News 19(6),
       1964. Primarily architectural preservation.
1188. Marwick, Claire S. An Historical Study of Paper
       Document Restoration Methods. Washington, D. C. :
       1964. Unpublished Master's Thesis, The American
       University.

II. The Nature of Library Materials

GENERAL [See also IX. General References--Bibliographies]

1189. Ainsworth, J. H. Paper: The Fifth Wonder. Kau-
       kauna, Wisconsin: Thomas Printing & Publishing
       Co., 1967. This expanded third revision of the
       1959 basic manual includes the highly simplified
       but extremely useful style of the original chapters
       on printing processes, composition, industrial
       binding, ink and condensed but useful terminologies
       on paper, graphic arts, and ink.
1190. Barrow, W. J. 'New Device Tests Performance of
       Library Bindings, " Book Production March, 1964.
1191. _____. Permanence/Durability of the Book. Rich-
       mond: W. J. Barrow Research Laboratory, 1963
       to - A continuing series of pamphlets reporting
       various aspects of conservation research.
1192. _____. Strength and Other Characteristics of Book
       Papers. Richmond, Virginia: W. J. Barrow Re-
       search Laboratory, Inc., 1967. Permanence/Dura-
       bility of the Book - V.
1193. Coleman, D. G. Woodworking Factbook. New York:
       Robert Speller, 1966. A handbook of basic infor-
       mation on wood.
1194. Employing Bookbinders of America. Research Divi-
       sion. Special bulletins on glue, book cloth,
       pyroxylin-treated fabrics, imitation gold leaf. New
       York: 1933.
1195. Encyclopaedias Britannica and Americana. (Look un-
       der heading of material in question.)
1196. Grant, Julius. Books and Documents: Dating, Per-
       manence and Preservation. London: Grafton &
       Co., 1937.
1197. Greathouse, G. A. and C. J. Wessel. Deterioration
       of Materials. New York: Reinhold Publishing
       Corporation, 1954.
1198. Groome, G. T. Bookbinding Materials. Washington:
       U. S. Government Printing Office, c.1948.

89

1199. Heaton, Noel. "The Permanence of Artists' Mate-
       rials, " Journal of the Royal Society of Arts
⁌   80(4137), March 4, 1932.
1200. "How Long do Books Last?" Angew andte chemie
       71(20), 1959. Suppl. 347.
1201. Huber, L. R. "Materials and Methods in Book Fin-
       ishing and Repairing, " American Library Associa-
       tion Bulletin 49:326-330, 1955. An appraisal of
       newer materials developed for the repair of books,
       such as pressure-sensitive tapes, adhesive cloths,
       plastic tapes, and the like, which finds in them
       merits the more conservative will perhaps ques-
       tion.
1202. ibn Bādis, Al - Muizz. "Staff of the Scribes and
       Implements of the Discerning with a Description of
       the Line, the Pens, Soot Inks, Liq, Gall Inks,
       Dying and Detail of Bookbinding. (c. A. D. 1025). "
       Transactions of the American Philosophical Society
       52(4), 1962. A rich repository of Arab practical
       chemistry in the fields of tanning and dying leath-
       er, glues and their use, the preparation of inks,
       paper and paper making.
1203. Jacob, P. L. Curiosités de l'Histoire des Arts.
       Paris: 1858. Includes article on parchment and
       paper with a bibliography.
1204. Kettle, D. W. Pens, Ink and Paper. London: Pri-
       vately printed, 1885. An introduction to the
       calligraphic arts. Only 235 copies printed for the
       Sette of Odd Volumes.
1205. Koops, M. Historical Account of the Substances
       Which Have Been Used To Describe Events, and
       To Convey Ideas from the Earliest Date to the In-
       vention of Paper. 2nd ed. London: Jaques &
       Co. , 1801.
1206. Lamb, C. M. (ed.). The Calligrapher's Handbook.
       London: Faber & Faber, Ltd. , n. d. Articles on
       pigment, ink, skins, gilding, binding of manu-
       scripts, binding.
1207. The Library Handbook of Genuine Trade Secrets and
       Instructions. London: Foyles, 1923.
1208. Lucas, A. and J. A. Harris. Ancient Egyptian
       Materials and Industries. London: F. Arnold
       Ltd. , 1962.
1209. Mayer, Ralph. The Artists Handbook of Materials
       and Techniques, (rev. ed.). New York: The Vik-
       ing Press, 1965. Much useful information on
       materials and techniques for conservation of paper.

1210. Nikitin, N. I. The Chemistry of Cellulose and Wood.
       New York: Davey, 1966. Translated from the
       Russian.
1211. Nitz, H. Die Materialien für Buch und Bucheinband.
       2nd ed. Halle: Wilhelm Knapp, 1950.
1212. Olin, Jacqueline S.; Maurice E. Salmon; Charles H.
       Olin. "Investigations of Historical Objects Utilizing
       Spectroscopy and Other Optical Methods," Applied
       Optics 8(1):29-39, January 1969. Includes UV radi-
       ation for identification of leather and parchment and
       the investigation of writing inks using the electron
       microprobe.
1213. Rozmarin, G. M. "Progress in the Study of the Ag-
       ing of Fibrous Materials - Cellulosic," Russian
       Chemical Reviews 34(11), 1965.
1214. Scriven, Margaret. "Preservation and Restoration of
       Library Materials," Special Libraries 47:439-448,
       December, 1956. Includes list of materials used
       in preservation and restoration.
1215. Sheridan, Jane. "Chemical Analysis of Materials of
       Art and Archeology," Exposition of Painting Con-
       servation. Brooklyn: Brooklyn Museum, 1962.
       Brief general guidance.
1216. Taylor, Isaac. History of the Transmission of An-
       cient Books to Modern Times. Liverpool: Edward
       Howell, 1875. Chapter on materials of ancient
       books.
1217. Thompson, Daniel V. Jr. Il Libro dell Arte, The
       Craftsman's Handbook. New Haven: Yale Univer-
       wity Press, 1933. The English text of a classical
       medieval text useful for source material on mate-
       rials and techniques.
1218. Thuma, Max. Die Werkstoffe des Buchbinders: Ihre
       Herstellung und Verarbeitung. 4th ed. Stuttgart:
       Max Hettler, 1960. This training manual discusses
       all materials used in books.
1219. "Trial Data on Painting Materials," Technical Studies
       in the Field of the Fine Arts. Vols. 5-10. Cam-
       bridge, Mass.: Fogg Museum, 1936-42. Includes
       lengthy description of solvents, inks, colors and
       other materials used in conservation.
1220. Walton, Robert P. Causes and Prevention of Deteri-
       oration in Book Materials. New York: The New
       York Public Library, 1929.
1221. Ward, W. H. The Seal Cylinders of Western Asia.
       Washington: Carnegie Institute, 1910. Contains
       section on origin and use of materials.

1222. Weidner, Marilyn K. "Damage and Deterioration of
       Art on Paper Due to Ignorance and Use of Faulty
       Materials," Studies in Conservation 12(5), 1967.
1223. Werner, A. E. A. "New Materials in Conservation of
       Antiquities," Museums Journal 64(1):1-16, 1964.

THE EXOTIC MATERIALS

1224. Abbot, E. "Ancient Papyrus and the Mode of Making
       Paper From It," Authorship of the Fourth Gospel.
       Boston: G. H. Ellis, 1880.
1225. Anna, Sister M., (O. S. F.). "Bark Cloth Making
       Among the Baganda of East Africa," Primitive Man
       9(1), 1936.
1226. Baer, N. S. and L. J. Majewski. "Ivory and Re-
       lated Materials in Art and Archaeology," Art and
       Archaeology Technical Abstracts 9(2), 1970-1971.
       An annotated bibliography of 190 titles on ivory
       bone and horn.
1227. "Bamboo," CIBA Review 1:39, 1969. Describes
       growth cycle of various bamboo plants and pro-
       cedures for processing them into paper.
1228. Boynton, R. S. Chemistry and Technology of Lime
       and Limestone. New York: Interscience, 1966.
1229. Brady, G. S. Materials Handbook. New York: Mc-
       Graw Hill, 1929. General information on stone.
1230. Brigham, W. T. "Ka Hana Kapa; the Making of
       Bark-Cloth in Hawaii," Bernice P. Bishop Museum,
       Memoirs 3, 1911.
1231. Buck, R. D. "A Note on the Effect of Age on the
       Hygroscopic Behavior of Wood," Studies in Con-
       servation 6(1), 1961.
1232. Bühler, A. and W. Naumann. "Bark Fabrics of the
       South Seas," CIBA Review 33:1166-1203, 1940.
1233. Burns, P. J. and P. B. Lee. "Copper and its Al-
       loys," South African Corrosian Journal 3(6):3-5,
       7, 9, 12, 1967.
1234. Chhabra, Bahadur Chand. "Seals of Ancient India,"
       Indian Archives 14:36-49, January 1961/December
       1962.
1235. Dobie, Sir James and Dr. J. J. Fox. "The Com-
       position of Some Mediaeval Wax Seals," Chemical
       Society Transactions 105:797, 1914 (London).

1236. Doblhofer, Ernst. Voices in Stone. New York: Au-
       gust M. Kelley, 1961. Translated by Mervyn
       Savill.
1237. Dureau de la Malle, D. J. C. A. "Le Papyrus et
       la Fabrication du Papier Chez les Ancions, " In-
       stitute Academie de Science 19(1), 1851 (Paris).
1238. Ebers, Georg. "The Papyrus Plant, " Cosmopolitan
       15:677-682, 1893.
1239. Filliozat, J. "Manuscripts on Birch Bark and their
       Preservation, " Indian Archives 1, 1947.
1240. Hedvall, J. Arvid. "Objects of Cultural Value and
       Knowledge of Materials, " Museum 5(1):39-52, 1952.
       Recommended reading.
1241. Hunt, G. M. "The Behavior of Wood, " Research 11,
       1953.
1242. Ivory: A Selected List of References. Washington:
       Library of Congress, 1919. Supplemented in 1946.
1243. Jenkinson, Hilary. Guide to Seals in the Public Re-
       cord Office. London: H. M. Stationery Office,
       1954.
1244. Kollmann, Franz, F. P. and Wilfred A. Cote, Jr.
       Principles of Wood Science and Technology. Vol. 1.
       New York: Springer-Verlag, 1968.
1245. Kribs, David, A. Commercial Foreign Woods on the
       American Market. Dover, N. Y. : 1968.
1246. Lander, E. T. "Ivory and its Imitations, " Galaxy
       24(6), 1877.
1247. Lucas, Alfred. Ancient Egyptian Materials and In-
       dustries. 3rd ed. rev. London: Edward Arnold
       & Co. , 1948.
1248. Mitraux, Alfred. "Bark Cloth, " Handbook of South
       American Indians 5:67-68, 1949.
1249. Moeller, G. Hieratische Palaeographie. 3 vols.
       Leipzig: J. C. Hinrichs, 1909-12. Describes
       origin and manufacture of papyrus writing material.
1250. Moncrieff, A. "Review of Recent Literature on Wood
       (January 1960-April 1968), " Studies in Conserva-
       tion 13(4), 1968. The 344 titles described include
       many on wood/moisture relationship, biological
       attack, etc. Of interest to librarians and con-
       servators.
1251. Nature of the Chemical Components of Wood. New
       York: Technical Association of the Pulp and Paper
       Industry, 1948.
1252. "Papyrus, " The Ecnclopaedia Britannica Vol. 22.
1253. Pliny. Natural History. Cambridge, Mass. : Har-
       vard University Press, 1952. Description of

papyrus making in Egypt about 50 A.D. is given
in vol. 8 chapters 11 & 12.
1254. Raven, H. C. "Bark Cloth Making in the Central
        Celebes, " Natural History Magazine 33, 1932.
1255. Schikorr, G. Atmospheric Corrosion Resistance of
        Zinc. New York: American Zinc Institute, 1965.
        Booklet.
1256. Schuyler, Montgomery Jr. "Notes on the Making of
        Palm-Leaf Manuscripts in Siam, " Journal of the
        American Oriental Society 29:281-283, 1908.
1257. Tachudin, Peter. "Papyrus, " The Paper Maker 1:3-
        15, 1965. Wilmington, Delaware.
1258. Theophrastus. Inquiry Into Plants. Cambridge,
        Mass. : Harvard University Press, 1946. (Loeb
        Classical Library.) The earliest accurate de-
        scription of papyrus.
1259. "To Distinguish Ivory, " Scientific American (Supple-
        ment 48) 1235, 1899. Describes the use of sul-
        furic acid to distinguish true ivory from vegetable
        ivory (seeds of the ivory nut tree).
1260. Webster, R. "Ivory, Bone and Horn, " The Gemolo-
        gist 27(322), 1958. Discusses the chemical nature
        of animal and vegetable ivory.
1261. _____. "Vegetable Ivory and Tortoise Shell, " The
        Gemologist 27(323), 1958. The detection of ivory
        substitutes.
1262. Williamson, G. C. "Some Suggestions Arising out of
        Experiments on Ivory, " The Book of Ivory. Lon-
        don: Muller, 1938. Discusses differences in
        color between varieties of ivory under u. v. light.

THE SKINS

1263. "Alaska Sealskins, " CIBA Review 94, October 1952.
1264. Graham, Rigby. "Bookbinding with Human Skin, "
        Private Library 6(1):14-18, 1965.
1265. _____. "Early Japanese Bookbinding, " Private
        Library 6(2):26-31, 1965.
1266. _____. "Human Leather for Books, " American
        Book Collector 17(5):24-30, 1967.
1267. Hides, Skins and Leather Under the Microscope.
        Milton Park, Egham, Surrey: The British Leather
        Manufacturers' Research Association, n. d.

PARCHMENT AND VELLUM

1268. Fahey, Herbert and Peter. Parchment and Vellum.
       San Francisco: Herbert and Peter Fahey, 1940.
1269. Lalande, Jerôme le Francais de. Art de Faire le
       Parchemin. Paris: Saillant et Nyon, 1761. Also
       in Descriptions des Artes et Metiers. Paris:
       l'Academie Royale des Sciences, 1771-1783. (vol.
       3, 1775).
1270. "Parchment, " American Archivist 1:5, 14, 16, 52,
       60, 73, 1938; 3:212, 1940; 16:119, 1953.
1271. Plenderleith, H. J. "Animal Skin and Skin Pro-
       ducts, ... Parchment, " The Conservation of Anti-
       quities and Works of Art. New York: Oxford
       Press-University Press, 1956.
1272. Ryder, Michael L. "Parchment-Its History, Manu-
       facture and Composition, " Society of Archivists,
       Journal 2:391-399, 1964. Abstract in American
       Archivist 28:117, 1965.
1273. Saxl, Hedwig. "Histology of Parchment, " Technical
       Studies in the Field of Fine Arts 8(1), 1939.
1274. _____. "A Note on Parchment," in: Singer, Ch.,
       et al. (ed.). A History of Technology, Vol. II.
       Oxford: Clarendon Press, 1956.
1275. Thompson, D. V. Jr. "The DeClarea of the so-
       called Anonymous Bernensis, " Technical Studies
       in the Field of Fine Arts 1(1&2), 1932.
1276. Thompson, Sir Edward M. "Parchment and Vellum, "
       Encyclopaedia Britannica 1945.

LEATHER [See also under IX--Bibliographies--
       Leather]

1277. Andrews, Duncan. "Footloose and Bookish in the
       British Isles, " Guild of Book Workers Journal 4(1),
       1965. Describes the preparation of vegetable   ✕
       tanned skins at G. W. Russell & Son.
1278. Archer, John. "A Ten-Year Test of Bindings, "
       Bulletin 40(1):97-100, 1936. New York Public Li-
       brary. Reports on superiority of leather vs. cloth
       and evaluates leather preservatives.
1279. Beebe, C. W. , R. W. Frey and M. V. Hannigan.
       "A Comparison of Gas Chamber Tests of Bookbind-
       ing Leather with a Long Time Atmospheric Ex-
       posure, " Journal of the American Leather Chemists
       Association 50:20-31, 1955.

1280. Bowker, Roy Clement and M. N. V. Geib. Compara-
       tive Durability of Chrome and Vegetable Tanned
       Leathers. Washington, D. C. : U. S. Government
       Printing Office, 1925. U. S. Bureau of Standards
       Technological Paper No. 286, pages 267-286.
1281. Breillat, Pierre. "Rare Books Section in the Li-
       brary, " UNESCO Bulletin for Libraries 19:174-194,
       251-263, 1965.
1282. Cheshire, A. "The Aging of Leather, " Journal Inter-
       national Society of Leather Trades Chemists 30:134-
       166, 1946.
1283.   . "Durability of Leather, " The Leather
       Trades' Review 82:101-108, 1948.
1284. Chivers, C. The Relative Value of Leathers and
       Other Binding Materials. Bath: Chivers Ltd. ,
       1911. Illustrated by diagrams and microphoto-
       graphs.
1285. Cobham, The Rt. Hon. Viscount, and Sir Henry True-
       man Wood. Leather for Bookbinding: Report of
       the Committee on. London: George Bell & Sons,
       1905. 93 pp., 11 plates, diags., leather samples,
       index.
1286. Cockerell, Douglas. "Leather for Bookbinding, "
       Journal of the Society of Arts 48:401-407, 1900.
1287. Davenport, Cyril. "Leather as Used in Bookbinding, "
       The Library 10, 1898.
1288. Davis, Charles Thomas. The Manufacture of Leather.
       Philadelphia: H. C. Baird & Co. , 1885.
1289. Davy, John (ed.). The Collected Works of Sir
       Humphry Davy. London: Smith, Elder & Co. ,
       1839.
1290. Dussance, H. A New and Complete Treatise on the
       Arts of Tanning, Currying and Leather-Dressing.
       Philadelphia: 1865.
1291. Edelstein, S. M. and H. C. Borghetty. "Dyeing and
       Tanning Leather in the Sixteenth Century, " Ameri-
       can Dyestuff Reporter 54:48-52, 1965.
1292. Elliot, R. G. H. "Long-term Durability Test for
       Bookbinding Leathers, a Review, " Journal of the
       Society of Leather Trade Chemists 53(8), 1969.
       Summarizes reports to date on the study begun in
       1931 by the British Leather Manufacturers Re-
       search Association.
1293. Fisher, L. E. The Tanners. New York: Franklin
       Watts, Inc. , 1966. Colonial American Craftsmen
       Series for Juveniles.

1294. Fiske, R. E. "Bookbinding Leather, " Harvard Library Notes March 1940. Reports on a series of leather tests. Also a bibliography of articles on leather in the 1920's and 1930's.

1295. Freudenberg, Walter. International Dictionary of the Leather and Allied Trades: German, English, French, Spanish, Italian. 2nd ed. New York: Springer-Verlag, 1968.

1296. Frey, R. W. "The Decay of Bookbinding Leathers, " Journal of the American Leather Chemists Association 26(9):461-482, 1931.

1297. _____. "Comparative Permanence of Chrome and Vegetable Leathers, " Journal of American Leather Chemists Association 29:489-511, 1934.

1298. Frey, R. W. and C. W. Beebe. "The Permanence to Acid Deterioration of Vegetable Leather Tanned with Alum, " Journal of the American Leather Chemists Association 35(1), 1940.

1299. _____. "Tannages and Treatments Resistant to Acid Rot, " Journal of American Leather Chemists Association 30(1), 1935.

1300. Gansser, A. "The Early History of Tanning, " CIBA Review (81):2938-2962, 1950.

1301. Glossary of Leather Terms. London: British Standards Institution, 1956. British Standard #2780.

1302. Green, G. H. "Leather Science: Some Recent Developments, " Research 11, 1958 (London).

1303. Gross, J. "Collagen, " Scientific American 204(5), 1961. Discussion of the structure and chemistry of collagen the basic substance in leather.

1304. Guldbeck, Per E. Leather: Its Understanding and Care. Nashville: American Association for State and Local History, 1969. Technical Leaflet No. 1.

1305. Hannigan, M. , J. Naghski, and W. Windus. "Evaluation of the Relative Serviceability of Vegetable and Chrome-tanned Leathers for Bookbinding, " Journal of the American Leather Chemists Association 60(9):506-518, 1965.

1306. Hide and Leathers Year Book. Chicago: Jacobson Publishing Co. , 1906.

1307. Houghton, George C. "Leather, Tanned, Curried and Finished, " in part 3, "Special Report on Selected Industries, " in vol. 9 of Twelfth Census of the United States, 1900. Washington: U. S. Government Printing Office, 1902.

1308. Howes, F. N. Vegetable Tanning Materials. London: Butterworth, 1953.

1309.   Hulme, E. W., et al. Leather for Libraries. Chi-
        cago: Library Supply Co., 1905.
1310.   Hulme, E. W. and E. Wyndom. Leather for Li-
        braries. London: The Sound Leather Committee
        of the Library Association, 1905. Samples of
        leather on inside of covers.
1311.   Innes, R. Faraday. "The Deterioration of Vegetable-
        Tanned Leather on Storage, " Journal of the Inter-
        national Society of Leather Trades' Chemists. Oc-
        tober 1931.
1312.   Jacobson, Fred. "Leather for Bookbinding, " Book-
        binding and Book Production 56(4):47, 1950 and
        56(5):41-42, 1950.
1313.   Julia de Fontenelle, J. S. E., and F. Malepeyre.
        The Arts of Tanning, Currying and Leather Dress-
        ing. Philadelphia: H. C. Baird Co., 1852. Edit.
        and transl. by Campbell Morfitt.
1314.   Kantrowitz, M. and G. T. Groome. Bookbinding
        Leather. Washington: U. S. Government Printing
        Office, 1948. G. P. O. -P. I. A. Joint Research
        Bulletin, Bindery Series no. 5.
1315.   Kennedy, David H. The Art of Tanning Leather.
        New York: Baker & Godwin, 1857.
1316.   Lalande, Jérôme Le Francais de. Art du Corroyeur.
        Paris: Saillant et Nyon, 1767. Description of the
        practice of currying leather. Also in Description
        des Arts et Métiers. Paris: l'Academie Royale
        des Sciences, 1771-1783. (vol 3, 1775.) [1428]
1317.   _____. L'Art de l'Hongroyer. Paris: Saillant et
        Nyon, 1761. Short description of the method for
        tanning Hungarian leather. Also in Description
        des Artes et Métiers. Paris: l'Academie Royale
        des Sciences, 1771-1783. (vol. 3, 1775.) [1428]
1318.   _____. L'Art de Faire le Moroquin. Paris:
        Saillant et Nyon, 1761. Also in Descriptions des
        Artes et Métiers. Paris: l'Academie Royale des
        Sciences, 1771-1783. (vol. 3, 1775.) [1428]
1319.   _____. Art du Megissier. Paris: Saillant et
        Nyon, 1761. Instructions for leather dressing.
        Also in Description des Artes et Métiers. Paris:
        l'Academie Royale des Sciences, 1771-1783. (vol.
        3, 1775.) [1428]
1320.   _____. Art du Tanneur. Paris: Saillant et Nyon,
        1764. Instructions for tanning leather. Also in
        Descriptions des Artes et Métiers. Paris:
        l'Academie Royale des Sciences, 1771-1783. (vol.
        3, 1775.) [1428]

1321. "Leather for Bookbinding," Library Association Record 2:250-253, 1900 (London).
1322. "Leather for Libraries," Library Association Record 6, 1905 (London).
1323. Leather in the Decorative Arts. New York: Cooper Union for the Arts of Decoration, ca. 1950. Includes use of leather on books.
1324. Leonard, Fred, et al. "Nylon-Coated Leather," Industrial and Engineering Chemistry April, 1953.
1325. Macbride, Davis. "Instructions to Tanners," Philosophical Transactions of the Royal Society of London 68:111-130, 1778.
1326. Martin, Thomas. The Circle of the Mechanical Arts. London: R. Rees, 1813. Includes sections on tanning leather, making parchment etc.
1327. McCloy, Shelby T. French Inventions of the Eighteenth Century. Lexington, Ky.: University of Kentucky, 1952.
1328. Metz, S. "Notes on the Bookbinding Leather Controversy," The Library Association Record 13:395-398, 1911.
1329. Mitton, R. G. and J. N. Turner. "A Study of Mould Growth on Chrome Tanned Leather and the Associated Changes in Physical Properties," Journal of the Society of Leather Trade Chemists 39:343-358, 1955.
1330. Modern American Tanning. 2 vols. Chicago: Jacobson Publishing Co., 1902-1910. A practical treatise on the manufacture of leather.
1331. O'Flaherty, F., et al. The Chemistry and Technology of Leather. 4 vols. New York: Reinhold, 1965.
1332. _____. "Leather and Its Care," Leather Manufacturer 71(3), 1954.
1333. [No entry.]
1334. Page, R. O. "The Mechanism of Vegetable Tanning," Journal Society Leather Trade Chemists 37, 1953.
1335. Parker, James Gordon. "Leather," The Encyclopaedia Britannica, 11th ed., vol. 16.
1336. _____. "Leather for Bookbinding," Society of Arts Journal 50:25-35, 1902 (London). Detailed report of the experiments leading to the conclusions by this committee on leather for bookbinding, 1901.
1337. Phillips, H. "The Chemistry of Leather," Journal of the Royal Society of Arts 102(4934):824-875, 1954.
1338. Poole, J. B. and R. Reed. "The Preparation of Leather and Parchment by the Dead Sea Scrolls Community," Technology and Culture 3(1):1-26, 1962.

1339. Proctor, Henry R. The Making of Leather. New
       York: Putnams's, 1914.
1340. Progress in Leather Science 1920-1945. London:
       British Leather Manufacturer's Research Associa-
       tion, 1946.
1341. "Report of the Committee on Leather for Bookbinding, "
       Society of Arts Journal 49, 1901. (London). This
       is the study that firmly pinpointed acid as the
       cause for deteriorated leather.
1342. Rogers, Allen. Practical Tanning. New York: Henry
       Carey Baird & Co., 1922. An excellent source of
       highly technical information on all aspects of the
       manufacture of chrome, vegetable and alum tanned
       leather by the former head of Industrial Chemistry
       and Leather Courses at Pratt Institute, Brooklyn,
       N. Y.
1343. The Romance of Leather. New York: Tanners'
       Council of America, 1937.
1344. Royal Society of Arts, London, and the Worshipful
       Company of Leathersellers. Report of the Com-
       mittee on Leather for Bookbinding. London: Soci-
       ety of Arts, 1905.
1345. Rye, W. B. "Leather for Bookbinding, " The Library
       Association Record 3:532-534, 1901.
1346. Seymour-Jones, A. 'Nigerian and Somalliland Leath-
       er, " Journal of the American Leather Chemists
       Association 10(5):258-273, 1915.
1347. "Some Fundamental Problems of the Leather Industry, "
       Chemistry and Industry pp. 296-298, March 13,
       1954. Discusses the problem of leather durability.
1348. Stambolov, T. Manufacture, Deterioration and Pres-
       ervation of Leather. Amsterdam: Central Research
       Laboratory for Objects of Art and Science, 1969.
       A paper presented at 1969 Plenary Meeting of
       ICOM's Committee for Conservation. This litera-
       ture survey, with 89 pages of text, presents all
       that a library conservator need know about leather.
       The bibliography of 223 titles covers modern theory
       as well as time proven techniques.
1349. "Tanning in Modern Times, " CIBA Review 118, Janu-
       ary 1957.
1350. Vallancey, Charles (trans.). The Art of Tanning and
       Currying Leather. Dublin: 1773. From the
       French of M. de Lalande and others.
1351. Veitch, F. P., et al. "Polluted Atmosphere a Factor
       in the Deterioration of Bookbinding Leather, " Jour-
       nal of American Leather Chemists Association 21,

1926. Describes tests demonstrating the effect of sulphur dioxide on leather.

1352. Ward, A. G. "Tanning in the United States to 1850, " Nature 206(4988):991-992, 1965. (London).

1353. Warner, John. "Modern Bookbinding Leathers, " The Library Association Record 2nd series, 7:153-164, 1929.

1354. Waterer, John William. "Leather, " A History of Technology vol. 2. London: Oxford University Press, 1957.

1355. _____. Leather and Craftsmanship. London: Faber and Faber, 1950.

1356. _____. Leather in Life, Art and Industry. London: Faber and Faber, 1943.

1357. Welsh, Peter C. Tanning in the United States to 1850. Washington: Smithsonian Institution, 1964. Excellent descriptions of vegetable tanning processes that produced durable leather. Lengthy bibliography.

1358. Wheatley, H. B. "Leather for Bookbinding, " The Library 2nd series, 2:311-320, 1901.

1359. Wilson, J. A. The Chemistry of Leather Manufacture. New York: The Chemical Catalog Co. , Inc. , 1928. Highly technical treatise. Lengthy bibliographies after each chapter.

1360. Young, Laura S. "Leather, " Guild of Book Workers Journal 8(1):11-17, 1969. A brief description of the material, its manufacture, properties, and suitability for bookbinding.

PAPER [See also under IX. --Bibliographies--Paper]

1361. Ainsworth, J. H. Paper: The Fifth Wonder. Kaukauna, Wisconsin: The Thomas Publishing Co. , 1958. (3rd rev. 1967.) A simplified but excellent and well illustrated story of the technical aspects of the transformation of wood into pulp and thence into paper.

1362. Alibaux, Henri. Les Premières Papeteries Françaises. Paris: 1926.

1363. Alley, Harold R. "Japanese Handmade Paper Industry, " Paper Industry 33:932-933, 1951. Brief, well-illustrated article dealing with establishments in the Ogawa region.

1364. American Paper and Pulp Association. The Dictionary of Paper Including Pulps, Paper Boards, Paper Properties and Related Papermaking Terms. 3rd ed. New York: American Pulp and Paper Association, 1965.

1365. Andes, Louis Edgar. The Treatment of Paper for Special Purposes. London: Greenwood and Son, 1907.

1366. "An Enquiry Concerning the Materials that May be Used in Making Paper," Select Essays: Collected from the Dictionary of Arts and Sciences, and from Various Modern Authors. Philadelphia: George Bell, 1777.

1367. Archer, John and W. R. Thurman. "When Did Newspapers Begin to Use Wood Pulp Stock?" Bulletin 33:743-749, 1929. New York Public Library. A report compiled by the Superintendent of Printing and Binding and the Foreman of the Bindery of the beginnings of the use of wood pulp stock compiled by actual examination of the papers on file in the New York Public Library.

1368. Argy, M. and H. L. Supper. Vocabulaire Papetièr des Industries Papetières et Graphiques. Paris: La Papeterie, 1948. French-English and English-French.

1369. [No entry.]

1370. Armitage, F. D. Atlas of Paper Making Fibers. Epsom, England: Guildhall Publishing Co., 1957. Contains microphotographs of fibers.

1371. Baker, W. E. B. "Relationship of Impurities to Paper Permanence," Paper Trade Journal 91(4):51-52, 1930.

1372. Barker, E. F. "Swiss Mill Produces Paper Containing Substantial Quantities of Nylon," Paper Trade Journal 145(7):48-51, 1961.

1373. Barrow, W. J. "Migration of Impurities in Paper," Archivum 3:105-108, 1953.

1374. _____. Physical Strength of Non-Fiction Book Papers, 1900-1949. Richmond: W. J. Barrow Research Laboratory, 1957.

1375. _____. Permanent/Durable Book Paper. Richmond: Virginia State Library, 1960.

1376. _____. The Manufacture and Testing of Durable
Book Papers. Richmond: Virginia State Library,
1960.

1377. _____. Permanence and Durability of Library
Catalog Cards. Chicago: American Library Association, 1961. Gives librarians objective criteria
by which to test their cards for permanence and
durability.

1378. _____. "Establishing Least Squares Regression
Lines for Data of Aged Paper," Tappi 45(9):209A-
210A, 1962. Two figures and bibliography.

1379. _____. Permanence/Durability of the Book-II.
Test Data of Naturally Aged Paper. Richmond:
W. J. Barrow Research Laboratory, 1964.

1380. _____. "Strength and Other Characteristics of
Book Papers 1880-1899," Permanence/Durability
of the Book-V. Richmond: W. J. Barrow Research Laboratory, 1967.

1381. Barrow, W. J. and A. M. Carlton. "Durability of
Three Current Laminating Tissues," The American
Archivist 30(3):526-529, 1967.

1382. _____. "Permanence of Laminating Tissue," The
American Archivist 31(1):88-91, 1968. Supplements
authors' report on the durability of laminating
tissues.

1383. Barrow, W. J. and R. C. Sproull. "Permanence in
Book Paper," Science 129, April 1959.

1384. Battista, O. A. Synthetic Fibers in Papermaking.
New York: Wiley, 1964.

1385. Bayldon, O. The Paper Makers Craft. Leicester:
Twelve by Eight Press, 1965. Verse, illustrated.
This modern translation of Imberdis' 17th century
poem, Papyrus, is illustrated by Rigby Graham.

1386. Beadle, C. "The Recent History of Paper Making,"
Journal of the Society of Arts 46:405-417, 1898.

1387. _____. Comprising a Series of Lectures Delivered
on Behalf of the Battersea Polytechnic Institute in
1902. Vol. 1. London: H. H. Grattan, 1907.
Chapters on papermaking.

1388. Blanchet, A. Essai sur l'Histoire du Papier et de
sa Fabrication. Paris: E. Leroux, 1900.

1389. Blank, M. G. and Y. P. Nyuksha. "Effects of Some
Polymers on Paper Strength," Causes of Decay of
Written and Printed Monuments Leningrad: Laboratory for Preservation and Restoration of Documents, 1967. In Russian.

1390.   Blum, André.   Les Origines du Papier, de l'Im-
        primerie et de la Gravure.   Paris: Editions du
        Trianon, 1935.
1391.   _____.   On the Origin of Paper.   New York: R. R.
        Bowker Co., 1934.   Translated from the French
        by Harry Miller Lydenberg.   Seventy-nine pages
        of which three or four are devoted to Asiatic pa-
        per.
1392.   Bojesen, C. C. and Rewi Alley.   "China's Rural Pa-
        per Industry," The China Journal 28(5), 1938
        (Shanghai).
1393.   The Book of Specimens Stanhope Press.   Boston:
        F. H. Gilson Co., 1904.   This publisher's reference
        includes technical information on paper, illustration
        techniques, presswork, bookbinding, book cloth,
        leather and bound-in specimens of seven illustrative
        processes, twenty-nine book papers, sixty book
        cloths, and sixteen leathers.   An important source
        of information on the technical details of early
        20th century book materials.
1394.   (Book Paper).   Paper for Books.   London: Robert
        Horne & Co., 1953.   A comprehensive survey of
        various types of paper used in book production in
        Great Britain.
1395.   (Book Paper).   Strathmore Bay Path Book Papers.
        Woronoco, Mass.:   Strathmore Paper Co., 1925.
        Pamphlet illustrating the use of eight different
        printing papers for book production.
1396.   Boxshus, J. P., et al.   "Permanence of Paper,"
        Tappi 37, 1954.   Rag vs. wood pulp paper.
1397.   Britt, K. W. (ed.).   Handbook of Pulp and Paper
        Technology.   New York: Reinhold Publishing Co.,
        1964.
1398.   Bromley, H. A.   Paper and Its Constituents.   Lon-
        don: E. & F. N. Spon, 1920.
1399.   Browning, B. L.   "The Nature of Paper," The Li-
        brary Quarterly 40(1):18-38, 1970.   The Senior
        Research Associate, Institute of Paper Chemistry,
        discusses the chemical make-up of paper, the na-
        ture of cellulose, paper manufacture, measuring
        the properties of paper, and paper stability.
1400.   Browning, B. L. and W. A. Wink.   "Studies on the
        Permanence and Durability of Paper. I.   The Pre-
        diction of Paper Permanence," Tappi 51:156-163,
        1968.
1401.   Burnston, M. A.   "A Philatelic View of the Pulp and
        Paper Industry," Tappi 53(4):544-545, 1970.

Illustrated monograph on stamps illustrating various aspects of paper and its use.

1402. Burton, John O. "Permanence Studies of Current Commercial Book Papers, " Bureau of Standards Journal of Research 7:429-439, 1931. Also available as U. S. Bureau of Standards Research Paper RP 349.

1403. Buyn, K. E. C. "Paper Permanence, " Bulletin Associated Tech. Ind. Pap. , 5:231-238, 1951.

1404. Byrne, J. and J. Weiner. Permanence. Appleton, Wis. : Institute of Paper Chemistry, 1965.

1405. Calkin, J. B. Modern Pulp and Paper Making. New York: Reinhold Publishing Corp. , 1957.

1406. Casey, J. P. "Papermaking, " Pulp and Paper: Chemistry and Chemical Technology 2nd ed. New York: Interscience Publishers, 1960.

1407. _____. "Properties of Paper and Converting, " Pulp and Paper: Chemistry and Chemical Technology vol. 2. New York: Interscience Publishers, 1952.

1408. Chalmers, T. W. Papermaking and Its Machinery. London: Constable & Co. , 1920.

1409. Charpentier, P. Le Papier. Paris: V. Dunod, 1890. Includes 167 illustrations of paper making.

1410. Chaudhary, Yadovrao S. Handmade Paper in India. Lucknow: J. S. Kumarappa, 1936. Eight pages text on paper made in India.

1411. Chivers, Cedric. "The Paper and Binding of Lending Library Books, " ALA Bulletin 3:231-259, 1909.

1412. Church, Randolph W. (ed.). The Manufacture and Testing of Durable Book Papers. Richmond: Virginia State Library, 1960. Based on the investigations of W. J. Barrow.

1413. Clapp, Verner W. "Permanent/Durable Book Papers, " ALA Bulletin 57:847-852, 1963.

1414. Clapperton, George. Practical Papermaking. London: C. Lockwood & Son, 1894. Now outdated but a good source of information on paper technology at the end of the 19th century.

1415. Clapperton, R. H. Paper and its Relationship to Books. London: London School of Printing, 1935. The fourth of the J. M. Dent Memorial Lectures given at the London School of Printing, October 26, 1934.

1416. Clapperton, R. H. and W. Henderson. Modern Papermaking. 3rd ed. London: Blackwell, 1952.

1417. Corte, H. "Fundamental Properties of Paper, " School Science Review 47(162):331-344, 1966 (London).

1418. Cowper, E. "On Recent Improvements in Papermaking, " in "Proceedings of the Royal Institution, " Journal of the Royal Institution 1:252-254, 1831.

1419. Cross, C. F. and E. J. Bevan. "Report on Wood-Pulp Processes, " in Rattray J. and H. R. Mill. Forestry and Forest Products. Edinburgh: Rattray Mill, 1885 [1598].

1420. _____. A Text Book of Paper Making. London: E. & F. N. Spon, 1920. Seventeen plates and ninety-nine other illustrations.

1421. Curwen Press. Specimen Book of Pattern Papers. London: Curwen Press, 1928. Contains actual specimens of binding papers used in edition binding by this firm.

1422. Davis, C. T. The Manufacture of Paper. Philadelphia: H. C. Baird & Co., 1886.

1423. Dawe, Edward A. Paper and Its Uses, a Treatise for Printers, Stationers and Others. London: C. Lockwood & Son, 1929.

1424. [No entry.]

1425. [No entry.]

1426. DeCew, J. A. Process of Treating Paper-Pulp. Washington: U.S. Patent Office, April 15, 1919. (U.S. Patent No. 1, 300, 357)

1427. Della Robbia Papers. Springfield, Mass.: William E. Rudge, 1926. Large folio. This opulent sample book contains an original etching by Joseph Pennell.

1428. Descriptions des Arts et Metiers Faites ou Approuvees par Messieurs de l'Academie Royal des Sciences de Paris. Neuchatel, France: Imprimerie de la Societe Typographique, 1771-1783. 19 volumes include much information on paper manufacturing and other crafts associated with bookmaking.

1429. Dictionary of Paper. 3rd ed. New York: American Pulp and Paper Association, 1965.

1430. Dorce, C. The Methods of Cellulose Chemistry. 2nd ed. London: Chapman and Hall, 1947.

1431. Dunbar, J. Notes on the Manufacture of Wood Pulp Papers. Leith, England: 1892.

1432. The Durability of Paper. London: Library Association, 1930. Report of a special committee. The cover is printed on a grade 1-a stock as specified in the report; the title-plate and the postscript on a grade 1-b; the text on a grade 2 stock.

1433. "The Durability of Paper," Report of the Librarian of
Congress for the Fiscal Year Ended June 30, 1898.
Washington: U. S. Government Printing Office, 1898.

1434. Emerson, H. W. Monograph on Papermaking and
Papier-mâché in the Punjab. Lahore: 1908. 25
pages text.

1435. Esparto Paper. Newman Neame, Ltd., 1956. The
object of this book is to show the unique properties
of esparto paper. Traces pictorially the progress
of the grass from its growth in North Africa
through all the manufacturing processes to the
finished sheets of paper. Bound-in samples of all
the types of paper made from esparto.

1436. Erfurt, Julius. The Dyeing of Paper Pulp. London:
1901. Translated from the German by Julius Hubner. 175 pages text; 157 specimens of coloured
papers.

1437. Facts and Views of Papermaking. Boston: S. D.
Warren Company, 1968. A discussion of the
methods and aims of papermaking from the manufacturers point of view. Excellent simplified technical data.

1438. Fairbanks, Thomas Nast. "A Generalization of the
Manufacture of Paper, Modern Papermaking in
Japan," The Dolphin 2:120-130, 1935. New York.
11 pages text; 15 illustrations.

1439. Fisher, L. E. The Papermakers. New York:
Franklin Watts, Inc., 1965. An introduction to
the craft, written for children. Excellent illustrations and clear, concise text.

1440. Flyate, D. M. and M. P. Lumielskaja. "New Type of
Transparent Restoration Paper," Causes of Decay of
Written and Printed Manuscripts pp. 88-97. Leningrad. Laboratory for Preservation and Restoration
of Documents, 1967. In Russian. English summaries.

1441. Fox, C. J. J. "Paper," Encyclopaedia Britannica.
1945 ed.

1442. Franklin, Benjamin. "Description of the Process to
be Observed in Making Large Sheets of Paper in
the Chinese Manner, with One Smooth Surface,"
Transactions of the American Philosophical Society
3:10-12, 1793.

1443. Gee, W. H. Monograph on Fibrous Manufactures in
the Punjab. Lahore: 1891. 52 pages text.

1444. Gilmour, F. C. (ed.). Paper, Its Making, Merchant-
ing and Usage. London: Longmans Green, 1955.

1445. Goto, Seikichiro. Japanese Paper and Papermaking.
      Tokyo: 1958-1960. Vol. 1, Northeastern Japan;
      Vol. 2, Western Japan.
1446. _____. Japanese Handmade Paper. Kyoto: 1953.
      Small folio, 2 vols. This work, one of several
      on the subject by this author, contains forty-seven
      specimens of paper. There is a forward by Bunsho
      Jugaku. One of 300 copies.
1447. _____. Japanese Handmade Paper. Tokyo:
      Bijutso Shuppan Sha, 1960. 2 vols. Translated
      into English by Iwa Matsuhara. Beautifully illus-
      trated text printed on hand made paper describes
      all of the papers made in the different regions of
      Japan. Many samples of local papers tipped in.
      Books are bound oriental style (Tsuzuri-Toji) in
      hand made paper covers. The best modern trea-
      tise on Japanese papermaking available.
1448. Grant, Julius. A Laboratory Handbook of Pulp and
      Paper Manufacture. London: Edward Arnold,
      Ltd., 1960. Much information on chemical and
      physical testing of paper useful in the examination
      and dating of old paper.
1449. _____. Cellulose Pulp. London: Leonard Hill,
      1958.
1450. Green, J. Barcham. Notes on the Manufacture of
      Handmade Paper. London: The London School of
      Printing, 1936. A brief well illustrated (drawings)
      monograph on making of paper by hand as it is
      still practiced in England.
1451. _____. Papermaking by Hand. London: S. C.
      Phillips & Co., 1953. Sixteen pages with 22 half-
      tone illustrations all on handmade paper.
1452. Griffin, R. B. and A. D. Little. The Chemistry of
      Paper Making. New York: 1894.
1453. Guthrie, J. A. The Newsprint Paper Industry.
      Cambridge, Mass.: The Harvard University Press,
      1941.
1454. Hagen, Victor W. von. The Aztec and Maya Papermakers.
      New York: J. J. Augustin, 1944. 120 pp., 39
      pls.
1455. _____. Paper Making Amongst the Aztecs and
      Mayas. Mexico: Editorial Nuevo Mundo, 1945.
1456. _____. "Mexican Papermaking Plants," Journal of
      the New York Botanical Garden 44(517): 1943.
1457. Hand-made Papers of Japan. Tokyo: IIS Crafts,
      1963. This catalog of paper samples contains an
      abridged reproduction (with English translation) of

the 1798 illustrated classic Kamisuki Chôhôki (handbook of paper making).

1458. "Handmade Paper Still Flourishes," Publisher's Weekly September 5, 1966. Describes activities of Douglas Howell, one of few remaining craftsmen in the American handmade paper industry.

1459. A Handy Guide to Papermaking. Berkeley: The Book Arts Club, 1948, [see 1515]. Translated by Charles E. Hamilton after the Japanese edition of 1798.

1460. Hansen, F. S. "Resistance of Paper to Natural Aging," Paper Industry and Paper World 20:1157-1163, 1939.

1461. Hardman, H. and E. O. Cole. Paper-making Practice. Manchester, Eng.: Manchester University Press, 1960. Detailed technical treatment with 150 diagrams.

1462. Harpham, J. A.; A. R. Reid; and J. W. Turner. "A New Cotton Fiber Pulp for Fine Papermaking," Tappi 41:758-763, 1958.

1463. Henser, E. The Chemistry of Cellulose. New York: Wiley, 1944.

1464. Herring, Richard. Paper and Papermaking, Ancient and Modern. London: Longman, Brown, Green and Longmans, 1855. 125 pages text, 4 illustrations, 25 bound-in specimens. A good account of early 19th century paper making by machine.

1465. Higham, Robert R. A. A Handbook of Papermaking. London: Oxford University Press, 1963. An excellent handbook of practical information on the science and technology of paper making.

1466. Hirsch, Olga. "Decorated Papers," The Penrose Annual 51:48-53, 1957. A brief illustrated discussion of old and new types of decorated paper.

1467. Hoernle, A. F. R. "Who Was the Inventor of Rag Paper?" Royal Asiatic Society Journal October 1903.

1468. Hofmann, C. A Practical Treatise on the Manufacture of Paper in All Its Branches. Philadelphia: Henry Carey Baird Co., 1873.

1469. Honeyman, J. Recent Advances in the Chemistry of Cellulose and Starch. London: Heywood, 1959.

1470. Hopkins, E. A. Paper Trade Dictionary. London: 1906.

1471. Howell, Douglas. "Handmade Paper Still Flourishes," Publisher's Weekly September 1966. Description of one of the few remaining American handmade

papermakers.
1472. Hunter, Dard. "Fifteenth Century Papermaking, " <u>Ars</u>
<u>Typographica</u> 3(1):37-51, 1926.
1473. _____. "Hand-made Paper and Its Relation to
Modern Printing, " The Dolphin no. 1. New York:
Limited Editions Club, 1933.
1474. _____. Old Papermaking. Chillicothe, Ohio: The
Mountain House Press, 1923. 114 illus. Now very
scarce.
1475. _____. Papermaking Through Eighteen Centuries.
New York: W. E. Rudge, 1930. 354 pp., 214
illus.
1476. _____. "Laid and Wove, " Smithsonian Institution
Annual Report for 1921. Washington: 1922. pp.
587-593.
1477. _____. Old Papermaking in China and Japan.
Chillicothe, Ohio: The Mountain House Press,
1932. 71 pages text; 36 illus.; 19 specimens.
1478. _____. A Papermaking Pilgrimage to Japan, Korea
and China. New York: Pynson Printers, 1936.
150 pages text; 69 illus.; 50 specimens.
1479. _____. Papermaking in Southern Siam. Chillicothe, Ohio: Mountain House Press, 1936. 40
pages text; 18 illus.; 4 specimens.
1480. _____. Primitive Papermaking. Chillicothe, Ohio:
The Mountain House Press, 1927. Descriptions of
paper and papermaking methods in Mexico, South
America, Java, and Islands in the South Pacific.
Contains 31 specimens of primitive paper, either
actual or fascimile and numerous text figures and
photographs.
1481. _____. (Philpott, A. J. ed.). Lesson in Paper
Making at the Club of Odd Volumes, February
1934. Boston: Club of Odd Volumes, 1934. Only
sixty copies printed.
1482. _____. Chinese Ceremonial Paper. Chillicothe,
Ohio: The Mountain House Press, 1937. 82 pages
text; 15 illus.; 47 specimens.
1483. _____. Papermaking by Hand in India. New York:
Pynson Printers, 1939. 129 pages text; 84 illus.;
27 specimens.
1484. _____. Papermaking in Indo-China. Chillicothe,
Ohio: The Mountain House Press, 1947. 102
pages text; 2 mounted samples. Limited edition
of 250 copies.
1485. _____. Papermaking in Pioneer America. Philadelphia: University of Pennsylvania Press, 1952.

(A Rosenbach Fellowship in Bibliography publication.)

1486. _____. Papermaking, The History and Technique of an Ancient Craft. New York: Alfred A. Knopf, 1943. Revised and enlarged 1947. The best book on the subject. Fine bibliography. Contains all a librarian needs to know about paper.

1487. _____. Papermaking in the Classroom. Peoria, Illinois: The Manual Arts Press, 1931.

1488. _____. My Life with Paper: An Autobiography. New York: Knopf, 1958.

1489. Imberdis, Jean. Papyrus, Sive Ars Conficiendae Papyri... Le Papier, ou l'Art de Fabriquer le Papier, 1693. Traduction par Augustin Blanchet. Paris: C. Beranger, 1899.

1490. _____. Papyrus or the Craft of Paper. Holland: Hilversum, 1952. Modern translation of the 1693 original. [1489]

1491. Inoue, Keijiro. Watashi Wa Goseishi: Sekiyu Kara Umareta. Tokyo: Nikkan Kogyo Shimbun Sha, 1969. This first book made of pulp-free synthetic paper (title reads, 'I am Synthetic Paper: Born of Petroleum') a product of Japan's booming petrochemical industry, describes the need for synthetic paper, method of manufacture, characteristics and future prospects of the product.

1492. Irvine, R. and G. S. Woodhead. "On the Presence in Paper of Residual Chemicals Used in Its Preparation," Journal of the Society of Chemical Industry 13:131-133, 1894.

1493. Jarrell, T. D. "Effect of Atmospheric Humidity on the Moisture Content of Paper," Paper Trade Journal 85(3):47-51, 1927.

1494. Jarrell, T. D., et al. Deterioration of Book and Record Papers. Washington: Department of Agriculture, 1936. Technical Bulletin # 541.

1495. Johnson, Rossiter. "Inferior Paper, a Menace to the Permanency of Literature," Library Journal 16:241-242, 1891. Reprinted from the New York World.

1496. Jugaku, Bunshō. Hand Made Paper of Japan. Tokyo: Tourist Library, 1942. This is an earlier version of the author's 1959 book.

1497. _____. Paper Making by Hand in Japan. Tokyo: Meiji-Shobu Ltd., 1959. Current methods; bound-in samples; well illustrated; early history; bibliography of literature 1600 A.D. to present.

1498. _____. Washi-Danso. (Symposium on Japanese
Handmade Paper.) Kyōto Japan: 1936. Only vol.
1 published. 100 pages text; 2 illustrations; 20
specimens.
1499. Kaempfer, Engelbert. The History of Japan, with a
Description of Siam, 1600-1692. 2 vols. London:
1727. 7 pages text and 3 illustrations devoted to
old Japanese paper making.
1500. Karabacek, Josef V. Das Arabische Papier. Vienna:
K. K. Hof, 1887.
1501. Kato, H. "Studies on Japanese Paper," Kami-pa
Gikyoshi 16:835-847, 1962. In Japanese with English summaries. Environ. Eff. Mater. and Equip.
Abstr. 4(1):48, 1964.
1502. Kay, John. Paper: Its History. London: Smith,
Kay & Co., 1893.
1503. Kenneison, W. C. and A. J. B. Spilman. Dictionary
of Printing, Papermaking and Bookbinding. London: George Newnes, 1963.
1504. Keppel, R. A., et al. "Paper from Inorganic Fibers,"
Industrial Engineering Chemistry 1, 1962.
1505. Khaddari, Munnalal. Handmade Paper Industry of
India. Kalpi, India: 1937. Textbook of the Kalpi
Handmade Paper School. 25 pages text.
1506. Khoodke, S. B. Handmade Paper. Wardha, India:
All India Village Industries Association, 1936. Indian papermaking as practiced in the Mohandas K.
Gandhi School of Papermaking, Wardha. Cover
printed on Indian paper.
1507. Kimberley, A. E. and J. F. G. Hicks. "Light Sen-
sitivity of Rosin Sized Paper Sizing Materials,"
U. S. National Bureau of Standards. Journal of
Research 6:819-827, 1931.
1508. Kimberly, Arthur E. and Adelaide L. Emley. Study
of the Deterioration of Book Papers in Libraries.
Washington: Bureau of Standards, 1933. Publication # 140.
1509. Kingery, Robert E. "The Extent of the Paper Problem in Large Research Collections and the Comparative Costs of Available Solutions," Permanent/
Durable Book Paper. Richmond: The Virginia
State Library, 1960. Summary of a conference
held in Washington, D. C., September 1960. Sponsored by the American Library Association and the
Virginia State Library.
1510. Kirkham, A. "Alum and Sodium Aluminate in Paper
Manufacture," Paper-Maker and British Paper

Trade Journal pp. 105-112, February 1951.

1511. Kiyofusa, N. Japanese Paper Making. Tokyo: 1954.

1512. Kôgei (Crafts). Articles on Japanese Handmade Papers by Naoyuki Ohta, Kazu Makamura, Muneyoshi Yanagi, Bunshō Jugaku, Naokatsu Nakamura, T. Iwai, and Dr. Torajiro Naitô. Tokyo: Nippon Mingei Kyokwai, 8th Year of Showa. 14 illustrations and 18 specimens.

1513. Kozulina, O. U. and Z. P. Barysnikova. "Biological Resistance of Paper to Insect Attacks, " Starenige Bumagi pp. 68-74, 1965 (Moscow).

1514. Kunihigashi, Jihyoe (or Kunisaki, Jihei). Kamisuki Chôhô-Ki. (Papermakers' Treasury). Osaka, Japan: 1798. The oldest book in the Japanese language devoted to papermaking. Woodblocks by Tôkei Niwa. Reprinted in part in IIS Crafts Catalog (Tokyo 1963), and in full in color by Parkes, H. S. (1871) and Clapperton, R. H. (1934) [884] and the University Arts Club, Berkeley (1948) [1515].

1515. Kunisaki Jihei. A Handy Guide to Papermaking. Berkeley: The Book Arts Club, 1948. After the Japanese edition of Kamisuki Chôhôki of 1798 [1514] with a translation by Charles E. Hamilton. 78 pp. illus.

1516. Labarre, E. J. Dictionary and Encyclopedia of Paper and Paper Making. 2nd ed. Revised and enlarged. Amsterdam: Swets & Zietlinger, 1952. (Reprinted 1969.)

1517. La Fabrication du Papier et du Carton. Paris: Payen, Vigreux et A. Prouteaux, 1866.

1518. Lalande, J. J. Le F. de. Art de Faire le Papier. vol. 1. Paris: Saillant et Nyon, 1761.

1519. _____. "Art de Faire le Papier, " Description des Artes et Metiers, Faites ou Approvees par les Messieurs de l'Academie Royale des Sciences, Neuchatel, France: 1776. [1428].

1520. Lane, Gerould T. Permanence of Paper. Rochester, N.Y. : Eastman Kodak Co. , 1935.

1521. Langwell, W. H. "The Permanence of Papers, Part 2, " Technical Bulletin, Technical Section, British Paper and Board Makers Association 29, 1952.

1522. _____. "The Permanence of Paper, Part 3, " Technical Bulletin, Technical Section, British Paper and Board Makers' Association 30:170-175, 1953.

1523. _____. "The Permanence of Paper, Part 5, "
Proceedings of the Technical Section, British Paper and Board Makers' Association 37:495-500,
1956.

1524. _____. "The Permanence of Paper in Temperate
Climates, " Tappi 38(9), 1955.

1525. _____. "The Permanence of Paper Records, " Library Association Record 55:212-215, 1953.

1526. Latour, A. and G. Schaefer. "Paper, " CIBA Review
72:2630-2656, 1949.

1527. Laufer, Berthold. Paper and Printing in Ancient
China. Chicago: The Caxton Club, 1931.

1528. Launer, Herbert F. , and William K. Wilson. "The
Photo-chemical Stability of Papers, " Paper Trade
Journal 116:28-36, 1945.

1529. Le Clert, L. Le Papier. 2 vols. Paris: du
Pégase, 1926. Colored frontpiece and many other
plates and facsimiles. The finest work on the history and manufacture of paper in France.

1530. Lehner, A. "Manufacture of Paper with Synthetic
Fibers, " Social Rhodiaceta Fr. 3, 1958.

1531. Lenz, Hans. Mexican Indian Paper: Its History and
Survival. Mexico: Editorial Cultura, 1961.
Translated from the Spanish by H. M. Campbell.

1532. Lewis, Harry F. "The Deterioration of Book Paper
in Library Use, " American Archivist 22:309-322,
1959.

1533. Libby, C. Earl (ed.). Pulp and Paper Science and
Technology. New York: McGraw Hill, 1962. 2
vols. including bibliography. Prepared under the
direction of the Joint Textbook Committee of the
paper industry.

1534. Library Association. "The Durability of Paper, "
Library Association Record 8:281, 1930.

1535. _____. "The Durability of Papers, " Library Association Record 8(Suppl.):1-24, 1930.

1536. Library of Congress. Paper Making Art and Craft.
Washington: Library of Congress, 1968. An ac-
count derived from the exhibition presented in the
Library of Congress, 1968.

1537. Lingen, A. W. Dictionary of Technical Words, Paper
and Printing. Paderborn: Ferdinand Schöningh,
1947. (Eng. -Ger. & Ger. -Eng.)

1538. Luner, Philip. "Paper Permanence, " Tappi 52(5),
1969. Reviews factors related to paper permanence. Discusses testing procedures and suggests
avenues for further study. This reference and

USGPO Technical Bulletin No. 22, Kantrowitz Permanence and Durability of Paper, (a bibliography) 1940, [4732] should be available to anyone desiring an understanding of this subject.

1539. Lydenberg, Harry Miller. "Inferior Paper Endangering the Permanence of the Printed Page, " New York Times Book Review August 2, 1925.

1540. MacAlister, J. Y. W. "The Durability of Modern Book Papers, " Library 10:295-304, 1898.

1541. Machine-Finish End Paper. Proposal for Furnishing Paper for the Public Printing and Binding, Beginning November 1, 1960. Washington: U. S. Government Printing Office, 1960. U. S. Congress Joint Committee on Printing.

1542. MacKenzie, K. J. "Permanence of Paper, " Tappi 37(4):178A, 1954.

1543. Maddox, H. A. Paper, Its History, Sources and Manufacture. London: 1933.

1544. The Manufacture of Pulp and Paper. Reprinted 1945. 3rd edition. New York: McGraw-Hill, 1939. Prepared under the direction of the Joint Textbook Committee of Paper Industry of the United States and Canada.

1545. Manufacture and Testing of Durable Book Papers. Conducted by W. J. Barrow. Edited by Randolph W. Church, Richmond, Va., 1960. Virginia State Library Publication No. 13.

1546. Marston, A. Norman. "Paper With a Working Life of Five Centuries, " The Publisher 1968. Describes the development of archive text paper (selected for the National Union Catalog) by P. F. Bingham, Ltd. of Croyden, England.

1547. Mason, John. Twelve Papers. London: Faber and Faber, 1959. Small folio. Although Mason's interest in hand made paper antedates this work and he had printed several ephemeral pieces on paper of his making, this is his first published work on his own paper. It is actually a portfolio of small specimens mounted on boards and includes descriptive notes about materials used.

1548. _____. Papermaking as an Artistic Craft. Leicester: The Twelve by Eight Press, 1962, quarto. Specimens of the author's own paper and issued under his imprint. It contains a foreword by Dard Hunter. Provides complete instructions for the home craftsman using easily obtained tools, equipment and materials.

1549. _____. More Papers Handmade by John Mason.
London: John Mason, 1966. Small folio. Another
sampling of the author's papers made from various
materials, the book contains 35 specimens, well
printed by the best of English presses, and often
amusingly conceived and illustrated. Less than
100 copies of this book were completed.

1550. _____. The Paper Makers Craft. Leicester: The
Twelve by Eight Press, 1965. Small folio. The
text is a verse translation by Oliver Bayldon of
1693 poem by Fr. Imberdis, S. J., and was
printed on a variety of English handmade papers,
including the author's own, by Will Carter. Illustrated by Rigby Graham.

1551. McClure, F. A. "The Native Paper Industry in
Kwangtung, " Lingnan Science Journal 5(3), 1927.
Canton, China. 10 pages text; 7 illustrations.

1552. _____. "Some Chinese Papers Made on the Ancient Wove, Type of Mould, " Lingnan Science Journal 60:1, 2, 1930 (Canton, China.) 13 pages text;

1553. Means, P. S. Ancient American Paper Making. Reprinted from ISIS 35(99), 1944.

1554. Mookerjee, D. N. A Monograph on Paper and Papier
Maché in Bengal. Calcutta: 1908.

1555. Morris, Henry. Papyrus. North Hills, Penn. : The
Bird & Bull Press, 1961. This translation of
Imberdis poem was printed by Morris on paper
made by him and watermarked with a bird and
bull. There were 113 copies of the book issued.

1556. _____. Five on Paper. North Hills, Penn. : The
Bird & Bull Press, 1963. Printed by Henry Morris on paper made by him, the book was bound by
him in full leather as well. The papermaking as-
sociations of this inspired volume do not end with
its physical makeup, for the writers of the essays
are Dard Hunter, J. Barcham Green, English papermaker, John Mason, Norman Strouse, advertis-
ing man, bibliophile and private printer, and Henry
Morris himself. Two specimens of Morris' earlier
paper are included with his essay. Mason's article
is delightfully illustrated, and there are six wood
engravings of papermaking as well, along with ex-
cerpts from the Imberdis poem Papyrus. The edition was 169 copies.

1557. _____. Omnibus. Instructions for Amateur Papermakers With Some Notes and Observations on
Private Presses, etc. North Hills, Penn. : The

Bird and Bull Press, 1967. 121 pages, illustrations, samples of hand-made papers.
1558. Moss, L. A. "Rag Stock vs. Wood Pulp," Paper & Paper Products 81(8), 1940.
1559. Munsell, J. A. A Chronology of Paper and Papermaking. Albany: J. Munsell, 1856. 58 pp. Five editions, under slightly varying titles, appeared by 1876.
1560. Murdock, H. R. "Tsuso-rice Paper," Paper Trade Journal 136, 1953. A description of the "rice paper" which is neither paper nor produced from rice.
1561. Natwick, A. G. and others. Making Paper. 3rd ed. Washington: Crown, Camos, 1953.
1562. Newell-Stephenson, J. (ed.). Paper and Paper Manufacture. 4 vols. New York: McGraw-Hill, 1950-1955.
1563. Nikitin, N. I. The Chemistry of Cellulose and Wood. New York: Davey, 1966.
1564. Norris, F. H Paper and Paper Making. London: New York: 1952.
1565. Nuttall, G. H. The Theory and Operation of the Fourdrinier Paper Machine. 1966. Well illustrated 626 page text.
1566. Nyuksha, J. P. "On the Fungoid Resistance of Experimental Paper Samples," Problema Dolgovechnosti Documentov I Bumagi 53:8, 1964. In Russian. Moscow-Leningrad, U. S. S. R.
1567. Okamura, S. and H. Inagaki. "Papylon - Synthetic Papers," Paper Making 136(5):74, 1958.
1568. Orraco, José and Sadako. "A National Treasure: Hand-Crafted Paper," IIC-AG Bulletin 11(1):32-33, 1970.
1569. Page, D. H. et al. The Structure and Physical Properties of Paper. London: British Paper and Board Research Association, 1960.
1570. "Paper," American Archivist 3:102, 1940; 18:92, 1955.
1571. "Paper," Rees' Cyclopaedia. London: 1819.
1572. "Paper and the Book," Publishers' Weekly 196(22):50-51, 1969. A review by William Chesholm of the enormous variety of grades and finishes of book paper now available.
1573. "Paper, Chemistry," American Archivist 12:9, 1949.
1574. "Paper, Dictionary of," American Archivist 10:18, 1947.

1575. Paper From Corn. New York: U.S. Corn Fibre
      Company, 1866. Pamphlet explaining the use and
      benefit of the utilization of the corn plant for pa-
      per-making amongst other things.

1576. Paper in Foreign Countries. Washington: U.S. House
      of Representatives, 56th Congress, 1st Session,
      1900. Special consular reports.

1577. The Papermakers Handbook & Guide to Papermaking,
      by a Practical Papermaker. London: Chil-
      worth, 1878.

1578. Paper Making. Kenley, Surrey, England: British
      Paper and Board Makers Association, 1950.

1579. Papermaking, Art and Craft. Washington: Library
      of Congress, 1968. A short account derived from
      the exhibition presented in the Library of Congress
      beginning April, 1968. Excellent illustrations with
      their sources.

1580. "Paper, Rag," American Archivist 1:3, 1938; 12:9,
      1949.

1581. "Paper, Wood Pulp," American Archivist 12:9, 1949.

1582. Parkinson, R. A Treatise on Paper. London: 1894.

1583. Parley, Norman. "Enduring Paper," The Book Col-
      lector's Quarterly 3:29-38, 1931 (London).

1584. Payen, A. "Exposition Universal Papiers de Bois,"
      Revue de D. Mondes December, 1867.

1585. Pearl, Irwin A. The Chemistry of Lignin. New
      York: Marcel Dekker, Inc., 1970. The book will
      familiarize the reader with the chemistry of lignin
      and with the theories and hypotheses extant at the
      present time.

1586. Pearson, R. S. The Indian Forest Records. Cal-
      cutta, India: 1916. Note on the utilization of
      bamboo for the manufacture of paper-pulp. 121
      pages text; 2 illustrations; folding map.

1587. Permanence of Paper. Appleton, Wisconsin: The In-
      stitute of Paper Chemistry, 1964. An annotated
      bibliography containing most of which has been
      published on the permanence of paper to 1962.
      Short abstracts and criticisms.

1588. The Permanence of Paper Archives and Related Mate-
      rials: A Research Proposal. December, 1969.
      A suggestion by the National Bureau of Standards
      to the National Archives (and co-sponsor) the Soci-
      ety of American Archivists, for a five-year pro-
      gram of research into the stability of archival pa-
      per and related materials, environment optimums
      for paper storage, the development of test methods,

and the establishment of standards.

1589. Phillips, G. O. "Radiation Chemistry of Carbohy-
drates, " Advances in Carbohydrate Chemistry
16:13-58, 1961.

1590. Plinius Secundus, Gais. Naturalis Historia, Book 13,
Chaps. 26-27. Trans. J. Bostock and H. T.
Riley as The Natural History of Pliny. London:
Henry G. Bohn, 1855. Volume 3 is on paper.

1591. (Pliny). Natural History. Cambridge, Mass.: Harvard University Press, 1952. Volume 4 is on
paper.

1592. Pound, A. "Wood, Water and Brains, " Industrial
America 1936. "Modern" paper making from a
commercial point of view.

1593. Poyser, J. Norman. Experiments in Making Paper
by Hand. Valois, Quebec: J. N. Poyser, 1966.

1594. Pravilova, T. A. and T. N. Strel'tzova. "Types of
Paper Suitable for Use in Restoration, " New
Methods for the Restoration and Preservation of
Documents and Books. Moscow: Academy of Sci-
ences of the U. S. S. R. , 1960. Translation avail-
able from National Technical Information Service,
Springfield, Va.

1595. Publisher's Library of Paper Samples. 6 vols. Boston: S. D. Warren Paper Co., 1908. This is a
handy reference for identifying early 20th century
book papers.

1596. Raitt, W. "Kashmir Papermaking in Photographs, "
The Papermaker and British Paper Trade Journal
London: February, 1930.

1597. Rasch, R. H.; M. B. Shaw and G. W. Bicking.
"Highly Purified Wood Fibers as Paper-making
Material, " Bureau of Standards Journal of Re-
search 7:765-782, 1931. Also available as U. S.
Bureau of Standards Research Paper RP-372.

1598. Rattray, J. and H. R. Mill. Forestry and Forest
Products. Edinburgh: Rattray Mill, 1885. Prize
essays of the Edinburgh International Forestry Exhibition, 1884.

1599. Recknagel, A. B. "Albrecht Pagenstecher and Wood
Pulp Paper Stock, " Bulletin 34:239-240, 1930. New
York Public Library. A brief description of the
man who brought the first samples of wood pulp
stock to the U. S. from Germany and was instru-
mental in the establishment of the wood pulp industry here.

1600. Reichardt, G. "The Durability of Paper, " Library
       Quarterly 8:510-520, 1938.
1601. Renker, A. Das Buch vom Papier. Leipzig: Insel,
       1935.
1602. Report From the Select Committee on Paper. London
       House of Commons, 1861.
1603. "Report of the (Technical Association of the Pulp and
       Paper Industry) Committee on Permanence and
       Durability of Paper, " Paper Trade Journal pp. 33-
       36, July 27, 1933.
1604. Richter, George A. "Relative Permanence of Papers
       Exposed to Sunlight, " Industrial and Engineering
       Chemistry 27:177-185; 432-439, February-April,
       1935.
1605. Robinson, John M. Making of Handmade Paper in
       Japan and England. Paper presented at the Febru-
       ary 1970 meeting of the Washington Region Con-
       servation Guild.
1606. Rossman, J. "Methods of Producing Insect Repellent
       Paper, " Paper Trade Journal 100:39-40, 1935.
1607. Royle, J. Forbes. The Fibrous Plants of India
       Fitted for Cordage, Clothing, and Paper. London:
       Smith Elder & Co. , 1855.
1608. Santucci, L. "Report on Paper Stability, Part 1.
       Survey of Literature, Discussion and Some Experi-
       mental Contributions, " Bollettino dell'Istituto di
       Patologia del Libro 22:65-104, 1963. An outstand-
       ing critical review of literature on the causes of
       paper degradation, testing methods, etc. Fully
       documented.
1609. _____ . "Resistenza e Stabilita della Carta, "
       Bollettino dell'Istituto di Patologia del Libro 19:162,
       1960; 20:141, 1961; 20:145, 1961; 20:158, 1961. A
       series of highly technical papers on paper stability.
       Good English summaries at end of each.
1610. Schäffer, J. C. Attempts Toward Making Paper from
       Plants and Wood. (in German) Regensburg: 1765.
       A fully documented research into the use of mate-
       rials other than rags for paper.
1611. _____ . Proefnemingen en Monster-bladen, om
       Papier te Maaken Zonder Lompen. Amsterdam:
       J. C. Sepp, 1770. 2 vols. Extremely rare.
       Samples of paper are made of wasps' nests, saw-
       dust, hops and vines, straw, leaves, curly Kale
       stalks, nettles, reedmare, remains of aloe and
       hemp, various mosses, and various sorts of wood.

1612. Scribner, B. W. "Comparison of Accelerated Aging
       of Record Paper with Normal Aging for 8 Years, "
       Journal of Research of the National Bureau of
       Standards 23:405-413, 1939. Research Paper RP-
       1241.
1613. Shatzkin, Leonard. "Publishing on Permanent Paper, "
       The Library Quarterly 40(1):113-127, 1970. Vice
       President for Manufacture, McGraw-Hill Book
       Company, discusses the quality of permanence vs.
       the other qualities of paper important in book
       manufacture, and the effect on the industry of a
       wholesale shift to neutral paper. Mr. Forest
       Carhart, Director, Library Technology Project,
       ALA, offers some suggestions for librarians in
       their relations with publishers in the matter of
       long lasting books.
1614. Shaw, Merle B. and M. J. O'Leary. Effect of Fill-
       ing and Sizing Materials on Stability of Book Pa-
       pers. Washington: U.S. Government Printing Of-
       fice, 1938. U.S. National Bureau of Standards
       Research Paper, RP-1149.
1615. Shaw, Merle B. , et al. A Study of the Relation of
       Some Properties of Cotton Rags to the Strength
       and Stability of Experimental Papers Made from
       Them. Washington: U.S. Government Printing
       Office, 1935. U.S. National Bureau of Standards
       Research Paper, RP-794.
1616. Shigeru S. , et al. "Synthetic Fiber Papers. III
       Manufacture of Nylon Papers, " Parupu Kami Kogyo
       Zasshi 12:385-392, 1958.
1617. Siamese Papermaking. A lecture on the making of
       Khoi (Steblusasper) paper by Phya Kasikan Banca
       (in Siamese language). This pamphlet was distri-
       buted at the cremation of Madame Aphiraksh
       Amphorsathan at Wat Amarintraram, 10th of Feb-
       ruary B. E. 2477. Bangkok, Siam.
1618. Simmonds, P. L. "On the Utilization of Waste Sub-
       stances, " Journal of the Society of Arts 7:175-
       183, 1859. Suggests using waste for paper making.
1619. Smith, J. E. A. A History of Paper. Holyoke,
       Mass. : Clark W. Bryan & Co. , 1882.
1620. Smith, R. D. "A Comparison of Paper in Identical
       Copies of Books from the Lawrence University,
       the Newberry, and the New York Public Li-
       braries, " Manuscript June 24, 1969. Available
       from author, 5029 22nd Ave. , N. E. , Seattle,
       Washington, 98105.

1621. Spalding and Hodge's. Paper Terminology. London:
       Spalding & Hodge, 1954.
1622. Specimens. New York: The Stevens-Nelson Paper
       Company, 1953. Probably the most varied sample
       book of handmade and mould made papers ever
       done. This book contains the work of more than
       150 designers, printers, papermakers of ten
       countries. Papers of both West and the Orient are
       included.
1623. (Specimens). Old Paper, A Few Scratches in Black
       Ink - Some Red. New York: Stevens Nelson Pa-
       per Co., 1963. A catalogue in which the signa-
       tures are made up of samples of the finest of
       European and Oriental handmade papers.
1624. Stamm, A. J. Wood and Cellulose Chemistry. New
       York: Ronald Press, 1964. Highly scientific
       treatment, often too much so for general reading.
1625. Stephenson, J. N. (ed.). The Manufacture of Pulp
       and Paper, A Textbook of Modern Pulp and Paper
       Mill Practice. New York: 1939. 3rd ed. Com-
       piled by many writers prominent in American pa-
       permaking. The best work in any language on the
       technique of modern paper fabrication. Five
       volumes, exhaustive text, hundreds of illustrations,
       figures, etc.
1626. _____. Pulp and Paper Manufacture. 4 vols.
       New York: McGraw-Hill, 1950.
1627. Stevenson, L. T. The Background and Economics of
       American Papermaking. New York: Harper, 1940.
1628. Stonehill, W. S. "Paper Pulp from Wood, Straw,
       etc.," Forestry and Forest Products. Edinburgh:
       Rattray Mill, 1885.
1629. _____. "Paper Pulp from Wood and Other Fibres."
       Forestry and Forest Products. Edinburgh: Rat-
       tray Mill, 1885. [1585]
1630. The Strathmore Quality Deckled Edge Book Papers.
       Mittineague, Mass.: Mittineague Paper Company,
       1906. Large octavo. This early sample book was
       printed in a variety of permutations and combina-
       tions of methods.
1631. Stratton, B. L. 'Harvard University Press Specifies
       a New Paper For Books," Publishers Weekly
       179(6):94-96, 1961.
1632. Studeny, John; J. D. Pollard and C. G. Landes.
       Permanent Paper and Method of Making Same.
       U.S. Patent 2,492,821 filed Sept. 28, 1948, issued
       Dec. 27, 1949.

1633. Sutermeister, Edwin. Chemistry of Pulp and Paper
      Making. New York: John Wiley & Sons, 1941.
1634. _____. The Story of Paper Making. Boston: The
      S. D. Warren Company, 1954.
1635. Swan, R. T. Paper and Ink. Chicago: American
      Library Association, 1895. A paper on technical
      considerations read at a meeting of the Massachu-
      setts Library Club, March 1, 1895, by the Com-
      missioner of Public Records of the State of Massa-
      chusetts.
1636. "Syntosil - A New Paperlike Material," Textil-Rund-
      schau 15:674-677, 1960.
1637. Thomas, Joseph J. "Alkaline Printing Papers:
      Promise and Performance," The Library Quarterly
      40(1):99-112, 1970. The research director of S. D.
      Warren Paper Company describes the beneficial
      effect on paper permanence of alkaline fillers
      (calcium carbonate). Some of the problems of
      printing on alkaline papers are added by the mana-
      ger of the University of Chicago printing depart-
      ment.
1638. Tindale, T. K. et al. The Handmade Papers of
      Japan. Tokyo and Rutland, Vt.: Charles E. Tut-
      tle Co., 1952. Regarded by Dr. Bunsho Jugaku
      of Kónan University in Japan as the best work on
      the subject.
1639. Torrey, W. V. and E. Sutermeister. "A Brief Study
      of Some Old Papers," Paper Trade Journal 96:45-
      46, 1933.
1640. Tsuchibayashi, S.; T. Sakai, and T. Nagaosa. "Syn-
      thetic Fiber Papers. IV Manufacture of Nylon
      Fiber Paper," Parupu Kami Kogyo Zasshi 12:725-
      733, 1958.
1641. UNESCO. "Paper for Printing: Today and Tomor-
      row," The Economist 1952. The Intelligence Unit
      of the Economist draws attention to the possibility
      of an acute shortage of paper unless raw materials
      other than wood pulp are developed on a commer-
      cial basis.
1642. Valentini, J. J. "Mexican Paper," Proceedings of
      the American Antiquarian Society. Worchester,
      Mass.: 1881.
1643. Vegetable Substances. London: Charles Knight, 1833.
      Includes chapters on vegetable fibers available for
      paper making in Europe, Orient and America in
      the early 19th century.

1644. Veitch, F. P. "Suitable Paper for Permanent Records," 1908 Yearbook of the Department of Agriculture pp. 261-266. Washington: U. S. Government Printing Office, 1908.

1645.   . Paper-making Materials and Their Conservation. Washington: U. S. Government Printing Office, 1908. Department of Agriculture, Bureau of Chemistry, Circular # 41.

1646.   . "Paper Specifications," in H. W. Wiley and C. H. Merriam (eds.). Durability and Economy in Papers for Permanent Records. Washington: U. S. Government Printing Office, 1909. U. S. Department of Agriculture, Report # 89.

1647. Veitch, F. P. and J. L. Merrill. Pulp and Paper and Other Products From Waste Resinous Woods. Washington: U. S. Dept. of Agriculture, 1913. Bulletin No. 159.

1648. Venkajee, Tekumalla. "Handmade Paper Industry in India," Paper Trade Journal 45 (Oct. 28), 1926. Four pages of text and 12 illustrations.

1649. Von Hagen, Victor W. "Mexican Papermaking Plants," Journal of the New York Botanical Garden 44(517): 1943.

1650. Voorn, H. "In Search of New Raw Materials," Paper Maker 21:1-14, 1952.

1651.   . "A Brief History of the Sizing of Paper," Paper Maker 30:47-52, 1961.

1652. Wang, C. J. K. "Preliminary Report on the Fungous Flora Pulp and Paper in New York," Tappi 44(2):785-788, 1961.

1653. S. D. Warren Paper Company. Publishers' Library of Paper Samples. Boston: S. D. Warren Co., 1908. Bound in samples of some book papers available in 1908.

1654. Watt, A. The Art of Paper Making. New York: D. Van Nostrand, 1907.

1655. Weeks, L. H. A History of Paper-Manufacturing in the United States, 1690-1916. New York: The Lockwood Trade Journal Co., 1916.

1656. Weiner, Jack and Lillian Roth. Paper Making Materials: Two Bast Fibers. Appleton, Wisconsin: Institute of Paper Chemistry, n. d. (Bibliog. Ser. No. 176, Supp. 1.)

1657. West, C. J. Classification & Definitions of Paper. New York: Lockwood Trade Journal Co., 1924.

1658.   . Papermaking Materials. Appleton, Wisconsin: Institute of Paper Chemistry, 1945-50.

Bibliographic Series Nos. 171 and 176.
1659. Wheelwright, W. B. Printing Papers. Chicago: University of Chicago Press, 1936. 133 p. illus.
1660. _____. Paper Trade Terms. Boston: Callaway Associates, 1947. A useful dictionary.
1661. _____. Practical Paper Technology. Cambridge, Mass.: M. J. & W. B. Wheelwright, 1951.
1662. "When Did Newspapers Begin to Use Wood Pulp Stock?" Bulletin 33(10), 1929. New York Public Library.
1663. Wiley, Harvey W. and C. Hart Merriam. Durability and Economy in Papers for Permanent Records. Washington, D. C.: Government Printing Office, 1909. Department of Agriculture Report # 89.
1664. Wilson, William K. "Reflections on the Stability of Paper," Restaurator 1(2), 1969.
1665. Wilson, W. K. and R. L. Hebert. "Evaluation of the Stability of Record Papers," Tappi 52:1523-1529, 1969.
1666. (Woodpulp). "When Did Newspapers Begin to Use Wood Pulp Stock?" New York: Newsprint Service Bureau, February 13, 1930. A reprint of the same article in New York Public Library Bulletin 33(10), 1929.
1667. Worth, John T. "Permanent Paper," American Association of Medical Record Librarians Journal 20:60-61, 66, 1949. Reprinted from U. S. Census Bureau Registrar 10(3):2-4, 1945.
1668. Wrist, P. E. "New Concepts Concerning Paper Structure and Paper Physics," Tappi 49, July 1966.
1669. Zöbisch, Albert. Terms for Paper and Boards. n. d.

AUDIO-VISUAL MATERIALS

FILMS AND PHOTOGRAPHS

1670. Adelstein, P. Z. and J. L. McCrea. "Permanence of Processed Ester Polyester Base Photographic Films," Photographic Science and Engineering 9:305-313, 1965.
1671. Bradley, John G. "Motion Pictures as Government Archives," Journal Society Motion Picture Engineers

26(6):653, 1936.

1672. Calhoun, J. M. "The Physical Properties and Dimensional Behavior of Motion Picture Film," Journal Society Motion Picture Engineers 43:227-266, 1944.

1673. Carver, E. K.; R. H. Talbot, and H. A. Loomis. "Film Distortions and Their Effect upon Projection Quality," Journal Society Motion Picture Engineers 41:88-93, 1943.

1674. Clapp, V. W. and R. T. Jordan. "Re-evaluation of Microfilm as a Method of Book Storage," College and Research Libraries 24, 1963. Reports that microfilming costs exceed that of new construction.

1675. Clerc, L. P. Photography Theory and Practice. 2nd ed. New York: Pitman, 1937. Photographic materials.

1676. Cobb, A. L. "Burning Characteristics of 'Safety' Film," Quarterly of the Nat. Fire Protection Assoc. 50:135-138, 1956.

1677. Cummings, J. W.; A. C. Hutton, and H. Silfin. "Spontaneous Ignition of Decomposing Cellulose Nitrate Film," Journal Society Motion Picture Engineers 54:268-274, 1950.

1678. Fordyce, C. R. "Improved Safety Motion Picture Film Support," Journal of the Society of Motion Picture Engineers 51:331-350, 1948.

1679. Fordyce, C. R., et al. "Shrinkage Behavior of Motion Picture Film," Journal of the Society of Motion Picture and Television Engineers 64:62-66, 1955.

1680. Harding, Bruce C. Microfilm, Its Use in Public Offices. Lansing, Mich.: Michigan Historical Society, n. d.

1681. Henn, R. W. and D. G. Wiest. "Properties of Gold-treated Microfilm Images," Photo Science Engineering 10(1):15-22, 1966. Describes protective treatment.

1682. Hill, J. R. and C. G. Weber. Evaluation of Motion-Picture Film for Permanent Records. Washington: National Bureau of Standards, 1937. Miscellaneous Publication, M158.

1683. Hill, J. R. and C. G. Weber. "Stability of Motion Picture Films as Determined by Accelerated Aging," Journal of the Society of Motion Picture Engineers 27:677-690, 1936.

1684. Larson, G. W.; D. C. Hubbell, and L. E. West. "Application of Two Analytical Test Methods to

Predict Processed Image Stability," Journal of the
Society of Motion Picture and Television Engineers
71:495-501, 1962.

1685. McCamy, Calvin S. "Summary of Current Research
on Archival Microfilm," National Bureau of Standards Technical Note 261. Washington, D. C. :
1965.

1686. McCamy, C. S. and C. I. Pope. "Current Research
on Preservation of Archival Records on Silver
Gelatin-type Microfilm in Roll Form," Journal of
Research 69A:385-395, 1965. Washington. National Bureau of Standards.

1687. "New Kodak Microfilm," American Archivist 31:407,
1968.

1688. Nuckolls, A. H. and A. F. Matson. "Some Hazardous Properties of Motion Picture Film," Journal
Society Motion Picture Engineers 27:657-661, 1936.

1689. Scribner, B. W. Summary Report of Research at the
National Bureau of Standards on the Stability and
Preservation of Records on Photographic Film.
Washington: National Bureau of Standards, 1939.
NB. S. Miscellaneous Publication M162.

1690. Shor, M. I. "Domestic Photographic Papers for
Printing Documents and Texts," U. S. S. R. Zhurnal
Nauchnoy i Prikladnoy Fotografi i Kinematografi
2, 1961. Translated by U. S. Joint Publications
Research Service, 1966.

1691. White, D. R., et al. "Polyester Photographic Film
Base," Journal of the Society of Motion Picture
and Television Engineers 64:674-678, 1955.

1692. Wilson, W. K. and B. W. Forshee. "Degradation of
Cellulose Acetate Films," Society of Plastics Engineers Journal 15:144-156, 1959.

TAPES AND DISCS

1693. Hard, Herbert G. "What Do You Know About Recording Tapes?" Radio and Television News 59(2):111,
1958.

1694. "High Stability Magnetic Tape," American Archivist
31:406, 1968.

1695. Latham, W. S. "Tape Life," U. S. Navy Underwater
Sound Laboratory, IRE Convention Record 1955.

1696. _____. "A Study of Limitations of Magnetic
Tapes," Audio Engineer September 1952. U. S.
Navy Underwater Sound Laboratory Report No. 140.

1697. "Literature Survey on the Properties of Plastics In-
fluencing Their Stability in Storage," Battelle Memorial Institute. Contract W33-019-ORD-5333,
May 31, 1946.
1698. Pearson, Mary D. Recordings in the Public Library.
Chicago: American Library Association, 1963.
1699. Radocy, Frank. Magnetic Tape as a Recording Medium. Audio Devices, Inc., New York, n. d.
1700. Some Plain Talk About Sound Recording Tape. Rochester, New York: Eastman Kodak Company, 1965.
1701. Welch, Walter L. "Recorded Music and Re-recording
Processes," American Archivist 31(4), 1968.

INK [See also under IX--Bibliographies--Ink]

1702. Adrosko, R. J. Natural Dyes in the United States.
Washington: Smithsonian Press, 1968. Basic information on dyes used by American craftsmen before the advent of indigo colors.
1703. _____. Summary of Natural Dyestuffs Commonly
Used in the United States. Rome: Rome Centre,
1967. Includes excellent bibliography. Main
sources for information presented were dye manuals printed in the U. S. before 1870. A practical
dyers guide.
1704. Barrow, William J. "Black Writing Ink of the Colonial Period," The American Archivist 11:291-307,
1948.
1705. _____. Manuscripts and Documents: Their Deterioration and Restoration. Charlottesville, Virginia: University of Virginia Press, 1955. Bibliography. Covers the history of papers, inks, and
restoration methods. Lengthy information on ink,
ink making, effect of ink on paper.
1706. _____. "New Non-Acid Permanent Iron Ink,"
The American Archivist 10:338, 1947.
1707. Blagden, C. "Some Observations on Ancient Inks,"
Transactions Royal Society 77(2):451, 1787.
1708. Bowles, Reginald F. Printing Ink Manual. Cambridge, England: University Press, 1961.
1709. Carvalho, David N. Forty Centuries of Ink. New
York: The Banks Law Publishing Co., 1904.

1710. Casey, R. S. "Writing Ink," Encyclopaedia of Chemical Technology. Brooklyn, N.Y.: Polytechnic Institute of Brooklyn, n.d.

1711. Davids, T. The History of Ink. New York: T. Davids & Co., 1860.

1712. Fagan, M. M. "The Uses of Insect Galls," American Naturalist 52:155-176, 1918.

1713. Gamble, W. B. and H. M. Lydenberg. "Chemistry and Manufacture of Writing and Printing Inks," Bulletin 29:579-591, 625-677, 706-741, 1925. New York Public Library. An excellent bibliography of 2167 entries, 728 of which are books and articles in professional journals, etc., and the remaining 1439 items European and American patents. To make the list even more useful, the almost 1500 patents are indexed by subject and patentee.

1714. "Inks," American Archivist 1:55, 76, 142, 147, 1938; 2:9, 1939; 3:7, 102, 109, 209, 212, 1940; 4:130, 1941; 10:106, 338, 345, 1947.

1715. (Inks). Article in Encyclopaedia Brittanica. 14th ed., 1929.

1716. "Ink, Early Analyzed," American Archivist 11:291, 1948.

1717. Jametel, Maurice (trans). L'Encre de Chine. Paris: Ernest Leroux, 1882. Translated from early Chinese documents. Covers history, manufacture and use of ink in Orient. Illustrated with 27 Chinese woodcuts and figures.

1718. Kantrowitz, Morris S. and Earl J. Gosnell. Alkaline Writing Ink. Washington: U. S. Government Printing Office, 1947. U. S. Government Printing Office, Technical Bulletin No. 25.

1719. Lehner, S. Manufacture of Inks. Philadelphia: H. C. Baird & Co., 1892. Translated, with additions, by W. T. Branut.

1720. Lindsly, G. H. and R. S. Casey. "Behaviour of the Ballpoint Pens and Inks as Seen by a Principal Manufacturer," American Bar Asso. Journal 34, 1948.

1721. Lucas, A. "The Inks of Ancient and Modern Egypt," The Analyst 47, 1922.

1722. Mally, Rudolf. "The Ball Point Pen," Kriminalistik 10(2):55-60, 1956.

1723. Manginni, James P. Reservoir, Stylographic, and Fountain Pens. London: Royal Society of Arts, 1905. The Cantor Lectures for 1905.

1724. "Manuscript-marking Ink, " American Library Association Bulletin No. 56, April 1962.
1725. "Manuscript-Marking Ink Being Tested, " American Library Association Bulletin No. 56, March 1962.
1726. Margival, F. Les Encres. Paris: Gauthier-Villars, 1912.
1727. Mitchell, C. A. "Blacklead Pencils and Their Pigments in Writing, " Journal of the Society of Chemical Engineers 38, 1919.
1728. _____. "Graphites and Other Pencil Pigments, " The Analyst 47, 1922.
1729. _____. Ink. London: Griffin, 1922.
1730. Mitchell, C. A. and T. C. Hepworth. Inks, Their Composition and Manufacture. 4th ed. London: C. Griffin & Company, 1937. Philadelphia, Pa.: Lippincott, 1937.
1731. Mitchell, C. A. and D. R. Wood. "Action of Molds on Ink in Writing, " The Analyst pp. 63-111, 1938.
1732. Moffatt, Mariet. "Official Ink Will Soon Disappear in the Bay State, " Times Beverly, Mass., June 5, 1969. A report to the effect that the Commonwealth of Massachusetts is using less and less fluid ink in favor of ball points.
1733. Padfield, Tim and Sheila Landi. "The Light Fastness of the Natural Dyes, " Studies in Conservation 2(4), 1966.
1734. Schmitt, Charles A. "The Chemistry of Writing Inks, " Journal of Chemical Education 21:413-414, 1944.
1735. The Science of Color. Washington: The Optical Society of America, 1963.
1736. Souder, W. "Composition, Properties and Behaviour of Ballpoint Pens and Inks, " Journal of Criminal Law and Criminal and Police Science 45, March-April, 1945.
1737. Swan, Robert T. Paper and Ink. Chicago: American Library Asso., 1895. An early discussion of the importance of quality in the production of writing materials by the Massachusetts Commissioner of Public Records.
1738. Underwood, N. and T. V. Sullivan. Chemistry and Technology of Printing Inks. New York: D. Van Nostrand Co., 1915.
1739. Waters, C. E. "Quick-drying Stamp-pad Inks, " Journal of Research 20:543-547, 1938. Washington, National Bureau of Standards.

1740. _____. Inks. Washington: U. S. Government
Printing Office, 1940. U. S. National Bureau of
Standards, Circular C426. The history and technology of writing ink with formulas. Section on
restoration of faded writing ink. An excellent
source of general information with a selective
bibliography.

1741. Weiss, H. B. "The Writing Masters and Ink Manufacturers of New York City, " Bulletin 56:383-394,
1952. New York Public Library.

1742. Wiborg, F. B. Printing Ink. New York: Harper &
Bros., 1926. An illustrated history with a treatise on the modern methods of manufacture and
use of ink.

1743. Wolfe, H. F. The Manufacture of Printing and Litho-
graphic Ink. New York: MacNair-Dorland Co.,
1933.

1744. Zimmerman, E. W. "Coloured Waterproof Drawing
Inks, " Industrial Engineering Chemist 25:1033,
1933.

1745. _____. Iron Gallate Inks--Liquid and Powder.
Washington: National Bureau of Standards, 1935.
NBS Research Report R 297.

ADHESIVES [See also under IX--Bibliographies--Adhesives]

p. 369

1746. (Adhesives). "Some Library Adhesives-A Laboratory
Evaluation of PVA's, " ALA Bulletin October, 1962.
An evaluation of adhesives for library book repair.

1747. "Adhesives--Chiefly for Paper, " Consumers' Research
Bulletin 24(2):21-24, 1949.

1748. "Adhesives for Book Repair, " American Archivist
1:3, 1938; 13:318, 1950.

1749. Adhesives Red Book. New York: Palmerton Publishing Co., annually. Directory of manufacturers
with brand names and product types.

1750. Blomquist, Richard F. Adhesives--Past, Present,
and Future. Philadelphia: American Society for
Testing and Materials, 1963.

1751. Braude, Felix. Adhesives. New York: Chemical
Publishing Co., 1943. Theory and application.

1752. Brooke, N. "Laboratory Adhesives, " Journal Chemical Education 31, 1954.

1753. DeBruyne, N. A. and R. Houwink. Adhesion and
        Adhesives. Amsterdam: Elseveir Publishing Com-
        pany, 1951. Part 1: theories relating to adhesion.
        Part 2: technology and practices.
1754. Delmonte, J. The Technology of Adhesives. New
        York: Reinhold Publishing Company, 1947. Syn-
        thetic adhesives.
1755. Dulac, R. Industrial Cold Adhesives. London: J. L.
        Rosebaum (C. Griffin & Co., Ltd.), 1937.
1756. Feller, R. L. "Polymer Emulsions," Bulletin of the
        American Group - IIC 6(2), 1966; 7(1), 1967; 9(2),
        1969; 10(2), 1970.
1757. Gray, V. R. "Understanding Adhesives," New Sci-
        entist 19, 1963, London.
1758. Houwink & Solomon (eds.). Adhesion and Adhesives.
        New York: Elzevier Publishing Co., 1965. Re-
        quires acquaintance with scientific language but
        excellent treatment of the subject.
1759. Hurd, Joyce. Adhesives Guide, Research Report M.
        39. London: British Scientific Instruments Re-
        search Association, 1959.
1760. Iwasaki, Tomokichi. "Scientific Preservative Methods
        for Cultural Properties. VIII. Adhesives for Re-
        pairs of Cultural Properties," Museum (Tokyo)
        154:32-33, 1964. A general description of adhe-
        sives used for repairs is given.
1761. Kantrowitz, M. S., et al. Miscellaneous Bookbinding
        Adhesives. Washington: U. S. Government Print-
        ing Office, 1953. Bindery series No. 4. Includes
        formulas for various adhesives.
1762. Katz, Irving. Adhesive Materials, Their Properties
        and Usage. Long Beach: Foster Publishing Co.,
        1964. Slanted toward industrial production.
1763. Macbeth, James A. and Alfred C. Strohlein. "The
        Use of Adhesives in Museums," Museum News
        43:9, 1965. Technical Supplement No. 7.
1764. (National Bureau of Standards). Adhesives for Every-
        day Use. Washington: U. S. Government Printing
        Office, 1970. Consumer Information Series C 13,
        53:3. Hints on selecting adhesives for various
        requirements and instructions for their application.
1765. Parker, R. S. R. and P. Taylor. Adhesion and Ad-
        hesives. New York: Pergamon Press, 1966.
1766. "Paste making," Repairers' News Sheet 18:5, 1971.
        Society of Archivists, England. Gives formula for
        a hot climate paste developed at the National Ar-
        chives of Malaysia.

1767. Reports of the Adhesive Research Committee. London: His Majesty's Stationery Office, 1922, 1926, 1933.
1768. Skeist, I. (ed.). Handbook of Adhesives. New York: Reinhold Publishing Co., 1962.
1769. Smith, Richard E. Using Adhesives in Small Plants. Washington: Small Business Administration Technical Aid No. 92, March 1969. Primarily for industry but a concise informative monograph on modern adhesives.
1770. Stout, G. L. and M. H. Horwitz. "Experiments with Adhesives for Paper," Technical Studies in the Field of Fine Arts 3(1), 1934. Reports results of tests of the adhesive properties and resistance to deterioration of various adhesives.
1771. "Trial Data on Painting Materials - Mediums, Adhesives and Film Substances," Technical Studies in the Field of Fine Arts 6(2), 1937. Includes a six-page bibliography.
1772. Wetherall, W. F. "Adhesives, Their Properties and Selection," Holtztechnologie 5:15-20, 1964. Leipzig. A survey of synthetic adhesives.

ANIMAL GLUES

1773. "Animal Glues," Forest Products Laboratory Report No. 492, 1955.
1774. Belaya, I. K. "Glue for the Restoration of Leather Bindings," Collection of Materials on the Preservation of Library Resources. (Moscow 1958) Springfield, Va.: National Technical Information Service, 1964.
1775. Belyakova, L. A. "Sodium Pentachlorophenate as an Antiseptic Protecting Glue from Mould," Microbiology 25(6):713-717, 1956. Moscow.
1776. Clad, W. O. "Glues and Gluing. A Survey of the Years 1963-1966," Holz-Roh-Werstoff 26(1):1-9, 1968.
1777. Hunt, George M. and W. L. Jones. The Selection and Testing of Animal Glue for High-Grade Joint Work. Madison, Wis.: Forest Products Laboratory, n. d.
1778. Kantrowitz, M. S., et. al. Bindery Glues. Washington: U. S. Government Printing Office, 1948. The manufacture, testing, preparation and storage of bookbinding glues. USGPO Research Bulletin B-3,

Bindery Series.

1779. _____. Flexible Glues for Bookbinding. Washington: U. S. Government Printing Office, 1941. Technical Bulletin No. 24.

1780. _____. Miscellaneous Bookbinding Adhesives. Washington: U. S. Government Printing Office, 1953. GPO-PIA Joint Research Bulletin B-4. Supplement added 1954.

1781. Monceau, M. Duhamel du. "Art de Faire les Colles, " Descriptions des Artes et Métiers, etc. vol. 8. Paris: Académie Royale des Sciences, 1771-1783. [1428.] Eighteenth century gluemaking illustrated.

VEGETABLE PASTES

1782. Bookbinding Pastes. Washington: U. S. Government Printing Office, 1953. Bindery Series No. 2.

1783. Clark, R. G. "Waterproof Starch Adhesives, " Canadian Pulp and Paper Industries 14(4):88-90, 1961.

1784. Fowler, George Herbert. "Paste, " British Records Association. Technical Section Bulletin 1:3, 1938. London. Mimeographed. A formula for making paste of good adhesive qualities.

1785. Gairola, T. R. "Pastes and Adhesives for Paper and Textiles, " Journal of Indian Museums 8, 1952.

1786. Kishore, R. and Y. P. Kathpalia. "A Note on Dextrin Paste, " Indian Archives 9:55, 1955. Gives recipe for a flour paste incorporating insecticidal poisons.

1787. Mantell, C. L. "Dextrin and British Gum: Modified Starches, " IIC-AG Bulletin 11(1):52, 1970. From Mantell's book, The Water Soluble Gums. [1788.]

1788. _____. The Water Soluble Gums. New York: Hafner Reprint, 1965.

1789. Morris, J. "Gum Arabic, " Adhesives and Resins 1, 1953.

1790. "Resinous Adhesives for Book Binders, " Chemical Age 69:547-548, 1953.

1791. Smith, Lee T. and R. M. Hamilton. "Starch Adhesives, " Chemical Engineering News 22, 1944. A review presenting a history of the development and uses of starch adhesives, together with a discussion of adhesion theories, adhesive requirements for specific purposes and methods of determining the comparative properties of different types. One hundred forty-seven references.

1792. Verrier, Lindsay. "A Pressure-cooked Non-moulding
       Adhesive Flour Paste," Nature 164:545, 1949.
       London. Lindsay Verrier claims this receipe
       gives a paste of uniform consistency which is not
       messy to make and nonpoisonous.

SYNTHETIC ADHESIVES

1793. Barrow, W. J. Permanence /Durability of the Book -
       IV, Polyvinyl Acetate (PVA) Adhesives for use in
       Library Bookbinding. Richmond, Va.: W. J.
       Barrow Research Laboratory Publications, 1965.
1794. Berger, G. A. "A New Adhesive for the Consolida-
       tion of Paintings, Drawings and Textiles," Bulletin
       American Group - IIC 11(1):36-38, 1970. Reports
       on a polyvinyl acetate copolymer, the result of
       research done in cooperation with the Conservation
       Center at the Institute of Fine Arts, New York
       University.
1795. Delmonte, J. The Technology of Adhesives. New
       York: Reinhold Publishing Co., 1947. Primarily
       synthetic adhesives.
1796. Feller, R. L. "Polymer Emulsions," Bulletin Amer-
       ican Group - IIC 6(2), 1966; 7(1), 1967; 9(2), 1969.
       An introduction to the characteristics and properties
       of polymer emulsions and guidance for selecting
       emulsions for restoration work.
1797. Galbreich, E. I. "Adhesive Properties of Polyvinyl
       Alcohol," Saltykov-Shchedrin 93-95, 1963. Lenin-
       grad, State Public Library.
1798. "Guide to Household Adhesives," Consumers Report
       32(4):230-232, 1967. The typical uses, advantages,
       and disadvantages of white glues, epoxy glues,
       contact cements and clear cements are discussed.
       25 brands are listed.
1799. Gutttmann, W. H. Concise Guide to Structural Adhe-
       sives. New York: Reinhold Publishing Co., 1961.
1800. Mason, J. P. and J. Manning. Technology of Plas-
       tics and Resins. Princeton: Van Nostrand, 1945.
       A complete college textbook.
1801. McLaren, A. D. and Charles J. Seiler. "Adhesion
       III. Adhesion of Polymers to Cellulose and
       Alumina," Journal Polymer Science 4:63-74, 1949.
1802. Phelan, W. H., et al. "Adhesives Used in Paper
       Conservation - A Preliminary Review," Bulletin

American Group - IIC 11(1), 1970.   Authors con-
clude that polyvinyl acetate is not in general a
recommended adhesive for paper objects.

1803.   Piez, Gladys T.   "Some Library Adhesives--A Laboratory Evaluation of P. V. A. 's," American Library
Association Bulletin 56:838-843, 1962.

1804.   Polyvinyl Acetate (PVA) Adhesives for Use in Library
Binding.   Richmond, Va.:   W. J. Barrow Research
Laboratory, 1965.

1805.   Sutton, D. A.   "Modern Natural Synthetic Glues and
Adhesives," Journal Royal Society of Arts 3, 1963.

1806.   Venkov, I.   "Epoxy Resins and Restoration," Musei i
pamegnitsi na Kulturata 3:43, 1966.   Discusses
using epoxy resin in conservation.

1807.   Webb, R. F.   "Modern Glues," Research 13, 1960.

1808.   Yabrova, R. R.   "Polymethacrylate Emulsion--A New
Glue for Book Restoration and Bookbinding," Col-
lection of Materials on the Preservation of Library
Resources (Moscow: 1958).   Springfield, Va.:
National Technical Information Service, 1964.

BOARDS

1809.   Kantrowitz, M. and F. Blaylock.   Paper Boards for
Bookbinding.   Washington: U. S. Government Printing Office, 1950.   Description of the manufacture
of and standards for boards.

1810.   Lalande, Jérôme Le Francais de.   Art de Cartonnier.
Paris: Saillant et Nyon, 1761.   Description of the
method for making paper book boards.   Also in
Descriptions des Artes et Metiers, Vol. 4, Paris:
l'Academie Royale des Sciences, 1776.   [1428.]

1811.   _____.   Art de Cartonnier.   Paris: J. Moronval,
1820.   This new edition of the 1761 volume contains additional material on making paper book
boards as it was done in Germany, Sweden, England and Italy.

1812.   Paper and Paper Board: Characteristics, Nomenclature and Significance of Tests.   Philadelphia:
American Society for Testing and Materials, 1963.

1813.   Zöbisch, Albert.   Terms for Paper and Board.   n. d.

CLOTH

1814. Bowyer, W. "Publishers' Binding Cloth," The Book
       Collector's Quarterly 6:57-59, 1932.
1815. Carter, John. "The Origin of Publisher's Cloth Bind-
       ing," The Colophon 8, 1931.
1816. _____. Publisher's Cloth. London: Constable,
       1935. (New York: Bowker, 1935) An outline his-
       tory of publisher's cloth bindings in England 1820-
       1900.
1817. Consult, C. Flax and Its Products. Belfast: 1862.
1818. Cook, J. G. Handbook of Textile Fibres. 2nd ed.
       Watford, Herts, England: Merrow Publishing Co.,
       1960.
1819. "Cover Materials," Publishers' Weekly 196(22):51,
       1969. An outline of the kinds of woven and non-
       woven book cover materials available today.
1820. Dictionary of Bookcloth. London: Thomas Goodall
       & Co., 1944. Spiral-bound sample sheets.
1821. Elder, Hamish M. "Cellulose and Protein Fibers,".
       Paper presented at a meeting of the IIC-UK Group,
       April 1968. Describes the difference in properties
       of wool and cotton fibers and fabrics.
1822. "A Guide to Man-Made Fibers," New Scientist 13,
       1962.
1823. Identification of Textile Materials. Manchester, Eng-
       land: The Textile Institute, 1965.
1824. "Impact Wear Test for Bookcloths Described in Labo-
       ratory Report," Patra News 94:1-2, 1958.
1825. "The Influence of Contaminants on the Water Repellency
       of Fabrics," American Dyestuff Reporter 52:P1059-
       P1067, 1963. American Association of Textile
       Chemists and Colorists Northern Piedmont Section.
1826. Kantrowitz, M. S., et al. Pyroxylin Treated Book
       Cloths. Washington: U. S. Government Printing
       Office, 1948. G. P. O. -P. I. A. Joint Research
       Bulletin, bindery series No. 7. Pam.
1827. Kinery, Irene. The Primary Structures of Fabrics.
       Washington: The Textile Museum, 1966. This
       volume clears the way for greater understanding
       of the confused realm of textile classification and
       terminology. Basic information on bark, papyrus,
       fibrous materials.
1828. Leggett, W. F. The Story of Linen. New York:
       Chemical Publishing Co., 1945.

1829. _____. The Story of Silk. New York: Lifetime
        Editions, 1949.
1830. Leighton, Douglas. "Canvas and Bookcloth: an Essay
        on Beginnings, " The Library 5th series, 3(1):39-
        49, 1948.
1831. Making of Bookbinding Fabrics. Being an illustrated
        story showing the various processes required to
        transform raw cotton into a finished bookbinding
        fabric. Norwood, Mass. : Holliston Mills, circa
        1951.
1832. Mathews, J. M. Textile Fibres. London: Chapman
        and Hall; New York: J. Wiley & Sons, 1967.
1833. Moore, A. S. Linen. London: 1914.
1834. "Nomenclature of Nineteenth-century Cloth Grains, "
        The Book Collector 2(1):54-58, 1953.
1835. Review of Textile Progress: a Survey of World Lit-
        erature. New York: Plenum Press, 1967.
1836. Sadleir, Michael. Evolution of Publishers' Binding
        Styles, 1770-1900. London: Constable, 1930.
        First systematic attempt to classify the basic
        fabrics used in publishers' bindings.
1837. _____. "XIX Century Fiction, " The Book Col-
        lector 2(1), 1953. Includes an expansion of the
        author's earlier classification of binder's cloth.
1838. Sadleir, Michael and John Carter. "The Nomen-
        clature of Nineteenth-Century Cloth Grains, " The
        Book Collector 2(1):54-58, 1953. Twenty-four
        photographs of named varieties of book cloth used
        in the 19th century.
1839. Schaefer, G. "Flax and Hemp, " CIBA Review
        (49):1762-1795, 1945. Basle.
1840. Spoor, H. and K. Ziegler. "Chemistry and Fine
        Structure of Natural Silk, " Angewandte Chemie
        Weinheim, Germany 72: 1960.
1841. "Technical Note on Silk Chiffon, " Archives and Manu-
        scripts Australia Library Association. June 1956.
        Discusses shrinking.
1842. Walton, Perry. The Story of Textiles. New York:
        Tudor, 1937.
1843. Watkins, James L. King Cotton. New York: Wat-
        kins & Sons, 1908.
1844. Weibel, A. C. Two Thousand Years of Textiles.
        New York: Pantheon Books, 1952. Published for
        the Detroit Institute of Arts.
1845. Woodhouse, T. The Finishing of Jute and Linen
        Fibers. London, 1928.

1846.   Woolman, M. S. and E. B. McGowan. Textiles.
        New York: The MacMillan Co. , 1943.

GOLD STAMPING MATERIALS

1847.   Barnes, Richard H.   Gilding and the Making of Gold
        Leaf. Philadelphia: Butler and Ferrigno Litho-
        graphic Co. , 1962.
1848.   Hobson, Kenneth.   "Some Notes on the History and
        Development of Bookbinder's Stamps and Tools, "
        Print 8(4), 1953.
1849.   Holt, Penelope and Edmund Thorpe. Gold & Books.
        Mellon Mowbry, Leicestershire: Brewhouse, 1969.
        Illustrated by Rigby Graham.   The story of the
        preparation of gold and its used in decorating
        books and bindings through the ages.
1850.   Kantrowitz, M. S. and F. Blaylock. Bronze Stamp-
        ing Leaf. Washington: U. S. Government Printing
        Office, 1952.   Research Bulletin B-6, Bindery
        series.
1851.   Whiley, George M.   Leaves of Gold: An Account of
        the Ancient Craft of Goldbeating and its Develop-
        ment into a Modern Industry.   Privately printed,
        1951.

SEWING MATERIALS

1852.   Castellini, Luigi.   "Hemp, " CIBA Review No. 5,
        1962.
1853.   Consult, C. Flax and Its Products. Belfast: 1862.
1854.   Hemp. Washington: U. S. Government Printing Of-
        fice.   U. S. Plant Industry Bureau Bulletins 46 and
        221.
1855.   Levenberger, Dr. H. R.   "Thread, " CIBA Review
        (3):22-28, 1965.   Illus.   The processes for twist-
        ing yarns to make threads are described.   Different
        types of threads are illustrated in microphotos.
1856.   Linen, Jute and Hemp Industries. Washington: U. S.
        Government Printing Office.   U. S. Foreign and

Domestic Commerce Bureau, Special Agents Series No. 74.

1857. Menzi, K. and N. Bigler. "Identification of Bast Fibers (Flax, Hemp, Ramie, Jute), " CIBA Review 123:33-36, 1957. Basle.

1858. Plonka, F.; P. Hermant, and P. Gayet. "Flax, " CIBA Review 2:1-38, 1965. 53 photographs, 1 diagram, bibliography, (33 refs). The domestication and cultivation of flax is discussed and diagramed and photomicrographs of the plant illustrate the text. The processes of retting, scutching and production of linen threads and fabrics are outlined and photographs of the flax from raw material to finished product are shown.

1859. Schaefer, G. "Flax and Hemp, " CIBA Review 49:1762-1795, 1945. Basle.

1860. Select Essays: Containing the Manner of Raising and Dressing Flax and Hemp. Also the Whole Method of Bleaching or Whitening Linen-Cloth. Philadelphia: Printed by Robert Bell, 1777.

MISCELLANEOUS

1861. Barrow, William J. Permanence and Durability of Library Catalog Cards. Chicago: American Library Association, 1961. LTP Publications, No. 3.

1862. Kashima, M. and Y. Nose. "Physiochemical Investigation of Rust Preventive Oil, " National Association of Corrosion Engineers Proceedings 612-623, 1963. Houston, Texas.

VARNISHES

1863. Barrett, O. W. "Roach-proof Book Varnish, " Philippine Agricultural Review 6:49, 1913.

1864. Barry, T. H. Natural Varnish Resins. London: Ernest Benn Ltd., 1932. A history.

1865. Block, S. S. "A Protective Lacquer for Books,"
Florida Public Library Newsletter 3(9), 1949.

1866. Coating Technology. Philadelphia: Federation of Societies for Paint Technology, 1964-1968. A series
of nine pamphlets on technology of paint, varnish,
etc. No. 5, Resins; No. 6, Solvents; No. 8, Inorganic Color Pigments; and No. 9, Organic Color
Pigments. Contains much useful information for
conservators.

1867. Martens, Charles R. (ed.). Technology of Paints,
Varnishes and Lacquers. New York: Reinhold,
1968.

SIZES

1868. Kimberly, A. E. and J. F. G. Hicks. Light Sen-
sitivity of Rosin Paper-sizing Materials. Washington: National Bureau of Standards Research Paper
372, n. d.

1869. Kowalik, R. and E. Czerwinska. "Sizes Used in
Paper-making and Paper Binding," BLOK Notes
Muzeum Michiewicza pp. 153-154, 1960. Warsaw.

1870. Radley, J. A. Starch and Its Derivatives. London:
Chapman and Hall, 1953.

SYNTHETICS

1871. Barker, E. F. "Swiss Mill Produces Paper Containing Substantial Quantities of Nylon," Paper Trade
Journal 145(7):48-51, 1961.

1872. Bennet, H. Commercial Waxes. New York: Chemical Publishing Co., 1956. Includes information on
synthetics used in conservation.

1873. Blegen, J. R. and W. R. Fuller. Alkyd Resins.
Philadelphia: Federation of Societies for Paint
Technology, 1967. Unit five of a series of pamphlets on coatings. An excellent concise introduction
to this important group of polyester resins.

1874. Brydson, J. A. Plastic Materials. Princeton, N. J. :
      Van Nostrand, 1966. A comprehensive introduc-
      tion to history, properties, structure, use, etc. of
      all plastics.
1875. Bolding, Brace. Polymers and Resins. New York:
      Van Nostrand, 1959.
1876. Dick, Marshall and Charles E. Feazel. "Resistance
      of Plastics to Ethylene Oxide, " Modern Plastics
      35:148, 1960.
1877. Gallo, F. "Experimental Research on Resistance to
      Biological Agents of Materials Used in Book Res-
      toration, Pt. 5, " Bolletino dell'Istituto di Patologia
      del Libro 24(1-4):95-105, 1965. Tests on plastic
      films and discussion of their properties. Summar-
      ized in English.
1878. Gettens, Rutherford. "Polymerized Vinyl Acetate and
      Related Compounds in the Restoration of Works of
      Art, " Technical Studies in the Field of the Fine
      Arts 4:15-27, 1935. A technical discussion of
      polyvinyl acetate and its use in lieu of the natural
      resins.
1879. Gruetzner, N. K. and J. J. Shay. "Acrylic Resins
      in Aerosol Surface Coatings, " Paint Varnish Pro-
      ducts 52:40-44, 1962.
1880. Haynes, William. Cellulose, The Chemical That
      Grows. Garden City, N. Y. : Doubleday & Co. ,
      1953.
1881. Heuser, E. The Chemistry of Cellulose. New York:
      Wiley, 1946.
1882. Jorner, J. "Photochemistry of Cellulose Acetate, "
      Polymer Science 37, 1959.
1883. Lee and Neville. Handbook on Epoxy Resins. New
      York: Reinhold Publishing Co. , 1967.
1884. Maranyl, Nylon Soluble Polymers. London: Imperial
      Chemical Industries Information Service Note 611,
      n. d.
1885. Mason, J. P. and J. F. Manning. The Technology
      of Plastics and Resins. New York: Van Nostrand,
      1945. See especially the sections on cellulose
      (pp. 150-162), acrylic resins (pp. 239-259), and
      polyvinyl acetate (pp. 272-278).
1886. Morrison, J. A. S. Plastics in the Printing and
      Bookbinding Industries. London: London School
      of Printing and Kindred Trades, 1948.
1887. Okamura, S and H. Inagaki. "Papylon-Synthetic
      Papers, " Paper Making 136(5):74, 1958.

1888.   Ott, Emil (ed.). Cellulose and Cellulose Derivatives.
        New York: Interscience Publishers, Inc., 1946.
1889.   Petukhov, B. V. The Technology of Polyester Fibers.
        New York: The MacMillan Co., 1963. The theo-
        retical and experimental fundamentals of the pro-
        duction of polyester fibers.
1890.   Roff, W. J. Fibres, Plastics and Rubbers. London:
        Butterworths, 1956.
1891.   Schildknecht, C. E. Vinyl and Related Polymers.
        New York: Wiley, 1952.
1892.   Shigeru, S., et al. "Synthetic Fiber Papers, III
        Manufacture of Nylon Papers," Parupu Kami Kogyo
        Zasshi 12:385-392, 1958.
1893.   Stannett, Vivian. Cellulose Acetate Plastics. New
        York: Chemical Publishing Company, 1951.
1894.   Synthetic Materials Used in the Conservation of Cul-
        tural Property. Rome: International Centre for
        the Study of the Preservation and the Restoration
        of Cultural Property, 1963. Scientific description
        of synthetic adhesives, varnishes, resins, etc.
        with manufacturers and trade names.
1895.   "Syntosil--a New Paperlike Material," Textil-Rund-
        schau 15:674-677, 1960.
1896.   Tsuchibayashi, S., et al. "Synthetic Fiber Papers,
        IV Manufacture of Nylon Fiber Paper," Parupu
        Kami Kogyo Zasshi 12:725-733, 1958.
1897.   Werner, A. E. A. "New Materials in the Conserva-
        tion of Antiquities," Museum Journal 64, 1964.
        Discusses wide range of synthetic materials.
1898.   _____. "Synthetic Waxes," Museum Journal 57:3-
        5, 1957-1958. Discusses modern waxes in relation
        to book protection.
1899.   _____. "Technical Notes on a New Material in
        Conservation," Chronique d'Egypte 33(66), 1958.
        On soluble nylon.
1900.   Zaguliaeva, Z. A. "Biological Resistance of Some
        Methylcellulose Grades for Paper Restoration
        Work," Stareniye bumagi 112-116, 1956. Moscow.

III. The Enemies of Library Materials

GENERAL

1901. Alekseeva, T. V. and N. G. Belenkaja. "Cellulose
Functions and Their Influence on Paper-ageing.
III. Carbonyl Groups," in Flyate, D. M. Causes
of Decay of Written and Printed Documents Leningrad: Laboratory for Preservation and Restoration
of Documents, 1967. In Russian but with English
summaries.

1902. Animals Injurious to Books. London: Science Museum, 1938. Science Library Bibliographical Series
No. 377.

1903. [No entry.]

1904. (Anon.). "Les Ennemis des Livres: Histoire Natur-
elle, Leur Constitution, Leurs Ravages, Les
Moyens de s'en Preserver," Magasin Pittoresque
46:146-149, 1878. Paris.

1905. _____. "Why Dyed Cellulose Fibres Rot," Chemical and Engineering News 35(26), 1957.

1906. Archer, John. "A Ten Year Test of Bindings,"
Bulletin 40(2), 1936. New York Public Library.

1907. Arts, Society of. Report on the Deterioration of Paper. London: 1898.

1908. Baker, W. E. B. "Relationship of Impurities to Paper Permanence," Paper Trade Journal 91(4):51-
52, 1930.

1909. Barrow, W. J. "An Accelerated Aging Study of
Several Writing Papers. Reevaluation of Data,"
Tappi 47:105-107, 1964.

1910. _____. "Migration of Impurities in Paper,"
Archivum 3:105-108, 1953. Tables and bibliography. The migration of impurities due to non-
cellulosic material, acidic material from ground
wood papers, acid from writing ink, and other
materials is considered.

1911. Barrow, W. J. and R. C. Sproull. "Permanence in
Book Papers," Science 129(3356):1075-1084, 1959.

144

Investigation of deterioration in modern papers and
suggestions for practical basis for remedy.

1912.   Barrow Research Laboratory. Strength and Other
Characteristics of Book Papers, 1800-1899. Richmond, Virginia: W. J. Barrow Research Laboratory, 1967. Pinpoints acid primarily from rosin
size as the arch enemy of book paper.

1913.   Basu, Purnendu. "Enemies of Records," Indian Archives 4, 1950. Names time, fire, water, light,
heat, dust, humidity, air pollution, fungi, vermin,
acts of God and people.

1914.   _____. "Common Enemies of Records," The Indian Archives 5(1), 1951.

1915.   Belaya, I. K. "The Action of Certain Antiseptics on
Paper," Collection of Materials on the Preservation
of Library Resources. Moscow, 1958. Springfield,
Va.: National Technical Information Service, 1964.

1916.   _____. "The Action of Short Wave Ultraviolet Irradiation by Bacteriocidal Lamps on Paper,"
(ibid).

1917.   Belenkaja, N. G.; T. V. Alekseeva, and V. F. Gor-
shenina. "Effect of Sizing With Alkylketene-dimer
on the Aging of Sulfite Cellulose Paper," Causes
of Decay of Written and Printed Monuments Leningrad: Laboratory for Preservation and Restoration
of Documents, 1967. In Russian with English
summary.

1918.   Bhargava, K. D. Repair and Preservation of Records. New Delhi: Archives of India, 1959. Care
and repair of birch bark, palm leaf, paper, ink,
leather.

1919.   Blades, W. The Enemies of Books. London: Elliot
Stock, 1888. Reprinted 1902.

1920.   Blank, M. G. and others. "Aging of Restored Paper," Stareniye bumagi 57-67, 1965. Moscow.
Describes effects of water, chloramine, magnesium
carbonate, etc. on new and old paper.

1921.   Brommelle, N. S. and A. E. A. Werner. "Deteriora-
tion and Treatment of Wood," ICOM's Problems of
Conservation in Museums. London: George Allen
& Unwin, Ltd., 1969.

1922.   Brooks, C. E. P. "Climate and the Deterioration of
Materials," Quarterly Journal of the Royal Meteorological Society 72:87-97, 1946.

1923.   Browning, B. L. and W. A. Wink. "The Prediction
of Paper Permanence," Tappi 51(4):156-163, 1968.
Reprint of a report to the April 1967 meeting of the

American Chemical Society.   Discusses the factors
affecting the durability of paper.

1924. Bureau, W. H.   "Static: Unwelcomed Guest in Paper, "
Graphic Arts Monthly 38(3):106, 108, 110, 1966.

1925. Calvert, F. C.   "On Decay in the Binding of Books, "
Transactions of the Society of Arts 57:120-122,
1851.

1926. "Cause of Paper Turning Yellow, " Paper Trade Journal 58(18), 1914.

1927. Chakravorti, S. K.   "Effect of 'Gammexane' on the
Durability of Paper, " Nature 163(607), 1949.

1928. Chapman, J. A.   "An Inquiry Into the Causes of the
Perishing of Paper, " Calcutta Review 301-307,
1919.

1929. _____. "The Perishing of Paper, " Calcutta Review
223-246, 1920.   Chapman identified bleaching
practices and new fiber sources as probable causes
for paper deterioration in early 19th century.

1930. _____. "The Imperial Library - Past and Future, "
Calcutta Review 447-457, 1922.   Author suggests
moving library into foothills to escape all the ills
of tropical climate in Calcutta.

1931. Charlesby, A.   Atomic Radiation and Polymers.   Oxford: Pergamon, 1960.

1932. Chesebrough, T. W.   "Death of Books, " University
Quarterly 2:284, 1861.

1933. Cheshire, A.   "The Ageing of Leather, " Journal of
the International Society of Leather Trades' Chemists 30:134-166, 1946.

1934. Church, R. W. (ed.).   Deterioration of Book Stock:
Cause and Remedies.   Richmond, Va.: Virginia
State Library, 1959.   Two studies on the perman-
ence of book paper conducted by W. J. Barrow.
Virginia State Library Publication No. 10.

1935. Clapp, Verner W.; Francis H. Henshaw, and Donald
C. Holmes.   "Are Your Microfilms Deteriorating
Acceptably, " Library Journal 80(6):589-595, 1955.

1936. "Climatology and Conservation in Museums, " Museum
13(4):202-289, 1960.   A study by the Rome Center.
Reviewed by N. Stolow in Studies in Conservation
7(1):33-34, 1962.

1937. "Conference of Italian Librarians, " Library Journal
23:667, 1898.   U. S. Library of Congress.   Report
of the Librarian of Congress for the Fiscal Year
Ended June 30, 1898.   Washington, D. C.: U. S.
Government Printing Office, 1898.   Includes comments on deteriorating book paper.

1938. Corbett, W. M. "The Alkaline Degradation of Chemically Modified Cellulose, " Journal Society Dyers and Colourists 76:265-271, 1960.

1939. Coremans, Paul. Problems of Conservation in Museums. London: George Allen & Unwin, Ltd. , 1969. Contains sections on the deterioration of cellulose, the deacidification of paper and the deterioration and conservation of wood.

1940. Csapodi, C. "Conservation of the Manuscript and Old Book Collections at the Library of the Hungarian Academy of Science, " Publications Academie Scientiarium Hungarie 44. Budapest: Academy of Science, 1954. Includes English translation.

1941. Cummings, J. W. , et al. "Spontaneous Ignition of Decomposing Cellulose Nitrate Film, " Journal of the Society of Motion Picture and Television Engineers 54:268-274, March 1950.

1942. Dahl, S. "The Effects of Fungicides on Deterioration of Leather, " Journal American Leather Chemists Association 52(11):611-621, 1957.

1943. Dahl, S. and A. M. Kaplan. "Laboratory and Field Exposure Studies of Leather Fungicides, " Journal American Leather Chemists Ass. 51(3):118-136, 1956.

1944. "Destroyers of Early Books, " Hogg's Instruction 3:220, 1851.

1945. Deterioration of Book and Record Papers. Washington: U. S. Dept. of Agriculture, 1936. Technical Bulletin No. 541.

1946. The Deterioration and Preservation of Book Material Stored in Libraries. Garston, England: Building Research Station, 1949. Note No. D. 62.

1947. DeZeih, C. J. Effects of Nuclear Radiation on Cork, Leather and Elastomers. Washington: U. S. Atomic Energy Commission, 1957.

1948. Evans, D. M. "The Deterioration of Bookbinding Materials, " Microbiological Deterioration in the Tropics. London: Society of Chemical Industry, 1966.

1949. Evans, J. (Chairman). "Report of the Committee on the Deterioration of Paper, " Society of Arts Journal 46:597-601, 1898.

1950. Faria, Diego de. Os Inimigos dos Nossos Livros. São Paulo: Serbico Sanitario Estado de São Paulo, 1919. 42 p. illustrated.

1951. Flieder, Francoise. LaConservation des Documents Graphiques: Recherches Expérimentales. Paris: Libraire de l'Enseignement Technique, 1969. A

joint publication by UNESCO's Rome Centre and
ICOM's Committee on Museum Laboratories of
Madam Flieder's important contributions to the
study of the factors contributing to the deterioration
of paper.

1952. Frey, R. W. and C. W. Beebe. 'The Decay of
Bookbinding Leathers, " Journal of the American
Leather Chemists Association 26(1), 1931.

1953. Galbreich, E. I. and others. "Some Properties of
Paper Restored With the Help of Synthetic Polymers, " Part II. O sokhranenii bumagi 42-61,
1963. Leningrad. Reports the action of sulphur
dioxide, light, etc. on plastic coatings.

1954. Gale, R. O. and A. L. Williams. "Factors Affecting
Color Film Dye Stability: Related Printing Problems and Release Print Quality, " Journal of the
Society of Motion Picture and Television Engineers
72:804-809, 1963.

1955. Gallo, A. Le Malattie del Libro. Milano: Monda-
dori, 1935.

1956.   . "Libri Mallati, " Academie e Biblioteche
d'Italia 10:334-335, 1936.

1957.   . "Patologia e Terapia del Libro, " Enci-
clopedia Poligrafica Vol. 1, monograph 3. Roma:
Editrice Raggio, 1951.

1958.   . "The Pathology of Books, " East and West
1:54-58, 1950. The director of the Istituto di
Patologia del Libro in Rome reviews the afflictions
to which books are subjected.

1959. Greathouse, G. A. and C. J. Wessel (eds.). Deterioration of Materials: Causes and Preventative
Techniques. New York: Reinhold Publishing Co.,
1954.

1960. Greenwood, F. W. P. "Uses and Abuses of Books, "
Christian Examiner 10:240, 1907.

1961. Grove, Lee E. "Paper Deterioration--an Old Story, "
College and Research Libraries 25:365-374, 1964.

1962.   . "John Murray and Paper Deterioration, "
Libri 16:194-204, 1966.

1963. Guarnieri, A. C. Notas sôbre o problema do môfo
nos livros. São Paulo: Universidade de Sao
Paulo, 1948.

1964. Haight, Anne Lyon. Books and Printing. New York:
World Publishing Co., 1963. Miss Haight refutes
very successfully Andrew Lang's 1881 statement
that women are the natural enemies of books
[1993.]

General 149

1965. Hamilton, Robert M. "The Library of Parliament Fire," American Archivist 16:141-144, 1953.

1966. Hanson, Fred S. "Resistance of Paper to Natural Aging," The Paper Industry and Paper World 1939.

1967. Hill, F. P. "The Deterioration of Newspaper Paper," The Library Journal 35, 1910. Also in American Library Association Bulletin 4, 1910.

1968. Hill, J. R. and G. G. Weber. "Stability of Motion Picture Films as Determined by Accelerated Aging," Journal of the Society of Motion Picture Engineers 27(6):677 ff, 1936.

1969. Hitchins, Alfred B. "The Yellowing of Paper," Paper July 24, 1918. Pinpoints rosin size as a principal cause of yellowing.

1970. Hoffman, W. F. and S. R. Olsen. "The Deterioration of Paper: A Review," Paper Trade Journal 90:171-173, 1930.

1971. "How Long Do Books Last?" Agnewandte Chemie 71:20, 1959. Supply No. 347.

1972. Hudson, F. L. "Review of The Manufacture and Testing of Durable Book Papers," Paper Technology 2:21, 1961.

1973. _____. The Absorption of Sulfur Dioxide on Printing Papers and Their Chemical Stability. Lecture given in Munich April 27, 1967. Published as "Die Sorption von Schwefeldioxid durch Druckpapiere und deren chemische Bestandigkeit," Wochenblatt fur Papierfabrikation 16:660-662, 1967.

1974. _____. "Acidity of 17th and 18th Century Books," Paper Technology 8:189-190, 1967.

1975. Hudson, F. L. and W. D. Milner. "Factors Affecting the Permanency of Paper: Tests with Labelled Sulphur," Nature 178:590, 1956.

1976. Hudson, F. L. and C. J. Edwards. "Some Direct Observations on the Aging of Paper," Paper Technology 7(1):27, 1966.

1977. Hummer, Charles W. Jr.; Charles R. Scuthwell, and Allen A. Alexander. "Corrosion of Metals in Tropical Environment--Copper and Wrought Copper Alloys," Materials Protection 7(1):41-47, 1968.

1978. Hutchinson, G. L., et al. "Film Decomposition Tests," Journal of the Society of Motion Picture and Television Engineers 54:381-383, 1950. Summary from British Government reports.

1979. Iglesias, L. "Contra la polilla de los libros," Association de Bibliotecarios y Bibliografia 2:89-100, 1935. Madrid.

1980. Innes, R. F. "The Corrosion of Metals by Contact
       With Leather, " Journal of the International Society
       of Leather Trades' Chemists 19:548-563, 1935.

1981. _____ . "The Deterioration of Vegetable Tanned
       Leather on Storage, " Journal of the American
       Leather Chemists Association 26(2):114-115, 1931.

1982. Jarrel, T. D.; J. M. Hankins, and F. P. Veitch.
       Deterioration of Book and Record Papers. Wash-
       ington: U. S. Government Printing Office, 1936.
       U. S. Department of Agriculture, Technical Bulletin
       No. 541. An early proof of the necessity for
       positive action to save paper records in libraries
       and archives.

1983. _____ . "The Effect of Inorganic Acids on the
       Physical Properties of Waterleaf Rag Bond Paper, "
       Paper Trade Journal 95:28-33, 1932.

1984. _____ . Deterioration of Book and Record Paper
       as Indicated by Gas Chamber Tests. Washington:
       U. S. Government Printing Office, 1938. U. S.
       Department of Agriculture Technical Bulletin No.
       605.

1985. Jedrzejewska, H. "The Damaging Influence of Disin-
       fecting Agents on Sensitive Ancient Materials, "
       Museum Climatology. London: International In-
       stitute for Conservation, 1968.

1986. Kathpalia, Y. P. "Deterioration and Conservation of
       Paper. I: Biological Deterioration, " Indian Pulp
       and Paper 15, July 1960.

1987. _____ . "Deterioration and Conservation of Paper.
       II: Physical Deterioration, " Indian Pulp and Paper
       15, January 1961.

1988. _____ . "Deterioration and Conservation of Paper.
       III: Chemical Deterioration, " Indian Pulp and Pa-
       per 16, November 1961.

1989. Kimberly, A. E. and A. L. Emley. A Study of the
       Deterioration of Book Papers in Libraries. Wash-
       ington: U. S. Government Printing Office, 1933.
       National Bureau of Standards. Miscellaneous Pub-
       lication No. 140.

1990. Kleinert, T. N. "Primary chain scission in cellu-
       lose, " Papier 23(12):885-887, 1969. This short
       work in German reviews 25 references on cellulose
       degradation by ultraviolet radiation, heat, mechani-
       cal action and free radicals.

1991. Koller, L. R. Ultraviolet Radiation. New York:
       Wiley and Sons, 1965.

1992. Kowalik, R. "The Influence of the Ink Upon the Paper. Ink for Permanent Documents," Blok-Notes Muzeum Mickiewicza 152, 1960. Warsaw.

1993. Lang, Andrew. "On the Enemies of Books," The Library 1881. In this article, Lang includes women as one of "The natural enemies of books" and describes them to be as dangerous to collections as damp, dust, dirt, bookworms, borrowers, stealers, and careless readers. He singles out "Stingy wives who begrudged their husbands purchase of books" as the worst of all. For a rebuttal by Anne Haight see [1964].

1994. Langwell, W. H. "The Permanence of Paper Records," Library Association Record 55:212-215, 1953.

1995. Lawrence, Virginia. "Preservation of Manuscripts," Manuscripts 6, 1954. A warning on effects of light, heat, moisture.

1996. Leighton, John. "On Library Books and Binding, Particularly with Regard to Their Restoration and Preservation," Royal Society of Arts Journal 7:209-219, 1858-1859. Early and accurate recognition of some of the causes of book decay such as light, acid, sulphur dioxide, shortcuts in tanning, etc.

1997. Lewis, Harry F. "The Deterioration of Book Paper in Library Use," American Archivist 22:309-322, 1959.

1998. Libby, W. F. "Dosages From Natural Radioactivity and Cosmic Rays," Science 122:57-58, 1955.

1999. Library Association. "The Durability of Paper," Library Association Record, 1930. Findings by the special committee set up by the Library Association in 1930. Also see Supplement: 1-24 in the same issue of the Record.

2000. Lollar, R. M. "Leather," Deterioration of Materials by Glenn A. Greathouse and C. J. Wessel. New York: Reinhold Publishing Co., 1954.

2001. Lydenberg, Harry Miller. "Inferior Paper Endangering the Permanence of the Printed Page," Pulp and Paper Magazine of Canada August 27, 1925.

2002. _____. "Present Discontents with Newspaper Stock," ALA Bulletin 12:211-216, 1918.

2003. McCamy, C. S. and C. I. Pope. Cause and Prevention of Microfilm Blemishes. Washington: National Bureau of Standards, 1970. Report of research that has shown that blemishes result from the

oxidation reduction reaction of the silver image by
peroxides and other gaseous products evolved by
the degradation of paper storage cartons.   Recommends measures to prevent such damage.

2004. _____ . Redox Blemishes: Their Causes and Prevention.   Paper presented at the National Microfilm Association Meeting in Boston, May 7, 1967.
Reports on the causes for blemishes on microfilm.

2005. McCamy, C. S.; S. R. Wiley, and J. A. Speckman.
"A Survey of Blemishes on Processed Microfilm, "
Journal of Research National Bureau of Standards,
73A, 79, 1969.   This is the study of 7400 rolls of
microfilm that led to the identification of the
causes of the blemishes and suggested remedial
measures.

2006. Microbiological Deterioration in the Tropics.   London:
Society of Chemical Industry, 1966.   Published papers of the Symposium at London School of Hygiene
and Tropical Medicine April 1965.   Much of interest to those concerned with archival conservation.

2007. "Newspaper Files Disintegrate Soon, " New York
Times September 3, 1917.

2008. Nyuksha, J. P. "Changes in Alkali-soluble Fraction
of Paper Fibers as the Result of Some Physical
and Chemical Actions, " O sokhraneii bumagi 69-87,
1963.   Leningrad.   Reports the effect of water,
alcohol, formaldehyde, hypochlorite, etc. on
mildewed paper.

2009. _____ . "Some Causes of Book Damage, " Priroda
11:94-95, 1955.   Moscow.   Discusses dust, sulphur
dioxide, moisture, insects, fungi.

2010. Padfield, Tim.   The Deterioration of Cellulose: a
Literature Review.   London: Victoria and Albert
Museum, 1965.   A review of the literature on the
effects of exposure to light, ultra-violet and high
energy radiation.   Bibliography keyed to text.   A
report for ICOM's Committee for Museum Laboratories in Washington, September 1965.

2011. _____ . "The Rate of Fading of Natural Dyes, "
Paper delivered at I. I. C. Conference.   Delft, 1964.

2012. "Paper, Diseases of, " American Archivist 1:165,
1938.

2013. Parker, J. C.   The Causes of Decay in Book Binding
Leather.   London: Library Supply Co. , Brieg
House, n. d.

2014. Perl'stein, E. Ia. "Changes in the Physical and
       Mechanical Properties of Paper as a Result of
       Natural Aging, " Stareniye bumagi 148-149, 1965.
       Moscow.

2015. _____ . "Step-solubility of Paper in Caustic Soda
       Solutions, " Stareniye bumagi 30-45, 1965. Mos-
       cow.

2016. Permanent/Durable Book Paper, Summary of a Con-
       ference Held in Washington, D. C. , September 16,
       1960. Richmond: The Virginia State Library,
       1960. Sponsored by the American Library Asso-
       ciation and the Virginia State Library, a good
       presentation of the problem of paper deterioration
       and a comparison of suggested solutions.

2017. Pravilova, T. A. "Aging of Paper, " New Methods
       for the Restoration and Preservation of Documents
       and Books, Moscow, 1960. Springfield, Va. :
       1965. National Technical Information Service,
       1965.

2018. Rabald, Erich. Corrosion Guide. 2nd ed. New
       York: Elsevier, 1968.

2019. Rasch, Royal H. and B. W. Scribner. "Comparison
       of Natural Aging of Paper with Accelerated Aging
       by Heating, " Bureau of Standards Journal of Re-
       search 11:727-732, 1933. Research Paper RP
       620.

2020. "Report of the Committee on the Deterioration of
       Paper, " Society of Arts Journal 46:597-601, 1898.

2021. Santucci, L. "Degradation of Paper Treated with
       Oxidants: Effect of Lamination on the Aging of
       Paper, " Problems of Conservation in Museums.
       London: George Allen & Unwin, 1969.

2022. _____ . "Report on Paper Stability, " Bollettino
       dell'Istituto di Patologia del Libro 22:67-104, 1963.
       A literature survey.

2023. Scarone, Arturo. El Libro y sus Enimigos. Monte-
       video: 1917.

2024. Schoeller, V. "Concerning the Yellowing of Paper, "
       Mitteilungen der Arbeitsgemeinschaft der Archiv-
       restauratoren 6:54-57, 1960; 7:59-68, 1960. Frei-
       burg, West Germany.

2025. Sée, Pierre. Les Maladies du Papier Piqué. Paris:
       Dion et Fils, 1919.

2026. Shaw, Merle B. and Martin J. O'Leary. Effect of
       Filling and Sizing Materials on Stability of Book
       Papers. Washington: U. S. Government Printing
       Office, 1938. U. S. National Bureau of Standards,

Research Paper RP 1149.

2027. _____. Study of the Effect of Fiber Components on the Stability of Book Papers. Washington: U. S. Government Printing Office, 1936.   U. S. National Bureau of Standards, Research Paper RP 949.

2028. Shearon, Will H., Jr.   "The Old Grey Book," Industrial Engineering Chemistry 49:25A-26A, 1957.

2029. Sinha, S. N.   "Loss of Mechanical Strength of Paper Due to Aging," Indian Print and Paper 11:31, 1946.

2030. Smith, R. D.   "Paper Impermanence as a Consequence of pH and Storage Conditions," Library Quarterly 153-195, April 1969.   Describes the effects of excessive acid and inferior storage conditions on books.

2031. Stolow, N.   "The Action of Environment on Museum Objects," Curator 9, 1966.   New York.

2032. Sugimatsu, A.; S. Senda, and Y. Harada.   "Degradation of Cellulose by Gamma Irradiation," Kogyo Kagaku Zasshi 62:576, 1959.

2033. Suri, V. S.   "Some Hints on the Health of Contents of Libraries," Indian Librarian 147-153, March 1954.

2034. Takamuru, S.; Y. Miyamato, and Y. Hachihama. "Effect of Gamma Irradiation on the Hydrolysis of Cellulose," Kogyo Kagaku Zasshi 64:2027, 1961. Cited in Chemical Abstracts 57:3663 a.

2035. Teszler, O. et al.   "The Effect of Nuclear Radiation on Fibrous Materials," Textile Research Journal 28:456-462, 1958.

2036. Thomson, Garry.   "Impermanence - Some Chemical and Physical Aspects," Museums Journal 64(1):16-36, 1964.   A review of certain aspects of museum climatology which are equally applicable to libraries.

2037. Toishi, Kenzo and Toshiko Kenjo.   "Changes of Art Objects in a Newly Constructed Concrete Storage Room," Science for Conservation 3:30-34, 1967.

2038. Van den Akker, J. A. et al.   "The Nature of the Colour Changes in Ground Wood," Tappi 43:187-192, 1949.

2039. Vely, V. C.; N. D. Gallagher, and M. B. Neher. "Effect of Gamma-Radiation on Leather and Pickled Calfskin," Journal American Leather Chemists Assoc. 55:202-219, 1960.

2040. Wallace, John William.   An Address of Welcome from the Librarians of Philadelphia to the Congress of Librarians of the United States, Assembled October

4, 1876, in the Hall of the Historical Society of
Pennsylvania. Philadelphia: Sherman & Co.,
1876. Reprint Boston: G. K. Hall & Co., 1965.
Also found in Library Journal 1:92-95, 1876.
Discusses the problem of deteriorating book paper.

2041. Walton, Robert P. "Causes and Prevention of
Deterioration in Book Materials," Bulletin 33:235-
266, 1929. New York Public Library.

2042. _____. "Paper Permanence," Publishers' Weekly
116:979, September 7, 1929.

2043. Weber, Charles G. et al. "Effect of Fumigants on
Paper," Journal of Research 15, September 1935.
Washington: U.S. Bureau of Standards, Research
Paper 828.

2044. Wessel, Carl J. "Environmental Factors Affecting
the Permanence of Library Materials," The Library Quarterly 40(1):39-84, 1970. A detailed
discussion with a bibliography of 116 references
of these environmental factors and their effect on
library and museum artifacts:- atmosphere, light,
temperature, humidity, vibration, insects, fungi,
people, acts of God, mechanical failure.

2045. White, D. R. and N. E. Weston. "Electron Micro-
probe Examination of Aging Blemishes on Microfilm," Photographic Science and Engineering March-
April, 1967.

2046. Williams, Edwin E. "Magnitude of the Paper-Deteri-
oration Problem as Measured by a National Union
Catalog Sample," College and Research Libraries
23:499. 543. 1962.

2047. _____. "Deterioration of Library Collections Today," The Library Quarterly 40(1):3-17,
1970. This paper discusses the solution for
deteriorating books suggested by the Association
of Research Libraries, by forming a national
repository where one copy of everything that is
in research libraries can be stored for posterity
under optimum conditions of temperature, humidity,
etc. Author is the Chairman of the ARL Committee on the Preservation of Research Library Materials.

2048. Wilson, William K. "Reflections on the Stability of
Paper," Restaurator 1(2), 1969. Discusses variables in the composition of paper and effect on
stability. Describes new approaches to research
on preservation.

2049. _____ and J. L. Harvey; John Mandel, and Thelma
        Worksman. "Accelerated Aging of Record Papers
        Compared with Normal Aging," Tappi 38(9):543-
        548, 1955.
2050. _____ and B. W. Forshee. "Degradation of Cellu-
        lose Acetate Films," Society Petroleum Engineers
        Journal 15, February 1959.
2051. Yabrova, R. R. "Artificially Accelerated Aging of
        Paper," Collection of Materials on the Preservation
        of Library Resources. (Moscow, 1958). Spring-
        field, Va.: National Technical Information Service,
        1964.
2052. Zimmerman, Elmer W.; Charles G. Weber, and
        Arthur E. Kimberly. Relation of Ink to the Pres-
        ervation of Written Records. Washington: U. S.
        Government Printing Office, 1935. U. S. National
        Bureau of Standards, Research Paper RP 779.

PEOPLE

2053. Adams, R. G. "Librarians as Enemies of Books,"
        Library Quarterly 7:317-331, 1937.
2054. "Adhesive Tape, Damage from," American Archivist
        16:122, 1953.
2055. Hatson, C. W. "Abuse of Books," Southern Maga-
        zine 9:536, 1916.
2056. Land, Robert H. "Defense of Archives Against Hu-
        man Foes," American Archivist 19:121-138, 1956.
        With comments by Lucile M. Kane and Richard D.
        Higgins.
2057. Mearns, David C. The Declaration of Independence:
        The Story of a Parchment. Washington: U. S.
        Government Printing Office, 1950. Includes an
        account of the physical abuse of this document
        since its origin which accounts for its present
        poor condition.
2058. Wagg, R. E. The Soiling of Textile Materials. Lon-
        don: The Clothing Institute, 1959.
2059. Weber, C. G. et al. "Effects of Fumigants on Pa-
        per," Journal of Research 15(3):271, 1935. Wash-
        ington: National Bureau of Standards.
2060. Weidner, Marilyn Kemp. "Damage and Deterioration
        of Art on Paper Due to Ignorance and the Use of

Faulty Materials, " Studies in Conservation 12(2),
1967.

THE AIR WE BREATHE

2061. Air Pollution Control Program Support Under the Air
Quality Act of 1967. Washington: U.S. Dept. of
Health, Education and Welfare, December 1968.
Provides general information on the program and
guidance in the obtaining of grants. (Primarily for
State agency use.)

2062. Air Pollution Prevention and Control. Washington:
U.S. Congress, Public Law 90-148, 1967. The
"Air Quality Act" of 1967 is a blueprint for a
systematic effort to deal with air pollution problems
on a regional basis under the direction of the Dept.
of Health, Education and Welfare.

2063. Air Quality Criteria for Sulfur Oxides. Washington:
U.S. Dept. of Health, Education and Welfare, Public Health Service, 10-1 to 10-22, 1969.

2064. Altshuller, A. P. "Air Pollution, " Analytical Chemistry 41(5), 1969. Reviews papers published in
1967 and 1968. 328 references.

2065. Altshuller, A. P. and J. J. Bufalini. "Photochemical
Aspects of Air Pollution: A Review, " Environmental Science and Technology 5(1):39-64, 1971.

2066. Berryhill, J. "Our Troubled Urban Environment, "
Nation's Cities 5:5-7, 1967.

2067. Brooks, C. E. P. "Climate and the Deterioration of
Materials, " Quarterly Journal of the Royal Meter-
ological Society 72:87-97, 1946.

2068. Carroll, J. F. and J. M. Calhoun. "Effect of Nitro-
gen Oxide Gases on Processed Acetate Film, "
Journal Society Motion Picture and Television Engineers 64:501-507, 1955.

2069. Church, A. H. "Destruction of Leather by Gas, "
Chemical News 36:179, 1877. London.

2070. Commission on Lighting Picture Galleries by Gas.
"Opening of Galleries of Art in the Evening, "
Journal of the Society of Art 7:605, 1859.

2071. Control Techniques for Particulate Air Pollutants.
Washington: U.S. Department of Health, Education
and Welfare, 1969. National Air Pollution Control

Admin.   Publication No. AP-51.   The first of a
series of documents to be produced under a program established to develop and distribute control
technology information.

2072.   Denmead, C. F.   "Air Pollution by Hydrogen Sul-
phide from a Shallow Polluted Tidal Inlet, Auckland, New Zealand," Proceedings of the Clean Air
Conference 1962.   Sydney.

2073.   "Discussion of Injuries to Bindings by Gas and Heat,"
Library Journal 1:124-125, 1876.

2074.   Edwards, C. J.   "Some Aspects of the Sorption of
Sulphur Dioxide by Paper," unpublished PhD. dissertation, University of Manchester, 1967.

2075.   Edwards, C. J.; F. L. Hudson, and J. A. Hockey.
"Sorption of Sulfur Dioxide by Paper," Journal of
Applied Chemistry 18:146-148, 1968.

2076.   Emoto, Yoshimichi.   "Effects of Air Pollution on Art
Objects," Gekkan-Bunkazai 83:11-16, 1970.   Includes description of deterioration by sulfur dioxide
and hydrogen sulfide of paper, leather and cloth.

2077.   _____ and Takeo Kadokura.   "Results of Investigation on Air Pollution as Environment for Preservation of Cultural Properties in Various Areas,"
Science for Conservation 3:1-22, 1967.

2078.   Environmental Effects on Materials and Equipment,
Section A.   Washington: Preservation from Deterioration Center, Division of Chemistry and Chemical Technology, National Academy of Sciences,
National Research Council, 1962.

2079.   Environmental Quality.   Washington: U. S. Government Printing Office, 1970.   The first annual report of the Council on Environmental Quality and
the President's Message to Congress, August,
1970.   326 pp. with illustrations and appendices.

2080.   Evelyn, John.   Fumifugium: or The Inconveniencie
of the Aer and Smoak of London Dissipated.   London: 1661.   In this very early recognition of the
problem of air pollution, Evelyn deplored the per-
petual cloud of smoke hanging over London and
proposed freeing the city of the problem by removing the smoke producing trades some miles out of
London and planting a green belt around the metrop-
olis.

2081.   Faraday, Michael.   On the Ventilation of Lamp Burn-
ers.   Royal Institution Lecture 7, April 1843 in
which he names combustion products as one source
of leather decay.

2082. Frey, R. W. "Gaseous Pollution of the Atmosphere, a Cause of Leather Decay," Library Journal 52:405-414, 1932.

2083. Greenburg, L. et al. "Corrosion Aspects of Air Pollution," American Paint Journal 39, 1955.

2084. Haagen-Smit, A. J. "Air Pollution and Preservation of Art," Papers Presented at IIC-AG Annual Meetings, 1968-1970. New York: New York University Conservation Center, 1970.

2085. _____. "The Chemistry of Atmospheric Pollution," Museum Climatology. London: International Institute for Conservation, 1968.

2086. Hudson, F. L.; R. L. Grant and J. A. Hockey. "Atmospheric Sulphur and Durability of Paper," Journal Society of Archivists 2, 1961.

2087. _____. "The Pick-up of Sulphur Dioxide by Paper," Journal of Applied Chemistry 14:444-447, 1964.

2088. Huey, N. A. "Lead Dioxide Estimation of Sulphur Dioxide Pollution," Journal Air Pollution Control Assoc. 18(9):610-611, 1968.

2089. Iwasaki, Tomokichi. "Scientific Preservative Methods for Cultural Properties," Museum 143:28-29, 1963. Tokyo.

2090. Jacobs, M. B. The Chemical Analysis of Air Pollutants. New York: Interscience Publishers, Inc., 1960.

2091. Kimberly, A. E. "Deteriorative Effect of Sulfur Dioxide upon Paper in an Atmosphere of Constant Humidity and Temperature," Bureau of Standards Journal of Research 8:159-171, 1932. Also available as U.S. Bureau of Standards Research Paper RP 407.

2092. Kimberly, A. E. and A. L. Emley. A Study of the Deterioration of Book Stock in Libraries. Washington: U.S. Government Printing Office, 1933. U.S. Bureau of Standards Miscellaneous Publication No. 140.

2093. _____. A Study of the Removal of Sulphur Dioxide from Library Air. Washington: U.S. Government Printing Office, 1933. U.S. Bureau of Standards Miscellaneous Publication No. 142.

2094. Kleinert, T. N. and L. M. Marraccini. "Aging and Colour Reversion of Bleached Pulps, Part 2. Influence of Air and Moisture," Svensk Papperstidning 66:189-195, 1963.

2095. Kobayashi, Y. et al. "Studies on the Behavior of Air Pollutants Outdoors and Indoors," Clean Air Journal

7(2), 1969. Tokyo.

2096. Kowalik, R. and I. Sadurska. "Micro-organisms
       Destroying Paper, Leather and Wax Seals in the
       Air of Archives, " Acta Microbiologica Polonica
       5(1/2):277-284, 1956.

2097. Langwell, W. H. "How Does Air Pollution Affect
       Books and Paper?" Royal Institution of Great
       Britain. Proceedings 37(2):210-214, 1958.
       Address before the Library Circle Meeting, May
       12, 1958.

2098. _____. "Permanency of Paper, " Process and
       Technical Section of the British Paper and Board
       Makers Association 36:199, 1955; 29:21, 1952;
       30:170, 1953. Tappi 38:190A, 1955.

2099. _____. "Sulphur Dioxide Pollution of the Atmos-
       phere, " Journal of the Society of Archivists
       1(10):291-293, 1959.

2100. Mallette, F. S. (ed.). Problems and Control of Air
       Pollution. New York: Reinhold Publishing Co. ,
       1955.

2101. Marsh, Arnold. "Smoke, the Problem of Coal and
       the Atmosphere, " The Destruction of Property
       London: Faber and Faber, 1947. Chapter 6:
       94-107.

2102. McCabe, L. C. "Atmospheric Pollution, " Industrial
       Engineering Chemistry 48, 1953.

2103. Meetham, A. R. Atmospheric Pollution, Its Origins
       and Prevention. 3rd ed. New York: Macmillan, 1964.

2104. Middleton, J. T. "Air Pollution: How 65 Metropoli-
       tan Areas Rank in Severity, " Nation's Cities 5:8-
       11, 1967.

2105. Morris, M. A. et al. "The Effect of Air Pollution
       on Cotton, " Textile Research Journal 34:563-564,
       1947.

2106. Parker, A. "The Destructive Effects of Air Pollution
       on Materials, " Chemical Abstracts 52, 1958.

2107. Progress in the Prevention and Control of Air Pollu-
       tion. Washington: U. S. Government Printing Of-
       fice, 1968. First report of the Secretary of HEW
       to Congress on the progress in control of air pol-
       lution pursuant to the Air Quality Act of 1967.

2108. Progress in the Prevention and Control of Air Pollu-
       tion. Washington: U. S. Government Printing Of-
       fice, 1969. Second report of the Secretary of HEW
       to Congress on the control of air pollution pursuant
       to the Air Quality Act of 1967.

2109. Race, Edward. "The Degradation of Cotton during
         Atmospheric Exposure, Particularly in Industrial
         Regions, " Journal of the Society of Dyers and
         Colourists 65:56-63, 1949.
2110. Report on Air Pollution. London: H. M. Stationery
         Office, 1954.
2111. Report on the Commission Appointed to Inquire Into
         the Questions of Housing the Raffaelle Cartoons.
         London: H. M. Stationery Office, 1891. A very
         early awareness of the problem of acidity.
         Recommended use of barium hydroxide.
2112. Report of the Panel on Electrically Powered Vehicles.
         The Automobile and Air Pollution: A Program for
         Progress. Washington: U. S. Government Printing
         Office, 1967. A report to the Commerce Technical
         Advisory Board, U. S. Department of Commerce.
2113. Salmon, Richard L. Systems analysis of the effects
         of air pollution on materials. (Final report) Kansas
         City: Midwest Research Institute, 1970.
2114. Salvin, V. S. "The Effect of Atmospheric Contami-
         nants on Light Fastness, " Journal Society Dyers
         Colourists 79:687-696, 1963. Celanese Fibers Co.,
         Charlotte, N. C.
2115. Schreiber, Walter T.; Austin L. Bullock, and Wendell
         L. Ward. "Resistance of Partially Acetylated
         Cotton Fabric to Nitrogen Dioxide and to Hydrogen
         Chloride, " Textile Research Journal 819-822, 1954.
2116. Special Committee to Investigate Air Pollution. Air
         Pollution in New York City: M-970, an Interim
         Technical Report of the Special Committee to In-
         vestigate Air Pollution. New York: Council of the
         City of New York, June 22, 1965.
2117. Study of Air Pollution. Cambridge, Mass.: Harvard
         Law Conservation Society, 1969. A study by the
         Union of Concerned Scientists' Committee on En-
         vironmental Pollution.
2118. Thomson, Garry. "Air Pollution--A Review for Con-
         servation Chemists, " Studies in Conservation 10(4),
         1965. Should be read by all librarians.
2119. _____. "Sulfur dioxide damage to antiquities, "
         Atmospheric Environment 3(6):687, 1969.
2120. Thring, M. W. (ed.). Air Pollution. London: But-
         terworths, 1957.
2121. Toishi, K and T. Kenjo. "A Simple Method of
         Measuring the Alkalinity of Air in New Concrete
         Buildings, " Studies in Conservation 13(4), 1968.

2122.   Trewartha, G. T.   An Introduction to Climate.   New
        York: McGraw-Hill, Inc. , 1954.
2123.   Veitch, F. P. et al.   "Polluted Atmosphere a Factor
        in the Deterioration of Bookbinding Leather, "
        American Leather Chemists Association Journal
        21:156-176, 1926.
2124.   Vernon, W. H. J.   "Second Report to the Atmospheric
        Corrosion Research Committee, " Transactions of
        the Faraday Society, 1927.   Effect of atmosphere
        on metals.
2125.   Waller, R. E.   "Studies on the Nature of Urban Pol-
        lution, " Museum Climatology.   London: Interna-
        tional Institute for Conservation, 1968.
2126.   Woodward, C. J.   "The Action of Gas on Leather
        Bookbindings: A Preliminary Experimental Inquiry, "
        The Library Chronicle 5:25-29, 1888.

LIGHT AND DARK

2127.   Allison, J. P.   "Photo-degradation of Polymethyl
        Methacrylate, " Journal Polymer Science Part
        A-1(4):1209-1221, 1966.
2128.   Apps, E. A.   "The Fading of Printed Matter, " Paper
        and Print 31, 1958.
2129.   Balder, J. J.   "The Discolouration of Coloured Ob-
        jects Under the Influence of Daylight, Incandescent
        Lamplight and Fluorescent Lamplight, " Lichttechnik
        8(2):57-61, 1956.   Leiden: The Netherlands Mu-
        seums Association.   Reviewed by R. L. Feller,
        Studies in Conservation 4:155, 1959.
2130.   Barr, G. and I. H. Hadfield, "The Nature of the
        Action of Sunlight on Cotton, " Journal Textile In-
        stitute 18:T490-493, 1927.
2131.   _____.   "Some Physio-chemical Studies on the Ef-
        fect of Sunlight on Cotton, " Reports and Memoranda
        No. 1016, 1926.   Aeronautical Research Committee.
2132.   Belaya, I. K.   "Effect of Shortwave Ultraviolet Radia-
        tion from Bactericidal Lamps on Paper, "
        Bumazhnaya Promyshlennost 32:9-10, 1957.
2133.   Brommelle, N. S.   "The Russell and Abney Report
        on the Action of Light on Water Colours, " Studies
        in Conservation 9(4), 1964.   An analysis of the
        often quoted but not readily accessible 19th-century

pioneer work on the effect of light on color.

2134. Brommelle, N. S. and J. B. Harris. "Museum Lighting, Part 2," Museums Journal 61, 1961. Effect of light on deterioration.

2135. Charlesby, A. "The Degradation of Cellulose by Ionising Radiation," Journal Polymer Science 15:263-270, 1955.

2136. Cooper, B. S. "Fluorescent Lighting in Museums," Museums Journal 53, 1954. An examination of the effect of light on materials.

2137. Dudley, R. A. and A. M. Brues. (eds.). Low Level Irradiation. Washington: American Association for Advancement of Science, 1959.

2138. Edge, S. R. H. and H. M. McKenzie. "The Discolouration of Wood Pulp by Light and Heat," Paper Makers Association Great Britain and Ireland, Technical Section Proceedings 17:437-456, 1937.

2139. Egerton, G. S. "The Action of Light on Dyed and Undyed Cloth," American Dyestuff Reporter 36:561, 1947.

2140. _____. "Some Aspects of the Photochemical Degradation of Nylon, Silk and Viscose Rayon," Textile Research Journal 18:659-669, 1948.

2141. Ellis, Carleton; Alfred A. Wells, and Francis F. Heyroth. The Chemical Action of Ultraviolet Rays. New York: Reinhold Publishing Corp., 1941.

2142. Faraday, Michael. "On Light and Ventilation," The Repertory of Patent Inventions and Other Discoveries and Improvements 2:174-181, 238-250, 1843.

2143. Feller, Robert L. "The Deteriorating Effect of Light on Museum Objects," Museum News (Technical Supplement) 42(10):1-8, 1964. 5 Charts. 49 Refer.

2144. Flynn, J. H. "An Equation for Calculating the Number of Chain Scissions in the Photochemical Degradation of Solid Polymers," Journal Polymer Science 27:83-86, 1958.

2145. Flynn, P. J.; J. E. Sands, and K. S. Campbell. "Cellulose Behaviour with Filtered Sunlight," Textile Research Journal 18:350-375, 1948.

2146. Genard, J. "Extreme Ultra-Violet Radiation from Tubular Fluorescent Lamps and Its Effect on Museum Lighting," Museum 5(1), 1952; and Museums Journal 52(1):5, 1952.

2147. Giles, C. H. "The Fading of Colouring Matters," Journal of Applied Chemistry 15:541-550, 1965. London.

2148.   . "The Fading of Coloring Matters," Curator
        9(2):95-102, 1966. New York.
2149. Harrison, L. S. "An Investigation of the Damage
        Hazard in Spectral Energy," Illuminating Engineer-
        ing 49:253-257, 1954.
2150.   . "Evaluation of Spectral Radiation Hazards
        in Window-Lighted Galleries," Recent Advances in
        Conservation. London: Butterworth, 1963.
2151.   . Report on the Deteriorating Effects of
        Modern Light Sources. New York: Metropolitan
        Museum of Art, 1954.
2152. Jones, J. I. M. "Further Notes on the Tendering
        and Fading of Cellulose Materials on Exposure," Jour-
        nal Society Dyers and Colourists 51:285-299, 1936.
2153. Judd, Deane B. Radiation Hazard of Museum Light
        Sources. Washington: National Bureau of Stand-
        ards, 1953.
2154. Kato, H. "Studies on Japanese Paper," Kami-pa
        Gekyoshi 16, October 1962. Discusses paper de-
        terioration due to light. English summary.
2155. Koller, L. R. Ultraviolet Radiation. New York:
        Wiley and Sons, 1965.
2156. Lanigan, H. "The Photochemical Degradation of Un-
        dyed and Dyed Cellulose Irradiated by the Mercury
        Spectrum," Journal Textile Institute 39:285-292,
        1948.
2157. Launer, Herbert F. and William K. Wilson. "Photo-
        chemical Stability of Papers," Journal of Research
        of the National Bureau of Standards 30:55-74, 1943;
        and Paper Trade Journal 116:28-36, 1943.
2158.   . "The Photochemistry of Cellulose: Ef-
        fects of Water Vapor and Oxygen in the Far and
        Near Ultraviolet Regions," Journal of the American
        Chemical Society 71:958, 1949.
2159. Lewis, H. F.; E. A. Reineck, and D. Fronmuller.
        "The Fading of Groundwood by Light," Tappi
        28:157-161, 1945.
2160. Little, A. H. "The Effect of Light on Textiles,"
        Tappi 47:527-534, 1964.
2161. Lodewijks, J. "The Influence of Light on Museum
        Objects," Recent Advances in Conservation. Lon-
        don: Butterworth, 1963. Describes the damage to
        cellulose by ultraviolet light and to colors by
        visible light.
2162. MacClaren, R. H. et al. "Brightness Reversion of
        Cellulose Exposed to Ultraviolet Light," Tappi
        45:789-793, 1962.

2163. McLaren, K. "The Action of Light on Coloring Matters, " American Perfumer Cosmetician 81(11), 1966.

2164. _____. "The Spectral Regions of Daylight Which Cause Fading, " Journal, Society of Dyers and Colorers 72, 1956.

2165. Mohrberg, W. "The Yellowing and Resistance to Aging of Paper, " Bulletin Institute Of Paper Chemistry 23, 1952-1953. Effect of light on paper ingredients.

2166. Norton, J. E. "A Study of the Variables Encountered in Natural Light Fading, " American Dyestuff Reporter 46:861-883, 1957.

2167. Padfield, Tim and Sheila Landi. "The Light Fastness of the Natural Dyes, " Studies in Conservation 2(4), 1966.

2168. Phillips, G. O. "Chemical Effects of Light on Cotton Cellulose and Related Compounds, " Textile Research Journal 34:497-505; 572-580, 1964.

2169. Plexiglass Ultraviolet Filtering Formulations. Philadelphia: Rohm and Haas Co. , 1968. Bulletin No. PL-612a. Includes an introduction to the mechanism of radiation damage.

2170. "Problems of Artificial Lighting, " ICOM News 3(1), 1950.

2171. Rabek, J. F. "The Effect of UV-light on Polymers, " Wiadomosci chemiczne 20:291-300; 355-372; 435-447, 1966. Warsaw.

2172. Rawlins, F. I. G. and W. E. Rawson-Bottom. "Ultra-Violet Radiation from Fluorescent Lamps, " Museums Journal 52(3):84, 1952.

2173. Richardson, A. "On the Action of Light on Water Colours, " Report British Association of Advanced Science 58:641-642, 1888.

2174. Richter, G. A. "Relative Permanence of Papers Exposed to Sunlight I, " Industrial and Engineering Chemistry 27, February 1935.

2175. _____. "Relative Permanence of Papers Exposed to Sunlight, II, " Industrial and Engineering Chemistry April 1935.

2176. Russell, J. W. and W. Abney. Report on the Action of Light on Water Colours. London: Her Majesty's Stationery Office, 1888. A report to the Science and Art Department of the Committee of Council on Education.

2177. Senebier, J. Memoires Physico-chemiques sur l'Influence de la Luminière Solaire. Geneva, 1782.

Vol. 3.
2178. Simionescu, C. R.; G. J. Rozmarin, and V. Bula-
chovski. "Research in the Field of the Photochemical Destruction of Cellulose," Cellulose 14(7, 8, 9):
319-335, 1965.
2179. Stillings, R. A. and R. J. Van Nostrand. "The Action of U. V. Light on Cellulose," Journal American
Chemical Society 66:753-760, 1944.
2180. Stolow, N. "The Action of Environment on Museum
Objects, Part II - Light," Curator 9(4), 1966.
2181. Taylor, A. H. and W. G. Pracejus. "Fading of
Colored Materials by Light and Radiant Energy,"
Illuminating Engineer 45(3), 1950.
2182. Thomson, Garry. "Deterioration Under Light," Conference on Museum Climatology. London: International Institute for Conservation, 1967.
2183. _____. "Visible and Ultraviolet Radiation," Museums Journal 57:27, 1957.
2184. van Beek, H. C. A. and P. M. Heertjes. "Fading
by Light of Organic Dyes on Textiles," Studies in
Conservation 11(3), 1966.
2185. Vely, V. C.; N. D. Gallagher, and M. B. Neher.
"Effect of Gamma-radiation on Leather and Pickled
Calfskin," Journal American Leather Chemists Association 55:202-219, 1960.
2186. Wilson, William K. and Jack L. Harvey. "Effect of
Light on Coated Groundwood Papers," Tappi
36(10):459-461, 1953.

HEAT

2187. Baer, N. S. et al. "The Effect of High Temperature
on Ivory," Studies in Conservation 16(1):1-8, 1971.
2188. Belaya, I. K. "Aging of Cotton and Flax Fiber Papers Under the Simultaneous Influence of Heat and
Humidity," Stareniye bumagi 46-56, 1965. Moscow.
2189. Bowes, J. H. and A. S. Raistrick. "The Action of
Heat and Moisture on Leather, Part I: The Storage
of a Variety of Commercial Leathers at 40° C and
100% R. H. ," American Leather Chemists Association Journal 56, July-December 1961.

2190. _____. "The Actions of Heat and Moisture on
       Leather. Part VI: Degradation of the Collagen,"
       American Leather Chemists Association Journal
       62(4):240-257, 1967.

2191. Coremans, Paul. "Climate and Microclimate," The
       Conservation of Cultural Property. Paris:
       UNESCO, 1968.

2192. Grove, L. E. "What Good is Greenland?" Wilson
       Library Bulletin 36:749, 1962. New thinking on
       book preservation and temperature.

2193. Gullichsen, J. E. "The Influence of Temperature and
       Humidity on the Colour Reversion of Pulp,"
       Paperi ja Puu--Papper och Trä 4a:215-222, 1965.
       Special Number.

2194. Hamlin, Arthur T. "The Libraries of Florence--No-
       vember 1966," American Library Association Bul-
       letin February 1967.

2195. MacKay, G. D. M. "Mechanism of thermal degrada-
       tion of cellulose: a review of the literature,"
       Aerospace Reporter 6(8):1285, 1968.

2196. Raistrick, A. S. "The Effect of Heat and Moisture
       in Leather," Journal of the Society of Leather
       Trades' Chemists 44:167-168, 1960.

2197. Yabrova, R. R. "Influence of Temperature and
       Moisture on the Aging of Paper," Bumazhnaya
       Promyshlennost 32:15-16, 1957. Available in
       translation from the National Translations Center,
       John Crerar Library, Chicago, Ill.

MOISTURE

2198. Ambler, H. R. and C. F. Finney. "Brown Stain
       Formed on Wet Cellulose," Nature 179:1141, 1957.

2199. Ashton, D. and M. E. Probert. "A Simple Technique
       for Investigating the Effect of Humidity on the Fad-
       ing and Degradation of Dyed Fabrics by Sunlight,"
       Journal Textile Institute 44:T1-11, 1953.

2200. Block, S. S. "Humidity Requirements for Mold
       Growth," Engineering Progress 7(10):287-293, 1953.
       University of Florida.

2201. Block, S. S.; R. Rodriguez-Torrent; M. B. Cole,
       and A. E. Prince. "Humidity and Temperature
       Requirements of Selected Fungi," Developments in

Industrial Microbiology 3:204-216. New York:
Plenum Press, 1962.

2202. Bowes, J. H. et al. "Action of Heat and Moisture
on Leather, " Journal American Leather Chemists
Association 56, 1961.

2203. Bowes, J. H. and A. S. Raistrick. "The Action of
Heat and Moisture on Leather. Part VI: Degrada-
tion of the Collagen, " Journal of the American
Leather Chemists Association 62(4):240-257, 1967.

2204. Carson, F. T. Effect of Humidity on Physical Properties of Paper. Washington: U.S. Government
Printing Office, 1944. National Bureau of Standards Circular C-445.

2205. Crook, D. M. and W. E. Bennett. The Effect of
Humidity and Temperature on the Physical Properties of Paper. The British Paper and Board Industry Research Association, February 1962.

2206. Hutcheon, N. B. Humidity and Building. Ottawa:
National Research Council, 1964. The Council's
Technical Paper No. 188.

2207. Jarrell, T. D. "Effect of Atmospheric Humidity on
the Moisture Content of Paper, " Paper Trade Journal 85(3):47-51, 1927.

2208. Kimberly, Arthur E. "Deteriorative Effect of Sulphur
Dioxide Upon Paper in an Atmosphere of Constant
Humidity and Temperature, " Bureau of Standards
Journal of Research 8:159-171, 1932.

2209. Little, A. H. and J. W. Clayton. "Photochemical
Tendering and Fading of Dyed Textiles at Different
Humidities, " Journal Society Dyers and Colourists
79:671-677, 1963. Shirley Institute, Manchester,
England.

2210. Richter, George A. and Frank L. Wells. "Influence
of Moisture in Accelerated Aging of Cellulose, "
Tappi 39(8):603-608, 1956.

2211. Rose, C. D. and J. N. Turner. "Mold Growth on
Leather as Affected by Humidity Changes, " Journal
Society of Leather Trades' Chemists 35, 1951.

2212. Rubinstein, Nicolai. "Libraries and Archives of
Florence, " Times Literary Supplement page 1133,
December 1, 1966.

2213. Tribolet, Harold W. Flood Damage to Florence's
Books and Manuscripts. Chicago: The Lakeside
Press, 1967.

2214. Wexler (ed.). Humidity and Moisture. 4 vols. New
York: Reinholdt, 1965.

2215.   Wink, W. A.   "The Effect of Relative Humidity and Temperature on Paper Properties," <u>Tappi</u> 44(6): 171A-180A, 1961.

2216.   Yabrova, R. R.   "Influence of Temperature and the Air Humidity on the Aging of Paper," <u>Chemical Abstracts</u> 54, 1960.

VERMIN

2217.   <u>Animals Injurious to Books</u>.   3rd ed.   London: Science Museum, 1938.   Science Library Bibliographical Series No. 377.

2218.   Collins, P. B.   <u>Household Pests; Their Habits, Prevention and Control</u>.   London: Pitman, 1936.

2219.   Wälchli, O.   "Paper-damaging Pests in Libraries and Archives," <u>Textil-Rundschau</u> 17:63-76, 1962.

INSECTS

2220.   Acloque, A.   "Les Insectes Bibliophages," <u>Cosmos. Revue des Sciences et de leurs Applications</u> 68:205-207, 1913.   Paris.

2221.   Araujo, R. L.   "Notas e Informacoes; Notas Sobre Insectos que Prejudicam Livros," <u>Biologico</u> 1:32, 1945.   São Paulo.

2222.   Aristotle.   <u>Historia Animalium</u> Ca 335 BC.   Book 4, Chapter 7 and Book 5, Chapter 32.   Aristotle found in books a creature resembling a scorpion and also other "animalcules."

2223.   Back, E. A.   <u>Book-Lice or Psocids</u>.   Washington: U. S. Government Printing Office, 1922.

2224.   _____ .   <u>Bookworms</u>.   Washington: U. S. Department of Agriculture, 1940.

2225.   _____ .   "Bookworms," <u>The Indian Archives</u> 1(2), 1947.

2226.   _____ .   "Bookworms," <u>Smithsonian Institution Annual Report</u>.   Washington: U. S. Government Printing Office, 1939.   An excellent summary with 18 illustrations of the insects dangerous to books.

2227.   _____ .   <u>The Silverfish as a Pest of the Household</u>.   Washington: U. S. Department of Agriculture, 1931.   Farmer's Bulletin No. 1665.

2228. Ballou, H. A. Insect Pests of the Lesser Antilles.
       Bridgetown, Barbados: Advocate Co., 1912. Im-
       perial Department of Agriculture for the West In-
       dies. Pamphlet Series No. 71.
2229. Baryshnikova, Z. P. "Some Observations of the
       Development and Nutrition of Booklice," Restau-
       rator 1(3), 1970. Refutes common concept that
       booklice are merely a nuisance. Proves by
       laboratory tests that these insects can damage
       books, paper, photographs, and that they prefer
       cloth, artificial natural silk and leather and that
       even parchment is not immune from them.
2230. Boyer, J. "Insect Enemies of Books," Scientific
       American 98:413-414, 1908.
2231. British Museum, Economic Series: The Cockroach,
       No. 12, 1951; Clothes Moths and House Moths,
       No. 14, 1951; Furniture Beetles, No. 11, 1954;
       Silver Fish and Firebrats, No. 3, 1957; Psocids,
       Book Lice, etc.," No. 4, 1940.
2232. Broadhead, E. "The Book-Louse and Other Library
       Pests," British Book News 77-81, 1946.
2233. Brown, Carl D. "Temperature and Relative Humidity
       as Factors in the Ecology of Liposcelis Divinatorius
       (book-louse)," Journal of Science 26, 1951-1952.
       Iowa State College.
2234. Burns-Brown, W. "The Disinfection of Furniture with
       Methyl Bromide for Control of the Bedbug," The
       Sanitarian June, 1959.
2235. Carruthers, R. H. and H. B. Weiss. "Insect Pests
       of Books," Bulletin 40:829-841, 985-995, 1049-
       1063, 1936. New York Public Library. An an-
       notated bibliography to 1935 of 493 references
       covering a period of 2200 years. Includes 23
       previous bibliographies and 20 references in classi-
       cal literature to insect enemies of books.
2236. Clothes Moths and Carpet Beetles: How to Combat
       Them. Washington: U. S. Government Printing
       Office, 1953.
2237. Clothes Moths and House Moths; Their Life-History,
       Habits, and Control. 5th ed. London: British
       Museum 1951.
2238. Cockroaches - How to Control Them. Washington:
       U. S. Government Printing Office, 1958.
2239. "Color Slides Nibbled," American Archivist 31:207,
       1968.
2240. The Common Furniture Beetle. (Anobium Punctatum
       de Geer.) Sydney: New South Wales Forestry

Commission, Division of Wood Technology, 1964.
Pamphlet No. 13.

2241. Crick, C. E. "Bookworm," Northamptonshire Notes
and Queries 2:33, 1888.

2242. Ealand, G. A. Insects Enemies. London: Richards,
1916.

2243. Evans, D. M. "Cockroaches and Bookbinding," The
Penrose Annual 54:118-120, 1960. Illustrated
discussion of the ravages of these insects.

2244. Feytaud, J. R. "Les Insectes Ravageurs d'Archives;
Comment les Combattre?" Archives, Bibliothèques,
Collections, Documentation 6:147-156, 1952.

2245. Fullaway, D. T. "Termites, or White Ants, in
Hawaii," Hawaiian Forester and Agriculturist
23:68-88, 1926.

2246. Gahan, C. J. Furniture Beetles; Their Life History
and How to Check or Prevent the Damage Caused
by the Worm. London: British Museum, 1954.
Economic Series No. 11.

2247. Gallo, A. "La Lotta anti-Termitica in Italia,"
Bolletino dell Istituto di Patologia del Libro 11:3-
34, 1952.

2248. Gallo, F. "Fatti e Misfatti del Pesciolino d'Argento,"
Bolletino dell Istituto di Patologia del Libro 13,
1954.

2249. Ghani, M. A. and Harvey Sweetman. "Ecological
Studies of the Book-louse," Ecology 32, 1951.

2250. Godwin, A. J. H. "Insects and Human Culture in
Africa," Scientia 43:324-329, 1958.

2251. Golledge, C. J. "The Insect Pests of Books," Library Association Record 7:240-242, 1929.

2252. Grassi, Pierre P. "Archive Destroying Termites,"
A Manual of Tropical Archivology. Paris: Mouton
& Co., 1966.

2253. Green, S. A. Ravages of Bookworms. Boston: 1893.
Includes a brief description of insect pests including
the "buffalo bug" (carpet beetle).

2254. Griffiths, J. R. and O. E. Tauber. "The Nymphal
Development of the Roach Peri Planeta Americana,"
Journal New York Entomology Society 50:263-272,
1943.

2255. Hagen, H. A. "Insect Pests in Libraries," Library
Journal 4:251-274, 1879.

2256. _____. "Literature Concerning Injuries to Books
by Insects," Library Journal 4:373-374, 1879. An
annotated bibliography of 18 titles.

2257. Harris, W. V. Termites: Their Recognition and
      Control. London: Longmans, 1961.
2258. Hickin, N. E. Woodworm: Its Biology and Exter-
      mination. London: Privately Printed, 1954.
2259. ———. Household Insect Pests. London: Hutchin-
      son Company, 1964.
2260. Hinton, H. E. "The Ptinidae of Economic Import-
      ance, " Bulletin of Entomological Research 31:331-
      381, 1941.
2261. Hoffman, W. A. "Rhizopertha Dominca as a Library
      Pest, " Journal of Economic Entomology 26:293-
      294, 1933.
2262. Hooke, Robert. Micrographia. London: J. Martyn
      and J. Allestry, 1665. pp. 208-210. Describes
      a "small silver-colour'd bookworm" later identified
      as the silverfish.
2263. Horace. Epistularum Lib 1, 20, line 12. Horace
      here expresses the fear that his books will become
      food for vandal moths.
2264. Houlbert, C. V. Les Insectes Ennemis des Livres.
      Paris: Picard, 1903. One of the few books avail-
      able devoted exclusively to the study of book in-
      sects.
2265. Howard, L. O. and C. L. Martlett. The Principal
      Household Insects of the United States. Washing-
      ton: U. S. Government Printing Office, 1896.
2266. Illuminati, G. "Introduzione alla Studio della fauna
      carticola, " Bollettino dell Istituto di Patologia del
      Libro 4(2):25-33, 1942.
2267. "Insect Attacks on Wood, " Review 28:725-726, 829-
      830, 1955.
2268. "Insects, Damage From, " American Archivist 16:377,
      1953.
2269. Jepson, F. P. "Sitadrepa Damages Books, " Fiji De-
      partment of Agriculture Annual Report 1919.
2270. Jones, H. "Insects Destructive to Books, " Library
      Association Record 14:286-287, 1912. London.
      Includes 35 references to literature on the subject.
2271. Kalshoven, L. G. E. "Book-beetle in the Netherlands
      Indies, " Entomologische mededeelingen van Neder-
      landsch-Indie 4:10-16, 1938.
2272. Kett, F. S. L. "Insect Pests of Books, " The Book
      Collector 5(1):57-62, 1966. Brief description of
      insects found in books in England.
2273. Kimberly, A. E. "Insect and Bacterial Enemies of
      Archives, " American Archivist 11:246-247, 1948.

2274. Kofoid, C. A. et al. Termites and Termite Control.
      Berkeley: University of California Press, 1946.
2275. Kotinsky, J. "A New Book and Leather Pest, " Ha-
      waiian Forester and Agriculturist 3:117-118, 1935.
      Honolulu.
2276. Laing, F. "Borkhausenia pseudospretella and Other
      House Moths, " Entomologist's Monthly Magazine
      68:77-80, 1932.
2277. Langton, L. R. Insect Pests in Ethnographical Speci-
      mens. London: International Institute for Con-
      servation, 1968. A brief monograph on the
      clothes moth, woodworms and termites.
2278. Lepigre, A. L. Insects du Logis et du Magasin.
      Algiers: Insectarium Jardin d'Essai, 1951.
2279. Light, S. F. Termites and Termite Damage. Berke-
      ley: University of California, 1929. College of
      Agriculture Circular No. 314.
2280. Lindsay, E. "The Biology of the Silverfish. Cteno-
      lepisma Longicaudata Esch. with Particular Refer-
      ence to Its Feeding Habits, " Proceedings Zoological
      Society 52, 1947. Victoria, B. C.
2281. Mallis, A. "The Silverfish, " Pest Control and Sanita-
      tion 1(1), 1946.
2282. Marshall, M. "The Termite Menace, " Technical
      Studies in the Field of Fine Arts 4(3), 1936.
2283. McCall, Floyd C. "Carpet Beetle Larvae Nibble
      Color Slides, " Sunday Denver Post February 5,
      1967.
2284. McDaniel, E. I. Cockroaches, Silverfish, and Book-
      Lice. East Lansing: Michigan State College,
      1934. Agricultural Experiment Station Circular
      Bulletin 101.
2285. McKenny Hughes, A. W. "Insect Pests of Books and
      Paper, " Indian Archives 7(1), 1953.
2286. Metcalf, C. L. and W. P. Flint. Destructive and
      Useful Insects. New York: McGraw-Hill Book
      Co. , 1962.
2287. Morita, H. "Some Observations on the Silverfish,
      Lepisma Saccharina, " Proceedings of the Hawaiian
      Entomological Society 6:271-273, 1925.
2288. O'Conor, Rev. J. F. X. Facts About Bookworms.
      New York: Francis P. Harper, 1898. A short
      account that is accurate textually but very poorly
      illustrated.
2289. Osler, Sir William. "Illustrations of the Book Worm, "
      Bodleian Quarterly Record 1(12):355-357, 1917.
      Photographs of "anobium hirtim" native to France.

2290. Peignot, E. F. "Insectes Qui Rongent les Livres,"
       Dictionnaire Raisonne de Bibliologie. Paris: Vil-
       leir, 1802.
2291. Perotin, Yves. Le Problème des Termites et Autres
       Agents Destructeurs aux Archives de la Reunion.
       Paris: Archives Department Reunion, 1953.
2292. Petrova, G. I. "Insects in Book Storerooms," Col-
       lection of Materials on the Preservation of Library
       Resources. Moscow: USSR State Library, 1953.
       English translation available from National Techni-
       cal Information Center, Springfield, Va.
2293. Plenderleith, H. J. "Insects Among Archives,"
       British Records Association Bulletin 18:2-6, 1945.
2294. Robinow, B. H. "Books and Cockroaches: An At-
       tempt to Cope With the Menace," South African
       Libraries 24(2):40-42, 1956.
2295. Rosewall, O. W. "The Biology of the Booklouse,"
       Annals of the Entomological Society of America
       23:192-194, 1930.
2296. Scarone, Arturo. El Libro y sus Enemigos. Monte-
       video: 1917. One of the few books devoted ex-
       clusively to book insects.
2297. Silverfish and Firebrats. Washington: U.S. Govern-
       ment Printing Office, 1957.
2298. Skaife, S. H. Dwellers in Darkness. London: Long-
       mans, 1955.
2299. Snyder, T. E. Our Enemy the Termite. Ithica, New
       York: Comstock Printing Co., 1935.
2300. _____. Our Enemy the Termite. 2nd ed. Lon-
       don: Constable, 1948.
2301. Stored Grain Pests. Washington: U.S. Government
       Printing Office, 1962. Farmers Bulletin No. 1260.
       Includes identification of pests known to attack
       books and paper.
2302. Terlecki, E. "Book Scorpions," Bibliotekarz 21,
       1954.
2303. Termites in the Humid Tropics. Paris: UNESCO,
       1960.
2304. Termites, Wood-borers and Fungi in Buildings. Re-
       port of the Committee on the Protection of Building
       Timbers in South Africa against Termites, Wood-
       boring Beetles and Fungi. Pretoria: South African
       Council for Scientific and Industrial Research, 1950.
       National Building Research Institute.
2305. Towne, C. M. E. Autobiography of Master Book-
       worm. Lansing, Michigan: Ellison Book Shop,
       1935.

2306.   Wahls, A.   "Woodboring Pests and Their Remedies,"
        Maltechnik 72:18-23, 1966.   Munich.
2307.   Watson, J. R.   "A Tropical Bookworm in Florida,"
        Florida Entomologist 26(4):61-63, 1943.
2308.   Weiss, H. B. and R. H. Carruthers.   "The More
        Important Insect Enemies of Books," Bulletin
        40:739-752, 827-828, 1936.   New York Public Li-
        brary.   An account of the commoner species of
        insects found in libraries together with suggestions
        for their control.   The description and illustrations
        of these pests are excellent but the treatments
        suggested are in some cases outdated.
2309.   Weiss, H. B. and Carruthers, R. H.   Insect Enemies
        of Books.   New York: New York Public Library,
        1945.   Their 1936 essay in Bulletin of the New
        York Public Library, updated.

        FUNGI

2310.   Abrams, Ed.   Microbiological Deterioration of Organic
        Materials.   Washington: U.S. Government Printing
        Office, 1948.   Bureau of Standards Misc. Pub.
        188.
2311.   Ambler, H. R. and C. F. Finney.   "Brown Stain
        Formed on Wet Cellulose," Nature 179:1141, 1957.
2312.   (Anonymous).   Mildew in Books.   Chicago: American
        Library Association, 1948.   A Library
        Technology Project Leaflet.
2313.   Armitage, F. D.   The Cause of Mildew on Books and
        Methods of Preservation.   London: Printing, Pack-
        aging and Allied Trades Research Association,
        1949.   PATRA Bulletin No. 8.
2314.   Aufsess, H. von; H. von Pechmann, and Graessle
        Pechmann.   "Fluorescence Microscope Investiga-
        tions with Fungus-Attacked Wood," Holz Roh-
        Werkstoff 26(2):50-61, 1968.
2315.   Barghoorn, E. S.   "Historical Study of the Action of
        Fungi on Leather," Journal American Leather
        Chemists Association 45:688-700, 1950.
2316.   Barr, P.   "Mildew in Libraries--Prevention and
        Treatment," New Jersey Library Bulletin 13:123-
        129, 1945.
2317.   Beckwith, Theodore D.; W. H. Swanson, and Thomas
        Marion Iiams.   "Deterioration of Paper; The Cause
        and Effect of Foxing," University of California
        Publications in Biological Science 1(13):299-356, 1940.

2318. Belyakova, L. A.   "The Mold Species and Their In-
       jurious Effect on Various Book Materials," Resto-
       ration and Preservation of Library Resources
       Documents and Books.   London: Oldbourne Press,
       1964.

2319. _____.   "The Mold Species and Their Effect on
       Book Materials," Collection of Materials on the
       Preservation of Library Resources.   Moscow:
       U. S. S. R. State Library, 1958.   English translation
       available from National Technical Information Ser-
       vice, Springfield, Virginia.

2320. Block, S. S.   "Humidity Requirements for Mold
       Growth," Engineering Progress 7(10), 1953.   Uni-
       versity of Florida.

2321. Block, S. S.; R. Rodriguez-Torrent; M. B. Cole;
       and A. E. Prince.   "Humidity and Temperature
       Requirements of Selected Fungi," Developments in
       Industrial Microbiology 3:204-216, 1962.   New
       York: Plenum Press, 1962.

2322. Bracken, A.   The Chemistry of Micro-organisms.
       London: Pitman and Sons, 1955.

2323. Brown, A. E.   "Report on the Problems of Fungal
       Growth on Synthetic Resins, Plastics and Plasticis-
       ers," U. S. Office of Scientific Research and De-
       velopment Report 6067.   Washington: USGPO, 1945.

2324. Christensen, Clyde M.   The Molds and Man.   New
       York: McGraw-Hill, 1965.   Combines authoritative
       scholarship with an unusually clear knack of com-
       munication.

2325. Czajnik, Michal.   "Biological Agents Causing De-
       composition and Destruction in Ancient Objects.
       Means and Methods of Protection, Disinfection and
       Disinsectization," Materialy Muezeum Budownictwa
       Sanoku 19-26, 1966.   Poland.

2326. Czerwinski, E. and R. Kowalik.   "Penicillia Destroy-
       ing Archival Papers," Acta Microbiologica Polonica
       5(1-2):299-302, 1956.

2327. Czerwinska, E.; I. Sadurska, and D. Kozlowska.
       "Actinomyces Damaging Old Manuscripts and Docu-
       ments," Acta Microbiologica Polonica 2(2-3):190-
       207, 1953.

2328. Dahl, Sverre.   "The Effects of Fungicides on Deteri-
       oration of Leather," Journal of the American
       Leather Chemists Association 52(11), 1957.

2329. Fahraeus, G.   "Studies in the Cellulose Decomposition
       by Cytophaga," Symbolae Botanicae Upsalienses
       9(2), 1947.   Uppsala.

2330. Flieder, F. "Etude de la Résistance Biologique des Procédés de Renforcement des Documents Graphiques," Recent Advances in Conservation. London: Butterworth's, 1963. Mme. Flieder's findings on the resistance of reinforced paper to mold.

2331. _____. "Lutte Contra Les Moisissures des Materiaux Constitutifs des Documents Graphiques," Recent Advances in Conservation. London: Butterworth's, 1962. Summarizes Mme. Flieder's investigation of molds and preventive measures.

2332. Gallo, Fausta. "Aspetti della lotta preventiva e curativa contro i microorganismi dannosi al materiale bibliographico e i archivistico," Bollettino dell Istituto di Patolgia del Libro 22:29-66, 1963. A review of damage to library materials done by bacteria and fungi and the ways to prevent it. 96 bibliographical references.

2333. _____. "Biological Agents Which Damage Paper Materials in Libraries and Archives," Recent Advances in Conservation. London: Butterworth's, 1963.

2334. _____. "Bli agenti biologici che danneggiano il materiale cartaceo degli archivi e delle bibliotheque," Bollettino dell Istituto de Patologia del Libro 22:36-60, 1961. A lengthy review with over 100 references of the problems of insects and micro-organisms in libraries and archives.

2335. _____. "Ricerche spirimentali sulla resistenza agli agenti biologici dei materiale impiegati nel restauro dei libri," Bollettino dell Istituto di Patologia del Libro 22:6-24, 1961. Report on the resistance to micro-organisms of organic and synthetic adhesives.

2336. Gascoigne, J. A. and M. M. Biological Degradation of Cellulose. London: Butterworth's, 1960.

2337. Gupta, R. C. Effects of Clenofix and Other Common Insecticides on the Durability of Paper. Paris: International Council of Museums, 1963. A paper presented at 1963 Moscow Meeting of ICOM Committee for Museum Laboratories.

2338. Harmsen, L. and T. Vincentsnissen. "Bacterial Attacks on Wood," Holz-Roh und Werkstoff 23:389-393, 1965. Berlin.

2339. Henn, R. W. and D. G. Wiest. "Microscopie Spots in Processed Microfilm: Their Nature and Prevention," Photographic Science and Engineering 7:253-261, 1963.

2340.   Iiams, T. H.   Foxing and Deterioration of Books.
        MA thesis., University of Chicago, n. d.

2341.   Iiams, T. M. and T. D. Beckwith.   "Notes on the
        Causes and Prevention of Foxing in Books," Li-
        brary Quarterly 45(4):407-418, 1935.

2342.   Inouye, Y., Y. Iizuka, and T. Tazima.   "Studies on
        Leather Fungi.   I-Morphology and Enzyme Activity
        of the Leather Fungi.   II-Selection of the Test
        Strains and the Antifungal Action of Phenolic Com-
        pounds.   III-The Antifungal Activity of Organic
        Mercury Compounds," Bulletin Japanese Associa-
        tion Leather Technologists 3:95-100, 1957; 4:163-
        168, 1958.

2343.   Kanagy, J. A. et al.   "Effects of Mildew on Vege-
        table-Tanned Strap Leather," Journal of Research
        36, 1946.   National Bureau of Standards.

2344.   Kanevskaja, I. G.   "Acetylcellulose Destruction
        Caused by Fungi," Causes of Decay of Written
        Printed Monuments 74(6), 1967.   Leningrad, USSR:
        Laboratory for Preservation and Restoration of
        Documents.   In Russian with English summary.
        Experiments showed that acetylation of cotton fibre
        proceeds unevenly.   This leads to fungi develop-
        ment of untreated areas.   Presumably, a higher
        degree of cellulose acetylation will result in fungi
        resistant material.

2345.   Kowalik, R.   "The Micro-organisms That Destroy
        the Archival Papers," Prace Placowek Naukowo
        Badowzych 2:49-67, 1952.

2346.   _____.   Micro-organisms Destroying Paper, Leath-
        er and Wax Seals, Pathogenic for Man.   Warsaw:
        Museum Mickiewicza, 1960.

2347.   _____.   "Some problems of Microbiological Deteri-
        oration of Paper," Annali della Scuola Speciale per
        Archivisti e Bibliotecari dell'Università di Roma
        9(1-2):61-80, 1969.   In English.

2348.   Kowalik, R. and J. Sadurska.   "Micro-organisms
        Destroying Leather Bookbindings," Acta Micro-
        biologica Polonica 5(1-2):285-290, 1956.

2349.   _____.   "Micro-organisms Destroying Paper,
        Leather and Wax Seals in the Air of Archives,"
        Acta Microbiologica Polonica 5(1-2):277-284, 1956.

2350.   _____.   "Protection of Parchment Against Micro-
        flora," Annali della Scuola Speciale per Archivisti
        e Bibliotecari dell'Universita di Roma 9(1-2):51-62,
        1969.   Amongst other things the authors report
        that parchment is more prone to damage by fungi

after fumigation with ethylene oxide.   In English.

2351. Lawrence, C. A. and S. S. Block (eds.).   Disinfection, Sterilization and Preservation.   Philadelphia:
Fea and Febiger, 1968.   Discusses causes as well
as prevention of fungus damage.

2352. Levi Della Vida, M.   "I micro-organismi nemici del
libro, " Accademia Biblioteca Italia 10(4):234-250,
1936.

2353. Metcalf, C. L. and W. P. Flint.   Destructive and
Useful Insects.   New York: McGraw-Hill, 1951.

2354. Microbiological Deterioration in the Tropics.   London:
Society of Chemical Industry, n. d.

2355. "Micro-organic Attack on Textiles and Leather, "
CIBA Review 100, October 1953.

2356. "Mildew, " American Archivist 1:11, 1938.

2357. Minier, D. W.   "Mildew and Books, " Library Journal
57:931-936, 1932.

2358. Mitchell, C. A. and D. R. Wood.   "Action of Molds
on Ink in Writing, " Analyst 63-111, 1938.

2359. Mitton, R. G. and J. N. Turner.   "A Study of Mould
Growth on Chrome-Tanned Leather and the Associated Changes in Physical Properties, " Journal of
the Society of Leather Chemists 39:343-358, 1955.

2360. Moutia, A.   "Sitodrepa Panicea L. Infesting Books, "
Mauritius Department of Agriculture Annual Report,
1932.

2361. Nishira, H.   "The Tannin-decomposing Enzyme of
Molds. V. Paper Chromatographic Analysis of
Tannase Formation, " Hakko Kogaku Zasshi 37:85-
89, 1963.

2362. Nishira, H. and N. Mugibayashi.   "Tannin-decomposing Enzyme of Molds. XI. Formation of Tannase
by Various Molds on Wheat Bran Medium, " Hyogo
Noka Daigaku Kenkyu Hokoku Nogeikaku Hem 4:113-
116, 1960.

2363. Nyuksha, Y. P.   "Changes in the chemical and mechanical qualities of paper contaminated by Gimnoa-
cus setosus, " Microbiologiya 29(2):276-280, 1960.
Moscow.

2364. _____.   "Microscopic Study of Paper Stained by
the Fungus Gymnoascus Setosus, " Microbiologiya
29(1):133-136, 1960.   Moscow.

2365. _____.   "Mycoflora of Books and Paper, "
Botanicheski Zhurnal 41:797-809, 1956.

2366. _____.   "Physical Investigation of Gimnoascus
Setosus Eidam, " Microbiologiya 22(1):15-22, 1953;
25(3):306-312, 1957.   Reports on one of the most

common book pests.

2367.   . "The Action of Bacterial Radiation on
         Fungi Spores, " Microbiologiya 22(2):678-681, 1953.
         Moscow.

2368.   . "Experimental Pigmentation of Paper
         Samples by Fungi, " Stareniye bumagi 82-93, 1965.
         Moscow.

2369.   . "A Taxonomic Survey of Fungi Dwelling
         on Paper, Books and Pulp, " Botanicheski Zhurnal
         46:70-79, 1961.

2370. [No entry.]

2371.   . "On Paper Permanence and Resistance to
         Fungi, " Causes of Decay of Written and Printed
         Monuments 51-73, 1967.   Leningrad, USSR: Lab-
         oratory for Preservation and Restoration of Docu-
         ments.   In Russian with English summary.

2372. Plenderleith, H. J.   "Mould In the Muniment Room, "
         Archives 7:13, 1952.

2373. Rose, C. D. and J. N. Turner.   "Mold Growth on
         Leather as Affected by Humidity Changes, " Journal
         Society Leather Trades' Chemists 35:37-42, 1951.

2374. Siu, Ralph G. H.   Microbial Decomposition of Cellu-
         lose, with Special Reference to Cotton Textiles.
         New York: Reinhold Publishing Corp. , 1951.

2375. Smirnowa, B. I.   Problems of Micro-organisms in
         Parchments.   Moscow: USSR Academy of Sciences,
         1962.

2376. Tate, Vernon D.   Checklist of Information About
         Microscopic Spots on Microfilm.   Society of Amer-
         ican Archivists, 1964.   Paper distributed at the
         October 1964 meeting.

2377. Walters, A. H. and J. S. Elphick.   Biodeterioration
         of Materials.   London: Elsevier, 1969.   This is
         the proceedings of the first International Biodeteri-
         oration Symposium in Southampton in 1968.

2378. Wang, C. J. K.   "Preliminary Report on the Fungus
         Flora Pulp and Paper in New York, " Tappi 44(2):
         785-788, 1961.

2379. Wiest, D. G. and R. W. Henn.   "Microscopic Spots:
         a Progress Report, " National Micro-News 70:249-
         264, June 1964.

2380.   W. J. Barrow Research Laboratory.   Permanence/
        Durability of the Book.   6 vols.   Richmond, Va.:
        William J. Barrow Research Laboratory Inc.,
        1963-1969.   The Barrow Laboratory is one of the
        centers for research into the problems of deteri-
        oration of library materials.   This series of pub-
        lications reports the findings of major projects
        concerning the problem of acidity and the develop-
        ment of standards for paper, bindings and adhe-
        sives.
2381.   Barrow, W. J.   "Acidity: An Undesirable Property
        in Paste and Mending Tissue," American Archivist
        30:190-193, 1967.
2382.   Bennett, H. G.   'On the Acidity of Leather," Journal
        of the American Leather Chemists Association
        26:200-201, 1931.
2383.   Bishop, William W.   'One Problem for 1950--Wood-
        pulp Paper in Books," Bookmen's Holiday 407-415,
        1943.   New York Public Library.
2384.   Blackaddert, T.   "Effect of Acid Upon Vegetable
        Tanned Leather," Committee Report.   Journal of
        the American Leather Chemists Association 26(9):
        482-490, 1931.
2385.   Brecht, W. and E. Liebert.   "The Effect of Writing
        Inks on the Strength of Paper," Papier-Fabr. /
        Wochbl. Papierfabr. 9:330, 1943.
2386.   Briggs, J. F.   "Rosin as a Factor in Paper Dis-
        coloration," Pulp and Paper Magazine of Canada
        11(20), 1913.
2387.   The Cause and Prevention of Decay in Bookbinding
        Leather.   (two reports)   London: St. Brides In-
        stitute, 1933 and 1936.   Findings of the Printing
        Industry Research Association and the British
        Leather Manufacturer's Research Association.
2388.   Chene, M.   "Unfavorable Influence of Acidity on Pa-
        per and Board Quality," Bulletin, Association Tech.
        Ind. Papetiere 5:74, 1947.
2389.   Coward, H. F. and G. M. Wigley.   "The Detection
        and Estimation of Acidity and Alkalinity in Cotton
        Fabrics," Journal Textile Institute 13:121-126,
        1922.
2390.   Ede, J. R. and W. H. Langwell.   "Sulphur Dioxide
        and Vapor Phase Deacidification," Museum Clima-
        tology.   London: International Institute for

Conservation, 1968.

2391. Evelyn, John. The Diary of. 6 vols. Oxford: Clarendon Press, 1958. On 24 August 1678, Evelyn's diary reports a visit to a paper mill in London where he saw dried sheets being dipped in allume (sic) water then polished. This early evidence of the use of alum in papermaking probably accounts for some of the embrittlement of 17th and 18th century book pages that "being made of rag paper sized with gelatin" should still be strong and durable.

2392. Herzberg, W. "Destruction of Paper by Writing Ink, " Paper Trade Journal 76(10), 1923.

2393. Hoffman, W. F. "Deterioration of Paper by Excessive Acidity, " Paper Trade Journal 88(12):59-60, 1929.

2394. _____. "Effect of Residual Acid on Rate of Deterioration of Paper, " Paper Trade Journal 86(9):58-60, 1928.

2395. Hudson, F. L. "Acidity of 17th and 18th Century Books in Two Libraries, " Paper Technology 8:189-190, 1967.

2396. "Ink, Acidity, " American Archivist 10:338, 1947; 11:291, 1948; 12:11, 1949.

2397. Jarrell T. D.; J. M. Hankins, and F. P. Veitch. The Effects of Inorganic Acids on the Physical Properties of Waterleaf Rag Bond Paper. Washington: U.S. Department of Agriculture, 1932. Technical Bulletin No. 334.

2398. Kanagy, J. R. "The Pick-Up of Sulfur Dioxide by Paper, " Journal of Applied Chemistry 14:444-447, 1964.

2399. Kowalik, R. "The Influence of the Ink Upon the Paper. Inks for Permanent Documents, " Blok Notes 175-176, 1960. Warszawie: Muzeum Mickiewicza.

2400. Kubelka, V. and R. Wollmarker. "Free Acid in the Analysis of Vegetable Leather, " Journal of the American Leather Chemists Association 26(8):435-439, 1931.

2401. Laurent, Gavonne. "Acidification of Atmospheric Water, " Tele Medd. Televerket 4:267-275, 1968. In Swedish.

2402. "Paper, Acidity, " American Archivist 6:151, 1943; 12:9, 1949.

2403. Report of the Committee on Leather for Bookbinding. London: Royal Society of Arts, 1905. Covers the sources of leather decay - mainly acid.

2404. "Rosin in Paper and Paperboard," Technical Association of the Pulp and Paper Industry T-408, 1961. Tappi Standard test procedure.

2405. Smith, R. D. "Paper Impermanence as a Consequence of pH and Storage Conditions," Library Quarterly 39:153-195, 1969. Provides basic information references to further information and a sense of proportion about the action of hydrogen ions and storage conditions on paper. An excellent well documented study of one of the most serious causes of the deterioration of library materials.

2406. _____. The Preservation of Leather Bookbindings from Sulphuric Acid Deterioration. Unpublished thesis, University of Chicago, 1964. Discusses acid contamination.

2407. _____. "Paper deacidifcation; A preliminary report," Library Quarterly 36:273-292, 1966. Includes description of the sources of acid.

2408. Zaguliaeva, Z. A. "The Influence of Acidity on Fungi Growth in Paper," Stareniye bumagi 75-81, 1965. Moscow.

2409. Zimmerman, E. W.; C. G. Weber, and A. E. Kimberly. "Relation of Ink to the Preservation of Written Records," Journal of Research 14:463-468, 1935. Washington, National Bureau of Standards.

IV. Preventive Care

OVERALL

2410. Alden, John E. "Reproduction vs. Preservation, "
Library Journal 91:5319-5322, 1966.

2411.   . "Why Preserve Books?" Catholic Library
World 30:267-272, 1959. An attempt to explore
reasons other than the obvious ones for the preservation of books as physical objects.

2412. American Library Association. Protecting the Library and Its Resources A Guide to Physical Protection and Insurance. Chicago: American Library Asso. , 1963. A Report on a Study Conducted
by Gage-Babcock and Associates, Inc.

2413. American Library Association. Permanence and
Durability of Library Catalog Cards. Chicago:
American Library Association, 1961. A study
conducted by W. J. Barrow for the Library Tech-
nology Project. Publication No. 3 of the Library
Technology Project.

2414. America's Museums--The Belmont Report. Washington: The American Association of Museums, 1969.
Includes an evaluation of the problems of conservation and what must be done about them. Argu-
ments are equally applicable to library conservation.

2415. Archer, H. Richard (ed.). Rare Book Collections:
Some Theoretical and Practical Suggestions. Chicago: American Library Association, 1965. ACRL
Monograph No. 27. Suggestions for librarians and
students on the nature and importance of rare
books; the rare book library and the public; library
housing and equipment; and care maintenance and
storage.

2416. Bach, C H. and Y. Oddon. Petit Guide Du Biblio-
thecaire. 4th ed. Paris: Bourrelier, 1952.

2417. Banks, Paul N. Treating Leather Bookbindings. Chicago: Newberry Library, 1967.

2418. _____. "The Librarian as Conservator," The Library Quarterly 40(1):192-198, 1970. Defines book conservation, the qualifications of the book conservator, the role of the conservator in the library and the education of conservators in his comments on Henderson and Krupp's paper on the same subject in the same journal.

2419. _____. The Scientist, the Scholar and the Book Conservator: Some Thoughts on Book Conservation as a Profession. Chicago: The Newberry Library, n. d.

2420. Barr, Pelham. "Book Conservation and University Library Administration," College and Research Libraries 7:214-219, 1946.

2421. Barrow, W. J. "New Device Tests Performance of Library Bindings," Book Production 79:60-62, 1964.

2422. Basu, M. N. "Preservation of Books," Indian Librarian 17-20, June 1953.

2423. Baughman, Roland. "Conservation of Old and Rare Books," Library Trends 4(3):239-247, 1956.

2424. Belyakova, L. A. et al. "Book Preservation in U. S. S. R. Libraries," UNESCO Bulletin for Libraries 15, July 1961.

2425. Belyakova, L. A. and O. N. Kozulina (eds.). Collection of Materials on the Preservation of Library Resources. No. 3, Moscow, 1958. Translated from the Russian by Israel Program for Scientific translations for National Science Foundation, Washington, D. C. Available from the National Technical Information Service, Springfield, Virginia.

2426. Belmont Report, America's Museums. Washington: American Association of Museums, 1969. This report to the Federal Council on the Arts and the Humanities by a Special Committee of the American Association of Museums discusses museum problems many of which are applicable to libraries and historical societies. Includes recognition of the importance of museum libraries and the unmet needs of conservation and restoration.

2427. Belov, G. A. "New Techniques, New Materials, and New Experiences Concerning Restoration of Documents and Seals, Preservation of Maps and Plans, and Photography since 1950," Archivum 10:72-80, 104-105, 1960. Abstracted in American Archivist 26:256, 1963.

2428. Bhargava, K. D. Repair and Preservation of Records. New Delhi: National Archives of India, 1959.

2429. Bhowmik, S. K. "A Concise History of Conservation of Antiquities and Works of Art," Museum Bulletin 21, 1969. Baroda. Describes the growth of certain crafts into a scientific discipline.

2430. Blanchard, Ralph H. and Albert H. Mowbray. Insurance, Its Theory and Practice in the United States. 5th ed. New York: McGraw-Hill, 1961.

2431. "Books and Documents," American Archivist 10:188, 1947.

2432. Boston Museum of Fine Arts. Application of Science in Examination of Works of Art: Proceedings of the Seminar, September 15-18, 1958. New York: October House, 1959.

2433. Bowditch, George and H. J. Swinney. Preparing Your Exhibits: Methods, Materials and Bibliography. Nashville: American Association for State and Local History, 1969. Technical Leaflet No. 4.

2434. Brandi, Cesare. "Il Fondamento Teorico del Restauro," Bolletino Istituto Centrale Restauro I, 1950. Theoretical considerations and the importance of the esthetic point of view.

2435. Brooks, Philip C. "The Selection of Records for Preservation," American Archivist 3(4):221-234, 1940.

2436. Buck, Richard D. "An Experiment in Co-operative Conservation," Studies in Conservation 2(3), 1956. Report on the establishment of the Intermuseum Conservation Association.

2437. _____. "The Inspection of Art Objects and Glossary for Describing Condition," Museum Registration Methods 164-170, 1968. American Association of Museums and the Smithsonian Institution.

2438. _____. "On the Conservation of Works of Art," Indianpolis Art Association Bulletin 54(1), 1967. Summary of the history of conservation of art objects and speaks of ethical considerations.

2439. "Care and Conservation in the Home," Toledo Museum of Art Museum News 8(3), 1965.

2440. Casford, E. L. "Periodicals; Their Use and Preservation," Wilson Library Bulletin 13:593-596, 1939.

2441. "Cercle des Alumni des Fondations Universitaires, Art et Science," Alumni 19:246-387, 1950. This issue of the journal is devoted to the relationship of art, science and conservation.

2442. Chasse, J. Conservation des Documents: (Instructions sommaires pour l'organisation et le

fonctionnement des bibliothèques publiques. 3)
Paris: Ministere de l'Education Nationale, Direction des Bibliothèques de France, 1954.

2443. Chastukin, V. "Scientific Research on Book Hygiene," Bibliotekar 9, December 1948.

2444. Church of Jesus Christ of Latter-Day Saints, Genealogical Society. Records Protection in an Uncertain World. Salt Lake City: 1969.

2445. Clark, John Willis. The Care of Books. Cambridge: Cambridge University Press, 1901.

2446. Clayjus, F. H. "The Prevention of Damage to Books and Manuscripts," Bulletin Institute of Paper Chemistry 27, 1956-1957.

2447. Cobden-Sanderson, T. J. Industrial Ideals and the Book Beautiful. London: Hammersmith Publishing Co., 1902.

2448. Coleman, Laurence Vail. "The Museum Library," Manual for Small Museums. New York: G. P. Putnam, 1927.

2449. Collection of Materials on the Preservation of Library Resources. Moscow: 1953. In English. Many informative articles on Russian preservation and restoration methods. Available from National Technical Information Service, Springfield, Virginia.

2450. Collis, I. P. "Technical Care of Records; Document Conservation in the Local Repository," Archives 6:4-7, 1963.

2451. Comité pour les Laboratoires de Musées. Groupe de Travail pour l'Etude de la Conservation des Materiaux Constitutifs des Documents Graphiques. Paris: Bibliothèque Nationale, 1960.

2452. Condon, Edward Uhler. Preservation of the Declaration of Independence and the Constitution of the United States. Washington: U. S. Government Printing Office, 1951. National Bureau of Standards Circular 505.

2453. The Conservation of Cultural Property; Museums and Monuments XI. Paris: United Nations Educational Scientific Cultural Organization (UNESCO), 1968.

2454. Constable, W. G. "Curators and Conservation," Studies in Conservation 1(3), 1954.

2455. _____. "Curatorial Problems in Relation to Conservation," Museum News 24(9):6-8, 1946.

2456. _____. "Curatorial Problems in Relation to Conservation," Bulletin Fogg Museum of Art 10, 1946.

2457. Coremans, Paul. Problems of Conservation in Muse-
       ums. London: George Allen and Unwin, Ltd.,
       1969. A selection of papers presented to the
       ICOM Committee Meetings in Washington and New
       York in 1965. Includes sections on deterioration
       of cellulose (a literature review), the conservation
       of wood, and a review of the methods of paper
       lamination, an evaluation of lamination processes,
       and paper deacidification.
2458. Council on Library Resources, Inc. Annual Report
       for the Year Ended June 30, 1967. Washington:
       Council on Library Resources, 1968. Record
       preservation.
2459. Dauze, Pierre. "La question de la conservation du
       papier dans les bibliothèques publiques et privées
       et un moyen de la résoudre," Procès-verbaux et
       Mémoires (of the) Congrès International des biblio-
       thécaires, Paris, August 20-23, 1900. Paris:
       Welter, 1901.
2460. David, Charles. "The Conservation of Historical
       Source Material," American Documentation 7:76-
       82, 1956.
2461. The Deterioration and Preservation of Book Material
       Stored in Libraries. Garston, England: Building
       Research Station, 1949. Great Britain Department
       of Scientific and Industrial Research, Note No.
       D 62.
2462. Dodd, L. V. "Examination of Documents and Paint-
       ings," Art and Archaeology Journal 31-35, 52,
       1930.
2463. Eckles, Robert B. "The Importance of Photocopy
       Projects for Local and Regional History," The
       American Archivist 25(2):159-163, 1962.
2464. Edlund, P. E. "The Continuing Quest: Care of Li-
       brary of Congress Collections," Library Journal
       90, 1965. Care of books, maps, manuscripts,
       film, tape, etc.
2465. Ellis, R. H. "An Archivist's Note on the Conserva-
       tion of Documents," Journal of the Society of
       Archivists 1(9):252-254, 1959.
2466. _____. "Latest Information for the Private Owner
       and Smaller Repository," Archives 4, 1963. Ar-
       chive repair.
2467. (Ethics). The Murray Pease Report: The Code of
       Ethics for Art Conservation. New York: Con-
       servation Center, Institute of Fine Arts, New York
       University, 1968.

2468. Evans, Luther H. "The Preservation of the Docu-
       mentation on the History of the Americas,"
       Quarterly Journal of Current Acquisitions 7(1):3-8,
       1949. U. S. Library of Congress. An address
       developing principles to be observed in cooperative
       efforts to preserve catalogs and disseminate the
       basic documents of national history.

2469. Fall, F. K. Art Objects: Their Care and Preserva-
       tion. A Reference for Museums and Collectors.
       Washington: Museum Publications, 1967.

2470. Fitzpatrick, John C. Notes on the Care, Cataloging,
       Calendaring and Arranging of Manuscripts. Wash-
       ington: U. S. Library of Congress, Division of
       Manuscripts, 1928.

2471. Fleetwood, Gustaf. "Sur la Conservation des Sceaux
       de cire du moyen age, desposes aux Archives du
       Royaume de Suede," Medelanden fran Svenska
       Riksarkivet 1:ff, 1945.

2472. Flyate, D. M. (ed.). Preservation of Documents and
       Papers. Washington: National Science Foundation,
       1968. A companion volume to the two Russian
       manuals previously translated by Israel Program
       for Scientific Translations. Much important infor-
       mation on paper aging, paper preservation, book
       restoration, document examination. Excellent
       bibliographies of Eastern Europe literature on the
       subjects. Available from the National Technical
       Information Service, Springfield, Virginia.

2473. Foster, Amy G. "Archives and the Archivist," Indian
       Archivist 2:59-67, 1948. Reprinted from Library
       Association Record 49:164-168, 1947.

2474. Friedman, H. B. "Preservation of Library Mate-
       rials: The State of the Art," Special Libraries
       59:608-613, 1968.

2475. Gairola, T. R. Handbook of Chemical Conservation
       of Museum Objects. Baroda: University of Baro-
       da, 1960.

2476. "General Library Conservation," Library Journal
       90(3), 1965.

2477. Grant, Julius. Books and Documents: Dating, Per-
       manence and Preservation. London: Grafton and
       Co., 1937. The section on preservation is devoted
       to preventive rather than curative measures.

2478. Greathouse, G. A. and C. J. Wessel and others.
       Deterioration of Materials. New York: Reinhold
       Publishing Corp., 1954. Discusses the climatic,
       chemical, physical and biological agents of

deterioration and outlines protective methods for
wood, paper, textiles, cordage, leather, plastics,
rubber and paints and varnishes.

2479. Grove, Lee E. "What Good is Greenland? New
Thinking on Book Preservation and Temperature,"
Wilson Library Bulletin 36:749, 757, 1962.

2480. _____. "Predictability of Permanence in Perfect
Library Bindings," College and Research Libraries
22:341-344, 1961.

2481. Guha Roy, K. K. "How to Preserve Books," Modern
Librarian 9:79-87, 1939.

2482. Gupta, R. C. "A Review of Work in Conservation in
the National Archives of India," Conservation of
Cultural Property in India. New Delhi: National
Museum, 1966. Reviews work done for the rehabilitation of documents since 1950. Discusses
insecticides, fungicides, adhesives and practical
measures for smaller institutions.

2483. A Handbook on the Care and Preservation of Works
of Art. New York: American Federation of Arts,
1963. A condensed manual (26 pages) primarily
for private collectors.

2484. "Handling Prints, Drawings, Books," Museum News
43, 1964.

2485. Hanson, J. C. M. et al. "Rare Books," American
Library Institute Papers and Proceedings 191-193,
1917. A discussion of a few aspects of the responsibility of rare books.

2486. Harding, Bruce C. and Robert L. Damm. Preservation of Library and Museum Collections. Columbus: Ohio State Museum, 1959.

2487. Harrison, T. "The Care of Books," The Book Collector's Quarterly 3:1-14, 1931. London.

2488. Haseldon, R. B. Scientific Aids for the Study of
Manuscripts. London: Bibliographical Society,
1935.

2489. Held, J. S. A Preliminary List of Basic Reference
Works in the Fine Arts. New York: American
Group, International Institute for Conservation,
1966.

2490. Henderson, J. W. Memorandum on Conservation of
the Collection. New York: New York Public Library, 1970. Describes the measures and organization for protection of the Research Libraries at
the NYPL.

2491. Henderson, J. W. and R. G. Krupp. "The Librarian
as a Conservator," The Library Quarterly

40(1):176-192, 1970. Considers the problems of the "library director" insofar as it concerns policy and decision making in the various aspects of conservation.

2492. Hobbs, John L. Local History and the Library. London: Andre Deutsch, 1962. With a forward by H. M. Cashmore. Partial contents: Manuscript records; local records, the present position; the care and treatment of archives. Includes bibliography.

2493. "How Long Do Books Last?" Bulletin Institute of Paper Chemistry 30, 1959-1960. (Abstract.)

2494. Hutchins, C. J. et al. "The Care and Preservation of Books," The American Book Collector 1(1), 1932.

2495. Iiams, Thomas M. "Preservation of Rare Books and Manuscripts in the Huntington Library," Library Quarterly 2, 1932.

2496. International Council of Museums. Problems of Conservation in Museums. London: George Allen and Unwin, Ltd., 1969.

2497. (Imperial Record Department, New Delhi). Notes on Preservation of Records. Simla: Government of India Press, 1941.

2498. Innes, R. F. "The Preservation of Vegetable-tanned Leather Against Deterioration," Progress in Leather Science. London: British Leather Manufacturers Research Association, 1948.

2499. Instructions for the Preservation of Books. Achimota: University College of Ghana Library, 1956.

2500. Jenkinson, Hilary. A Manual of Archive Administration. London: Percy Lund, Humphries and Co., 1965. Appendices III and IV are of interest to conservation. Appendix III: Specifications. (a) Racking and shelving, (b) Boxes, (c) Trays to contain fragile documents, (d) Folders and portfolios, (e) Filing press and file boards, (f) Repairs of bindings. Appendix IV: Some enemies of manuscripts. The book contains in addition an excellent introduction and bibliography.

2501. _____ . "Some Notes on the Preservation, Moulding and Casting of Seals," Antiquaries Journal 4:388-403, 1924. Society of Antiquaries of London.

2502. Johnson, Charles. The Care of Documents and Management of Archives. London: Society for Promoting Christian Knowledge, 1919.

2503. Jones, H. G. The Records of a Nation: Their Man-
       agement, Preservation and Use. New York:
       Atheneum, 1969. This book, by the State Archi-
       vist of North Carolina, includes constructive criti-
       cism of present archives and archives manage-
       ment.

2504. Jones, Louis C. "Primer for Preservation: A Look
       at Historic Preservation, " History News 19(6):17-
       19, 1964.

2505. Kaser, D. The Library in the Small Historical Soci-
       ety. Nashville: American Association for State
       and Local History, 1965. This Technical Leaflet
       No. 27 is good information for setting up a small
       library. It contains no information on conserva-
       tion.

2506. Kathpalia, Y. P. "Care of Books in the Libraries, "
       Indian Archives 9:147-154, 1955.

2507. Keck, Caroline. "History and Philosophy of Conser-
       vation, " Bulletin American Group International In-
       stitute for Conservation 5(1):1-3, 1964.

2508. _____. "Technical Assistance: Where to Find It;
       What to Expect, " Curator 8:3, 1965. New York.

2509. _____ (ed.). Exposition of Painting Conservation:
       Materials, Methods, Machines. Brooklyn: The
       Brooklyn Museum, 1962. These proceedings of the
       October 1962 meeting on easel painting preservation
       includes sections on ultra-violet and infra-red ex-
       amination of pictures, photography, solvents, en-
       vironment control, lighting, house keeping, etc. ,
       all of interest to librarians, archivists and histor-
       ical societies.

2510. _____. "Relationship of Conservators to Collec-
       tions and Acquisitions, " Paper read at American
       Association of Museums annual Meeting, Denver,
       May 1971.

2511. _____ and S. Keck. "Conservation in the U. S. A. :
       A Scandal, " Art News 57, 1958.

2512. Kimberly, Arthur E. "Recent Developments in Re-
       cord Preservation, " Indian Archives 3:69-72, 1949.

2513. Kimberly, A. E. and B. W. Scribner. Summary Re-
       port of the Bureau of Standards Research on Pres-
       ervation of Records. Washington: Bureau of
       Standards, 1934. Miscellaneous Publication No.
       144. This is a milestone in American library
       conservation studies and an excellent point of de-
       parture for a detailed study of the overall problem.

2514. King, A. "Suggestions for Research and Testing
       Projects Related to Paper Conservation, " Bulletin,
       American Group - International Institute for Con-
       servation 9(1):29-30, 1968.

2515. Kingery, Robert E. "The Extent of the Paper Prob-
       lem in Larger Research Collections and the Com-
       parative Costs of Available Solutions, " Permanent/
       Durable Book Paper, Summary of a Conference
       Held in Washington, D. C. , September 16, 1960.
       Richmond: Virginia State Library, 1960.

2516. Kowalik, R. and E. Czerwinska. "Sizes Used in Pa-
       per-making and Paper-binding, Their Deterioration
       and Preservation, " Blok-Notes p. 184, 1960. War-
       saw, Muzeum Mickiewicza.

2517. Kurth, W. H. and R. W. Grim. Moving a Library.
       Metuchen, N. J. : The Scarecrow Press, 1966. A
       textbook of very detailed instructions that can be
       be used as a blueprint for moving.

2518. Lamb, C. M. (ed.). The Calligrapher's Handbook.
       London: Faber and Faber, Ltd. n. d. (circa 1956).
       Contains useful information for libraries on ink,
       skins, paper, gilding and manuscript binding.

2519. Land, Robert H. "Defense of Archives Against Hu-
       man Foes, " American Archivist 19:121-138, 1956.

2520. Lawson, William P. (ed.). "A panel on conserva-
       tion: paintings, paper and wood, " Museum News
       49(5), 1971. Includes criteria for protection of
       works of art on paper.

2521. Leene, Dr. J. E. (ed.). Textile Conservation. Lon-
       don: Butterworth and Co. , 1971. A wide ranging
       treatment of the subject with contributions from
       nineteen conservators on everything from tapestries
       to leatherwork.

2522. Lewis, Harry F. "Research for the Archivist of To-
       day and Tomorrow, " The American Archivist 12:9-
       17, 1949.

2523. _____ . "The Deterioration of Book Paper in Li-
       brary Use, " The American Archivist 22, 1959.

2524. (Library Quarterly). "Deterioration and Preservation
       of Library Materials, " Library Quarterly 40, 1970.
       This volume contains the proceedings of the Thirty-
       fourth Annual Conference of the Graduate Library
       School, the University of Chicago, on the deteri-
       oration and preservation of library materials.
       Comprehensive in scope, it contains articles on
       paper, film, books, binding practices, printing,
       mass deacidification, environmental factors and

general conservation programs in libraries.
2525. Lister, Raymond. How to Identify Old Maps and
       Globes. London: George Bell and Sons, 1965.
2526. Lovett, Robert W. "Care and Handling of Non-Gov-
       ernmental Archives, " Library Trends 5:380-389,
       1957. A Bibliography is included.
2527. _____. "Care in the Handling of Manuscripts and
       Archives, " Proceedings: Literature of the Law-
       Techniques of Accession. South Hackensack, N. J. :
       Rothman & Co., 1962. American Association of
       Law Libraries, Institute for Law Libraries.
2528. _____. "The Appraisal of Older Business
       Records, " The American Archivist 15:231-239,
       1952. Contains information on storage.
2529. Lucas, A. Antiques, Their Restoration and Preser-
       vation. London: E. Arnold & Co., 1924.
2530. Ludwig, H. "Some Hints on the Care and Treatment
       of Graphics, Drawings, etc., " Neue Museumskunde
       3:158-160, 1960. Leipzig.
2531. Marconi, Bodhan L. Aesthetic Problems in Conser-
       vation of Art Objects on Paper and Parchment.
       Paris: ICOM Committee for Conservation, 1969.
       A paper presented at the 1969 Plenary Session of
       ICOM's Committee for Conservation. Amsterdam.
2532. Melia, J. A. "La conservación de libros y manu-
       scritos, " Anuario de biblioteconomia y archivono-
       mis 81-97, 1962. Universidad Nacional Autónoma
       de Mexico.
2533. Montgomery, Charles. Restoration--How Much if Any
       to Decorative Art Objects. Winterthur: The H. F.
       Dupont Winterthur Museum, 1962. A paper read
       before the 1962 American Association of Museums
       meeting. Discusses the responsibilities of cura-
       tors and conservators in regard to preservation.
2534. Mortimer, E. A. Library Books: Their Care and
       Repair. Auckland, N. Z. : University of Auckland,
       1967. Basic guidance for librarians.
2535. Moss, A. A. Application of X-rays, Gamma Rays,
       Ultra-Violet and Infra-Red Rays to the Study of
       Antiquities. London: The Museums Association,
       1954. Handbook for Museum Curators B4.
2536. Mühlethaler, Bruno. Manual on Conservation Tech-
       niques. Bern, Switzerland: Paul Haupt Verlag,
       1967. 124 pp. A short and practical introduction
       into the processes of deterioration of antiquities,
       the preventive measures and a selection of conser-
       vation treatment. Intended as a guide for small

museums and private collectors.   In German.

2537.   New Methods for the Restoration and Preservation of
Documents and Books.   Moscow: 1960.   Transla-
tion available from National Technical Information
Service, Springfield, Virginia.

2538.   "New Rx for Old Books Offered by Vatican Institute, "
Library Journal 88(12), 1963.   Vitamins for paper.

2539.   (New York State Library).   Your Book Collection: Its
Care.   Albany, N. Y. :   New York State Library,
1957.

2540.   Nordstrand, Ove K.   "The Conference on the International Cooperation for the Preservation of the
Book, " Restaurator 1(3), 1970.   Reports on the
formation of a committee for the study of an international center for book preservation and its mis-
sion to prepare a plan for the same to present to
UNESCO.

2541.   Nyuksha, J. P.   "To Preserve for Centuries, "
Bibliotekar 12:38-40, 1963.   Moscow.   Describes
the restoration practices at the State Public Library, Leningrad.

2542.   _____ .   "Lighting Appliance for Book Restoration, "
Bibliotekar 10:41-42, 1956.   Moscow.   A lighting
device for use between book pages.

2543.   Organ, R. M.   Design for Scientific Conservation of
Antiquities.   Washington: Smithsonian Institution,
1968.   Although concerned primarily with conservation of archaeological objects some of the information is equally relevant to graphic art.

2544.   "Paper Clip Investigation, " American Archivist 32:289,
1969.   Report on tests of plastic clips by University of Virginia Library, and aluminum ones by
the Barrow Laboratory.

2545.   Papers Presented at IIC - American Group Annual
Meetings, 1968-1970.   New York: Conservation
Center, New York University, 1970.   Twenty-six
papers on various aspects of conservation from
air pollution to specific techniques for restoring
artifacts.

2546.   Papritz, J.   New Methods, New Materials and New
Results in the Restoration and Conservation of Archives and in Documentary Photo Techniques Since
1950.   Report to the International Council of Archives.   Gotteborg, 1960.

2547.   The Permanence of Paper--Archives and Related
Materials: A Research Proposal.   Washington:
National Bureau of Standards, 1969.

2548. Pérotin, Yves (ed.). A Manual of Tropical Archivol-
       ogy. Paris: Mouton & Co., 1966.
2549. Petrova, L. G. "Requirements for the Preservation
       of Book Collections in the Book Storerooms of the
       Lenin State Library," Collection of Materials on
       the Preservation of Library Resources Moscow:
       1953. [2552] Available from National Technical
       Information Service, Springfield, Virginia.
2550. _____ . "Instructions for Dusting Book Collections
       and for Leaf-by-Leaf Treatment of Damaged and
       Dirty Books," (ibid.)
2551. _____ . "Instructions for Inspecting Book Collec-
       tions," (ibid.)
2552. Petrova, L. G. and L. A. Belyakova (eds.).
       Collection of Materials on the Preservation of Li-
       brary Resources. Moscow: U.S.S.R. State Li-
       brary, 1953-1958. Translation available from the
       National Technical Information Service, Springfield,
       Virginia.
2553. Plenderleith, H. J. The Conservation of Prints,
       Drawings, and Manuscripts. London: Oxford Uni-
       versity Press, 1937.
2554. _____ and A. E. A. Werner. The Conservation
       of Antiquities and Work of Art. London: Oxford
       University Press, 1971. This revised and updated
       edition of Dr. Plenderleith's 1956 volume is gen-
       erally regarded as the standard reference in the
       conservation field.
2555. _____ . "The New Science of Art Conservation,"
       UNESCO Courier 18, 1965. Some conservation
       techniques and the work of the Rome Centre.
2556. _____ and P. Philippot. "Climatology and Con-
       servation in Museums," Museum 13:243-289, 1960.
2557. Plumbe, W. S. The Preservation of Books. London:
       Oxford Press, 1964. Of particular interest for
       custodians of libraries in the tropics.
2558. Pollak, H. "Dehumidification for the Preservation of
       Documents," Mechanical World 268-270, August
       1961; 302-304, September 1961.
2559. Poole, Frazer G. "Preservation Costs and Stand-
       ards," Special Libraries 59:614-619, 1968.
2560. _____ . "Report on the 34th Annual Conference of
       the Graduate Library School of the University of
       Chicago," Library of Congress Information Bulletin
       August 1969. Summarizes the papers presented at

this conference on the deterioration and preservation of library materials.

2561. "Preservation Capsule," Manuscripts 20(2):56-60, 1968.
2562. "The Preservation of Deteriorating Books," Library Journal 91:51-56, 189-194, January 1966.
2563. "The Preservation of Deteriorating Books: An Examination of the Problem with Recommendations for a Solution," Minutes of the Sixty-fifth Meeting of the Association of Research Libraries, Washington, D.C., January 24, 1965.
2564. "Preservation of Records in Libraries," Science 79(2043):176, 1934. A summary of the U.S. Bureau of Standards studies.
2565. (Preservation Grants). "Massachusetts Council Preservation Grants," History News 59(5), 1969. Describes financial assistance available from Massachusetts Council on the Arts and Humanities.
2566. Problems of Conservation in Museums. Paris: International Council of Museums, 1969.
2567. "Protection of Documents," American Archivist 1:142, 1938; 14:372, 1951; 15:280, 1952; 16:125, 181, 234, 1953; 17:110, 370, 1954; 19:122, 130, 134, 1956; 20:36, 1957.
2568. "The Question of Paper Deterioration: Which Books Should be Saved?" Book Production Industry 46(1), 1970. The printing industry's point of view.
2569. [No entry.]
2570. Ranganathan, S. R. Social Bibliography or Physical Bibliography for Librarians. Delhi, India: University of Delhi, 1952. Library Science Series, No. 4.
2571. Rasch, R. H.; M. B. Shaw, and G. W. Bicking. "Highly Purified Wood Fibers as Paper-Making Material," Journal of Research of the National Bureau of Standards 7:765-782, 1931. Discussion of the increase in paper permanence as a result of the selection of high quality fibers for making it.
2572. Rawlins, F. I. G. "Science in the Care of Museum Objects," Museums Journal 54, 1955.
2573. _____. "Scientific Methods in the Care of Works of Art," Research 11, 1958. London.
2574. _____. "The Scientific Outlook in Conservation," Museums Journal 61, 1961.
2575. Ray, Gordon N. "The Future of the Book," American Library Association Bulletin September 1966.

2576. Recent Advances in Conservation. (Thomson, G. ed.)
       London: Butterworths, 1963.   Papers presented
       at the 1961 Rome Conference of the International
       Institute for Conservation.

2577. "Records Protection at Tenneco," OFFICE 63(6):101-
       112, 1966.

2578. Records Protection in an Uncertain World.   Salt Lake
       City: Church of Jesus Christ of Latter-Day Saints,
       1969.

2579. Reid of Robertland, David and Anne Ross.   The Con-
       servation of Non-Metallic Seals.   Glasgow: Glas-
       gow University Archives, 1968.   Discusses the
       preservation of thermoplastic seals and wafers.

2580. "Report of the Committee for Paper Problems," Bul-
       letin of the American Group--The International In-
       stitute for Conservation of Historic and Artistic
       Works 9:29-30, October 1968.

2581. Restoration and Preservation of Library Resources,
       Documents and Books.   (translated from the Rus-
       sian) Jerusalem: Israel Program for Scientific
       Translations, 1965.   A compendium on the restora-
       tion and conservation of books as practiced in the
       U.S.S.R.   This collection of the work by the State
       Library and Academy of Sciences of the U.S.S.R.
       is also available from the National Technical In-
       formation Service, Springfield, Virginia.   [2552].

2582. (Rome Centre).   Problems of Conservation in Muse-
       ums.   London: George Allen & Unwin, Ltd., 1969.
       This selection of papers to the joint meeting of the
       ICOM Committees on laboratories and the care of
       paintings is the 8th of the Rome Centre's important
       publications.   Subjects presented are training of
       restorers, deterioration and treatment of wood, the
       deterioration of cellulose, the lamination of docu-
       ments.

2583. Rorimer, J. J.   Ultraviolet Rays and Their Use in
       the Examination of Works of Art.   New York:
       Metropolitan Museum of Art, 1931.

2584. Roskova, Galina S.   "Hygiene and Restoration of Book
       Stock at Libraries," Restaurator 1(3), 1970.   De-
       scribes functions of the department's sections for
       preventive conservation, restoration and research.

2585. Ruscoe, Lewis D.   "On the Need of Caution in Scrap-
       ping Our Old Manuscripts," Old-Time New Eng-
       land 35(4):67-70, 1945.

2586. Sanders, J. P.   "The Preservation of Manuscripts
       and Bindings," Library Journal.

57:336-338, 1932 and Science 76:277-278, 1932.

2587. Santucci, L. "The Application of Chemical and Physical Methods to Conservation of Archival Materials," Recent Advances in Conservation. London: Butterworths, 1963. [2614] A review of the history of the scientific approach to conservation with detailed bibliographic references.

2588. Savage, George. The Art and Antique Restorer's Handbook. New York: Frederick A. Praeger, 1967. London: Barrie and Rockliff Ltd., 1967. A dictionary of materials and processes.

2589. Schulz, H. C. "The Care and Storage of Manuscripts in the Huntington Library," Library Quarterly 5:78-86, 1935.

2590. Scribner, B. W. "Report on Bureau of Standards Research on Preservation of Records," Library Quarterly 1:409-420, 1931.

2591. _____. Preservation of Newspaper Records. Washington: U.S. Government Printing Office, 1934. National Bureau of Standards Miscellaneous Publication No. 145.

2592. _____. "Preservation of Records in Libraries," Library Quarterly 4:371-383, 1934.

2593. Scriven, Margaret. "Preservation and Restoration of Library Materials," Special Libraries 47(10):439-448, 1956.

2594. Shaffer, Norman J. "Library of Congress Pilot Preservation Project," College and Research Libraries 30:5-11, 1969.

2595. Sherwood, P. W. "Corrosion Inhibitors," Australian Paint Journal 6(11):31-33, 35, 37, 1965.

2596. "Short-Term Course on Care of Museum Objects," ICOM News 20(6):210, 1967.

2597. Siegl, T. "Conservation at the Philadelphia Museum of Art," Philadelphia Museum of Art Bulletin 62(291), 1966.

2598. Smith, Richard D. "New approaches to preservation," The Library Quarterly 40(1):139-171, 1970. Discusses problems involved in preserving library materials and outlines an ideal preservation program.

2599. _____. "Guidelines for preservation," Special Libraries May - June 1968. Recommends a written preservation policy for each library.

2600. Spawn, Willman. "The Conservation of Books and Papers," Ontario Library Review 46:5-7, 1962.

2601. Spyers-Duran, Peter. Moving Library Materials.
       Chicago: American Library Association, 1965.
       A 63-page monograph on the problem of moving
       books from one building to another.

2602. Stevens, S. K.; Clifford L. Lord, and Albert B.
       Corey. "Making Our Heritage Live, " Bulletin of
       the American Association for State and Local His-
       tory 2(5), 1951. Nashville, Tenn.

2603. Stolow, Nathan. "The Importance of Traditional Art
       Museum Practice, " The Curator 12(1):23-24, 1969.
       Discusses the different points of view between con-
       servators and other museum personnel in regard
       to preservation.

2604. _____ . "The Technical Organization of an Interna-
       tional Exhibition, " Museum 21(3):181-240, 1968.
       This report of the planning before Expo 68 dis-
       cusses among other topics architectural planning,
       air conditioning, lighting, security, exhibiting,
       storage.

2605. Storm, Colton. "Care, Maintenance, and Restora-
       tion, " in H. Richard Ancher's Rare Book Collec-
       tions: Some Theoretical and Practical Suggestions
       for Use by Librarians and Students. Chicago:
       American Library Association, 1961.

2606. Subramanian, R. "Chemical Conservation, " Handbook
       of Museum Technique. Madras: Government of
       Madras, 1960. Includes treatment of paper.

2607. Suri, V. S. "Care and Preservation of Old and Rare
       Materials in Libraries, " Indian Librarian 8-13,
       March 1954.

2608. _____ . "Some Hints on the Health of Contents of
       Libraries, " Indian Librarian 147-153, March 1954.

2609. Tascon, D. Antonio Matilla. Administrative Archives.
       Madrid: September 1968. A paper presented at the
       Sixth International Congress on Archives. Contains
       information on buildings and shelving.

2610. Tauber, Maurice F. "Conservation Comes of Age, "
       Library Trends 4:215-221, 1956.

2611. _____ (ed.). Technical Services in Libraries. New
       York: Columbia University Press, 1954. See
       Chapters 15-17, "Conservation of Library Mate-
       rials. "

2612. Tests and Procedures for Books and Book Components.
       Hoboken, New Jersey: United States Testing Com-
       pany, 1957.

2613. Thompson, L. S. "Notes on Bibliokleptomania, "
       Bulletin 48(9), 1944. New York Public Library.

Dr. Thompson's review of book pilfering over the centuries will enlighten those whose duty is to protect their books. Many footnote references to other literature on same subject.

2614. Thomson, Garry (ed.). Recent Advances in Conservation. London: Butterworths, 1963. These contributions to the 1961 Rome Conference of the International Institute for Conservation of Historic and Artistic Works include articles on museum climate, fungicides and insecticides, and education and training of conservators all with detailed bibliographies.

2615. "Times to Print Copies on Durable Rag Paper," New York Times December 5, 1926.

2616. Tribolet, Harold. "Trends in Preservation," Library Trends 13(2), October 1964.

2617. _____. "Preservation and restoration," Manuscripts 18(4):6-10, 1966.

2618. Turner, Robert W. S. "To Repair or Despair?" American Archivist 20:319-334, 1957.

2619. (UNESCO). The Conservation of Cultural Property. Paris: UNESCO, 1968. Excellent information on climate control, materials, pest control, restoration techniques, etc.

2620. (U. S. Library of Congress). Annual Report of the Librarian of Congress for Fiscal Year Ended June 30, 1968. Washington: Government Printing Office, 1969. Includes report of progress in preservation.

2621. (U. S. National Archives). Annual Report of the Archivist of the United States for the Fiscal Year Ended June 30, 1936. Washington: U. S. Government Printing Office, 1936. Preservation of records.

2622. (U. S. National Bureau of Standards). Preservation of the Declaration of Independence and the Constitution of the U. S. Washington: U. S. Bureau of Standards, 1951. Circular No. 505.

2623. (U. S. National Park Service). "Museum Planning; The Exhibit Room and Its Equipment; Museum Exhibits," Field Manual for Museums. (Ned J. Burns). Washington: U. S. Government Printing Office, 1941.

2624. Usilton, Bertha M. Subject Index to Technical Studies in the Field of Fine Arts. Pittsburgh: Tamworth Press, 1965. Key to the wealth of information in the ten volumes (1932-1942) of the Fogg Museum's conservation journal.

2625. Vyskocil, Josef. "The central conservation workshop of the State Library of the Czechoslovak Socialist Republic," UNESCO Bulletin for Libraries 20:126-128, 1966.

2626. Walton, R. P. "Causes and Prevention of Deterioration in Book Materials," Bulletin 33:235-266, 1929. New York Public Library. Includes a chronological arrangement to 1929 of literature on the preservation of paper taken principally from paper periodicals.

2627. Warren, Jenney. "Permanence and Durability; Different Qualities and Needs," Publishers' Weekly 185(5):121, 124, 1964. Comments on the Barrow reports by the director of S. D. Warren Co.

2628. Waters, Peter. "In Search of a New Philosophy of Conservation and Restoration," Guild of Book Workers Journal 7(2), 1968-1969. Waters' talk to the Guild at the Morgan Library, 27 February 1969.

2629. _____. Problems of Restoring Old Books. Paper read to the Leeds Philosophical and Literary Society, March 1970. Explores the philosophical climate in which the restorer works and examines some of the requirements for establishing conservation principles in the general context of the preservation of library materials.

2630. Werner, Anthony E. "The Preservation of Archives," Journal of the Society of Archivists 1:282-288, 1959.

2631. Williams, Edwin E. "Magnitude of the Paper Deterioration Problem as Measured by a National Union Catalog Sample," College and Research Libraries 23, 1962.

2632. Williams, Gordon R. "The Preservation of Deteriorating Books," Library Journal 91:51-56, 189-194, 1966. A summary of findings with recommendations for a solution published by the Committee on Preservation of Library Materials of the Association of Research Libraries. The Committee, set up in 1960, concerned itself with preservation of materials in research libraries; the use of the best preservation methods; establishment of a central agency to assure the physical and lasting preservation of at least one specimen of all disintegrating books; the search for federal support; the establishment of bibliographical control of microforms through the National Register of Microforms.

2633. Wilson, W. K. "Discussion of New Approaches to Preservation," Library Quarterly 40:171-175, 1970.

2634. Winger, H. W. and R. D. Smith (eds). Deterioration and Preservation of Library Materials. Chicago: University of Chicago Press, 1970.

2635. Wood, G. W. "Books and Documents: Protection from Insect Damage. A Survey of the Problem and Methods of Control," Pesticides Abstracts and News Summary Section A, 2, Maggio, 1956.

2636. Yabrova, R. R. "Influence of Temperature and The Air Humidity on the Aging of Paper," Chemical Abstracts 54, 1960. Illustrates the importance of preventive measures to control damage by environment.

2637. _____. "The Prevention of Aging of Books and Newspapers," Collection of Materials on the Preservation of Library Resources (Moscow, 1953). Springfield, Va.: National Technical Information Service, 1964.

2638. Your Book Collection: Its Care. Albany, N.Y.: New York State Library, Library Extension Division, 1957.

2639. Zigrosser, C. and C. M. Gaehde. A Guide to the Collecting and Care of Original Prints. New York: Crown Publishers, 1965.

ENVIRONMENTAL CONTROL

2640. Baldwin, Malcolm and James K. Page, Jr. (eds.). Law and the Environment. New York: Walker and Company, 1970.

2641. Bhatnagar, J. L. and R. Kishore. "Use of Silica Gel for Reducing Relative Humidity on a Small Scale," Conservation of Cultural Property in India. New Delhi: National Museum, 1966.

2642. Brooks, C. E. P. "Climate and the Deterioration of Materials," Quarterly Journal of the Royal Meteorological Society 72:87-97, 1946.

2643. Cameron, Duncan. "Environmental Control: A Theoretical Solution," Museum News 46:17-21, 1968.

2644. Carver, T. H. "Control of Atmospheric Pollutants and Maintenance of Stable Climatic Conditions in Museum Buildings," Museum Climatology. London:

International Institute for Conservation, 1968.

2645. "Climatology and Conservation in Museums," Museum
13(4), 1960. A valuable review of the subject.

2646. Control of Museum Environment. London: International Institute for Conservation, 1967.

2647. Denninger, E. "Problems of Climate and Climate
Control," Nachrichtenblatt der Denkmalflege in
Baden-Wurttenberg 8(3):64-65, 1965. West Germany. Discussion of climate control in buildings.

2648. Environmental Effects on Materials and Equipment.
Washington: Prevention of Deterioration Center,
National Academy of Sciences--National Research
Council, 1945-1965.

2649. Feller, R. L. "Control of Deterioration Effects of
Light Upon Museum Objects," Museum 17:57-98,
1964.

2650. Franizitta, G. "Relative Humidity in Rooms and Its
Dependence Upon the Thermal Regime," La Termo-
tecnica 5:283-286, 1966. Milan.

2651. Gall, Gunter. "The Climatic Conditions in a Full-
Glass Showcase," Museumskunde 29(1):31-32, 1960.
In German.

2652. Gray, Oscar S. Environmental Law, Cases and
Materials. Washington: The Bureau of National
Affairs, Inc., 1970.

2653. Haagen-Smit, A. J. "Atmospheric Pollution," Paper
Given at IIC-AG Meeting, May-June 1969. Those
who are interested in preserving materials,
especially art objects, should be aware of the nature of the new pollutants and their effect in order
that the proper protection can be given against the
corrosive effects of the present day pollution in
the air.

2654. Hughson, R. U. "Controlling Air Pollution," Chemical Engineering News 73(8):71-90, 1966. Washington.

2655. Knightbridge, A. A. H. "Sulphur Dioxide Test Papers," Journal of the Society of Archivists 4(1),
1970. Describes W. H. Langwell's simple tests
for the presence of SO_2.

2656. Museum Climatology. London: International Institute
for Conservation, 1968. Proceedings of London
Conference on Museum Climatology.

2657. Museums Journal 64(1), June 1964. A special issue
devoted to the scientific aspects of museums and
art galleries. Much of this information is

applicable to library conservation.

2658. Plenderleith, H. J. and P. Philippot. "Climatology and Conservation in Museums," Museum 13(4):242-289, 1960.

2659. Poole, Fraser G. (ed.). The Library Environment: Aspects of Interior Planning. Chicago: American Library Association, 1965. Proceedings of the 1964 Library Equipment Institute in St. Louis.

2660. Stolow, Nathan. Controlled Environment for Works of Art in Transit. London: Butterworths, 1966.

2661. _____. "Temperature and Humidity as Regards Preservation of Collections." Paper read at American Asso. of Museums Annual Meeting, Denver, May 1971.

2662. Thomson, Garry (ed.). London Conference on Museum Climatology. London: International Institute for Conservation, 1968. Papers presented at the London Conference by international authorities.

2663. Tottle, H. F. "Strong Room Climate," Archives 2:393, 1950. British Records Association.

2664. Veitch, F. P. "Paper Specifications," U.S. Dept. of Agriculture Report 89, 1909. This early study of durability and economy in paper for permanent records stressed the importance of atmosphere control long before the advent of air conditioning.

2665. Vogt, Paul. "On the Control of the Climate Conditions in Museum Showrooms," Museumskunde 29(1):26-30, 1960. (In German) A description is given of a controlled heating system combined with air humidification installed in the new building of the Museum Folkwang in Essen.

AIR CONDITIONING

2666. "Air Conditioning and Lighting from the Point of View of Conservation," Museums Journal 63(1-2), 1963.

2667. Air Conditioning and Ventilating Systems Other Than Residence Type. Boston: National Fire Protection Association, 1961.

2668. Air Conditions and the Comfort of Workers. New York: Metropolitan Life Insurance Company, 1930. Industrial Health Series No. 5.

2669. Amdur, Elias J. "Humidity Control - Isolated Area Plan," Museum News 43:58-60, 1964. One chart. Technical Supplement No. 4, Part 2. Detailed information about applying this concept to existing

structures as well as to new construction, an alter-
native when total air conditioning is not feasible.

2670. Beach, R. F. and W. H. Martin. "Union Theological
Seminary Air-Conditions Its Library," College and
Research Libraries 18:297-301, 1957. Practical
experience and conclusions in the air-conditioning
of an existing library building, of value to the librarian considering such a step.

2671. Belaya, I. K. "Instructions on the Use of Bactericidal Circulation Devices for the Disinfection of Air
in Libraries," Collections of Materials on the
Preservation of Library Resources. Moscow,
1958. Available from National Technical Information Service, Springfield, Virginia.

2672. Bell, Morton. "The Cost of Clean Air," Air Conditioning, Heating and Ventilation 65:41-46, July
1968.

2673. Bhatnagar, J. L. and R. Kishore. "Use of Silica
Gel for Reducing RH on a Small Scale," Conservation of Cultural Property in India 1:102-105, 1966.
A proposal for humidity control without air conditioning.

2674. Boustead, W. M. "Dehumidification in Museum Storage Areas," Museum Climatology. London: International Institute for Conservation, 1968.

2675. Brommelle, N. S. "Technical Services - Air Conditioning and Lighting from the Point of View of
Conservation," Museums Journal 63(1-2):32-36,
1963.

2676. Buck, Richard D. "A Specification for Museum Air
Conditioning," Museum News 43:53-57, 1964.
Technical Supplement, No. 4, Part 1. One chart,
seven references. Applies equally to libraries and
archives.

2677. Buck, R. D. and others. "Humidity Indicators,"
ICA Newsletter 7(1), 1969. An interim report on
the behavior of two moderately priced non-record-
ing temperature/humidity indicators. Reports that
the accuracy of the humidity readings is subject
to question on this type of instrument.

2678. Carr, D. S. and B. C. Harris. "Solutions for Main-
taining Constant Relative Humidity," Industrial Engineering Chemistry 41:2014, 1949.

2679. Cecil, Raymond J. "Libraries: A Survey of Current
Lighting Practice," Light and Lighting 55:228-241,
1962.

2680. Chan Kai Meng. "A Dehumidifier For the Personal Library," Malayan Library Journal 1(2):13, 1961.

2681. Clayton, Nelson W. and George H. Fudge. "Chemical Dehumidification Protects Microfilm Records Stored in Mountain Vaults," Heating, Piping and Air Conditioning 38(10):127-129, 1966.

2682. Cutter, C. A. "Heat Regulation," Library Journal 11:365-366, 1886.

2683. Dauphinee, G. S.; F. H. Munkelt, and H. Sleik. Air Conservation Engineering. New York: W. S. Connor Engineering Corp., 1944.

2684. Gerassimova, N. G. "On the Use of Inhibitors of Atmospheric Corrosion for the Conservation of Metal Objects in Museums," Soob. VCNILKR 19:112-123, 1967. English summary.

2685. Grad, Ian and Alfred Greenberg. "Air Conditioning for Books and People," Architectural Record 121:231-234, 1957.

2686. Howarth, F. Hugh. "An Approach to Air Conditioning," Museum Climatology. London: International Institute for Conservation, 1968.

2687. Kaplun, E. A. "Stringent Air Conditioning Control for Library's Rare Works," Heating, Piping and Air Conditioning 36(2):103-105, 1964. Describes two air conditioning systems installed to fit the exacting requirements of the Berg collection in the New York Public Library.

2688. Keally, Francis and Henry C. Meyer. "Air Conditioning as a Means of Preserving Books and Records," American Archivist 12:280-282, 1949. A list of references on the subject of air conditioning.

2689. Kimberly, A. E. and A. L. Emley. A Study of the Removal of Sulphur Dioxide from Library Air. Washington: U. S. Government Printing Office, 1933. U. S. Bureau of Standards Miscellaneous Publication 142.

2690. Kuhn, H. "The Effect of Oxygen, RH and Temperature on the Fading Rate of Water Colours," Conference on Museum Climatology. London: International Institute for Conservation, 1967.

2691. Lewis, Logan L. "Air Conditioning for Museums," Museum 10(2):132-147, 1957.

2692. Macintyre, J. "Air Conditioning for Mantegna's Cartoons at Hampton Court Palace," Technical Studies in the Field of Fine Arts 2:171-184, 1934.

2693. Measurement of Humidity. London: National Physical Laboratory, 1953.

2694. "Modern Trends in Conservation," Museums Journal 60, 1961.

2695. Nelson, Elmer. "Do We Understand Museum Air Conditioning," Curator 11(2), 1968. Includes a carefully selected further reading list of forty-two references.

2696. Padfield, Tim. "The Control of Relative Humidity and Air Pollution in Showcases and Picture Frames," Studies in Conservation 11(1), 1966.

2697. Paribeni, M. "The Application of Air Conditioning Techniques to the Conservation of Works of Art," Acts of the 49th Conference 1967. Italian Society for the Progress of Science.

2698. Plenderleith, H. J. and P. Philippot. "Climatology and Conservation in Museums," Museum 13, 1960. Much useful data. Written for the keeper of small establishments as well as large organizations.

2699. Pollak, H. "Dehumidification for the Preservation of Documents," Mechanical World 141:268-270, 1961.

2700. _____. "Dehumidification for the Preservation of Documents," Mechanical World 141:302-304, 1961.

2701. Rawlins, F. I. G. "The Control of Temperature and Humidity in Relation to Works of Art," Museums Journal 41, 1942.

2702. Solvason, K. R. "Air Conditioning Processes," Canadian Building Digest 108, 1968. Describes the four basic processes of treating air for comfort air conditioning.

2703. _____. "Air Conditioning Systems," Canadian Building Digest 109, 1969. Describes the capabilities and limitations of some of the common systems.

2704. Sourwein, G. K. "Air Conditioning for Protection," Heating, Piping and Air Conditioning 13:311, 1941. Atmosphere control from the point of view of a rare book custodian.

2705. Stokes, R. H. and R. H. Robinson. "Standard Solutions for Humidity Control at 25 degrees C," Industrial Engineering Chemistry 41:2013, 1949.

2706. "Stolow on Air Conditioning," Museum News Nov. / Dec. 1965.

2707. Stolow, Nathan. "Fundamental Case Design for Humidity Sensitive Collections," Museum News 44:45-52, 1966. Washington, D. C.

2708. Stout, George L. "Air Conditioning in Storage,"
       W. A. M. News Bull. & Calendar 17:29-31, 1952.
       Illus.
2709. Thomson, Garry. "Air Pollution--A Review for Con-
       servation Chemists," Studies in Conservation 10(4),
       1965. The Journal of the International Institute for
       Conservation of Historic and Artistic Works.
2710. _____. "Relative Humidity Variation with Temper-
       ature in a Case Containing Wood," Studies in Con-
       servation 9(4):153-169, 1964.
2711. Toishi, K. "Humidity Control in a Closed Package,"
       Studies in Conservation 4:81-87, 1959.
2712. _____. "Relative Humidity in a Closed Package,"
       Recent Advances in Conservation. London: Butter-
       worths, 1961.
2713. Tottle, H. F. "Strong-Room Climate," Archives
       2:387-402, 1956.
2714. Werner, A. E. A. "Heating and Ventilation," Muse-
       ums Journal 57:159-166, 1957. Outlines measures
       to minimize danger to museum and library mate-
       rials.
2715. Whitby, Kenneth T.; Dale A. Lundgren; Andrew R.
       McFarland, and Richard C. Jordan. "Evaluation
       of Air Cleaners for Occupied Spaces," Journal of
       the Air Pollution Control Association 11:503-515,
       1961.
2716. Wilson, A. G. "Ventilation and Air Quality," Cana-
       dian Building Digest 110, 1970. A review of the
       nature of the ventilation process in controlling the
       level of contaminants in space.

       LIGHTING

2717. Black, Milton J. "Lighting," Museum News 47(5),
       1969. Within the case devices for artifact illumin-
       ation.
2718. Brommelle, N. S. "Air Conditioning and Lighting
       From the Point of View of Conservation," Museums
       Journal 63(1-2), 1965.
2719. _____ and J. B. Harris. "Museum Lighting, Part
       I," Museums Journal 61(3):169-177, 1961; "Part II,
       Artificial Lighting and Museum Display," Museums
       Journal 61(4):259-267, 1962; "Part III, Aspects of
       the Effect of Light on Deterioration," Museums
       Journal 62(1):337-346, 1962; "Part IV, Viewing the
       Object," Museums Journal 62(3):178-186, 1962.

2720.   Coleman, R. A. and W. H. Peacock. "Ultraviolet
        Absorbers," Textile Research Journal 28:784-791,
        1958. Lancaster, Pa.

2721.   Cooper, B. S. "Fluorescent Lighting in Museums,"
        Museums Journal 53(11):279-290, 1954.

2722.   Elenbaas, W. Fluorescent Lamps and Illumination.
        Paris: Dunod, 1963.

2723.   Feller, Robert L. "Considerations Regarding the Il-
        lumination of Museum Objects," Exposition of Paint-
        ing Conservation. Brooklyn: The Brooklyn Muse-
        um, 1962. Discusses the importance of distribu-
        tion, color and intensity of illumination of art ob-
        jects.

2724.   _____ . "Control of Deteriorating Effects of Light
        Upon Museum Objects," Museum 17(2), 1964. En-
        tire issue. Recommended reading.

2725.   _____ . "Control of Deteriorating Effects of Light
        on Museum Objects: Heating Effects of Illumina-
        tion by Incandescent Light," Museum News 46(9):33-
        47, 1968.

2726.   Geigy, A. G. "Protecting Organic Materials From
        the Effects of Ultraviolet Radiation and Oxidation,"
        British Patent 991, 320, May 5, 1965. Uses ad-
        ditives to plastic formulas.

2727.   Genard, J. "Extreme Ultraviolet Radiation from
        Tubular Fluorescent Lamps and Its Effect on Mu-
        seum Lighting," Museum 5(1), 1952.

2728.   General Anilin & Film Corporation. "Protecting
        Leather from U. V. and c. Radiations," Brit. Pat.
        1, 020, 507 (7. 3. 1962).

2729.   Hall, E. T. "An Ultraviolet Monitor for Museums,"
        Museum Climatology. London: International In-
        stitute for Conservation, 1968.

2730.   Harris, J. B. "Museum Lighting," Museums Journal
        63(1-2):36-42, 1963.

2731.   _____ . "Practical Aspects of Lighting as Related
        to Works of Art," Museum Climatology. London:
        International Institute for Conservation, 1968.

2732.   Harrison, Laurence S. "Museum Lighting Studies in
        a Laboratory," Architectural Record 104(6):137-142,
        1948.

2733.   Hatt, Robert T. "Seven Lighting Problems - Seven
        Solutions," Curator 3(4):361-370, 1960.

2734.   Hawthorne, J. O. et al. "Method of Protecting Mate-
        rial Against the Effects of Light," Prevention of
        Deterioration Abstracts 18, 1960. Protection by
        chemical treatment.

2735. Heorghita, F. "Light in Museums," Revista Muzeeler
       4:322-324, 1968.

2736. Hewitt, H. and A. Vause (eds.). Lamps and Lighting.
       New York: American Elsevier, 1966. A compre-
       hensive manual prepared by the British Lighting
       Industries.

2737. Holway, Alfred N. and Dorothea Janeson. Good
       Lighting for People at Work in Reading Rooms and
       Offices. Boston: Division of Research, Graduate
       School of Business Administration, Harvard Univer-
       sity, 1947. Summary of study on "good lighting"
       for reading purposes.

2738. Howard, Richard F. "Museum Lighting," Museum
       News 40(7):22-27, 1962.

2739. ICOM Commission for Lighting of Museum Objects.
       Use of Fluorescent Light in Museums. Paris:
       ICOM, 1953.

2740. Jones, William K. Preparing Exhibits: The Use of
       Plexiglass. Nashville: American Association for
       State and Local History, 1969. The Association's
       Technical Leaflet 49.

2741. Jordan, Robert T. "Lighting in University Libraries,"
       UNESCO Bulletin for Libraries 17:326-336, 1963.

2742. Kelly, Richard. "Museum Lighting, Part III," Muse-
       um News 37(3):16-19, 1959.

2743. Keyes, D. M. "Library Lighting," Library Journal
       86, 1961.

2744. Krollau, E. K. Effects of Lighting on Museum Col-
       lections and Preservation Means. Moscow: State
       Museum of Russia, n. d.

2745. Kühn, Hermann. "The Exhibition of Light Sensitive
       Museum Objects in Nitrogen Containing Show-cases,"
       Museumskunde 36(1):7-10, 1967. (In German.)
       The author was able to show that light damage also
       takes place when UV radiation is excluded. It is
       much easier to maintain permanently a nitrogen at-
       mosphere in a show-case than a vacuum.

2746. Lape, P. B and D. V. Ryer. How to Measure Light.
       Newburyport, Massachusetts: International Light
       Inc., 1968.

2747. "Lighting," Museums Journal 63(1-2), 1963.

2748. Lusk, Carroll B. "Museum Lighting," Museum News
       38(2):28-31, 1959.

2749. _____. "Museum Lighting I, II, III," Museum
       News 49(3, 4, and 6), 1970-71.

2750. Lynes, J. A. Principles of Natural Lighting. New
       York: American Elsevier, 1968. A thorough guide

to the principles of natural lighting including the
techniques and instruments used in lighting research.

2751. Mason, Ellsworth. "A Guide to the Librarian's Responsibility in Achieving Quality in Lighting and
Ventilation," Library Journal 92:201-206, 1967.

2752. McCandless, Stanley. "Museum Lighting, Part I,"
Museum News 37(1):8-11, 1959; "Museum Lighting,
Part II," Museum News 37(2):8-11, 1959.

2753. Padfield, Tim. "A Simple Ultraviolet Radiation De-
tector for Museum Use," Studies in Conservation
12(1), 1967.

2754. "Plastic Filters Reduce Light Damage in Museums,"
Plastics Industry 13, 1955.

2755. "Plastic Light Filters," Museums Journal 55, 1956.

2756. Plexiglass Ultraviolet Filtering Formulation. Philadelphia: Rohm & Haas Co., 1968. Bulletin
PL612a discusses filters for fluorescent lights and
windows.

2757. Protection of Exhibits from Degradation Caused by
U.V. Radiation. London: Imperial Chemical In-
dustries, n.d. Technical Data Sheet PX.TD 229.
Describes use of "Persfix" sheets for screening
U.V. component out of light.

2758. [No entry.]

2759. "Protection of Record and Exhibit Material Against
Light," News Bulletin June 1937. Washington:
National Bureau of Standards, 1937.

2760. Protective Display Lighting of Historical Documents.
Washington: U.S. Government Printing Office,
1953. U.S. National Bureau of Standards, Circular 538.

2761. Rawson-Bottom, W. E. and J. B. Harris. "Artificial
Lighting as Applied to Museums and Art Galleries,"
Transactions of the Illuminating Engineering Society
23(1), 1958.

2762. Rawson-Bottom, W. E. and B. S. Cooper. "Museum
Lighting," Museums Journal 57(7):167-173, 1957.
A review of lighting and effects of lighting on arti-
facts.

2763. Rohm & Haas Co. Plexiglass Ultraviolet Filtering
Formulations. Philadelphia: Rohm & Haas Co.,
November 1968. Bulletin No. 612a.

2764. Scott, H. P. "Lighting and Protection for an Art
Museum," Electrical Construction and Maintenance

35, 1956.
2765. Thomson, Garry. "A New Look at Colour Rendering, Level of Illumination and Protection from Ultraviolet Radiation in Museum Lighting," Studies in Conservation 6:49-70, 1961.
2766. _____. "Annual Exposure to Light Within Museums," Studies in Conservation 12(2), 1967.
2767. _____. "Calibration and Use of a Ultraviolet Monitor," Museum Climatology. London: International Institute for Conservation, 1968.
2768. _____. Conservation and Museum Lighting. London: Museums Association, 1970. A six-page information sheet by a well-known authority.
2769. _____. Products and Instruments Suitable for Use in Museums for Protection Against Damage by Light. Unpublished paper presented at 1969 plenary meeting of the ICOM Committee on Conservation in Amsterdam. Photostat copies available from Rome Centre, 256 Via Cavour, Rome.
2770. _____. "Visible and Ultraviolet Radiation," Museums Journal 57:27-32, 1957.
2771. _____; R. L. Feller; L. Gayward, and H. Kühn. Products and Instruments Suitable for Use in Museums for Protection Against Damage by Light. Paris: ICOM, Committee for Conservation, 1969. A discussion of filters, lamps, radiation detectors, controls, glazing, meters, etc. for museum use all of which is equally applicable to libraries and archives.
2772. _____ and E. T. Hall. "An Ultraviolet Monitor for Museums," Achaeometry 10:120-126, 1967.
2773. Thordemann, B. and G. H. Riviere. "The Use of Fluorescence Lamps in Museums," Museumskunde 31(3):89-94, 1962. (In German) A general consideration of the problems is followed by a sequence of practical recommendations for the use by museum directors and curators.
2774. Toishi, Kenzo and Rikuo Ishikawa. "Characteristics of Light Sources Suitable For Use in Museums and Selection of Fluorescent Lighting," Science for Conservation 4:1-10, 1968.
2775. Use of Fluorescent Lighting in Museums. Paris: ICOM, 1953. Practical advice on museum lighting of interest to librarians and archivists.
2776. Yoshida, Zenichi and Hiroshi Miyoshi. "Ultraviolet Absorbers," Yuki Gosei Kagaku Kyokaishi 25(11):1058-1062, 1967. Reviews the use of

ultraviolet absorbers, problems of practical use,
and recent studies on ultraviolet absorbers.
2777. Zittel, Bernhard. "Lighting and Ventilation of Archival Stacks," Belichtung und Beluftung von Archiv-
magazinen, 1969. (In German) Well documented
study of European and American literature on the
subject.
2778. Zoege Von Manteuffel, Claus. "Fluorescence Lamps
in the Museum," Museumskunde 31(3):95-102, 1962.
(In German) A short description of the essential
properties of fluorescence lamps--their advantages
and disadvantages in technical and esthetic terms.

FIRE PROTECTION [See under VI. When Disaster Strikes]

SECURITY

2779. (Alarm systems) American Archivist 30(3):288, 1969.
2780. Bostick, William A. "What is the State of Museum
Security?" Museum News 46(5):13-19, 1968.
2781. Chapman, Joseph M. "Stepping Up Security," Museum News 43(3):18-21, 1965.
2782. "Emerging Measures," Museum News 43(6), 1965.
2783. Francis, Sir Frank. "Security," Museums Journal
63(1-2):28-32, 1963.
2784. Grossman, Albert J. "Television - Museum Watch-
dog," Museum News 44(3):22-24, November 1965.
2785. Howard, Richard F. Museum Security. Washington:
American Association of Museums, 1958.
2786. Karl, Heinz. "Protection of Museums Against Loss,
Burglary and Theft," Museumskunde 31(3):25-45,
1962. The author who is a professional criminolo-
gist gives a critical review of the motives of the
wrongdoer, the experience made with several protective means and warning systems. By modern
technical means security for the museum collections can well be warranted. (In German).
2787. Keck, Caroline. Safeguarding Your Collections in
Travel. Nashville, Tenn.: American Association
for State and Local History, 1970. This manual
has useful information for librarians.

2788.   _____. "Security Depends on People, " Curator
         10(1):54-59, 1967. A plea for trained people to
         perform the myriad prerequisites of conservation
         in its steadily multiplying forms.

2789.   _____ et al. A Primer on Museum Security.
         Cooperstown, New York: New York State Historical
         Association, 1966. Edited tape transcripts of the
         NYSHA 1964 seminar on this subject.

2790.   Lawton, J. B. and H. T. Block. "Museum Insur-
         ance, " Curator 9(4), 1966.

2791.   Little, David B. "Safeguarding Works of Art: Trans-
         portation, Records and Insurance, " History News
         18(7), 1963.

2792.   Michaels, A. F. "Security and the Museum, " Muse-
         um News 43(3):11-16, 1964.

2793.   Montana, Joseph A. "Evaluating security equipment, "
         Administrative Management 28(4):66-73, 1967.

2794.   Noblecourt, Andre F. "The Protection of Museums
         Against Theft, " Museum 17(4), 1964. The entire
         issue of this UNESCO journal is devoted to the
         protection of museum objects against fire and theft.
         Much of the information is applicable to rare book
         libraries and archives.

2795.   Probst, Tom. "Electronic Eyes and Ears on Guard, "
         Museum News 44(3):11-17, 1965.

2796.   Protecting the Library and Its Resources. Chicago:
         American Library Association, 1963. A guide to
         physical protection and insurance.

2797.   "Proximity Alarm System, " American Archivist
         30:288, 1969. Describes a simple device for pro-
         tecting the security of file cabinets.

2798.   Rhoads, James B. "Alienation and Thievery: Ar-
         chival Problems, " American Archivist 29:197-208,
         1966.

2799.   Roberts, Matt. "Guards, turnstiles, electronic de-
         vices and the illusion of security, " College and Re-
         search Libraries 29(4):259-275, 1968.

2800.   Santon, Vernon B. and Howard W. Crocker. Pro-
         tecting Historical Societies' Records. Albany:
         University of the State of New York, State Educa-
         tion Department, 1951.

2801.   "Security, " Museums Journal 63(1-2), 1963.

2802.   Strickland, Robert L. "An Inexpensive Alarm System
         for the Small Museum, " Museum News 43(10):24-
         26, 1965.

2803.   Sugden, R. P. Safeguarding Works of Art. New
         York: Metropolitan Museum of Art, 1948.

Information on storage, packing, transportation and insurance.

2804. "Thiefproofing Museums," <u>UNESCO Courier</u> 18, 1965.

BUILDINGS

2805. Bean, Donald E. "Library Construction," <u>Illinois Libraries</u> 46:181-186, 1964.

2806. Beers, R. J. "High Expansion Foam Fire Control for Records Storage," <u>Fire Technology</u> May 1966.

2807. <u>Better Library Buildings</u>. Lewes, Sussex, England: British Library Association, 1969. These proceedings of a seminar organized by the Architect/Librarian Working Party of the London and Home Counties Branch of the British Library Association are available from the Library Association, East Sussex County Library, St. Annes Crescent, Lewes, Sussex, England.

2808. Bleton, Jean. "The Construction of University Libraries: How to Plan and Revise a Project," <u>UNESCO Bulletin for Libraries</u> 17:307-315, 345, 1963.

2809. Bradley, J. G. "Film Vaults: Construction and Use," <u>Journal Society Motion Picture Engineers</u> 53:193-206, 1949.

2810. <u>Buildings and Equipment for Archives</u>. Washington: National Archives, Division of Information and Publications, 1944. Bulletin of National Archives No. 6.

2811. Burchard, John E. et al. <u>Planning the University Library Building</u>. Princeton: Princeton University Press, 1949.

2812. Burgoyne, F. J. <u>Library Construction. Architecture Fittings and Furniture</u>, 1897.

2813. Chapman, J. M. "Stepping up Security," <u>Museum News</u> 44(3), 1965.

2814. Dominge, Charles Carroll and Walter O. Lincoln. "Building Construction as Applied to Fire Insurance and Inspecting for Fire Underwriting Purposes," <u>The Spectator</u> 4th ed., 1949. Philadelphia, New York.

2815. Duchein, M. <u>Les Bâtiments et Equipments d'Archives</u>. Paris: Conseil International des Archives, 1966.

Contains much information useful in planning the
construction of an archives repository.

2816. Eddy, Henry H. "Surveying for Archives Buildings,"
American Archivist 24:75-79, 1961.

2817. Galvin, Hoyt R. and Katherine A. Devereaux (eds.).
Planning a Library Building: Three Major Steps.
Chicago: American Library Association, 1955.

2818. _____ and Martin Van Buren. The Small Public
Library Building. Paris: UNESCO, 1959.

2819. Gondos, Victor, Jr. "American Archival Architecture," Bulletin of the American Institute of
Architects 1:27-32, 1947.

2820. _____. "Archival Buildings--Programming and
Planning," American Archivist 27:467-483, 1964.

2821. _____. "Collaboration Between Archivists and
Architects in Planning Archives Buildings," Build-
ings and Equipment for Archives, Washington: U.S.
National Archives, 1944. (Bulletin No. 6.)

2822. _____ (ed.). Reader for Archives and Records
Center Buildings. Washington: Society of American Archivists, 1970. This small volume contains
almost all the important literature on the subject
in the past 30 years.

2823. Horner, James W., Jr. "Planning the New Library:
Archer Daniels Midland Company Research Library," Special Libraries 55:36-40, 1964.

2824. Howard, Richard Foster. Museum Security. Washington: American Association of Museums, 1958.
Publications new series No. 18.

2825. Katz, William A. and Roderick Swartz. Problems in
Planning Library Facilities: Consultants, Archi-
tects, Plans and Critiques. Chicago: American
Library Association, 1964.

2826. Keally, Francis. "An Architect's View of Library
Planning," Library Journal 88:4521-4525, 1963.
Many of the observations are applicable to archival
buildings.

2827. MacGregor, W. D. The Protection of Buildings and
Timber Against Termites. London: H. M. Stat-
ionery Office, 1950. Great Britain, Department of
Scientific and Industrial Research, Forest Products
Research Bulletin No. 24.

2828. Metcalf, Keyes D. "Alternatives to a new library
building," College and Research Libraries 22, 1962.

2829. _____. Planning Academic and Research Library
Buildings. New York: McGraw-Hill Book Company,
1965. A study sponsored by the Association of

Research Libraries under a grant by the Council
on Library Resources.

2830. Nye, William. "Trends in Rare Book Library Facilities," College and Research Libraries 24, 1963.
Discusses handling, storage and conservation.

2831. Plumbe, Wilfred J. "Climate as a Factor in the
Planning of University Library Buildings," UNESCO
Bulletin for Libraries 17:316-325, 1963.

2832. Poole, Frazer G. (ed.). The Library Environment,
Aspects of Interior Planning: Proceedings of the
Library Equipment Institute. St. Louis, Mo.:
June 26-27, 1964.

2833. Poole, W. F. "The Construction of Library Buildings," Library Journal 6:69-77, 1881. (See also
Spofford, A. R. for comments on this article.)
[2846]

2834. _____. "Progress of Library Architecture," Library Journal 7:130-136, 1882.

2835. Posner, Ernst. "Records Center-Archives Buildings,"
American Archivist 29:111, 1966.

2836. Robison, Dan M. "Planning the Tennessee State Library and Archives Building," American Archivist
19:139-150, 1956.

2837. Roth, Harold L. Planning Library Buildings for Service. Chicago: American Library Association,
1964. Proceedings of the 1961 Library Buildings
and Equipment Institute.

2838. Ruskin, B. F. "Treatment of Museum Walls," Museum News 43(3):31-33, 1964.

2839. Sanchez Belda, Luis. "Construction of Archives
Buildings in the Last Ten Years," UNESCO Bulletins for Libraries 18:20-26, 1964. Includes pictures and plans.

2840. Schellenberg, T. R. "Modern Archival Buildings,"
Archivum 6:88-92, 1956.

2841. Schoenberner, Robert A. "What the Architect Needs
to Know About Archives," American Archivist
27:491-493, 1964.

2842. Sharman, R. C. "New building for old: the transmigration of the Queensland State Archives," Archives and Manuscripts 3(7):25-35, 1968.

2843. Shaw, Robert J. (ed.). Libraries: Buildings for the
Future. Chicago: American Library Association,
1967. Proceedings of the Library Buildings Institute and ALTA Workshop in Detroit, 1965.

2844. Simon, Louis A. "Some Observations on Planning
Archives Buildings," Buildings and Equipment for

Archives.   Washington: U. S. National Archives,
1944.   (Bulletin No. 6.)

2845.   Soule,   Charles C.   How to Plan a Library Building
for Library Work.   Boston: 1912.

2846.   Spoffard, A. R.   In discussion following W. F.
Poole's paper "The Construction of Library Buildings," Library Journal 6:69-77, 1881 [2833].

2847.   (Textiles).   The Housing of a Textile Collection.   North
Andover, Mass. :   Merrimac Valley Textile Muse-
um, 1968.   32 pp. paperbound.

2848.   Thomas, Anthony.   Library Buildings of Britain and
Europe: An International Study with Examples
Mainly from Britain and Some From Europe and
Overseas.   London: Butterworth, 1963.   Includes
plans, photographs, and bibliography for each build-
ing.

2849.   Ulveling, Ralph A.   "Problems of Library Construction," Library Quarterly 33:91-101, 1963.   Many
of the general observations are applicable to archives buildings.

2850.   Van Schreeven, William J.   "Equipment Needs to be
Considered in Constructing Post-War Archival
Depositories," Buildings and Equipment for Archives.   Washington: U. S. National Archives,
1944.   (Bulletin No. 6.)

2851.   Wheeler, J. L.   The Small Library Building.   Chicago: American Library Association, n. d.   (Small
libraries Library Project, Library Administration
Division.)

HOUSEKEEPING

2852.   Beecher, Reginald.   "Apparatus for keeping a showcase free of dust," Museums Journal 70(2):69-71,
1970.   Reports tests on an air intake appliance
capable of filtering out particles as small as one
micron.

2853.   Berkeley, Bernard.   Floors: Selection and Maintenance.   Chicago: American Library Association,
1968.   Library Technology Project Publication No.
13.

2854. Carlton, W. N. C. "The Housing Care of Special
       Collections, " The American Library Institute Pa-
       pers and Proceedings 181-190, 1917. Brief de-
       scription of practices employed by special libraries.
2855. Conover, Herbert S. Grounds Maintenance Handbook.
       2nd ed. New York: McGraw-Hill, 1958.
2856. Gilchrist, Agnes. A Primer on the Care and Repair
       of Buildings. Washington: National Trust For His-
       toric Preservation, 1963.
2857. Insall, Donald W. The Care of Old Buildings: A
       Practical Guide for Architects and Owners. Lon-
       don: Harrison & Sons, 1958.
2858. Kowalik, R. and I. Sadurska. "Disinfection of In-
       fected Stores in Rooms in Archives, Libraries and
       Museums, " Bulletino dell Istituto di Patologia del
       Libro 24(1-4):121-128, 1965.
2859. Kozulina, O V. The Hygiene and Restoration of
       Books in the City Library. Moscow: V. I. Lenin
       Library, 1960. Describes Soviet methods for
       cleaning and preserving books.
2860. Krogh, August. "The Dust Problem in Museums and
       How to Solve It, " Museum Journal 47:183-188,
       1948.
2861. Morrill, R. C. "Dust-proofing Exhibits by Air Pres-
       sure, " Curator 5, 1962.
2862. Sander, H. J. and R. E. Colwell. "An Electric Heat
       Pump for All Year Heating and Cooling in Li-
       braries, " Library Journal 79(22), 1954.
2863. Schwartz, Louis Edward. Accidents in Buildings:
       Spotter System. Brooklyn, New York: Trial At-
       torney Publications, Inc. , 1942.
2864. Werner, A. E. A. "Heating and Ventilation, " Muse-
       ums Journal 57, 1957.

STORAGE [See also under ROUTINE CARE--Photographic
Materials (below)]

2865. Abelson, Nathaniel. "A Method for Filing Rolled
       Wall Maps, " Special Libraries Association, Geog-
       raphy and Map Division. Bulletin No. 15 Febru-
       ary 1954. Describes the U. N. way of filing wall
       maps by putting screw eyes on the inner map rod
       and hooks at about 3-inch intervals on a 19-foot

long, 2 X 4 fastened on a wall 9 feet above the floor.

2866. Allen, Francis S. "Maps in the Library," Illinois Libraries 23(10):3-5, 1941. Summarizes the map storage problem.

2867. American Standard Practice for Storage of Microfilm. PH5.4- 1957. New York: American Standards Association, 1957.

2868. Archer, H. Richard. "Display and Exhibit Cases," Library Trends 13:474-480, 1965.

2869. Bahn, Catherine. "Map Libraries: Space and Equipment," Special Libraries Association, Geography and Map Division Bulletin, (46), December 1961.

2870. Barrow, W. J. "Archival File Folders," American Archivist 28(1):125-128, 1965. Table and bibliography. Two file folders with properties which make them suitable for archival use as described. Test data on physical strength, aging, pH, and fiber composition are given.

2871. Beers, R. J. "High Expansion Foam Fire Control for Record Storage," Fire Technology May 1966.

2872. _____. "New Fire Control Techniques for Records Storage," Records Management Journal 4(3):29-32, 1966.

2873. Bostwick, A. F. "Ready Filing of Sub-Pamphlet Material," American Library Institute Papers and Proceedings 187-190, 1917. Presents methods for storing broadsides, posters, book plates, post cards, programs, scrap books.

2874. Bradley, John G. "Film Vaults: Construction and Use," Journal Society of Motion Picture Engineers 53:193-206, 1949.

2875. Brown, H. G. "Problems of Storing Film for Archive Purposes," British Kinematography 20:150-162, 1952.

2876. Clayton, Nelson W. and G. H. Fudge. "Chemical dehumidification protects microfilm records stored in mountain vaults," Heating, Piping and Air Conditioning 38(10):127-129, 1966.

2877. Collison, Robert Lewis. Modern Storage Equipment and Methods for Special Materials in Libraries. Hampstead, England: 1955. Advocated roller shelves for large folio atlases and shallow drawers for maps. Issued in connection with an exhibition of modern storage equipment and methods for special libraries in London, January 1955. Includes

the names and addresses of exhibitors.
2878. Dabney, Virginius. "New Ways to Permanent Files,"
Saturday Review 67-68, 1964.
2879. Dunn, Walter S. Jr. Storing Your Collections. Nashville, Tenn.: American Association for State and
Local History, 1970. The Association's Technical
Leaflet No. 5 for museum storage has much of interest to librarians.
2880. Ellsworth, Ralph E. The Economics of Book Storage
in College and Research Libraries. Metuchen, New
Jersey: The Scarecrow Press, 1969. Describes
twelve book storage methods and the cost and other
factors involved.
2881. Gawrecki, Drahaslov. Compact Library Shelving.
Chicago: American Library Association, 1968.
Library Technology Project Publication No. 14.
Translated by Stanislov Rehak. The Chief of the
Czech State Library Technical Department discusses
the design and use of various types of compact
shelving.
2882. Gondos, Victor Jr. "A Note on Record Containers,"
American Archivist 17:237-242, 1954.
2883. Granier, Gerhard. "On Storage of Modern Records,"
Zur Magaziniering Moderner Akten 69-78, 1969.
(In German) A discussion of boxes, binders, etc.
and details of paper characteristics. Well documented.
2884. Henderson, George. Collection Storage and Preservation of Archives in Europe. Adelaid, Australia:
1915.
2885. Hill, J. Douglas. "Map and Atlas Cases," Library
Trends 13:481-487, April 1965.
2886. Hill, J. F. "Storage in University Library Buildings,"
UNESCO Bulletin for Libraries 17:337-345, November-December 1963.
2887. Jong, G. de. "De kaartenverzaneling," Bibliotheek-
leves 33:267-281, 1948. Rotterdam. A general
treatise on the care of maps in a library. Includes
bibliography.
2888. Josephson, A. G. S. "The Care of Maps at the John
Crerar Library," American Library Association
Bulletin 16(4):263, 1922. Maps are filed in special
boxes.
2889. Kimberly, Arthur E. "New Developments in Record
Containers," American Archivist 13:233-236, 1950.
2890. _____ and J. F. G. Hicks, Jr. A Survey of Storage Conditions in Libraries Relative to the

Preservation of Records. Washington: National
Bureau of Standards, 1931. Miscellaneous Publication No. 128.

2891. Langwell, W. H. "The Protection of Paper and
Parchment Against Dampness in Storage," Journal
Society of Archivists 3:82-85, 1965. London.

2892. LeGear, C. E. Maps, Their Care, Repair and Preservation in Libraries. Washington: Library of
Congress, 1956. A must reference for all curators
of map collections. Lengthy bibliography plus detailed instructions on processing, filing, preservation, repair and storage.

2893. Lewis, Willard P. "The Care of Maps and Atlases in
the Library," Library Journal 55:494-496, 1930.
Considers various types of map filing equipment.

2894. Metcalf, Keyes D. "The Design of Book Stacks and
the Preservation of Books," Restaurator 1(2), 1969.
A review of past mistakes, present standards, and
unsolved problems by Harvard's Librarian Emeritus.

2895. "Microfilm in an uncertain world," Records Management Quarterly 1(3), 1967. Describes the storage
facilities of the Genealogical Society of the Church
of Jesus Christ of Latter-Day Saints.

2896. Minogue, A. E. "The Use of Transparent Plastics
for the Protection of Manuscripts," Manuscript
8, 1956. New York. Envelopes, etc.--not lamination.

2897. Mitra, D. K. "Maps in Libraries; their storage and
preservation," Herald of Library Science 7(1):27-
32, 1968.

2898. Nelson, Harold. "Protection and Storage of EDP
Tapes," Records Management Journal 4(4):15-17,
1966.

2899. Nelson, Peter. "Maps and Atlases," American Library Association, Pamphlets and Minor Library
Material 23-29, 1917. Also A. L. A. Manual of
Library Economy, Chapter 25. A summary of the
acquisition, processing and care of maps in libraries.

2900. "New Document Storage Method," American Archivist
30(2):372-373, 1967. Describes a new method of
storing documents, including those with pendant
seals, by means of suspended sleeves of "Melinex"
polyester sheeting. The method has been approved
by the Central Research Laboratory for Objects of
Art and Science in Amsterdam. The sheeting which
is used in Holland is available also in the United

States.
2901. Noll, Daniel F. "The Maintenance of Microfilm
      Files," American Archivist 13:129-134, 1950. Re-
      lates to the physical care and storage of micro-
      film.
2902. Parsons, Francis H. "The Care of Maps," Library
      Journal 20(6):199-201, 1895. A good general dis-
      cussion, based on early experiences with the map
      collection of the U.S. Coast and Geodetic Survey.
2903. Phillips, Philip Lee. Notes on the Cataloging, Care,
      and Classification of Maps and Atlases, Including
      a List of Publications Compiled in the Division of
      Maps. Revised ed. Washington: U.S. Govern-
      ment Printing Office, 1921. Amplified from his
      earlier contributions. [2904].
2904. _____. "Preservation and Record of Maps in the
      Library of Congress," Library Journal 25(1):15-16,
      1900. A brief outline of the care of maps at the
      Library of Congress.
2905. Piez, Gladys T. "Archival Containers--A Search for
      Safer Materials," American Archivist 27:433-438,
      1964.
2906. Porter, James D. "Sound in the Archives," Ameri-
      can Archivist 27:327-336, 1964. Includes sections
      on the storage and processing of magnetic tape.
2907. Potter, Rex M. "The Map Collection in the Public
      Library: Acquisition, Cataloging and Care of the
      Collection," Wilson Library Bulletin 19(4):270-272,
      1944.
2908. Raisz, Erwin J. "Preservation and Cataloguing of
      Maps," General Cartography. New York: McGraw-
      Hill Book Company, 1938. Concerned primarily
      with university and college map collections.
2909. Rider, Fremont. Compact Book Storage. New York:
      Hadham Press, 1949. Some suggestions toward a
      new methodology for the shelving of less used re-
      search materials.
2910. Rieger, Morris. "Packing, Labeling, and Shelving at
      the National Archives," American Archivist 25:417-
      426, 1962.
2911. Ristow, Walter W. "The Library Map Collection,"
      Library Journal 67(12):552-555, 1942. A resume
      of acquiring, processing and preserving maps.
2912. Selva, Manuel. Guía para organización fichado 7
      catalogación de mapotecas. Buenos Aires: J.
      Suarez, 1941. Relates to the care and preserva-
      tion of maps on pages 53-62.

2913.   Skelton, Raleigh A. "The Conservation of Maps, "
        Society of Local Archivists Bulletin 14:13-19, 1954.
        London. A discussion of map storage and use
        problems in general, and the British Museum's
        plans and practices in particular.
2914.   Smith, R. D. "Paper Impermanence as a Consequence
        of pH and Storage Conditions, " Library Quarterly
        153-195, 1969. Considers the effects of excessive
        acidity and inferior storage conditions on the use-
        ful life of paper in libraries. Identifies tempera-
        ture as the second most significant cause of deteri-
        oration.
2915.   Smither, Reginald E. "The Treatment of Pamphlets,
        Maps, Photographs and Similar Items, " Library
        World 15:195-199, 1912-1913. A general discus-
        sion of non-book materials in a British library.
        Recommends that maps be dissected, mounted and
        folded to book size. Less satisfactory ways of
        handling them are to roll them, bind them, or keep
        them in portfolios.
2916.   Steckzén, Birger. "Storage and Preservation of Maps
        in Swedish Military Archives, " Indian Archives
        4(1):14-19, 1950. New Delhi. Describes also the
        classification, cataloging and indexing of the col-
        lection. Includes a floor plan of the map deposito-
        ry.
2917.   Stolow, Nathan. "Fundamental Case Design for Hu-
        midity Sensitive Museum Collections, " Museum
        News 44(6), 1966. Technical Supplement No. 11.
2918.   "The Storage and Conservation of Maps, " Geographi-
        cal Journal 121:182-189, 1955. A report prepared
        by a committee of the Royal Geographical Society,
        1954. A review of "Ideal Standards of Map Con-
        servation for the Guidance of Map Curators. "
2919.   "Storage of Maps, " Library Journal 39:936, 1914.
        Published also in American Library Annual, p. 220,
        1914-1915. Describes a map case designed by Dr.
        Charles Warren Hunt, Secretary of the American
        Society of Civil Engineers, for the Society's map
        collection in New York.
2920.   "Storage and Preservation of Microfilms, " Kodak Data
        Book No. P-108. Rochester, N. Y. : Eastman
        Kodak Co. , 1965.
2921.   Storage and Preservation of Motion Picture Film.
        Rochester, N. Y. : Eastman Kodak Co. , 1957.
2922.   Storage of Processed Color Films. Rochester, N. Y. :
        Eastman Kodak Co. , 1962.

2923.   Thirsk, J. W. "The Storage of Newspapers and
        Periodicals, " The Treatment of Special Material in
        Libraries, (by R. L. Collison). London: Aslib,
        1957.
2924.   Vanderbilt, Paul. Filing Your Photographs: Some
        Basic Procedures. Nashville: American Associa-
        tion for State and Local History, 1966. The Asso-
        ciation's Technical Leaflet No. 36.
2925.   Waddell, Gene. "Museum Storage, " Museum News
        49(5), 1971. Comments on relative merits of wood
        and metal shelves, fire protection, fumigation,
        security, air conditioning, and light control.
2926.   Wallace, J. H. Modern Storage Methods for Records.
        Sydney: University of Sydney, 1957.
2927.   Williams, W. Ogden. "Shelving of an Aluminum Al-
        loy, " Archives 2:30-32, 1949.
2928.   Wilson, W. K. Selection, Use, and Storage of Re-
        cords for the International Geophysical Year. Wash-
        ington: National Bureau of Standards, 1957. NBS
        Report 5321.
2929.   Winkler, J. Fred. "Cartographic Record Filing in
        the National Archives, " American Archivist 12:283-
        285, 1949. Contains useful suggestions for anyone
        planning the installation of map filing equipment.
2930.   _____. "One Solution to the Map Handling Prob-
        lem, " American Archivist 15(3):259-261, 1952.
        Describes how to make a handy truck for physically
        moving large maps in a library.

PEST CONTROL [See also under VIII. Appendices--N. ; and
IX. --Bibliographies--Pest Control]

2931.   Current Pest Control Recommendations. Washington:
        U. S. Armed Forces Pest Control Board, December
        1963. Technical Information Memorandum 6.
2932.   Donskoi, A. V. (and others). Disinfection of Books
        in an Electric Field of High Frequency. Leningrad:
        Saltykov-Shchedrin State Public Library, 1959.
2933.   Entoma. A Directory of Pesticide Materials Equip-
        ment Services. Madison: University of Wisconsin,
        Department of Entomology, 1957.
2934.   Frear, D. E. H. Pesticide Handbook. 13th ed. State
        College, Pennsylvania: College Science Publishers,

1961.

2935. _____. Pesticide Index. State College, Pennsylvania: College Science Publishers, 1961.

2936. Hartzell, A. and F. Wilcoxen. "Napthalene Fumigation at Controlled Concentrations," Journal Economic
Entomology 23:608-618, 1930.

2937. Kishore, R. and J. C. Bhatnagar. "Napthaline Fumigator," Conservation of Cultural Property in India.
New Delhi: National Museum, 1966.

2938. Mallis, Arnold. Handbook of Pest Control: The Behavior, Life History and Control of Household
Pests. 2nd ed. New York: MacNair-Dorland Co.,
1954.

2939. Markovitch, S. How to Control Certain Pests in the
Household. Knoxville: University of Tennessee,
1933. Tennessee Agricultural Experiment Station
Bulletin No. 147.

2940. Reddish, G. F. Antiseptics, Disinfectants, Fungicides
and Sterilization. London: H. Klimpton, 1957.

INSECTS

2941. Ant and Termite Control with Aldrine and Dieldrine.
Burmah Shell, India: Shell Chemicals for Agriculture Brochure, n. d.

2942. Armitage, F. D. "Prevention of Damage to Paper,
Books and Documents by Insect Pests," PATRA
Journal 8(2):40-49, 1944.

2943. Barnhard, C. S. "How to Control Cockroaches with
Dry Ice Fumigation," Pest Control 31(2):30, 1963.

2944. Becker, G. "Tests on the Effectiveness of Synthetic
Contact Insecticides Against Four Termite Species,"
Holz-Roh und Werkstoff 23:467-478, 1965. Berlin.

2945. Beesley, J. "Eradicating Termites (white ants) from
Buildings," Forest Products Newsletter 234-236,
1957.

2946. Bhatnagar, D. L. "Termite Infestation in Record
Depositories--Remedial Measures," Conservation
of Cultural Property in India 2:37-47, 1967.

2947. Block, S. S. "Protection of Paper and Textile Products from Insect Damage," Industrial and Engineering Chemistry 43(7):1558-1563, 1951.

2948. Bracey, P. and P. Barlow. "Ureaformaldehyde Resin
as a Vehicle for Semi-Permanent Insecticidal and
Fungicidal Coatings on Bookbindings and Bookcases,"
Journal of Documentation 9(3):157-168, 1953.

2949. Brown, A. W. A. Insect Control by Chemicals. New
        York: John Wiley Sons, 1952.
2950. Burns-Brown, W. "The Disinfection of Furniture with
        Methyl Bromide for Control of the Bedbug," The
        Sanitarian June 1959.
2951. Chakravorti, S. "Formaldehyde as a Preventive
        Against Bookworm," Science and Culture 9:251-252,
        1943.
2952. Control of Termites with Dieldrin and Protection of
        Buildings from Attack. Shell Company of West
        Africa, Ltd., 1958. Agricultural Circular No. 4.
2953. Cristol, Stanley J. and H. L. Haller. "The Chemis-
        try of DDT--A Review," Chemical Engineering
        News 23:2070-2075, 1945.
2954. Dyte, C. E. "Preliminary Tests of an Insecticidal
        Lacquer Containing Malathion," Pest Technology
        2:98-99, 1960.
2955. Ebling, W. and R. J. Pence. "UCLA Entomologists
        Evaluate Research Data in Drywood Subterranean
        Termite Control," Pest Control 1956.
2956. _____ and R. Wagner. "Rapid Dessication of Dry-
        wood Termites with Inert Sorptive Dusts and Other
        Substances," Journal Economic Entomology 52(2):
        190-207, 1959.
2957. Entomological Report--Dieldrin (Compound 497). Shell
        Chemicals Ltd., 1957.
2958. "Eradicating Termites from Buildings," Building Digest
        No. 30. Central Building Research Institute,
        Roorkee, India.
2959. Evans, D. M. Protection of Books Against Insects.
        Leatherhead: Printing, Packaging and Allied Trades
        Research Association, 1949. Bulletin No. 9.
2960. Fitzsimmons, K. R. "Termite Control in Historic
        Landmarks," Historic Preservation 22(4), 1970.
        Mr. Fitzsimmons, General Manager, Agricultural
        Division, Shell Chemical Co., describes successful
        operations on historic buildings.
2961. Fumigation with Methyl Bromide. London: HMSO,
        1960.
2962. Gahan, C. J. Furniture Beetles: Their Life History
        and How to Check or Prevent the Damage Caused
        by the Worm. London: British Museum, 1920.
        British Museum, Natural History Department,
        Economic Series No. 11.
2963. Gallo, P. "Problems in the Use of Insecticides on
        Occupied Premises," Recent Advances in Conserva-
        tion. London: Butterworths, 1963.

2964. Gay, F. J. "Soil Treatments for Termite Control in Australia," Building Lighting Engineering August, 1963.

2965. Goodhue, Lyle D.; Raymond L. Cobb, and Kenneth E. Cantral. Repelling Insects. Bartlesville, Okla.: Phillips Petroleum Co., 22, 1963. U. S. Pat. 3,108,037.

2966. Graveley, F. H. "Paraffin Wax as a Protection Against Termites," Journal of the Bombay Natural History Society 45(3):439-440, 1945.

2967. Gray, H. E. "Vikane a New Fumigant for Control of Drywood Termites," Pest Control 28:43-46, 1960.

2968. Gupta, R. C. "How to Fight White-Ants," The Indian Archives 8(2), 1954.

2969. Hall, I. N. "Microbial Control of Insects," Agricultural Chemistry 14:45-112, 1959.

2970. Harrick, G. W. and G. M. Griswold. "Napthalene as a Fumigant for the Immature Stage of Clothes Moths and Carpet Beetles," Journal Economic Entomology 26:446-451, 1933.

2971. Harris, W. V. Termites: Their Recognition and Control. London: Longmans, 1961.

2972. Heimpel, A. M. "Bacterial Insecticides," Bacteriological Reviews 24:266-288, 1960.

2973. Hint on How to Avoid Termite Damage in Libraries and Record Offices. Dehra Dun, India: Forest Research Institute, n. d.

2974. Holnes, R. F. G. "Use of Formaldehyde as a Fumigant," British Records Association Bulletin 14, 1942.

2975. Hutson, J. C. "Preservation of Book Covers from Cockroaches," Ceylon Department of Agriculture Report on the Work of the Entomological Division, 1932.

2976. Insecta-Lac, the Improved Insecticidal Lacquer. Maidstone, Kent, England: Sorex (London) Ltd., 1956.

2977. "Insects, Protection From," American Archivist 1:87, 111, 214, 1938; 2:21, 1939; 3:141, 212, 1940; 6:38, 197, 1943; 7:159, 1944; 11:246, 1948; 16:377, 1953.

2978. Jepson, F. P. "Preventing Injury to Books by Cockroaches," Fiji Department of Agriculture Report on the Work of the Division of Plant Pest Control 1934.

2979. Kenaga, E. E. "Some Biological Chemical and Physical Properties of Sulphuril Fluoride as an Insecticidal Fumigant," Journal Economic Entomology 50(1), 1957.

2980. Kirk-Othmer. "Insecticides and Fungicides," Paper
        Fillers. New York: Interscience Encyclopaedias
        Inc., 1947.

2981. Kishore, R. "Napthalene Fumigator," Conservation
        of Cultural Property in India 1:102-105, 1966. A
        method of area fumigation.

2982. Kleindienst, T. Note d'information sur la protection
        des collections contre les insectes et les champig-
        nons ou moisissures. Paris: Direction des Biblio-
        thèques de France, 1953.

2983. Kozulina, O. V. "Insect Control Methods Used in
        Moscow Libraries," UNESCO Bulletin for Libraries
        15:200-202, 1961.

2984. Lepesme, P. La protection des bibliothèques et des
        musees contre les insectes et les moisissures.
        Paris: Presses Documentaires, 1943.

2985. MacGregor, W. D. "The Protection of Buildings and
        Timber Against Termites," Forest Products Re-
        search Bulletin No. 24, 1950. London: H. M. S. O.,
        1950.

2986. "Making Bindings Insect Proof," Bookbinders Monthly
        10(7):2, 1929.

2987. Mallis, A. "Preliminary Experiments on the Silver-
        fish - Ctenolepisma Urbani Slabaugh (Ctenolepisma
        Longicaudata)," Journal Economic Entomology
        34:787, 1941.

2988. McKenny Hughes, A. W. "Protection of Books and
        Records from Insects," Indian Archives 7(1), 1953.

2989. Moncrieff, R. W. Mothproofing. London: Leonard
        Hill Ltd., 1950.

2990. Mori Hachirō. "Studies on the Control of Insects
        Noxious to Ancient Art Materials," Sci. Pap. Japn.
        Antiques 1:30-32, 1951. On the insecticidal meth-
        ods with reduced pressure.

2991. Noirot, C. and H. Alliot. La lutte contre les ter-
        mites. Paris: Masson, 1947.

2992. Nyuksha, Y. P. "Disinfection of Books in Chambers,"
        Saltykov-Shchedrin State Public Library 5-27, 1959.
        Leningrad. Reviews various methods of book dis-
        infection.

2993. Opfell, John B. et al. "Penetration by Gases to
        Sterilize Interior Surfaces of Confined Spaces,"
        Applied Microbiology 12:27-31, 1964. Pasadena,
        California: Dynamic Science Corp.

2994. Page, B. P. and O. F. Lubatti. "Fumigation of In-
        sects," Annual Review of Entomology 8:239-264,
        1963. Stanford, California.

2995. Parsons, D. E. "Fumigation on the site," Repairers'
       News Sheet 18:1, 1971. Society of Archivists,
       England. Describes a system for mass fumigation
       in a sealed room using Thymol.

2996. Pence, R. J. "Control of Fabric-Feeding Insects,"
       California Agriculture 14, 1960.

2997. _____. "Control of Powder-post Beetles," Califor-
       nia Agriculture 10, 1956. Infrared radiation.

2998. Plenderleith, H. J. "Protection of Records Against
       Bookworm," British Records Association Bulletin
       11, 1940.

2999. "Precautions Against Vermin and Dust," British
       Standard Code of Practice CP3. London: British
       Standards Institution, 1950. Chapter 10.

3000. Price, M. D. "Insecticidal Resins. A New Concept
       in Residual Insect Control," Pest Control 28:47-58,
       1960.

3001. _____. "Progress with Insecticidal Resins," Pest
       Technology 4:187, 1961.

3002. "Protection Against Spoilage by Micro-organisms,
       Insects, Mites and Rodents," British Standard
       Packaging Code. London: British Standards In-
       stitution, 1951. British Standard 1133, Section 5,
       1951.

3003. Roan, C. C. "What's New Among the Fumigants?"
       Pest Control 30(7):9, 1962.

3004. Robinow, B. H. "Books and Cockroaches: An At-
       tempt to Cope with the Menace," South African Li-
       braries 24(2):40-42, 1956.

3005. Rossman, Joseph. "Insect Repellent and Medicated
       Paper," Paper Trade Journal 100(7):39-40, 1935.
       Abstracts of 49 U.S. patents, 1855-1934 on methods
       of insect-proofing various kinds of paper.

3006. St. George, R. A. et al. Subterranean Termites:
       Their Prevention and Control in Buildings. Wash-
       ington: U.S. Government Printing Office, 1958.
       Dept. of Agriculture Home and Garden Bulletin No.
       64.

3007. Sahai, Y. "Insect Control in the Museum," Conser-
       vation of Cultural Property in India 2:82-90, 1967.
       Excellent categorization of various types of insect
       damage and recommended remedial action.

3008. Silverfish and Firebrats, How to Control Them. Wash-
       ington: U.S. Government Printing Office, 1957.

3009. Snyder, T. E.   Control of Non-Subterranean Ter-
         mites. Washington: U. S. Government Printing
         Office, 1958. Department of Agriculture Farmer's
         Bulletin No. 2018.

3010. _____ and S. Zetek. Effectiveness of Wood Pres-
         ervatives in Preventing Attack by Termites. Wash-
         ington: U. S. Department of Agriculture, 1943.
         Circular No. 683.

3011. Stored Grain Pests. Washington: U. S. Government
         Printing Office, 1962. Farmers Bulletin No. 1260.
         Includes information on control of beetles which
         have been known to infest libraries.

3012. Tarshis, I. B.   "UCLA Tests with Dessicant Dusts
         for Roach Control," Pest Control 27(6), 1959.

3013. (Termites). Damage to Buildings by Termites and
         Their Control. Washington: U. S. Department of
         Agriculture Farmer's Bulletin No. 1911.

3014. Tiunin, K.   "A Vacuum Gas-chamber for Disinfection
         in the State Ethnographic Museum in Warsaw,"
         Ochrana Zabytko 19(1):77-79, 1966. Warsaw.

3015. Tooke, F. G. C.   "The Use of Preservatives Against
         Wood-destroying Insects," Farming in South Africa
         235-240, 1943.

3016. Townsend, H. G.   "Insecta-lac: New Roach Killer
         Brushes on Like Paint," Pest Control 30(2):40,
         1962.

3017. Wolcott, G. N.   Termite Repellents: a Summary of
         Laboratory Tests. Puerto Rico: University of
         Puerto Rico, 1947. Agricultural Experiment Sta-
         tion Bulletin 73.

3018. Wood, G. W.   "Books and Documents: Protection
         from Insect Damage. A Survey of the Problem
         and Methods of Control," Pesticides Abstracts and
         News Summary 2(2), 1956.

3019. (United States National Pest Control Assoc.). Chemi-
         cals in Subterranean Termite Control. Elizabeth,
         New Jersey: 1963.

3020. Yadon, Vernal L.   "A Portable Fumigation Chamber
         for the Small Museum," Museum News 44(5):38-39,
         1966.

3021. "You are Old Father Ghinkgo," Chemistry 42(10),
         1969. Ghinkgo leaves are an insect repellant used
         in books to prevent silverfish damage.

RODENTS: The best general information available is in encyclopedias.

MILDEW

3022. [No entry.]
3023. Abrams, Edward. Microbiological Deterioration of Organic Materials; Its Prevention and Methods of Test. Washington: U.S. Government Printing Office, 1948. National Bureau of Standards Miscellaneous Publication No. 188.
3024. Armitage, F. D. The Cause of Mildew on Books and Methods of Preservation. London: Printing & Allied Trades Research Association, 1949. PATRA Bulletin No. 8.
3025. Arnold, J. "Parathion and Naphthalene as Closet Fumigants," Soap and Sanitary Chemicals, 1953.
3026. Barr, P. "Mildew in Libraries--Prevention and Treatment," New Jersey Library Bulletin 13:123-129, 1945.
3027. Belyakova, L. A. "Fungus Control in the Lenin State Library," UNESCO Bulletin for Libraries 15:198-200, 1961.
3028. [No entry.]
3029. _____. "Gamma-Radiation as a Disinfecting Agent for Books Infected with Mold Spores," Mikrobiologiya 29(5):299, 356, 762-765, 1960. Moscow.
3030. _____. "The Resistance of Fungi to Fungicides," Collection of Materials on the Preservation of Library Resources. Moscow: 1958. English translation available from the National Technical Information Service, Springfield, Virginia.
3031. Betto, E. The Bacterial and Fungicidal Activity of Ethylene Oxide in Vacuum Fumigation. Milan: Istituto di Patologia Vegetale dell'Universita di Milano, 1960. Booklet No. 52.
3032. Bhandari, N. D.; P. N. Agrawal; S. S. Nigam, and A. S. Raman. "Urea-Formaldehyde Resin Treatment for Protection of Woolen Fabrics Against Micro-organisms and Insects," Indian Journal Technology 1:255-256, 1963. Indian Defense Research Lab. Stores, Kanpur.
3033. Block, S. S. "Chemicals for Fungus Control," Chemical Week Report 26, 1952.
3034. _____. Experiments in Mildew Prevention. Florida Engineering and Industrial Experimental Station

Report, n. d.

3035. _____ . "Experiments in Mildew Prevention, " Modern Sanitation 3:61-67, 1951.

3036. _____ . "Opportunity for Manufacturers in Mildew Prevention, " Engineering Progress 7(7), 1953. U. of Fla.

3037. Bohatta, H. "Die Hygiene des Büches, " Einfubrung in die Büchkunde 301-307. Wien: Gilhofer & Ranschburg, 1927.

3038. Bracey, P. and F. Barlow. "Urea-Formaldehyde Resin as a Vehicle for Semi-Permanent Insecticidal and Fungicidal Coatings on Bookbindings and Bookcases, " Journal of Documentation 9(3):157-168, 1953. London.

3039. Buchanan, Estelle D. and Robert Earle. Bacteriology. 4th ed. New York: The MacMillan Company, 1938.

3040. CIBA Ltd. "Protecting Hides, Skins and Leathers, " Journal of the American Leather Chemists Association 58, 1963.

3041. Colin-Russ, A. "Further Observation on the Control of Mould Growth in Leather and Fabric Material, " Journal of the International Society of Leather Trades' Chemists 30(7):172-185, 1946.

3042. Dahl, Sverre. "Prevention of Microbiological Deterioration of Leather, " Journal of the American Leather Chemists Association 51(3), 1956.

3043. Dahl, Sverre and Arthur M. Kaplan. "5, 6 Dichloro-2-Benzoxazolinone as a Leather Fungicide, " Journal of the American Leather Chemists Association 56(12):686-698, 1961.

3044. _____ . "Fungicidal Effectiveness of Compounds Applied to Leather, " Journal of the American Leather Chemists Association 52(10):536, 1957. This report is a compilation of the test results on 126 compounds that have been screened as leather fungicides.

3045. _____ . "4-Nitrophenyl Esters, Including Mixed Carbonates and Bi-Carbonates, as Leather Fungicides, " Journal of the American Leather Chemists Association 55(9), 1960.

3046. _____ . "Studies in Leather Fungicides, " Journal of the American Leather Chemists Association 53(2):103-118, 1958.

3047. Deribere, M. "The Pathology of the Book and the Use of Ultra-violet Rays, " Papetérie 73:719, 721, 1951.

3048. Dow's Preservative Chemicals for the Adhesive Industry. Midland, Michigan: Dow Chemical

Company, n. d.

3049. Flieder, Françoise. "Techniques d'etudes de la composition physiochemique des enluminures de manuscrits, " Report to ICOM Committee for Museum
Laboratories, 1965.

3050. Gallo, Piero. "Alcuni problemi igienice riguardanti
l'impiego degli insetticidi negli edifici pubblici, "
Bollettino dell Istituto di Patologia del Libro 20:61-
85, 1961. A condensed review of fifty papers on
the hygienical and toxicological problems concerning employment of modern insecticides.

3051. _____. "Moderni orientamenti nella recerca e
nell'applicazione degli insetticidi utilizzabili negli
idifici pubblici, " Bollettino dell Istituto di Patologia
del Libro 22:1-28, 1963. A summary with 71
references of most important insecticides suitable
for public buildings including libraries and museums.

3052. "Heater Units Prevent Mildew in Book Stack, " Electrical World 107:574, 1937.

3053. Hetherington, D. C. "Mold Preventive for Bookbindings, " Science 101(2018):323, 1945.

3054. _____. "Mold Preventive for Bookbindings, " College and Research Libraries 7:246, 1946.

3055. Hueck van der Plas, E. "Survey of Commercial Products used to Protect Materials Against Biological
Deterioration, " Biodetn. Bull. 2(2):69, 1966.

3056. Husarska, M. "Fumigation of Archival Records and
Library Stocks, " Biul. Konserwatorski 2:30-44,
1954. Warsaw.

3057. Iiams, T. H. and T. D. Beckwith. "Notes on the
Causes and Prevention of Foxing in Books, " The
Library Quarterly 5(4), 1935. This report pinpoints the causes of foxing, suggests preventive
measures, but has little to say about removing foxing stains.

3058. Kenaga, E. E. "Biological, chemical and physical
properties of sulfuryl fluoride as an insecticidal
fumigant, " Journal of Economic Entomology 50:7-
11, 1957.

3059. Kleindienst, T. Note d'information sur la protection
des collections contre les insectes et les champig-
nons ou moisissures. Paris: Direction des Bibliotheques de France, 1953.

3060. Kowalik, R. and I. Sadurska. "The Disinfection of
Infected Stores or Rooms in Archives, Libraries
and Museums, " Bollettino dell Istituto di Patologia

del Libro 24:121-128, 1965.

3061. _____. "Fungi Protection for Archival Papers,"
Bolletino dell'Istituto di Patologia del Libro 27:37-
47, 1968.

3062. _____. "Microbiological Deterioration of Old Books
and Manuscripts - Remedies," Bolletino dell'Istituto
di Patologia del Libro 21:121-151, 1962. The problem of deterioration and prevention as it is understood and practiced in Poland. Text in English.

3063. Kurir, A. "The Possibility of Destroying Termites
with Atomic Waste," Holzforschung Holzverwertung
15, 1963.

3064. Lefeve, R. "Conservation of Archeological Leather
with Polyethyleneglycols," Bulletin Institut Royale
Patrimoine Artistique 3:98-102, 1960. Brussels.

3065. Lepesme, P. La protection des bibliothèques et des
musées contre les insectes et les moisissures.
Paris: Presses Documentaires, 1943.

3066. Mechalas, B. J. "Microbiological Pest Control,"
Pest Control 29(10):20, 1961.

3067. Munnecke, D. E.; F. A. Ludwig, and R. E. Samp-
son. "The Fungicidal Activity of Methyl Bromide,"
Canada Journal Botony 37:51-58, 1959.

3068. Nyuksha, Y. P. "High Frequency Currents as Instruments of Mould Control on Books," Bibliotekar
35-36, 1949. Moscow.

3069. Plenderleith, H. J. "Mould in the Muniment Room,"
Archives 7:13, 1952.

3070. Plumbe, W. J. "Protection of Books Against Mildew,"
Malayan Library Journal 1(2):11-13, 1961.

3071. Reddish, G. F. Antiseptics, Disinfectants, Fungicides and Sterilization. London: H. Kimpton,
1957.

3072. Rybakova, S. G. "Control of Mold Fungi on Books,"
Collection of Materials on the Preservation of Li-
brary Resources. Moscow, 1953. Available from
National Technical Information Center, Springfield,
Virginia.

3073. _____. "Preservation from Moulding of the Glue
Used for the Binding and Restoration of Books,"
Bibliotekar 39-40, 1949. Moscow.

3074. Schley, Donald G. and others. "Simple Improvised
Chambers for Gas Sterilization with Ethylene
Oxide," Applied Microbiology 8:15, 1960.

3075. Sharvelle, E. G. The Nature and Uses of Modern
Fungicides. Minneapolis: Burgess Publ. Comp.,
1961.

ROUTINE CARE [See also under IX. General References--
Bibliographies]

3076. Anthony, D. C. Caring for Your Collections: Manuscripts and Related Materials. Nashville: American Association for State and Local History, 1963.
Technical Leaflet No. 8.

3077. Banks, Paul N. "Some Problems in Book Conservation," Library Resources and Technical Services
12(3), 1968. A discussion of library binding techniques. See also rebuttal by D. A. Weiss, Executive Director of the Library Binding Institute, in
same Journal 13(2), 1969.

3078. Barrow, W. J. Permanence/Durability of the Book--
VI. Spot Testing for Unstable Modern Book and
Record Papers. Richmond: W. J. Barrow Research Laboratory, 1969. Describes simple procedures for spot testing for groundwood, acidity,
alum and rosin in modern papers.

3079. Beaufort, T. R. Pictures and How to Clean Them.
London: J. Lane, 1926 and New York: Frederick
A. Stokes, 1926. Deals mainly with the conserva-
tion and repair of pictures on paper.

3080. Berridge, Priscilla. Transparent Polyester Film
Used as a Protective Covering for Unbound Manuscripts. Paper presented at May 1970 meeting of
IIC (UK Group). The Conservation Officer, Cambridge University Library, describes how they have
protected an extensive collection of Second Century
manuscripts.

3081. Breillat, Pierre. The Rare Books Section in the Library. Paris: UNESCO, 1965. Includes section
on book conservation and restoration.

3082. Cox, Trenchard. Pictures, Handbook for Museum
Curators D1 & D2. London: The Museums Association, 1956.

3083. Cunha, G. M. "Vapor Phase Deacidification," American Archivist 30:614-615, 1967.

3084. _____. "Vapor Phase Deacidification," American
Archivist 31:84-86, 1968.

3085. Eisendrath, David B. "Some Comments and Suggestions Concerning Photography as an Aid to Conservation," Exposition of Painting Conservation.
Brooklyn: Brooklyn Museum, 1962.

3086. Flieder, F. La Conservation des Documents Graphiques: Recherches Experimentales. Paris:

Editions Eyrolles, 1969. The first part of this,
the 9th of the Rome Centre's publications, reviews
the history of writing materials, the enemies of
the same, preventive measures in conservation.
The author then goes on to describe the results of
her study of fungicides, bleaching agents, the effect of preservation techniques on paper, and the
colors used in illuminated manuscripts.

3087.   Friedman, Hannah B.   "Preservation of Library Materials: The State of the Art," Special Libraries
59:608-613, 1968.

3088.   A Guide to the Care of Manuscripts in Small Collections.   Albany: New York State Library, 1962.

3089.   Haney, Thomas V.   "To Clean or Not to Clean,"
The New York Times June 9, 1968.

3090.   Held, Julius.   "Alteration and Mutilation of Works of
Art," South Atlantic Quarterly 62(1):1-27, 1963.

3091.   Horton, Carolyn.   Cleaning and Preserving Bindings
and Related Materials.   2nd ed. rev.   Chicago:
American Library Association, 1969.   This Library
Technology Project Pub. No. 16 is also the first
of the LTP's series on the conservation of library
materials.

3092.   Iuga, Victoria G.   "Preserving Museum Goods," Revista Muzeumkundl 5(2):154-156, 1968.

3093.   Johnson, C.   The Care of Documents and the Management of Archives.   London: Society for Promoting
Christian Knowledge, 1919.

3094.   Keck, Caroline K.   How to Take Care of Your Pictures.   New York: The Museum of Modert Art, 1965.
A primer of practical information on easle paintings
but includes excellent general information.

3095.   Kimberley, A. E. and B. W. Scribner.   Summary
Report of Bureau of Standards Research on Preser-
vation of Records: U. S. Bureau of Standards,
Miscellaneous Publication No. 144.   Washington:
U. S. Government Printing Office, 1934.

3096.   Kingery, R. E.   Permanent/Durable Book Paper.
Richmond, Va.: Virginia State Library, 1960.
Report of a conference sponsored by the ALA and
the Virginia State Library to examine the extent
of the paper problem in large research libraries
and the comparative costs of available solutions.

3097.   Lawrence, George.   "Care and Preservation of Library Materials," Arnoldia 30(2), 1970.   An edited
version from a tape recording of a talk by Dr.
Lawrence at Mass. Horticultural Society Conference,

November 1969.

3098. Lawrence, Virginia N. "The Care of Autographs: Some Suggestions for the Collector," Autograph Collectors' Journal 2(1):8-10, 1949.

3099. Leighton, J. "On the Library, Books, and Binding; Particularly with Respect to Their Restoration and Preservation," Journal of the Society of Arts 7:209-215, 1859.

3100. Lydenberg, Harry Miller. "Preservation of Modern Newspaper Files," Library Journal 40:240-242, 1915.

3101. _____. "Saving the Newspaper Files for Posterity," New York Evening Post p. 11, April 2, 1921.

3102. Minogue, Adelaide E. "Physical Care, Repair and Protection of Manuscripts," Library Trends 5:344-351, 1957.

3103. New York State Library, Division of Library Extension. Care of the Book Collection, a Manual of Suggestions: Weeding, Mending, Binding, Discarding. Albany: New York State Library, 1948.

3104. "On the Preservation of Manuscripts and Printed Books," Library Journal 53:710, 712-715, 1928.

3105. Papritz, J. New Methods, New Material, and New Results in the Restoration and Conservation of Archives and in Documentary Photo Techniques Since 1950. Report of the International Congress of Archives, Göteborg, 1960.

3106. Plenderleith, H. J. and A. E. A. Werner. "Technical Notes on the Conservation of Documents," Journal Society of Archivists 1:195, 1958.

3107. "Preservation of Newspapers," ALA Bulletin 6:116-118, 1912.

3108. Preserve Your Pictures: A Handbook on the Care and Preservation of Works of Art. New York: American Federation of Arts, 1963.

3109. Protecting Essential Operating Records. Raleigh, N. C.: North Carolina State Department of Archives and History, 1967. A straight-to-the-point 16 page management handbook.

3110. "Rare Books and Special Material in Museum Libraries: A Roundtable," Special Libraries 52(1):9-21, 1961.

3111. Santucci, L. "The Application of Chemical and Physical Methods to Conservation of Archival Materials," Bollettino dell Istituto di Patologia del Libro 20:85-111, 1961. An excellent introduction to the scientific approach to conservation and restoration of library materials with comments. 182 other references pertinent to the subject.

3112.   Scott, Alexander.   The Cleaning and Restoration of
        Museum Exhibits.   London: H. M. Stationery Of-
        fice, 1921-23-26.   Three reports including clean-
        ing of pictures.

3113.   Scribner, B. W.   "Preservation of Records in Li-
        braries," Library Quarterly 4:371-383, 1934.

3114.   Seifert, J. W.   "Flash Photography of Ultra-Violet
        Fluorescence," Exposition of Painting Conservation.
        Brooklyn: Brooklyn Museum, 1962.

3115.   Smith, R. D.   "The Extension of Book Life," The
        Library Binder 18(2), 1970.   Practical suggestions
        regarding the choice of materials for book making
        and repair.   Also useful hints on handling books.

3116.   Stout, George L.   The Care of Pictures.   New York:
        Columbia University Press, 1948.   A scientific
        explanation of the proper treatment of all kinds of
        pictures.

3117.   Sugden, R. P.   Care and Handling of Art Objects.
        New York: Metropolitan Museum of Art, 1946.
        Includes information on drawings, prints, water
        colors, manuscripts and rare books.

3118.   Tauber, Maurice F. et al.   Technical Services in Li-
        braries: Acquisitions, Cataloging, Classification,
        Binding, Photographic Reproduction, and Circula-
        tion Operations.   New York: Columbia University
        Press, 1954.

3119.   "Times Files Saved by New Method," New York Times
        p. 12, August 12, 1921.

3120.   Tribolet, Harold.   "Protect Those Documents," Auto-
        graph Collectors Journal January 1950.

3121.   _____.   "Trends in Preservation," Library Trends
        13(2), 1964.

3122.   Vail, R. W. G. (Issue Editor).   "Manuscripts and
        Archives," Library Trends 6, 1957.   Entire issue.

3123.   Walton, R. P.   "Causes and Prevention of Deteriora-
        tion in Book Materials," Bulletin 33:235-266, 1929.
        New York Public Library.   A chronological ar-
        rangement of the literature on book preservation to
        1932, taken principally from leather and paper
        periodicals.

3124.   Weiss, D. A.   The Business of Librarians: Mainten-
        ance of Materials.   Boston: Library Binding In-
        stitute, 1961.

3125.   Winger, H. W. and R. D. Smith.   Deterioration and
        Preservation of Library Materials.   Chicago: The
        University of Chicago Press, 1970.   Papers

presented at the Thirty-fourth Annual Conference
of the Graduate Library School, August 4-6, 1969.
These papers are an excellent review of the causes
of deterioration, the technology of paper, binding
practices, conservation in library administration,
and a look at current research in preservation
techniques.

LEATHER [See also under IX. --Bibliographies--
Leather]

3126. Archer, John. "A Ten Year Test of Bindings," Bul-
       letin 40(1):97-100, 1936. New York Public Li-
       brary. Reports results after ten years use in
       reading room of fifteen identical books bound in
       various leathers and buckram.
3127. Banks, Paul N. Treating Leather Bookbindings. Chi-
       cago: Newberry Library, 1968. A leaflet sum-
       marizing treatments.
3128. _____ et al. "Program on Leather," Guild of
       Book Workers Journal 1(3), 1963. Treatment of
       decaying leather with potassium lactate.
3129. Baughman, Roland. "Conservation of Old and Rare
       Books," Library Trends 4, 1956.
3130. Belaya, I. K. "Preservation of Leather Bindings at
       the Lenin State Library in The U. S. S. R. ,"
       UNESCO Bulletin for Libraries 13:125-126, 1959.
3131. Belyakova, L. A. "Protection of Leather-bound Books
       from Mold Attack," Collection of Materials on the
       Preservation of Library Resources. Moscow, 1958.
       Available from National Technical Information
       Center, Springfield, Virginia.
3132. _____ and O. V. Kozulina. "Book Preservation in
       the U. S. S. R. Libraries," UNESCO Bulletin for Li-
       braries 15:198-202, 1961.
3133. Breillat, Pierre. "Rare Books Section in the Li-
       brary," UNESCO Bulletin for Libraries 19:174-194,
       251-263, 1965.
3134. The Care of Books. London: British Museum, n. d.
       Single sheet of excellent general instructions in re-
       gard to insect pests and mould growth.
3135. The Causes and Prevention of the Decay of Bookbind-
       ing Leather. London: Printing Industry Research
       Association, 1933. A pamphlet.
3136. Dahl, Sverre. "The Effects of Fungicides on Deteri-
       oration of Leather," Journal American Leather

Chemists Association 52(11):611-621, 1957.

3137. DeBeukelaer, F. L. "Preservation of Hides and
Skins," in O'Flaherty, F.; W. T. Roddy and R.
M. Lollar (eds.). The Chemistry and Technology
of Leather. New York: Reinhold Publishing Co.,
1956. pp. 194-218.

3138. Frey, R. W. and C. W. Beebe. "Preliminary Experiments on Prevention of Leather 'Red Rot',"
Journal American Leather Chemists Association
29, 1934.

3139. _____ and F. P. Veitch. Preservation of Leather
Bookbindings. Washington: U. S. Government
Printing Office, n. d. U. S. Department of Agricul-
ture Leaflet No. 69.

3140. Gairola, T. R. "Preservation of Parchment," Journal of Indian Museums 14, 1954 and 16, 1960.

3141. Gall, Günter. "The Conservation of Leather," Museumskunde 30(2):120-121, 1961. In German.

3142. Innes, R. F. "The Preservation of Bookbinding
Leathers," Library Association Record 52(12):458-
461, 1950.

3143. _____ . "The Preservation of Vegetable-tanned
Leather Against Deterioration," in Progress in
Leather Science. London: British Leather Manufacturers Research Association, 1948. An important authoritative work on the causes and prevention
of leather deterioration. Discusses potassium
lactate and other preservatives.

3144. "Leather Preservation," American Archivist 1:114,
1938; 9:228, 1946; 16:116, 125, 1953.

3145. Lollar, R. M. "Para-nitrophenol as a Fungicide for
Leather," Journal Society Leather Trades Chemists
49, 1954.

3146. Meldrum, R. S. "Rotproofing of Leather," Chemical
Products 12(1):4-6, 1948.

3147. Missar, Margaret du F. Preservation and Treatment
of Old Leather Bindings. Washington: National
Trust For Historic Preservation, n. d.

3148. "New Wax for Bookbindings," UNESCO Bulletin for Libraries 13:99, 1959. Describes use of Mme.
Flieder's CIRE 212.

3149. Plenderleith, H. J. "The Preservation of Leather,"
Museums Journal 27:217-218, 1928. London.

3150. _____ . The Preservation of Leather Bookbindings.
London: British Museum, 1946.

3151. Rogers, J. S. and C. W. Beebe. Leather Bookbindings, How to Preserve Them. Washington: U. S.

Government Printing Office, 1958. Department of
Agriculture Leaflet No. 398.

3152. Smith, R. D. The Preservation of Leather Bookbindings from Sulfuric Acid Deterioration. Unpublished
thesis, University of Chicago, 1964.

3153. Todd, William. Conservation of Skin and Leather.
Toronto: History Branch, Department of Travel
and Publicity, n. d.

3154. The Treatment of Leather Bookbindings. London:
British Museum, n. d. A single sheet of instructions based on practices at the British Museum.

3155. Tribolet, Harold W. "Binding and Related Problems,"
American Archivist 16:115-126, 1953. Comments
on what should and should not be done to care for
important library materials. Includes remarks on
binding, binding restoration, vellum and parchment,
paper restoration, framing, storage, and preserving
buildings.

3156. Veitch, F. P. The Care of Leather. Washington:
U. S. Government Printing Office, 1920. U. S. Department of Agriculture Farmer's Bulletin No.
1183.

3157. _____ and R. W. Frey. Preservation of Leather
Bookbindings. Washington: U. S. Government
Printing Office, 1930. U. S. Department of Agri-
culture Leaflet No. 69.

3158. Walton, R. P. "Causes and Prevention of Deterioration in Book Materials," Bulletin 33:235-236, 1929.
New York Public Library. Includes a chronological
arrangement to 1932 of literature on leather preservation taken principally from leather periodicals.

3159. Waters, Peter. "Some Technical Problems of Book
Conservation," Guild of Book Workers Journal 7(2),
1968-1969. Waters' talks at the Conservation
Center of the Institute of Fine Arts of New York
University, March 1, 1969.

PARCHMENT AND VELLUM

3160. Fackelmann, Anton. "Das Pergament: Seine Herstel-
lung und Seine Betreuung in den Bibliotheken,"
Biblos Oesterreichische Zeitschrift fur Buch und
Bibliothekswesen 10(3):118-130, 1961. Vienna. On
the care of parchment.

3161. Gairola, T. R. "Preservation of Parchment," Journal
of Indian Museums 14, 1958 and 16, 1960.

3162. Sadurska, Irena and Romuald Kowalik. "Protection of
       Parchment Against Microflora," Annali della Scuola
       Speciale per Archivisti e Bibliotecari dell'Universita
       di Roma 9(1-2):51-62, 1969. Amongst other things
       the authors report that parchment is more prone
       to damage by fungi after fumigation with ethylene
       oxide.
3163. Wächter, Otto. "Reflections on the Theme of Parch-
       ment Restoration," Allgemeiner Anzieger für Buch-
       bindereien 75(5), 1962. In German. Stuttgart.

       PAPER [See also under VIII. --J.; and IX. --Bibliog-
       raphies--Paper]

3164. American Library Association Committee. "Preser-
       vation of Newspapers," American Library Associa-
       tion Bulletin 6:116, 1912 and 7:22-26, 1913.
3165. Annon, G. L. "Paper Preservation: New Hope for
       Survival," Medical Library Association Bulletin
       53:384-387, 1965.
3166. Anthony, Donald C. "Caring for Your Manuscripts
       and Related Material," Hobbies Magazine 68(8):110-
       111, 126, 1964.
3167. Barrow, W. J. "An Evaluation of Document Restora-
       tion Processes," American Documentation 4:53-54,
       1953.
3168. _____. Stabilization of Modern Book Papers.
       Richmond: Virginia State Library, 1958. A
       preliminary report.
3169. Buyn, K. E. C. "Paper Permanence," Bulletin As-
       soc. Tech. Ind. Papetiere 5:231, 1951.
3170. Chakravorti, S. "Vacuum Fumigation: A New Tech-
       nique for Preservation of Records," Science and
       Culture 11, 1943-1944.
3171. Church, Randolph W. "Is There a Doctor in the
       House?" Publishers' Weekly 175:76, 78-80, 1959.
       An essay on the problems of paper conservation.
3172. _____. "Perish the Paper, Perish the Book,
       Perish the Thought: An Inquiry," Publishers'
       Weekly 172:54-58, 1957.
3173. Clapp, Anne F. "Curatorial Works of Art on Paper
       Supports," Intermuseum Conservation Assoc. News-
       letter 3, June 1965. Care of prints and pictures.
3174. Clarke, Carl D. Pictures, Their Preservation and
       Restoration. Butler, Md.: Standard Arts Press,
       1959.

3175. Dabney, Virginius. "New Ways to Permanent Files," Saturday Review 47(19):67-68, 1964. Discusses new permanent/durable papers.

3176. Dauze, Pierre. "La question de la conservation du papier dans les bibliothèques publiques et privées et un moyen de la résoudre," Procès-verbaux et mémoires. Congrès international des bibliothécaires tenu à Paris du 20 au 23 août 1900. Paris: Welter, 1901. pp. 227-231.

3177. Dolloff, Francis W. and R. L. Perkinson. How to Care for Works of Art on Paper. Boston: Museum of Fine Arts, 1971. Forty-six page pamphlet on the history of paper, the enemies of paper and matting and framing.

3178. Fitzpatrick, John C. Notes on the Care, Cataloging, Calendaring, and Arranging of Manuscripts. Washington: Library of Congress, 1913. Other editions were published in 1921, 1928, and 1934. A description of the practices of the Division of Manuscripts, Library of Congress, this work is still important for the observations on arranging and flattening.

3179. Grove, Lee E. "The Conservation of Paper," Museum News 42(2):15-20, 1963. Illus. A summary of Barrow's work on permanent/durable book paper and spray deacidification. Bibliography.

3180. _____. "Paper Deterioration--An Old Story," College and Research Libraries 25:365-374, 1964.

3181. India, Imperial Record Department, New Delhi. Notes on Preservation of Records. Simla: Government of India Press, 1941.

3182. Jaffar, S. M. "Protection of Paper," ICOM News 5:33, 1952.

3183. Kane, Lucile M. "A Guide to the Care and Administration of Manuscripts," Bulletin of the American Association for State and Local History 2:11, 1966. Contains a short but excellent section on manuscript preservation. Selective bibliography on care and administration of manuscripts.

3184. Kathpalia, Y. P. "Deterioration and Conservation of Paper, IV: Neutralization," Indian Pulp and Paper 17:245-251, 1962. Includes discussion of early attempts at gaseous deacidification with ammonia.

3185. Kimberly, A. E. and B. W. Scribner. Summary Report of National Bureau of Standards Research on Preservation of Records. Washington: National Bureau of Standards, 1937. NBS Publication No. 144.

3186. Kremer, Alvin W. "The Preservation of Wood Pulp
       Publications," College and Research Libraries
       15:205-209, 1954.

3187. Langwell, W. H. "The Preservation of Paper Re-
       cords," Archives 2(11), 1954.

3188. Lovett, Robert W. "Care and Handling of Non-Gov-
       ernmental Archives," Library Trends 5:380-389,
       1957. A bibliography is included.

3189. Ludwig, H. "Some Hints on the Care and Treatment
       of Graphics, Drawings, etc.," Neue Museumskunde
       3:158-160, 1960. Leipzig.

3190. Lydenberg, Harry M. "On the Preservation of Manu-
       scripts and Printed Books," Library Journal 53:712-
       716, 1928.

3191. _____. "Preservation of Modern Newspaper Files,"
       Library Journal 40:240, 1915.

3192. Minogue, Adelaide E. "Physical Care, Repair, and
       Protection of Manuscripts," Library Trends 5:344-
       351, 1957.

3193. Norton, Margaret C. "Handling Fragile Manuscripts,"
       Illinois Libraries 29:410-413, 460-464, 1947.

3194. Oregon State Public Welfare Commission. Drying of
       Flood Damaged Records of Marion County Welfare
       Office. Salem, Oregon: State Library, 1965. Ten
       pages.

3195. Peckham, Howard H. "Arranging and Cataloging
       Manuscripts in the William L. Clements Library,"
       American Archivist 1:215-229, 1938. Instructions
       for handling manuscripts in bulk.

3196. Plenderleith, H. J. and A. E. A. Werner. "Technical
       Notes on the Conservation of Documents," Journal
       of the Society of Archivists 1:7, 1958.

3197. Pravilova, T. A. et al. "Effect of a High-Frequency
       Electromagnetic Field on Paper," New Methods for
       the Restoration and Preservation of Documents and
       Books. Moscow, 1960. Available from National
       Technical Information Service, Springfield, Virginia.

3198. "Preservation of Newspapers," ALA Bulletin 6:116,
       1912 and 7:22-26, 1913.

3199. Redstone, L. J. and F. W. Steer. Local Records;
       Their Nature and Care. London: G. Bell and
       Sons Ltd., 1953.

3200. Rossiter, Henry Preston. "On the Care of Prints,"
       Print Collector's Quarterly 30:33-40, 1950. Recom-
       mendations are made on the care and handling of
       fine prints. Describes injuries caused by the cut-
       ting of margins, the abrasive action of dirt and

dust, careless handling, damp air, water drip and
poor mounts.

3201. Schraubstadter, Carl. Care and Repair of Japanese
Prints. Cornwall-on-Hudson, N. Y.: Idlewild
Press, 1948.

3202. Schulz, H. C. "The Care and Storage of Manuscripts
in the Huntington Library, " Library Quarterly 5:78-
86, 1935.

3203. Some Experiments Toward the Preservation of Paper
Made by the New York Public Library. Printed at
the New York Public Library for distribution at the
Paper Industries Exhibition, Grand Central Palace,
New York City, April 9-14, 1923.

3204. Tribolet, Harold. "Protect Those Documents, " Autograph Collectors Journal January 1950.

3205. Veitch, F. P. Paper-Making Materials and Their
Conservation. Washington: U. S. Government
Printing Office, 1911. U. S. Chemistry Bureau,
Circular 41. First issued December 31, 1908.
Reprinted March 31, 1909, January 31, 1911.

3206. Venter, J. S. M. "Aging and Preservation of Paper, " CSIR Development Study U. D. C. 676. 33. 017 /019.
Pretoria, South Africa, Sept. 1966. A bibliography
of 146 references with a general description complete to 1965.

3207. Volina, T. L. et al. Protection of Cardboard from
Biological Deterioration. Moscow: C. N. I. T. I. ,
1963.

3208. Weber, C. G. et al. "Effects of Fumigants on Paper, " Journal of Research, National Bureau of
Standards 15(3):271, 1935.

3209. Werner, A. E. A. "The Conservation of Manuscripts, " Research 11:166-172, 1957.

3210. _____. "The Preservation of Archives, " Journal
Society of Archivists 1, 1955-1959. Discusses atmosphere control, deacidification and lamination.

3211. Wilson, William K. "Record Papers and Their Preservation, " The Capital Chemist 6(2):46-51, 1956.

3212. Yabrova, R. R. "The Prevention of Aging of Books
and Newspapers, " Collection of Materials on the
Preservation of Library Materials (Moscow, 1953).
Springfield, Va.: National Technical Information
Service, 1964.

PHOTOCOPYING

3213. American Library Association, Resources and Technical Services Division, Reprinting Committee.
"Lending to Reprinters: A Policy Statement," Revised and adopted April 1968, 4 p. (Mimeographed).
Sets up guidelines for libraries interested in initiat-
ing a reprint program for lending to reprinters, or
for libraries acquiring reprints.

3214. Ballou, Hubbard W. (ed.). Guide to Microreproduction Equipment. 4th ed. Annapolis: National Microfilm Association, c1969. This guide is essential
for every library that uses or produces microforms. Descriptions and evaluations of cameras,
readers, printers, and auxiliary equipment are
given in detail.

3215. Binkley, Robert C. et al. Manual on Methods of Reproducing Research Materials. Ann Arbor, Mich.:
Edwards Brothers, Inc., 1936. A survey made for
the Joint Committee on Materials for Research of
the Social Science Research Council and the American Council of Learned Societies.

3216. "Copying," Kodak Data Book No. M-1. Rochester,
N.Y.: Eastman Kodak Co., 1968.

3217. Diaz, Albert. "Microreproduction Information
Sources," Library Resources and Technical Services 11:211-214, 1967.

3218. Doerner Institut, München. "Measures to be Taken
When Objects of Art are Filmed or Televised,"
Museumskunde 3:155-157, 1966. A few protective
rules are given. In German.

3219. Hawken, William R. Enlarged Prints from Library
Microforms: A Study of Processes, Equipment and
Materials. Chicago: American Library Associa-
tion, 1963. Library Technology Project Publication
No. 6.

3220. _____. Copying Methods Manual. Chicago: American Library Association, 1966. Library Technology
Project Publication No. 11. Evaluates and explains characteristics of materials and microforms,
processes, methods and techniques.

3221. _____. Photocopying from Bound Volumes: A
Study of Machines, Methods, and Materials. Chicago: American Library Association, 1962. Library Technology Project Publication No. 4.

3222. Kühn, Hermann. "The Use of Heat-Protection Filters
When Works of Art are Filmed or Televised,"

Studies in Conservation 12(3), 1967.

3223. Lewis, Chester M. and William H. Offenhauser, Jr. Micro-recording: Industrial and Library Application. New York: Inter-Science Publishers, 1956.

3224. Leisinger, A. H. Jr. Microphotography for Archives. Washington: International Council on Archives, 1968. A brief manual of introduction rather than an exhaustive treatise. Short but excellent bibliography.

3225. "Motion Picture Restoration Printer," American Archivist 31:83, 1968. Describes unique printer at Ohio State University.

3226. Nelson, Carl E. Microfilm Technology, Engineering and Related Fields. New York: McGraw-Hill, 1965. A basic book on the proper use of microfilm technology. It offers a wealth of factual material and solutions to technical problems.

3227. Papritz, John. Current Problems in the World of Archives. Stockholm: Ahnquist and Wiksell, 1960. A report to the 1960 International Council of Archives meeting.

3228. _____. New Methods, New Materials and New Results in the Restoration and Conservation of Archives and in Documentary Phototechniques Since 1950. Report to the International Congress of Archives, Goteborg, 1960.

3229. Skipper, James (ed.). "Photoduplication in Libraries," Library Trends 8:3, 1960. Entire issue.

3230. Sullivan, Robert C. "Developments in Reproduction of Library Materials and Graphic Communication, 1968," Library Resources and Technical Services 13:391-421, 1969. This covers computer-output-microfilm (COM), micropublishing projects, grants for microform research, copyright and photocopying, publications in the field, evaluation of equipment, and professional activities in the field.

3231. "Survey and Bibliography of Microreproduction Forms, Equipment, Technique and Problems," Special Libraries 51(2):59-76, 1960.

3232. Tholl, Joseph. "Ultra-violet Photography of Documents," Photographic Science and Technology Journal 17B:114-118, 1951.

3233. Ultraviolet and Fluorescence Photography. Rochester, N. Y.: Eastman Kodak Co. , 1968.

3234. U. S. Department of the Army. Copying Equipment. Washington: U. S. Government Printing Office, 1966. Technical Bulletin AG4, October 1965.

CLOTH COVERS

3235. Banks, Paul N. "Some Problems on Book Conserva-
       tion, " Library Resources and Technical Services
       12:330-338, 1968.
3236. Belyakova, L. A. and O. V. Kozulina. "Book Pres-
       ervation in USSR Libraries, " UNESCO Bulletin for
       Libraries 15(4):198-202, 1961.
3237. Chivers, C. The Paper and Binding of Recent Lend-
       ing Library Books. Chicago: American Library
       Association, 1909. Resume of an address before
       the ALA in 1909 expressing an awareness of the
       problems in connection with preserving books.
3238. Horton, Carolyn. Cleaning and Preserving Bindings
       and Related Materials. 2nd rv. ed. Chicago:
       American Library Association, 1969. Library
       Technology Project Publication No. 16. Any per-
       son who is charged with the care of books will find
       this volume invaluable. The procedures and tech-
       niques are clearly described, and the illustrations
       provide ample detail.
3239. Mortimer, E. A. Library Books: Their Care and
       Repair. Auckland, 1968. A hand book for library
       binding, instructors and librarians.
3240. Smith, R. D. "The Extension of Book Life, " The Li-
       brary Binder 18(2), 1970. Some important sugges-
       tions for improving the quality of cloth used in the
       manufacture of book covers, the nonaqueous de-
       acidification of paper, improving the formulation of
       pyroxylin coating for book cloth, and notes on
       handling, photocopying without damaging books.
3241. Tomlinson, John. The Conservation of Bound Volumes.
       London: Scottish Group, IIC, 1968. A twelve page
       monograph on preventive measures for book pres-
       ervation.
3242. Williams, Gordon. The Preservation of Deteriorating
       Books: An Examination of the Problem with Recom-
       mendations for a Solution. Library Journal 91:51-
       56, 189-194, 1966. Report by the Association of
       Research Libraries Committee on the Preservation
       of Research Library Materials. September 1964.

UNUSUAL MATERIALS

3243. Baer, N. S. and L. J. Majewski. "Ivory and Related
       Materials in Art and Archaeology, " supplement to

Art and Archaeology Technical Abstracts 8(2), 1970-1971. An annotated bibliography of 190 titles on care and preservation, etc. of ivory, bone and horn.

3244. Bhowmik, S. "Conservation of Palmleaf Manuscripts," Baroda Museum and Picture Gallery Bulletin 19:59-65, 1966.

3245. Bleck, R. D. "Conservation of Bronzes According to Thouvenin," Neue Museumskunde 9:47-50, 1966. Leipzig.

3246. Bosshard, H. H. "Actual Problems of Wood Protection," Holz-Roh-Werstoff 26(1):16-18, 1968.

3247. Cupr, V. and J. B. Pelikan. Elements of the Conservation of Metals in Museums. Prague: National Museum, 1964.

3248. Filliozat, J. "Manuscripts on Birch-Bark (Bhurjapatra) and Their Preservation," Indian Archives 1(2), 1947.

3249. Gladstone, B. "Guide to Marble Care," The New York Times Section 2, D27, November 27, 1966. How to remove stains and polish.

3250. Lewin, S. Z. "The Preservation of Natural Stone 1839-1965," Art and Archaeology Technical Abstracts 6(1), 1966. A thorough review of the literature on the conservation of stone.

3251. Mori, Toru and Ikno Asano. "Prevention of Decay and Insect Damage in Wood," Scientific Papers on Japanese Antiquities and Art Crafts. Tokyo: 1951.

3252. Murphy, J. F. and C. J. Armore. "Protective Oxides on Metal Surfaces," French patent 1,426,811, January 28, 1966. Describes a soap solution for achieving the same.

3253. Pinto, Edward H. and Eva R. Pinto. The Care of Woodwork in the Home: Cleaning, De-Worming, Repair and Surface Maintenance of Furniture and other Movables, as Well as the Protection and Treatment of the Timber of the Structure. Hollywood-by-the-Sea, Florida: Trans-Atlantic Arts, 1955.

3254. Rawlins, F. I. G. "The Cleaning of Stone Work," Studies in Conservation 3(1), 1957.

3255. Reisdorf, H. "Blue Stain on Lacquered Wood Surfaces, Its Prevention and Cure," Deutsche Malerblatt 39(3):106-108, 1968.

3256. Schlegal, M. "Tarnish-preventing Transparent Lacquer or Plastic Coatings for Silverware," German patent 1,207,244, December 16, 1965.

3257. Schulz, F. "Practical Hints on the Treatment and
       Care of Coins and Medals -- --, " Neue Museum-
       skunde 4:174-178, 1961. Leipzig.
3258. Telkes, T. "Protection of Wood by Paints and Var-
       nishes, " Travel Peinture 22(1):4-13, 1967.
3259. Tulka, J. and L. Cerveny. "Inhibition of the Cor-
       rosion of Silver, Copper and Their Alloys by Sul-
       phur Compounds, " Czech patent 115,779, August
       15, 1965.

PHOTOGRAPHIC MATERIALS

3260. Archives Handbook Series No. 3: Microfilm Proce-
       dures. Denver, Colorado: Division of State Ar-
       chives and Public Records, 1964. Contains basic
       information on care of film and equipment.
3261. Ballou, H. W. Guide to Microreproduction Equip-
       ment. Annapolis: National Microfilm Association,
       1959.
3262. Brown, H. G. "Problems of Storing Film for Ar-
       chival Purposes, " British Kinematography 20:150-
       162, 1952.
3263. Calhoun, J. M. "Air Conditioning in Storing and
       Handling Motion Picture Film, " Heating and Venti-
       lating 46:66-69, 1949.
3264. _____. "The Preservation of Motion Picture Film, "
       American Archivist 30:517-525, 1967. Sound guid-
       ance from Eastman Kodak laboratories.
3265. Clapp, Verner W.; Francis H. Henshaw, and Donald
       C. Holmes. "Are Your Microfilms Deteriorating
       Acceptably?" Library Journal 80(6):589-595, 1955.
3266. Clerc, L. P. Photography, Theory and Practice.
       2nd ed. New York: Pitman, 1937. Care of
       photographic materials.
3267. Crabtree, J. I. and C. E. Ives. "The Storage of
       Valuable Motion Picture Film, " Journal of the So-
       ciety of Motion Picture Engineers 15:289-305, 1930.
3268. DeMitri, C. "The Preservation of Colour in Mounted
       Colour Prints, " Journal of Photographic Science
       November-December 1960. Protecting color photo-
       graphs.
3269. Eaton, George T. "Preservation, Deterioration, Res-
       toration of Photographic Images, " The Library
       Quarterly 40(1):85-98, 1970. An Assistant Division
       Head, Eastman Kodak Research Laboratories,
       discusses the nature of photographic materials,

their processing from the point of view of permanence, post-processing steps for archival records, storage of photographic material and restoration of deteriorated photo records.

3270. État des Microfilms de Securité Conservés aux Archives Nationales. Paris: French National Archives, 1962.

3271. Fassett, D. W.; F. J. Kolb, Jr., and E. M. Weigel. "Practical Film Cleaning for Safety and Effectiveness," Journal of the Society of Motion Picture and Television Engineers 67:572-589, 1958.

3272. Filing Negatives and Transparencies. Rochester, N.Y.: Eastman Kodak Co., 1960. Kodak Pamphlet P-12.

3273. Fowler, E. W. and L. B. Newell. "Storage and handling of motion picture film," Journal of the Society of Motion Picture Engineers 16:773-786, 1931.

3274. Gallo, F. "About the Conservation of Microfilms," Bolletino dell Istituto di Patologia del Libro 24(1-4):107-110, 1965.

3275. Hawken, W. R. Photocopying From Bound Volumes. Chicago: American Library Association, 1962. An evaluation of twenty commercial book copying devices.

3276. Hazard in the Handling and Storage of Nitrate and Safety Motion Picture Film. Rochester, N.Y.: Eastman Kodak Company, 1951.

3277. Henn, R. W. and B. D. Mack. "A Gold Protective Treatment for Microfilm," Photographic Science and Engineering 9(6), 1965.

3278. _____; D. G. Wiest, and B. D. Mack. "Microscopic Spots in Processed Microfilm," Photographic Science and Engineering 9:121, 1965. Reports that iodide ions in film fixing solutions minimizes the formation of blemishes.

3279. _____. "Microscopic Spots in Processed Microfilm: Inspection of Collections to Evaluate the Effect of Iodide," Photographic Science and Engineering 13, 1969.

3280. Henry, Edward A. "Books on Film: Their Use and Care," Library Journal 57:215-217, 1932.

3281. Hutchinson, G. L.; L. Ellis, and S. A. Ashmore. "The Surveillance of Cinematographic Record Film During Storage," Journal of the Society of Motion Picture and Television Engineers 54:381-383, 1950. Report No. 2/R/48, Chemical Research and

Development Establishment and the Department of
the Government Chemist, Ministry of Supply (British), February 1948.

3282. Kolb, F. J. Jr. and E. M. Weigel. "Lubrication of
Motion Picture Film, " Journal of the Society of
Motion Picture and Television Engineers 74:297-
307, 1965.

3283. Leisinger, A. H. Jr. Microphotography for Archives.
Washington: International Council on Archives,
1968. An introduction for the archivist rather than
an exhaustive treatise.

3284. Lewis, Chester M. and W. H. Offenhauser. Micro-
recording. New York: Interscience Publishers,
1956.

3285. Lindgren, E. "The Permanent Preservation of Cinematograph Film, " Proceedings British Society International Bibliography 5:97-104, 1943.

3286. _____. "The Preservation of Cinematograph Film
in the National Film Archive, " British Kinematogr.
Sound Telev. 5(10):290-292, 1968. Previous treatments of the film preservation problem have tended
to concentrate on special aspects in isolation.
This paper stresses the importance of a total pro-
cedural pattern involving selection, acquisition,
storage, testing, cataloging and the safeguarding of
preservation masters, and describes the work of
the British National Film Archive in putting such
a pattern into practice. Details of storage and
restoration procedures are given and typical storage
facilities are described.

3287. McCamy, C. S. Inspection of Processed Photographic
Records for Aging Blemishes. Washington: U. S.
Government Printing Office, 1964. Bureau of
Standards Handbook No. 96.

3288. _____ and C. I. Pope. Cause and Prevention of
Microfilm Blemishes. Washington: U. S. Government Printing Office, 1970. National Bureau of
Standards Technical News Bulletin STR-3910. This
important paper identifies causes for microfilm
blemishes and outlines measures for preventing
them.

3289. "Microfilm Preservation, " Chemistry 39(9):28-29,
1966. Washington. Summarizes National Bureau
of Standards findings on microfilm blemishes.
Recommends storage procedures.

3290. Mo Och Domsjo Altiebolag. "Anticurl Treatment for
Photographic Paper, " Netherlands patent application

6,401,434, August 19, 1965. Gives permanent
anticurl to photographs.

3291. Neblette, Carroll B. Photography: Its Materials and
Processes. 6th ed. New York: Van Nostrand, 1962.

3292. Noll, D. F. "The Maintenance of Microfilm Files,"
American Archivist 13:129-134, 1950.

3293. Ostroff, E. "Preservation of Photographs," Photography Journal 107(10):309-314, 1967. Considers
long-term storage and preservation of photographs,
including those produced by historically early
processes.

3294. Peele, David. "Bind or Film: Factors in the Decision," Library Resources and Technical Services
8:168-170, 1964.

3295. Piez, Gladys T. "Film Coatings--Do They Really
Protect Microfilm?" National Micro-News 67:125-
139, 1963.

3296. Pope, C. I. "A Simplified Method for Determining
Residual Thiosulfate in Processed Microfilms,"
Photographic Science and Engineering September-
October 1969.

3297. Prevention and Removal of Fungus on Processed Film.
Rochester, N.Y.: Eastman Kodak Co., 1961.
Kodak Pamphlet E-22.

3298. "Protection by Microfilming," American Archivist
15:221, 1952.

3299. Ryan, J. V.; J. W. Cummings, and A. C. Hutton.
"Fire Effects and Fire Control in Nitrocellulose
Photographic-Film Storage," Building Materials and
Structures Report No. 145. Washington: U.S. Department of Commerce, 1956.

3300. Scribner, B. W. Summary Report of Research at the
National Bureau of Standards on the Stability and
Preservation of Records on Photographic Film.
Washington: National Bureau of Standards, 1939.
Miscellaneous Publication M162.

3301. Standard for Storage and Handling of Cellulose Nitrate
Motion Picture Film. Boston: National Fire Protection Association, 1953. NFPA No. 40.

3302. Storage of Cellulose Acetate Motion Picture Film.
New York: National Board of Fire Underwriters,
1950. Obtainable from National Board of Fire
Underwriters, 85 John St., New York, N.Y.
Special Interest Bulletin No. 283.

3303. Storage of Microfilms, Sheet Films and Prints. Rochester, N.Y.: Eastman Kodak Co., 1946.

3304. Storage of Microfilms, Sheet Films and Prints. Ro-
       chester, N.Y.: Eastman Kodak Co., 1951. Safety
       film base and paper base materials only.
3305. Storage and Preservation of Microfilms. Rochester,
       N.Y.: Eastman Kodak Co., 1965. Kodak Pamph-
       let P-108.
3306. Storage and Preservation of Motion Picture Film.
       Rochester, N.Y.: Eastman Kodak Co., 1957.
3307. Storage of Processed Color Film. Rochester, N.Y.:
       Eastman Kodak Co., 1962.
3308. Weber, C. G. and J. R. Hill. "Care of Slide-Films
       and Motion Picture Films in Libraries," Journal
       of the Society of Motion Picture Engineers 27:691-
       702, 1936.
3309. White, Deane R. et al. "Polyester Photographic Film
       Base," Journal of the Society of Motion Picture
       Engineers 64:674-678, 1955.

RECORDS AND TAPES

3310. Athey, S. W. Magnetic Tape Recording. Washington:
       National Aeronautics and Space Agency, 1966. Dis-
       tributed by Clearinghouse for Federal Scientific
       and Technical Information, Springfield, Virginia.
       Highly technical but very valuable summary of in-
       formation on all aspects of tape recording, preser-
       vation, etc.
3311. Davidson, Helen L. "Handling Pictures and Audio-
       Visual Materials in Company Libraries and Ar-
       chives," Special Libraries 53:326-329, 1962.
3312. Evaluation of Record Players for Libraries, Series 2.
       Chicago: American Library Association, 1964.
3313. Gifford, Woodland and Dahl. "A Method for Testing
       Quality of Phonograph Records," Modern Plastics
       34(12):140ff, 1957.
3314. Handling, Repair and Storage of 16 mm Films. Ro-
       chester, N.Y.: Eastman Kodak Co., 1965. Kodak
       Pamphlet D-23.
3315. Magnetic Tape Recording. Springfield, Virginia:
       Clearinghouse for Federal Scientific and Technical
       Information, 1967. A survey of the entire range
       of recorder technology by NASA. NASA SP-5038.
3316. Offenhauser, W. O. Jr. "16 mm Sound Motion Pic-
       tures," Interscience 11:355-363, 1949. Preserva-
       tion and Recording.

3317. Pickett, A. G. and M. M. Lemcoe. Preservation
       and Storage of Sound Recordings. Washington:
       Library of Congress, 1959. The results of a pro-
       tracted study financed by the Rockerfeller Founda-
       tion to fill a gap in the basic research in the field
       of library conservation. Highly technical, with a
       lengthy bibliography for specialists.
3318. Porter, James D. "Sound in the Archives," American
       Archivist 27:327-336, 1964. The problems of crea-
       tion, storage and use of sound-recording materials.
3319. _____. Use and Storage of Magnetic Tape Sound
       Recordings as Public Records. Salem, Oregon:
       Oregon State Library, 1963. State Archives Divi-
       sion, Bulletin No. 6, Publication No. 27.
3320. Radocy, Frank. "Tape Storage Problems," Journal
       of the Audio Engineering Society 5:32ff, 1957.
3321. Schuursma, R. L. "The Sound Archives of the Uni-
       versity of Utrecht," Recorded Sound 15:246-250,
       1964.
3322. Selsted and Snyder. "Magnetic Recording--A Report
       on the State of the Art," Transactions International
       Recording Engineers Sept. -Oct. 1954.
3323. The Testing and Evaluation of Record Players for Li-
       braries. Chicago: American Library Association,
       1962. A report based on studies by Consumer's
       Research, Inc.
3324. "Your investment in magnetic tapes - proper cleaning,
       handling, storage, protection," Administrative
       Management 29(12):34, 1968.

IN THE TROPICS

3325. Ballou, H. A. "Book Protection," Tropical Agricul-
       ture 3:212-213, 1926.
3326. Baynes-Cope, A. David. "The Conservator's Point
       of View," Microbiological Deterioration in the
       Tropics. London: Society of Chemical Industry,
       1966.
3327. Boustead, W. M. "Problems of Art Conservation,"
       Hemisphere 13(4), 1969. A warning to art custodi-
       ans in Pacific and Asian countries on the increas-
       ing problem of air pollution.

3328. _____. "The Surface pH Measurement and Deacidification of Prints and Drawings in Tropical Climates," Studies in Conservation 9(2):50-58, 1964.

3329. Brommelle, N. S. "The Conservation of Museum Objects in the Tropics," Museum Climatology. London: International Institute for Conservation, 1968.

3330. Clark, Thomas D. "Preservation of Southern Historical Documents," American Archivist 16(1):27-37,
1953. Lament of a dealer in regard to saving important material.

3331. Compton, K. G. "Corrosion in the Tropics," Transactions of the Electro-Chemical Society 1947. Page
705.

3332. Control of Termites with Dieldrin and Protection of
Buildings from Attack. Shell Company of West
Africa, Ltd., 1958. Agricultural Circular No. 4.

3333. Coremans, P. "Preservation of the Cultural Heritage
in Tropical Africa," Museum 18(3):168-182, 1965.
Discusses the influence of climate on deterioration.

3334. Cundall, F. "The Preservation of Books in the
Tropics," Handbook of Jamaica. Kingston: Government Printing Office, 1926.

3335. Doe, Brian. "Notes on Museum and Art Gallery
Lighting in the Tropics," Studies in Conservation
10(2), 1965.

3336. Edwards, W. H. The Preservation of Wooden Buildings in the Tropics, with Special Reference to
Conditions Existing in Jamaica. Kingston: Government Printing Office, 1939.

3337. Flieder, Françoise; R. Heim and J. Nicot. "Com-
batting the Moulds Which Develop on Cultural
Property in Tropical Climates," The Conservation
of Cultural Property. Paris: UNESCO, 1968.

3338. _____. "Protection of Archival Documents Against
the Effects of Tropical Climates," Pérotin, Yves,
Manual of Tropical Archivology. Paris: Mouton
& Cie, 1966. [3352].

3339. Gay, F. J. "Soil Treatment for Termite Control in
Australia," Building: Lighting and Engineering
August 1963.

3340. Graveley, F. H. "Paraffin Wax as a Protection
Against Termites," Journal of the Bombay Natural
History Society 45:439-440, 1945.

3341. Gwam, L. C. "The Construction of Archives Build-
ings in Tropical Countries," in Pérotin, Yves,
Manual of Tropical Archivology. Paris: Mouton
& Cie, 1966. [3352].

3342. Harris, J. "Notes on Book Preservation in West Africa," WALA News 2(4):102-105, 1956.

3343. Kalshoven, L. G. E. "Book-beetle in the Netherlands Indies," Entomologische Mededeelingen van Nederlandsch-Indie 4:10-16, 1938.

3344. Keller, G. W. "Preventing Fungus and Bacteriological Attack in the Tropical Monsoon Period," Chemical Abstracts 53, 1959.

3345. Kennedy, Robert A. "Conservation in Humid Tropical Zone," Museum News 38(7):16-20, 1960. Also in Technical Bulletin, Museums Association of Middle Africa 1:10, 1960.

3346. _____. "Conservation in Wet Tropics," Technical Bulletin Museums Association of Middle Africa 1, 1959.

3347. Kowalik, R. and E. Czerwinska. "The Preservation of Organic Coatings in Tropical Conditions," Acta Microbiologica Polonica 9:59-60, 1960.

3348. Leonard, John M. and A. L. Pitman. "Tropical Performance of Fungicidal Coatings; A Statistical Analysis," Industrial Engineering Chemistry 43, 1951.

3349. Mould-proofing Treatment and Mould Resistance Test for Leathers for Use in Tropical Conditions. Milton Park, Egham: British Leather Manufacturers' Research Association, 1950.

3350. Noirot, C. and H. Alliot. La Lutte Contre les Termites. Paris: Masson, 1947.

3351. Operation Tropical Wet. Environmental and Microbiological Observations. Panama Canal Zone, Republic of Panama, November-December 1960. Washington: U. S. Government Printing Office, 1962.

3352. Pérotin, Yves (ed.). A Manual of Tropical Archivology. Paris: Mouton and Co., 1966. Part II discusses archives buildings for tropical countries, the protection of archival documents from tropical climates, termites, and the restoration of documents.

3353. Plumbe, W. J. Preservation of Books and Periodicals in Arab Countries. Paris: UNESCO, 1961.

3354. _____. The Preservation of Books in Tropical and Sub-Tropical Countries. London: Oxford University Press, 1964.

3355. _____. "Preservation of Library Materials in Tropical Countries," Library Trends 8:291-306, 1959. A short history of insect damage and

                methods of control and preservation going back to
                ancient Greece and Rome leads up to a description
                of methods of preservation used in many modern
                tropical countries.
3356.   . "Protection of Books Against Mildew, "
                Malayan Library Journal 1(2):11-13, 1961.
3357.   . "Storage and Preservation of Books, Peri-
                odicals and Newspapers in Tropical Climates, "
                UNESCO Bulletin for Libraries 12:156-162, 1958.
                A select bibliography.
3358.   . "Tropical Librarianship, " Library Review
                99:161-166, 1951.
3359.   "Protection of Documents in Tropics, " American Ar-
                chivist 3:212, 1940; 6:197, 1943; 7:159, 1944;
                15:379, 1952 and 17:54, 1954.
3360.   Rauschert, Mansfred.   "Paper and Writing Materials
                in Moist Tropical Regions, " Allgem. Papier-Rund-
                schau 48-50, 1957.   There is an abstract in The
                Paper Industry May 1957.
3361.   Reports on Plastics in the Tropics. 14. Low-Pres-
                sure Glass-Fibre Laminates Bonded with Polyester
                Resins.   Great Britain Ministry of Aviation.   Re-
                port TIL(BR)631; ... ASTIA Doc. 407178, 1962.
3362.   Reports on Plastics in the Tropics. 15. Protected
                Polythene.   Great Britain Ministry of Aviation.
                Report TIL(BR)632; ... ASTIA Doc. 407511, 1962.
3363.   Robinow, B. H.   "Books and Cockroaches; an Attempt
                to Cope with the Menace, " South African Libraries
                24(2):40-42, 1956.
3364.   Shipley, Sir A. E.   "Enemies of Books, " Tropical
                Agriculture 2:223-224, 1925.
3365.   Termites in The Humid Tropics.   Proceedings of the
                New Delhi symposium jointly organized by UNESCO
                and the Zoological Survey of India.   Paris:
                UNESCO, 1960.
3366.   Termites, Wood-Borers and Fungi in Buildings.   Re-
                port of the Committee on the Protection of Building
                Timbers in South Africa Against Termites, Wood-
                Boring Beetles and Fungi.   Pretoria: South Afri-
                can Council for Scientific and Industrial Research,
                1950.
3367.   "Termite-Proofing of Timber for Use in the Tropics, "
                London: H. M. Stationery Office, 1944.   Forest
                Products Research Laboratory No. 38.
3368.   Tropic Proofing; Protection Against Deterioration Due
                to Tropical Climates.   London: H. M. S. O. , 1949.
                Great Britain, Ministry of Supply and Department

of Scientific and Industrial Research.

3369. UNESCO.   The Conservation of Cultural Property with
       Special Reference to Tropical Conditions.   Paris:
       UNESCO, 1968.   This manual prepared in coopera-
       tion with the "Rome Centre" includes guidance on
       climate, moulds, insect pests, textiles, air condi-
       tioning, leather, wood, bone and ivory, and archi-
       val materials.

3370. Williams-Hunt, P. D. R.   Preserving Books and
       Prints in the Tropics.   Kuala Lumpur: Museums
       Department, Federation of Malaya, 1953.   Muse-
       ums Popular Pamphlet No. 3.

3371. Wood, G. W.   "Books and Documents: Protection
       from Insect Damage.   A Survey of the Problem
       and Methods of Control," Pesticides Abstracts and
       News Summary 2(2), 1956.   Section A, Insecticides.

GENERAL

3372. All the King's Horses. Chicago: The Lakeside
      Press, n. d.
3373. Almela Meliá, Juan. Manual de Reparación y Con-
      servación de Libros, Estampas y Manuscritos.
      Mexico: Instituto Panamericano de Geografia e
      Historia, 1949. Comision de Historia. Publica-
      cion 10.
3374. Application of Science in the Examination of Works of
      Art. Boston: Museum of Fine Arts, 1967. Pro-
      ceedings of the Second Seminar at the Museum of
      Fine Arts in 1965.
3375. Banks, P. N. "Some Problems in Book Conserva-
      tion, " Library Resources and Technical Services
      12:330-338, 1968.
3376. Barrow Research Laboratory. A Two Year Research
      Program: Permanence/Durability of the Book Vol.
      1. Richmond, Va.: W. J. Barrow Research
      Laboratory, 1963. Progress report on work at the
      laboratory on development of performance standards
      for library binding, spray deacidification, stability
      of polyvinyl acetate adhesives.
3377. Baughman, Roland. "Conservation of Old and Rare
      Books, " Library Trends 4, 1956.
3378. Baynes-Cope, A. David. The Repair of Globes.
      Stockholm: Royal Library, 1966.
3379. Belen'Kaya, N. G. "Methods of Restoration of Books
      and Documents, " New Methods for the Restoration
      and Preservation of Documents and Books. Mos-
      cow: 1960. An outstanding summary of traditional
      as well as new techniques for paper restoration as
      practiced in Russia, Europe and the U. S. Avail-
      able from National Technical Information Center,
      Springfield, Va.
3380. Belyakova, L. A. and O. V. Kozulina. "Book Pres-
      ervation in U. S. S. R. Libraries, " UNESCO Bulletin

for Libraries 15:198-202, 1961.

3381. Belov, G. A. "New Techniques, New Materials and New Experiences Concerning Restoration of Documents and Seals, Preservation of Maps and Plans and Photography Since 1950," Archivum 10:72-80, 1960.

3382. Beyerman, J. J. "Een nistekend conserveringsmiddel voor leren banden," Nederlands Archievenblad 67:30-31, 1963. An unusual means of preserving books. Abstract in American Archivist 27:526, 1964.

3383. Bhargava, K. D. Repair and Preservation of Records. New Delhi: National Archives of India, 1959.

3384. Blaquière, Henri. "La Restauration: Un des Moyens de Sauvetage des Archives Communales," La Gazette des Archives 50, 1965. Paris.

3385. Bonnardot, A. Essai sur l'Art de Restaurer les Estampes et les Livres. New York: Burt Franklin, 1967. Reprint of 1858 text on bleaching, decolorizing, repairing, etc. of books, prints and drawings.

3386. Brandi, Cesare. "Il Fondamento Teorico del Restauro," Bolletino Istituto Centrale Restauro 1:5-12, 1950.

3387. Bull, David et al. "Blanching." London: IIC-UK Group, n. d. A mimeographed paper which summarizes the views of British conservators on the causes and treatment of the white "bloom" sometimes found on painted or varnished surfaces.

3388. Clark, J. W. The Care of Books. Cambridge, England: Cambridge University Press, 1901.

3389. The Cleaning and Restoration of Museum Exhibits. London: H. M. Stationery Office, 1921. Contains instructions for cleaning and bleaching prints and pictures.

3390. Collection of Articles About the Preservation of Books. Moscow: Lenin Library, 1958. Book Hygiene and Restoration Dept. Instructions for book care.

3391. Coremans, P. Training of Technical Personnel--Conservation. Report submitted to the Seventh General Conference of ICOM, New York, 1965.

3392. Cunha, George M. "Soluble Nylon: A New Tool for Restorationists," Guild of Book-Workers Journal 4(2), 1965-1966.

3393. Deobarats, Klaus; Otto Wächter, and L. Ritterpusch (eds.). Internationaler Restauratorentag

Arbeitsgemainschaft der Archiv-, Bibliotheks-, und
Graphikrestauratoren. Freiburg in Breisgau:
I. A. D. A. Informationsstelle, 1969. This is the
proceedings of the conference held by practicing
graphic art, library and archives restorers in
Freiburg, Basel and Zurich in September 1967.
Much good practical information but in German.

3394. The Deterioration and Preservation of Book Material
Stored in Libraries. Garston: Building Research
Station, 1949. Great Britain, Department of Sci-
entific and Industrial Research note No. D. 62.

3395. Ellis, Roger. The Principles of Archive Repair.
London: London School of Printing and Graphic
Arts, 1951.

3396. Flieder, Françoise. La Conservation Des Documents
Graphiques. Paris: Editions Eyrolles, 1969.

3397. France-Lanord, A. "How to Question an Object Before Restoring It, " Archeologia 6:8-13, 1965.
Paris. Stresses the importance of collaboration
between conservator, curator and scientist.

3398. Gairola, T. R. Handbook of Chemical Conservation
of Museum Objects. Baroda: University of Baroda, Department of Museology, 1959.

3399. Gibson, B. M. "The Use of the Air-Abrasive Process
for Cleaning Ethnological Materials, " Studies in
Conservation 14:155-164, 1969. Describes a device
for mechanical dry cleaning of ethnological specimens, including leather, paper, textiles, shell,
bone and ivory.

3400. Grabor, I. A. (ed.). Problems of Restoration and
Conservation of Objects of Art. Moscow: Academy
of Arts, 1960. A methodical guide. Text in Russian but 70 interesting illustrations. Lengthy summary and review in Studies in Conservation 8(2),
1963.

3401. Guha, Roy K. K. "How to Preserve Books, " Modern
Librarian 9:79-87, 1939.

3402. Gupta, R. C. "A Review of Work in Conservation in
the National Archives of India, " Conservation of
Cultural Property in India 1:54-61, 1960.

3403. Harrison, T. "The Care of Books, " Bookcollector's
Quarterly 3:1-14, 1931.

3404. Haslam, W. The Book of Trade Secrets, Recipes and
and Instructions for Renovating, Repairing, Improving and Preserving Old Books and Prints. London:
J. Haslam & Co. Ltd., 1910.

3405. _____ . Library Handbook of Genuine Trade Secrets and Instructions. London: Foyles, 1923.

3406. Henderson, James W. and Robert G. Krupp. "The Librarian as Conservator," The Library Quarterly 40(1):176-198, 1970. The Chief Research Libraries, and Chief, Science and Technology Division, Research Libraries, New York Public Library, consider the librarian's responsibility in administering their responsibilities in conservation. Excellent historical background; well documented. Offers suggestions for organization and management. Includes comments by Paul Banks on the role of the conservator under the librarian.

3407. Hensel, Evelyn. "Treatment of Nonbook Materials," Library Trends 2:187-198, 1953. Bibliography is included.

3408. Hey, Margaret. "The Use of the Scanning Electron Microscope in Document Restoration Problems," Restaurator 1(4):233-244, 1970. Describes the application of this instrument to document restoration and its advantages over other scientific devices. Well illustrated and has a bibliography of 24 pertinent articles.

3409. Hummel, Ray O. Jr. and W. J. Barrow. "Lamination and Other Methods of Restoration," Library Trends 4(3):259-268, 1956.

3410. ICOM. Problems of Conservation in Museums. London: George Allen and Unwin, Ltd., 1969.

3411. IIC-American Group - Technical Papers from 1968 through 1970. New York: Conservation Center, New York University. Twenty-seven articles on conservation by members of IIC-AG.

3412. Jenkinson, Sir Hillary. "The Principles and Practice of Archive Repair Work in England," Archivum 2:31-41, 1952.

3413. Kathpalia, Y. P. "Care of Books in Libraries," Indian Archives 9:147-154, 1955.

3414. Keck, Caroline. "Technical Assistance; Where to Find It; What to Expect," Curator 8(3), 1965. Primarily for museum staffs.

3415. Khovkina, K. Kh. "Recommendations of a Restorer," Saltykov-Shchedrin 33-40, 1958. Leningrad State Public Library. Practical advice for beginners.

3416. _____ . The Simplest Operations in Book Restoration. Leningrad: State Public Library, 1954. A 16-page practical guide for librarians. In Russian.

3417. Kimberly, Arthur E.   "Repair and Preservation in the
       National Archives," American Archivist 1:111-117,
       1938.
3418. Kremer, Alvin W.   "The Preservation of Wood Pulp
       Publications," College and Research Libraries
       15:205-209, 1954.
3419. Langwell, W. H.   The Conservation of Books and
       Documents. London: Pitman, 1957.
3420. Lawrence, George H. M.   "Care and Preservation of
       Library Materials," Arnoldia 30(2):56-66, 1970.
       The text of Dr. Lawrence's talk presented at the
       Massachusetts Horticultural Society's conference
       November 1969.
3421. Lowe, David K.   "The Case of the Vanishing Re-
       cords," American Heritage 20(5), 1969.   Summar-
       izes the work of W. J. Barrow.
3422. Lyon, R. Arcadius.   "Ultra-violet Rays as Aids to
       Restorers," Technical Studies in the Field of the
       Fine Arts 2:153-157, 1934.
3423. Mahmood, A.   "Preservation Methods," Granthalaya
       58-65, 1955.
3424. Marconi, B. L.   Aesthetic Problems in Conservation
       of Art Objects on Paper and Parchment.   Paper
       presented at the 1969 plenary meeting of the ICOM
       Committee for Conservation in Amsterdam.   Photo-
       stat copies available from Rome Centre, 254 Via
       Cavour, Rome.
3425. The Million Charms of Empress Shotoku.   Chicago:
       The Lakeside Press, 1966.   A collection of tales
       about the preservation of rare books and documents
       at the Lakeside Press rare book department.
3426. Minogue, Adelaide E.   The Repair and Preservation
       of Records.   Washington: U. S. National Archives,
       1943.   Bulletin No. 5.   Includes a classified bib-
       liography on causes and prevention of deterioration
       of paper, leather, and binding.
3427. _____ .   "Treatment of Fire and Water Damaged
       Records," American Archivist 9:17-25, 1946.
3428. Muhurkar, Kamla.   "Restoration of a Globe," Con-
       servation of Cultural Property in India 3:38-39,
       1968.
3429. "The Murray Pease Report," Studies in Conservation
       9:116-121, 1964.   A report by a Committee on
       Professional Standards set up by the American
       Group (IIC).   A useful outline of practical, ethical
       and legal aspects of conservation and technical
       examination for the professional conservator.

3430. Natu, K. S. "Use of Vacuum Hot Table for Conser-
       vation, " Conservation of Cultural Property in India
       2:76-79, 1967. Describes use of hot table for
       document repair.
3431. Nkrumah, J. and A. Cains. The Restoration System
       of The Biblioteca Nazionale Centrale Di Firenze.
       Florence: Biblioteca Nazionale, 1970. A small
       pamphlet describing in general terms the restora-
       tion effort underway to save the 17th and 18th cen-
       tury Magliabechi and Palatina Libraries. Includes
       descriptions of restoration processes.
3432. Nordstrand, O. K. "Chinese Double-Leaved Books
       and Their Restoration, " Libri 17, 1967.
3433. Pallenberg, Corrado. "Restoration of Ancient Books, "
       Catholic Market 3:82-83, 1964. Describes Institute
       for the Scientific Restoration of Books, Rome.
3434. Petrova, L. G. "Procedure for the Restoration of
       Books, Other Printed Matter, and Manuscripts, "
       Collection of Materials on the Preservation of Li-
       brary Resources. Moscow, 1953. English transla-
       tion available from National Technical Information
       Service, Springfield, Va.
3435. (Plastic Cleaning). Cleaning and Maintenance of
       "Perspex" Acrylic Sheet. London: Imperial Chem-
       ical Industries, n. d. Technical Data Sheet PX
       TD. 228. Describes methods for cleaning plexi-
       glass sheets.
3436. Plenderleith, H. J. "La Conservation des Estampes,
       Dessins et Manuscrits, " Mouseion 29-30, 81-104,
       1935; 33-34, 199-227, 1936. An early work of
       the author, most of which is included in his later
       The Conservation of Antiquities and Works of Art,
       1956.
3437. _____, and A. E. A. Werner. The Conservation
       of Antiquities and Works of Art. London: Oxford
       University Press, 1971. [2554].
3438. _____ and A. E. A. Werner. "Technical Notes on
       the Conservation of Documents, " Journal of the So-
       ciety of Archivists 1(7), 1958.
3439. Rawlins, F. I. G. Chemical Physics in the Museum
       and Gallery Laboratory. London: National Gallery,
       1959. A paper presented at Copenhagen meeting of
       ICOM Committee for Museum Laboratories, 1959.
3440. Redstone, L. J. and F. W. Steer. Local Records,
       Their Preservation and Care. London: G. Bell
       & Sons, Ltd. , 1953.

3441. Restoration and Preservation of Library Resources,
       Documents and Books. (Translated from the Rus-
       sian.) Jerusalem: Israel Program for Scientific
       Translations, 1965. A compendium on book con-
       servation as practiced in the Soviet Union. This
       collection of their works by the State Library and
       Academy of Sciences of the U. S. S. R. is also avail-
       able from the National Technical Information Ser-
       vice, Springfield, Virginia.
3442. Rorimer, James J. Ultra-violet Rays and Their Use
       in the Examination of Works of Art. New York:
       Metropolitan Museum of Art, 1931.
3443. Santucci, L. "The Application of Chemical and Phy-
       sical Methods to Conservation of Archival Mate-
       rials," Bollettino dell Istituto di Patologia del Li-
       bro 20:85-111, 1961.
3444. Savage, George. The Art and Antique Restorer's
       Handbook. New York: Frederick A. Praeger,
       1967. A standard reference brought up-to-date
       in light of recent scientific approaches to conser-
       vation. Some information on books and paper.
3445. Scott, Alexander. "Romance of Museum Restoration, "
       Journal of the Royal Society of Arts 80:488-498,
       1932. Interesting account of unusual restorations
       of museum artifacts.
3446. Scriven, Margaret. "Preservation and Restoration of
       Library Materials," Special Libraries 47(10):439-
       448, 1956.
3447. Smith, R. D. "Guidelines for Preservation, " Special
       Libraries 59:346-352, 1968.
3448. Spawn, Wilman. "The Conservation of Books and
       Papers," Ontario Library Review 46:5-7, 1962.
3449. Thompson, Daniel V. (trans.). The Craftsman's
       Handbook. New Haven: Yale University Press,
       1933. Modern edition New York: Dover Publica-
       tions, Inc. , 1954. An accurate translation of
       Cennini's 15th-century Il Libro dell Arte.
3450. Trey, E. N. "Methods of Restoration and Present
       Condition of the Ostromirovo Gospel, " Saltykov-
       Shchedrin 49-96, 1958. Leningrad State Public Li-
       brary.
3451. Tribolet, Harold W. "Trends in Preservation, "
       Library Trends 13(2), 1964. The Director of the
       Department of Extra Binding at the Lakeside Press
       discusses developments in library conservation.

3452. Turner, R. S. "To Repair or Despair?" American Archivist 20:319-329, 1957.

3453. Wachter, Otto. The Conservation of Globes and Maps. Bads Godesberg: 1968. In German. An extensive treatment of the subject. Detailed description of repair methods and formulas, both old and new. Bibliography.

3454. Waters, Peter. "Book Restoration After the Florence Floods," Penrose Annual 62, 1969.

3455. _____. "In Search of a New Philosophy of Conservation and Restoration," Guild of Book Workers Journal 7(2):12-21, 1968-1969. Mr. Waters philosophizes on the experience gained during the emergency program at the Bibliotica Nazionale Centrale di Firenze the first two years after the 1966 floods in Florence.

3456. _____. "Some Technical Problems of Book Conservation," Guild of Book Workers Journal 7(2):21-39, 1968-1969. Mr. Waters discusses the more technical problems of book repair based on his work on the restoration of the books damaged during the floods in Florence in 1966.

3457. Werner, A. E. A. "The Preservation of Archives," Journal of the Society of Archivists 1:282-288, 1959.

PAPER

3458. "Break for bibliophiles," Chemical Week 98(17):93-94, 1966. Describes chemical treatments for increasing durability of paper.

3459. "Lifebooster for paper," Chemical Week 98(26):80, 1966. Tells of chemical procedures for preserving documents and books.

3460. Pravilova, T. A. and T. N. Strel'tzova. "Types of Paper Suitable for Use in Restoration," New Methods for the Restoration and Preservation of Documents and Books. Moscow, 1960. English translation available from National Technical Information Service, Springfield, Va.

3461. "Restoration of Tracing Paper," New Methods for the Restoration and Preservation of Documents and Books. Moscow, 1960. English translation

available from the National Technical Information
Service, Springfield, Virginia.
3462. Santucci, L. "Restoration, Conservation and Durability of Paper; Some Chemical and Physical Problems," Bollettino dell Istituto di Patologia del Libro 18(1-2), 1959.
3463. U. S. National Archives. The Rehabilitation of Paper
Records. Washington, D. C.: U. S. National Archives, 1950. Staff Information Paper No. 16.

EXAMINATION [See under VIII. Appendices--J.]

TESTING

3464. Tests and Procedures for Books and Book Components. Hoboken, New Jersey: United States Testing Co., 1957.

MILDEW [See also under VIII. --N.]

3465. Almela Meliá, Juan. Higiene y terapeutica del libro.
Mexico: Fondo de Cultura Económica, 1956.
3466. Belyakova, L. A. "Choice of Antiseptic for Mold
Control on Book Glue," Collection of Materials on
the Preservation of Library Resources. Moscow,
1963. Available in English from the National Technical Information Service, Springfield, Virginia.
3467. _____. "Effect of Ultraviolet Radiation by Bactericidal Lamp on Spores of Mold Fungi," (ibid.).
3468. _____. "Instruction for Use of Sodium Pentachlorophenate as Glue Antiseptic," (ibid.).
3469. _____. "Fungus Control in the Lenin State Library,"
UNESCO Bulletin for Libraries 15:198-200, 1961.
3470. _____. "Gamma Radiation as a Disinfecting Agent,"
Environ. Eff. Mater. Equip. Abst. 2:117, 1962.
3471. _____. "The Resistance of Fungi to Fungicides,"
(ibid.).
3472. Betto, E. The Bactericidal and Fungicidal Activity
of Ethylene Oxide in Vacuum Fumigation. Milan:
Istituto di Patologia Vegetale dell'Universita di
Milano, 1960.
3473. Bloch, S. S. "Chemicals for Fungus Control,"
Chem. Week. 26, 1952.
3474. Dahl, Sverre et al. "Studies in Leather Fungicides,"
Journal American Leather Chemists Association

53, 1958.

3475. Helwig, H. "Books Infected by Mold: Possibilities for Disinfection and Preservation," Das Papier 7, 1953. Darmstadt.

3476. Holnes, R. F. G. "Use of Formaldehyde as a Fumigant," British Records Association Bulletin 14, 1942.

3477. Honig, Mervin. 'The Problem of Fungus Infestation of a Framed Pastel Portrait on Paper," IIC-AG Bulletin 2(2):129-130, 1971. Report with diagram of an actual treatment.

3478. Hubner, P. H. "Les Maladies du Papier et Leur Traitment," Mouseion 27-28, 1934. A unique method for restoration of mildewed paper utilizing ultra-violet light and other electric illumination to kill mold and mildew and reduce stains, followed by sizing with glue and coating with cellulose acetate. Not recommended for rare books and manuscripts.

3479. Petrova-Zavgorodnyaya, A. P. et al. "Disinfection of Books and Documentary Materials by a High-Frequency Electromagnetic Field," New Methods for the Restoration of Documents and Books. Moscow: 1960.

3480. _____. 'The Effect of High-Frequency Electromagnetic Fields on Paper-destroying Mold Fungi." New Methods for the Restoration of Documents and Books. Moscow: 1960.

3481. "Portable Fumigation Chamber," Museum News 44(6), 1966.

3482. Reddish, G. F. Antiseptics, Disinfectants, Fungicides and Sterilization. London: H. Kimpton, 1957.

3483. Santucci, L. "Rigenerazione dei documenti III," Bollettino dell'Istituto di Patologia del'Libro 18(3-4), 1959. On foxing. Summary in English.

3484. Sykes, G. Disinfestation and Sterilization. London: Spon, 1958.

3485. "Vacuum Fumigation Unit," Wilson Library Bulletin 38, 1963. Describes the Vacudyne Corp. unit.

3486. Winge-Hedén, K. "Ethylene Oxide Sterilization Without Special Equipment," Acta Pathologica et Microbiologica Scandinavica 58, 1963. Plastic bags.

3487. Yadow, V. L. "A Portable Fumigation Chamber for the Small Museum," Museum News 44(6), 1966.

3488. Zagulyaeva, Z. A. "The Lethal Effect of High Frequency Currents on Cellulose-destroying Mold Fungi," New Methods for the Restoration and Preservation of Documents and Books. Moscow: 1960. English translation available from the National

Technical Information Service, Springfield, Virginia.

INSECTS [See also under VIII. --N]

3489. Basu, M.   "Preservation of Books Affected with Insects, " Science and Culture 7:617, 1942.
3490. Beattie, W. R.   The Use of Hydrocyanic Gas for Exterminating Household Insects.   Washington: U. S. Department of Agriculture, Division of Entomology, 1902.   Bulletin No. 31.
3491. Blew, J. Oscar, Jr. and John W. Kulp.   Comparison of Wood Preservatives in Mississippi Post Study. Madison, Wis. : U. S. Forest Service, Forest Products Lab. , 1964.   Research Note FPL-01.
3492. Bollaerts, D. ; J. Quoilin and W. E. van den Bruel. "New Experiments on the Application of Micro-Waves to the Destruction of Insects Hiding In Wooden Materials, " Staat Gent. 26:1435-1450, 1961. Mededel. Landbouwhogeschool Opzoekingssta.   In French with English summary.
3493. Brown, A. W. A.   Insect Control by Chemicals. New York: Wiley and Sons, 1951.
3494. Bryan, J.   "Methods of Applying Wood Preservatives, " Forest Products Research Records 9, 1946.
3495. Chakravorti, S.   "Vacuum Fumigation - a New Technique of Preserving Records, " Science and Culture 9(2):77-81, 1943.
3496. Coaton, W. G. H.   "Toxic-smoke Generator for Termite Control, " Farming in South Africa September 1947.
3497. Cotton, R. T. and R. C. Roark.   "Ethylene Oxide as a Fumigant, " Industrial and Engineering Chemistry 1928.
3498. Dyte, C. E.   "Preliminary Tests of an Insecticidal Lacquer Containing Malathion, " Pesticide Technology 2:98, 1960.
3499. Ebeling, W. and R. Wagner.   "Rapid Desiccation of Drywood Termites With Inert Sorptive Dusts and Other Substances, " Journal of Economic Entomology 52(2):190-207, 1959.
3500. Gray, H. E.   "Vikane--A New Fumigant for Control of Dry Wood Termites, " Pest Control 28:43-46, 1960.
3501. Heimpel, A. M.   "Bacterial Insecticides, " Bacteriological Reviews 24:266, 1960.

3502. Kozulina, O. V. "Dermistid Book Pests and Mea-
       sures for Their Extermination," Collection of
       Materials on the Preservation of Library Resources.
       Moscow: 1958. Available in English from National
       Technical Information Service, Springfield, Virginia.

3503. _____. "Instructions for Use of DDT Preparations
       in the Extermination of Book Pests," (ibid.).

3504. Lepigre, A. L. Technique de la Désinsectisation.
       Paris: P. Lechevalier, 1947.

3505. Liberti, Sal. "A New Fumigant for Disinfestation
       with Lindane as a Base," Bollettino dell Istituto
       di Patologia del Libro 18(1-2), 1959. Smoke fumi-
       gation.

3506. "Making Bindings Insect Proof," Bookbinders Monthly
       10(7):2, 1929.

3507. Petrova, G. I. "Insects in Book Storerooms and Con-
       trol Measures," Collection of Materials on the
       Preservation of Library Resources. Moscow: 1953.
       A thorough, scientific study of the insect problem
       in libraries and ways to control it. English trans-
       lation available from National Technical Information
       Service, Springfield, Virginia.

3508. Petrova, L. G. "Instructions for the Use of DDT
       Preparations Against Insect Infestation of Books,"
       Collection of Materials on the Preservation of Li-
       brary Resources. Moscow: 1953. Available in
       English from National Technical Information Ser-
       vice, Springfield, Virginia.

3509. Plenderleith, H. J. "Bookworm; Treatment by Car-
       bon Disulphide," British Records Association Bul-
       letin 19:8, 1948.

3510. _____. "Protection of Records Against Bookworm,"
       British Records Association Bulletin No. 11, 1940.

3511. Stewart, D. "Precision Fumigation for Drywood Ter-
       mites with Vikane," Pest Control 30(2):24, 1962.

3512. "Vacuum Fumigation Unit for Destroying Insects and
       Mold In Graphic Records," Wilson Library Bulletin
       38:246, 1963.

3513. Walker, J. F. Formaldehyde. New York: American
       Chemical Society, 1944. Includes instructions for
       fumigation with this chemical.

RESTORATION OF PAPER [See also under IX. --Bibliog-
raphies--Paper]

3514. Analytical Techniques of Practical Use to Paper Con-
       servators. Paper presented at the February 1971
       meeting of the Washington Region Conservation
       Guild.
3515. Barrow, W. J. "Restoration Methods," American
       Archivist 6(3):151-154, 1943.
3516. The Barrow Method of Restoring Documents. Rich-
       mond, Va.: W. J. Barrow Restoration Shop, Inc.,
       1970. Discusses causes for degradation of paper
       and describes the Barrow deacidification and lam-
       ination techniques for preserving damaged paper.
3517. Belenkaja, N. G. and E. N. Kuznetsova. "The Use
       of Water Soluble Methylcellulose in Restoration of
       Books and Documents," Cause of Decay of Written
       and Printed Monuments. Leningrad: Laboratory
       for Preservation and Restoration of Documents,
       1967. In Russian.
3518. Bezdicek, Jaroslav. "Preservation of Historic Paper
       Documents," Czech. patent 126, 360, Cl. D. 21j)
       Feb. 15, 1968. Appl. 29, Nov. 1965.
3519. Blaquière, Henri. "La Restauration: un des moyens
       de sauvetage des archives communales," Gazette
       des Archives 50:117-119, 1965. "Restoration:
       one way of safekeeping the archives of the com-
       munes," Abstract in American Archivist 29:543,
       1966.
3520. Cutter, C. "Restoration of Paper Documents and
       Manuscripts," College and Research Libraries 28,
       1967.
3521. Deobarats, Klaus; Otto Wächter, and L. Ritterpusch
       (eds.). Internationaler Restauratorentag Arbeits-
       gemainschaft der Archiv-, Bibliotheks-, und
       Graphikrestauratoren. Freiburg in Breisgau:
       I. A. D. A. Informationsstelle, 1969. This is the
       proceedings of the conference held by practicing
       graphic art, library and archives restorers in
       Freiburg, Basel and Zürich in September 1967.
       Much good practical information but in German.
3522. Hey, Margaret. "The Use of the Scanning Electron
       Microscope in Document Restoration Problems,"
       Restaurator 1(4):233-244, 1970. Describes the ap-
       plication of this instrument to document restoration
       and its advantages over other scientific devices.

Well illustrated and has a bibliography of 24 pertinent articles.

3523. Kathpalia, Y. P. "Deterioration and Conservation of Paper, Part V - Restoration, " Indian Pulp and Paper April 1963.

3524. _____. "Trends in Restoration, " Indian Pulp and Paper September 1961.

3525. Santucci, L. Report on Paper Preservation. Paris: International Council on Museums, 1961. Paper presented at the ICOM 1961 meeting in Barcelona.

3526. Schweidler, Max. Die Instandsetzung von Kupferstichen Büchern USW. 2nd ed. Stuttgart: Max Hettler, 1950. Many "secret" paper restoration techniques for those who read German.

3527. Smith, Richard D. "New Approaches to Preservation, " The Library Quarterly 40(1):139-175, 1970. A review of existing technology on paper preservation and a progress report on Smith's important research in non-aqueous methods of paper deacidification. Smith also offers his ideas on protecting books from fungi, insects and rodents, about strengthening books and about book storage in research libraries.

3528. Tribolet, Harold W. "Preservation and Restoration, " Manuscripts 18(4):6-10, 1966.

3529. Wardle, D. B. Document Repair. London: Society of Archivists, 1971. A small volume presenting document restoration as it is done in England particularly at the Public Records Office. Includes information on map repair.

3530. Wendelbo, O. and B. Fosse. "Protein Surgery: A Restoring Procedure Applied to Paper, " Restaurator 1(4):245-248, 1970. Describes the use of enzymes for restoring library and archival material. Authors report their success in separating art (coated) paper stuck together into solid blocks after water damage. Also describes good results with similarly damaged 16th century books.

WASHING

3531. Price, Donald. Detergents, What They are and What They Do. New York: Chemical Publishing Co., 1952.

3532. Sheridan, Jane. "Enzymes, " Exposition of Painting Conservation. Brooklyn: The Brooklyn Museum,

1962.   Description of the chemical and suggestions for using them.

CLEANING

3533.   Banks, Paul N.   "Paper Cleaning," Journal of the Guild of Book Workers 5(1), 1966.

3534.   _____.   "Paper Cleaning," Restaurator 1(1):52-66, 1969.   A paper originally presented at the 1966 meeting in Chicago of the American Group, International Institute for Conservation.

3535.   Beaufort, Thomas Richard.   Pictures and How to Clean Them; To Which are Added Notes on Things Useful in Restoration Work.   London: J. Lane, 1926.   Also by New York: Frederick A. Stokes, 1926.

3536.   "Cold cleaning solutions," Repairers' News Sheet 18:2-3, 1971.   London: Society of Archivists.   Describes chemicals and lists suppliers in England.

3537.   (Erasing).   "A New Electric Eraser for Draftsmen, Artists, Library Workers," Consumers Bulletin February 1962.   Reports convenience for small erasures of a model tested for Library Technology Project.

3538.   Gunn, Maurice J.   Print Restoration and Picture Cleaning.   London: L. Upcott Gill, 1922.

3539.   Horton, Carolyn.   Cleaning and Preserving Bindings and Related Materials.   2nd ed.   Chicago: American Library Association, 1969.

3540.   Longo, Luigi et al.   "Experiments on a Method for Cleaning Discolored Paper Manuscripts," Bollettino dell Istituto di Patologia del Libro 18(3-4), 1959.

STAIN REMOVAL [See also under VIII.--K.]

3541.   Gerassimova, N. G. and Z. N. Ponomareva.   "The Removal of Grease and Oil Stains from Paper," Soob. VCNILKR 19:102-110, 1967.   English Summary.

3542.   Lewis, J. C.   Removing Residual Mud Stains from Paper.   Paper presented at meeting of IIC (UK Group) 30 April 1970.   Author's interim report on experiments at Imperial College with surface acting agents for loosening imbedded mud in paper fibers.

3543. Mellan, I. and E. Mellan. Removing Spots and
      Stains. New York: Chemical Publishing Co., Inc.,
      1959.
3544. Sheridan, Jane. "Enzymes," Exposition of Painting
      Conservation. Brooklyn: The Brooklyn Museum,
      1962.
3545. Randlett, J. C. and W. J. Nicklaw. Spotting. Silver
      Spring, Maryland: National Institute of Dry Clean-
      ing, 1956. Primarily for the removal of spots and
      stains from fabrics but much is of interest to pa-
      per restorers.
3546. Yabrova, R. R. "Instructions for Removing Ink
      Stains and Stamping Ink Stains From Paper," Col-
      lection of Materials on the Preservation of Library
      Resources. (Moscow, 1958). Springfield, Va.:
      National Technical Information Service, 1964.

      BLEACHING

3547. Bibikov, N. N. and N. A. Filippova. The Electro-
      chemical Method of Restoration of Library Mate-
      rials. Leningrad: State Public Library, 1959.
      Describes bleaching techniques.
3548. "Bleaching," American Archivist 1:76, 1938.
3549. de Fulvio, Silvano and Luigi Longo. "Use of Ozone
      for Bleaching of Browned Paper in Book Restora-
      tion," Bollettino dell Istituto di Patologia del Libro
      19, 1960.
3550. Feller, R. L. "Notes on the Chemistry of Bleach-
      ing," Bulletin American Group - IIC 2(2):39-57,
      1971. Excellent information on the basic concepts
      of bleaching.
3551. Filippova, N. A. "Methods of Removing Ink Spots
      From Paper," Saltykov-Shchedrin 23-32, 1958.
      Leningrad State Public Library.
3552. Flieder, F. "Chemical Bleaching of Mildew Spots on
      Old Papers," Association Technique de l'Industrie
      Papetière Bulletin 4, 1960. Paris. Comparison
      of 26 bleaching agents.
3553. _____. Studies of Chemical Bleaching of Stains in
      Old Paper. Paris: Laboratoire de Cryptogamie,
      1961. In French.
3554. Gerassimova, N. G. "Effect on Paper of Three Dif-
      ferent Methods of Chloramine Bleaching," Causes
      of Decay of Written and Printed Monuments. Lenin-
      grad: Laboratory for the Preservation and

Restoration of Documents, 1967.   In Russian with
English summaries.

3555. _____ and Z. V. Ponomareva.   "Protection of In-
scriptions in Iron-Gall Ink During the Bleaching of
Prints and Drawings, " Soob. VCNILKR 19:92-102,
1967.   English Summary.

3556. Gettens, Rutherford John.   "Bleaching of Stained and
Discoloured Pictures on Paper with Sodium Chlorite
and Chlorine Dioxide, " Museum 5:116-130, 1952.

3557. Holtz, G.   "The Chemistry of Bleaching and Oxidizing
Agents, " Chemistry Reviews 54:169-194, 1954.

3558. Keck, Sheldon.   "A Method of Cleaning Prints, " Technical Studies in the Field of Fine Arts 5(1), 1936.
Describes an effective method for reducing stains
in paper without leaving harmful residual chemicals
in the paper.

3559. Pravilova, T. A. and T. W. Istrubcina.   "The Bleaching of Documents on Paper With Sodium Chlorite, "
Woprosy Konserwacji i Restawracji Bumagi i Per-
gamena 5-27, 1962.   Moscow-Leningrad, U. S. S. R.
Academy of Sciences.   Diagrams.   22 References.
Problems of the conservation and restoration of
paper and parchment.

3560. Santucci, Ludovico.   "Chemical Restoration of Documents, " Bollettino dell Istituto di Patologia del
Libro 12(3-4), 1953.

3561. _____; B. Soto Y Galvez and R. Di Trapani.   "Protective Action of Paraloid in the Bleaching of Paper, " Bollettino dell Istituto di Patologia del Libro
18(1-2):87-96.   In Italian with English summary.
Paraloid will not protect ink from hypochlorite
bleach but it will strengthen paper.

3562. _____ and C. Wolff.   "Rigener Azione dei Documenti IV, " Bollettino dell Istituto di Patologia del
Libro 22(1-4):165-190, 1963.   A highly scientific
report on the revival and stabilization of iron inks.
In Italian with English summary.

3563. Yabrova, R. R.   "Instructions for the removal of ink
stains and stamping inks from paper, " Collection
of Materials on the Protection of Library Resources.
Moscow: 1958.   English translation available from
the National Technical Information Service, Springfield, Va.

3564. [No entry.]

DEACIDIFICATION

3565.   Barrow, W. J.   "Deacidification and Lamination of
        Deteriorated Documents, 1938-63, " American Ar-
        chivist 28:285-290, 1965.
3566.   .   Manuscripts and Documents, Their Deteri-
        oration and Restoration.   Charlottesville, Virginia:
        University of Virginia Press, 1955.   Deacidification
        techniques.
3567.   .   Permanence/Durability of the Book: a
        Two Year Research Program.   Richmond: W. J.
        Barrow Research Laboratory, 1963.   This first of
        an important series of Barrow Laboratory publica-
        tions reports on investigations of spray deacidifica-
        tion, the stability of PVA adhesives and the de-
        velopment of performance standards for library
        binding.
3568.   .   Permanence/Durability of the Book III:
        Spray Deacidification.   Richmond: W. J. Barrow
        Research Laboratory, 1964.
3569.   Baynes-Cope, A. D.   "The Nonaqueous Deacidification
        of Documents, " Restaurator 1(2-9), 1969.
3570.   Blanc, M. C. and J. P. Nyuksha.   "On the Stabiliza-
        tion of Paper with Calcium and Magnesium Car-
        bonates, " O sokhranenii bumagi 61-69, 1963.
        Leningrad.   Reports favorably on the Barrow
        process.
3571.   "Break for Bibliophiles, " Chemical Week 98(17):93-
        94, 1966.   Chemical treatments add to the dura-
        bility of paper.
3572.   Cunha, G. M.   "Vapor-Phase Deacidification, " Amer-
        ican Archivist 29:566-568, 1966; 30:614-615, 1967;
        31:84-86, 408, 1968.   Reports on tests of Lang-
        well's method for deacidifying paper with Cyclohexy-
        lamine carbonate.
3573.   [No entry.]
3574.   "Declaration of Independence, " The University of Chi-
        cago Magazine 62(6):31, 1970.   Describes use of
        magnesium methoxide to deacidify an early issue
        of this important document.
3575.   Dupuis, R. N. et al.   "Evaluation of Langwell's Vapor
        Phase Deacidification Process, " Restaurator 1(3),
        1970.   Finds that Langwell's process will effectively
        deacidify paper; that it destroys rosin sizing; it
        decreases the brightness of paper; and that CHC
        hydrolyzes to an odorous and toxic chemical on ex-
        posure to moist air.   This article is summarized

in Library of Congress Information Bulletin 29(22),
June 1970. (Appendix)

3576. Ede, J. R. and W. H. Langwell. "Sulphur Dioxide
and Vapour Phase Deacidification," Museum Climatology. London: International Institute for Conservation, 1968.

3577. Grove, L. E. "The Conservation of Paper," Museum
News 42(2):15-20, 1963. Discussion of the Barrow
Process including Barrows' work on spray deacid-
ification.

3578. Istrubtsina, T. V. and T. A. Pravilova. "Conservation of Paper Documents by Buffering," Problema
Dolgovechnosti Dokumentov i Bumagi 71-81, 1964.
Leningrad, Academy of Science of the USSR. English abstract in Chemical Abstracts 62:2911, 1965.

3579. Kathpalia, Y. P. "Deterioration and Conservation of
Paper, Part IV - Neutralization," Indian Pulp and
Paper 17(4), 1962. The author describes the Bar-
row process and others in use in India.

3580. Langwell, W. H. "Methods of Deacidifying Paper,"
Journal of the Society of Archivists 3(9):491-494,
1969. A concise review of all available methods.

3581. _____. "The Vapour Phase Deacidification of
Books and Documents," Journal of the Society of
Archivists 3, 1966.

3582. Lebel, R. G.; R. W. Schwartz, and O. Sepall. "A
Novel Approach to Dimensional Stabilization of Paper," Tappi 51(9):79A-84A, 1968.

3583. "Life Booster for Paper," Chemical Week 98(26):80,
1966. Procedure for preserving documents and
books.

3584. McCarthy, Paul. "Vapor Phase Deacidification: A
New Preservation Method," American Archivist
32:333-342, 1969.

3585. Process Materials Corporation. Vapor Phase Deacidification of Books and Documents (Langwell Method). Carlstadt, N. J.: Process Materials Corporation, 1968.

3586. Raff, R. A.; I. W. Herrick, and M. F. Adams.
"Archive Document Preservation," Northwest Science 40(1):17-24, 1966 and 41(4):184-195, 1967.
A report on a technique that the authors claim will
simultaneously deacidify and strengthen paper.

3587. Ruggles, Mervyn. "Practical Application of Deacidification Treatment of Works of Art on Paper,"
IIC-AG Bulletin 2(2):76-84, 1971.

3588. Schierholtz, Otto J. Process for the Chemical Stabil-
       ization of Paper and Paper Products. Washington:
       U. S. Patent Office, 1936. Patent #2,033,452 re-
       lates to the use of barium bicarbonate for deacidify-
       ing paper to make it more durable, inert with re-
       spect to inks and colors, and nontarnishing to
       metals.

3589. Smith, R. D. The Nonaqueous Deacidification of Pa-
       pers and Books. Chicago: University of Chicago,
       1970. This unpublished dissertation, available in
       Xerox or microfilm copies from the Photo-duplica-
       tion Department, Regenstein Library, University
       of Chicago, is a complete presentation of Smith's
       important studies.

3590. _____. "Paper Deacidification: A Preliminary
       Report, " Library Quarterly 36:273-292, 1966.

       RESIZING

3591. Belen'Kaja, N. G. et al. "The Use of Methyl-cellu-
       lose for the Restoration of Archival and Library
       Materials, " Stareniye bumagi 94-111, 1965. Mos-
       cow. Reports usefulness of the material for sizing
       paper and fixing ink.

3592. Cunha, George M. "Soluble Nylon, a New Tool for
       Restorationists, " Guild of Book Workers' Journal
       4(2), 1965-1966.

3593. Daniel, J. S. "Sizing Paper, " U. S. Patent 2,964,445,
       December 13, 1960.

3594. Gallo, Fausta. "Ricerche sperimenlati sulla resisten-
       za agli agenti biologici di materiali impiegati nel
       restauro dei libri VI Saggi su collanti puri o
       addizionati di fungicidi, " Bollettino dell Istituto di
       Patologia del Libro 28(1-2):9-47, 1969. The au-
       thor reports that the addition of fungicides to paper
       sizing is not recommended. Summary in English.
       Tables and bibliography.

3595. Kowalik, R. and E. Czerwinska. "Sizes Used in Pa-
       per-making and Paper Binding, Their Deterioration
       and Preservation, " Blok Notes 153-154, 1960.
       Warszawie, Muzeum Mickiewicza.

3596. Langwell, W. H. "The Preservation of Unstable Pa-
       pers, " Archives 4, 1949-1952. London. Emphasis
       on gelatin sizing.

3597. [No entry.]

3598.   Santucci, L. and M. G. Zappalà Plossi. "Resistance
        and Stability of Paper VIII - An Investigation on
        Sizing," Bollettino dell Istituto di Patologia del
        Libro 28(1-2):97-117, 1969. In Italian. Recom-
        mends polyvinyl alcohol and hydroxyethyl cellulose
        for reinforcing paper over gelatin, soluble nylon
        and acrylic resin. With English summary.
        Tables and graphs.
3599.   Shaw, M. B. and M. J. O'Leary. "Effect of Filling
        and Sizing Materials on Stability of Book Papers,"
        Journal Research 21(5):671-695, 1938. National
        Bureau of Standards.
3600.   "Sizing," American Archivist 1:4, 9, 64, 1938.

        MENDING

3601.   Andrews, R. "Japanese repair tissue," Repairers
        News Sheet 18:3-4, 1971. London: Society of
        Archivists. Describes method used in Florence
        for making heat sealing tissue with P.V.A. and
        Japanese tissue.
3602.   Bolsée, J. "La Restauration des Documents aux
        Archives Generales du Royaume," Archives Biblio-
        theques et Musees de Belgique 18(1):3-10, 1950.
3603.   Brown, M. W. Mending and Repairing of Books.
        Chicago: American Library Association, 1916.
3604.   Collis, I. P. "Document Conservation in the Local
        Repository," Archives 6, 1963. Tips for the small
        library conservators.
3605.   Das, Thakar and R. Kishore. "A Thin Paste for Re-
        pairs and Mending," Conservation of Cultural
        Property in India 3:32-37, 1968. Suggests 2.25
        per cent sodium carboxymethyl cellulose.
3606.   Gear, James L. "The Repair of Documents - Amer-
        ican Beginnings," American Archivist 26:469-475,
        1963.
3607.   "Inlaying Paper," American Archivist 16:123, 1953.
3608.   Jentink, R. L. "Notes on the Use of Mending Tapes
        on Paper," Bulletin IIC-American Group 2(1), 1961.
3609.   Kathpalia, Y. P. "Deterioration and Conservation of
        Paper. Part V, Restoration of Documents," Indian
        Pulp and Paper 17:565-573, April 1963.
3610.   _____. "Synthetic Fibers for Preservation of Pa-
        per," Conservation of Cultural Property in India
        20:54-61, 1966. Evaluation of non-woven synthetic
        fabrics for lamination.

3611. Maximova, N. N. "An Emulsive Adhesive for Res-
       toration of Paper and Textiles, " Soob. VCNILKR
       19:125-128, 1967.

3612. Minogue, Adelaide E. "Some Observations on the
       Flattening of Folded Records, " American Archivist
       8:115-121, 1945.

3613. _____. "Treatment of Fire and Water Damaged
       Records, " American Archivist 9:17-25, 1946.

3614. Nyuksha, J. P. "Application of Paper Pulp in Res-
       toration Work, " Saltykov-Shchedrin 41-48, 1958.
       Leningrad: State Public Library. Describes
       necessary apparatus.

3615. _____. "Restoration of Books and Documents by
       Application of Paper Pulp, " Saltykov-Shchedrin 47-
       56, 1959. Leningrad: State Public Library.
       Gives details of technique.

3616. "Paper, Restoration, " American Archivist 16:120,
       1953.

3617. "Paper, Splitting, " American Archivist 1:20, 1938 and
       16:121, 1953.

3618. Patri, Stella. "The Mending Program in Florence, "
       The Guild of Book Workers Journal 6(1), 1967.
       Describes mending using drymounting technique and
       lenz tissue impregnated with PVA.

3619. Schweidler, Max. Die Instandsetzung von Kupfersti-
       chen Ziechnungen, Büchern USW. 2nd edition.
       Stuttgart: Max Hettler, 1950. Many "secret" pa-
       per restoration techniques for those who read Ger-
       man.

3620. Smith, L. Herman. "Manuscript Repair in European
       Archives, " American Archivist 1:1-22, 51-77, Jan-
       uary, 1938. Paper mending.

3621. Stout, G. L. and M. Horwitz. "Experiments with
       Adhesives for Paper, " Technical Studies in the
       Field of Fine Arts 3(1), 1934.

3622. Wächter, Otto. "Paper Repairing Processes, " All-
       gemeiner Anzieger für Büchbindereien 7(9), 1958.
       Stuttgart. In German.

3623. Welch, C. E. "Repair of Documents, " Assistant Li-
       brarian 53:53-55, 1960.

3624. Williams, G. R. and H. Tribolet. "More Hints on
       the Preservation of Manuscripts, " Manuscripts 13,
       1961.

3625. Yabrova, R. R. "Treatment of Paper with Certain
       Polyacrylate Resins, " Collection of Materials on
       the Preservation of Library Resources (Moscow,
       1958). Available from National Technical

Information Service, Springfield, Virginia.
3626. _____ . "Instructions for the Reinforcement and
Restoration of Documents with Polymethylacrylate
Emulsion," Collection of Materials on the Preser-
vation of Library Resources (Moscow, 1958).
Springfield, Va.: National Technical Information
Service, 1964.

LAMINATION

3627. Barrow, W. J. "The Barrow Method of Laminating
Documents," Journal of Documentary Reproduction
2:147-151, 1939.
3628. _____ . The Barrow Method of Restoring Deteriorated Documents. Richmond, Va.: W. J. Barrow Research Laboratory, 1965.
3629. _____ . "An Evaluation of Document Restoration
Processes," American Documentation 4:50-54, 1953.
Discusses silk tissue and lamination processes with
full exposition of the latter.
3630. Belen'Kaja, N. G. "Methods of Restoring Books and
Documents," New Methods for the Restoration and
Preservation of Documents and Prints. Moscow,
1960. Includes a summary of lamination practices
in Europe and America and reviews the pros and
cons of lamination. English translation available
from the National Technical Information Service,
Springfield, Virginia.
3631. _____ (and others). "On Some Properties of
Laminated Papers," Stareniye bumagi 117-127,
1965. Moscow: Laboratory of Conservation and
Restoration of Documents.
3632. Boak, R. I. "Putting New Life in Old Volumes,"
Publishers' Weekly July 19, 1965. Describes the
Arbee Company's lamination services.
3633. British Records Association. The annual conference.
Archives 3:29-41, 1949. The report of the meeting of the Technical Section devoted to a consideration of lamination and related questions appears
on p. 29-32.
3634. Broadman, Joseph. Cellulose Acetate Sheetings as
Used for the Preservation of Permanent Records:
a Critical Analysis. New York: 1946. Gives
reasons why cellulose acetate cannot be considered
a permanent plastic.

3635. Chakravorti, S. A. "A Review of the Lamination
      Process," Indian Archives 1:304-312, 1947.

3636. Dadic, Vera and Ribkin Tatjana. "Techniques of
      Delaminating Polyethylene Laminates," Restaurator
      1(3), 1970. Examines solvents and techniques for
      delaminating cellulose acetate-coated documents as
      well as polyethylene.

3637. Darlington, Ida. "The Lamination of Paper Docu-
      ments," Journal Society of Archivists 1(4):108-110,
      1956. Describes methods in use in England at that
      time.

3638. de Valinger, Leon Jr. "Lamination of Manuscripts
      at the Delaware State Archives, 1938-1964," Amer-
      ican Archivist 28:290-293, 1965.

3639. "Document Lamination Applications Growing," Office
      63(2):183-186, 1966.

3640. Evans, D. L. "The Lamination Process, A British
      View," Bulletin 18:10-14, 1945. British Records
      Association, Technical Section.

3641. _____. "The Lamination Process--A British View,"
      American Archivist 9(4):320-322, 1946. An ex-
      cerpt from a review of Adelaide Minogue's Repair
      and Preservation of Records. [4024].

3642. Gear, J. L. "Lamination After 30 Years: Record
      and Prospect," American Archivist 28:293-297,
      1965.

3643. _____. "The Repair of Documents - American
      Beginnings," American Archivist 26:469-475, 1963.
      Describes the development of lamination techniques
      in the National Archives.

3644. Goel, O. P. "Repair of Documents with Cellulose
      Acetate on Small Scale," The Indian Archives 7:162-
      165, 1953.

3645. Hummel, Ray O. Jr. and W. J. Barrow. "Lamina-
      tion and Other Methods of Restoration," Library
      Trends 4(3):259-268, 1956.

3646. Kathpalia, Y. P. "Hand Lamination With Cellulose
      Acetate," The American Archivist 31(3), 1958.

3647. _____. "Synthetic Fibers for Preservation of Pa-
      per," Conservation of Cultural Property in India.
      New Delhi: National Museum, 1966. Describes
      lamination with acetone, cellulose acetate film and
      non-woven fabrics.

3648. Kremer, A. W. "NBS Study of Lamination Com-
      pleted," Library of Congress Information Bulletin
      16, 1957. Summary of study and findings.

3649.   "Lamination," American Archivist 1:114, 1938; 2:22,
        1939; 4:200, 1941; 6:37, 151, 259, 1943; 9:227,
        320, 1946; 16:122, 1953; 20:320, 324, 329, 332,
        1957.
3650.   "Laminators," American Archivist 4:68, 1941; 10:203,
        1947; 13:413, 1950; 14:364, 1951; 20:180, 321,
        1957.
3651.   "Laminator for Maps," American Archivist 15:81,
        1952.
3652.   Langwell, W. H.   "The Postlip Duplex Lamination
        Processes," Journal Society of Archivists 2:471-
        476, 1964.
3653.   Nixon, H. M.   "Lamination of Paper Documents with
        Cellulose Acetate Film Foil," Archives 2, 1949.
        London: The British Records Association.
3654.   Piez, G. T.   "Laminator for Libraries," ALA Bul-
        letin 53, 1961.
3655.   Procedures and Equipment Used in the Barrow Method
        of Restoring Manuscripts and Documents.   Rich-
        mond, Va.:   State Library, 1958.
3656.   "Putting New Life in Old Volumes," Publisher's Week-
        ly July 19, 1965.
3657.   Scribner, B. W.   Protection of Documents with Cellu-
        lose Acetate Sheeting.   Washington: U. S. Govern-
        ment Printing Office, 1940.   U. S. National Bureau
        of Standards, Miscellaneous Publication M168.
3658.   Tollenaar, D.   "L'Acetate de Cellulose et la Lamina-
        tion des Documents," Archivum 2:51-53, 1952.
3659.   Werner, A. E. A.   "The Lamination of Documents,"
        Journal of Documentation 20:25-31, 1964.
3660.   _____.   "The Lamination of Documents," Problems
        of Conservation in Museums.   London: George Al-
        len & Unwin, 1969.   A survey of the more impor-
        tant lamination techniques and the processes for
        paper deacidification.
3661.   Willis-Fear, M. J. W.   "The Repairers' Meeting at
        Southampton, June 28-29, 1966," Journal of the
        Society of Archivists 3(3):153-154, 1966.   Included
        in the report of the meetings is a brief technical
        note on the use of Maranyl soluble nylon in
        strengthening fragile documents.
3662.   Wilson, W. K. and B. W. Forshee.   Preservation of
        Documents by Lamination.   Washington: U. S. Na-
        tional Bureau of Standards, 1959.   Monograph No.
        5.

RECOVERY OF FADED INK [See also under VIII. --L.]

3663. Almy, L. H. "Restoration of Faded Ink Writings, "
Abstract Review 249, 1958.

3664. Arias, A. Charro. 'New Method for Restoring Falsified or Faded Documents, " Farm. nueva. 7:480-
485, 1942. Madrid: Chem. Zentr. 1:1916, 1943.
Summarized in Chemical Abstracts 38:M4065, 1944.

3665. Davis, Raymond. Action of Charred Paper on the
Photographic Plate and a Method of Deciphering
Charred Records. Washington: U. S. Government
Printing Office, 1922. U. S. Bureau of Standards,
Scientific Papers, No. 454.

3666. Erastov, D. P. "Control of Operating Conditions in
Reproduction Technique for Highlighting Faded
Images, " New Methods for Restoration and Preser-
vation of Documents and Books. Moscow, 1960.
Available in English from the National Technical
Information Service, Springfield, Virginia.

3667. "Faded Writing, " Archives 2(38), 1949. A note on
the method employed at the Public Record Office
to restore faded writing.

3668. Hamilton, D. H. "The Repair of Autographs, " Hob-
bies Magazine 63, November 1958.

3669. Hilton, Ordway. An Evaluation of Chemical Methods
for Restoring Erased Writing Ink. London: Swin-
don Press Ltd., (c1956). This short paper is primarily for examiners of questioned documents but
contains general information on ink revival useful
for librarians.

3670. "Infra-red Photographs of Illegible Leather Manuscripts, " British Museum Quarterly 8:52-53, 1933.

3671. "Ink, Restoration of, " American Archivist 1:16, 1938.

3672. Jones, G. A. "Decipherment of Charred Documents, "
Nature 147:676-677, 1941. Infra-red illumination.

3673. Kishore, Ranbir. "Preservation of Pencil Writing, "
Indian Archives 6:34-38, 1952.

3674. Komárek, Karel. "Restoration of Faded Ink Writings, "
Chemical Abstracts 54, 1960.

3675. O'Neill, M. E. "The Restoration of Obliterated Ink
Writing, " Journal of Criminal Law and Criminology
127(4), 1936.

3676. Shoichi, N. "Restoration of Erased Ink Writings with
Iron Complex, " Science and Crime Detection 8,
1955. Japan.

3677. Waters, C. E. Inks. Washington: U. S. Government
       Printing Office, 1940.   National Bureau of Stand-
       ards Circular C-426.   Includes section on ink re-
       vival.
3678. Yublinski, V. S.   "Two Difficult Cases of Restoration
       of Faded Text, " New Methods for the Restoration
       and Preservation of Documents and Books.   Mos-
       cow, 1960.   Describes use of photoanalytical meth-
       ods for deciphering faded texts.   Available in Eng-
       lish from the National Technical Information Ser-
       vice, Springfield, Virginia.
3679. Zimmerman, Elmer W. ; Charles G. Weber, and
       Arthur E. Kimberly.   Relation of Ink to the Pres-
       ervation of Written Records.   Washington: U. S.
       Government Printing Office, 1935.   U. S. National
       Bureau of Standards Research Paper RP 779.

LEATHER [See also under IX. --Bibliographies--Leather]

3680. Attwater, W. A.   Leathercraft.   London: Batsford
       Ltd. , 1961.
3681. Belaya, I. K.   "Instructions for Softening and Restor-
       ing Leather Bindings, " Collection of Materials on
       the Preservation of Library Resources.   Moscow:
       1958.   English translation available from National
       Technical Information Service, Springfield, Virginia.
3682. _____ .   "Methods of Strengthening the Damaged
       Leather of Old Bindings, " Restaurator 1(2), 1969.
       Describes the use of synthetic resins to strengthen
       weakened leather and soften hardened leather covers.
3683. _____ .   "Selecting and Testing Adhesives for the
       Restoration of Skinbindings and Parchment, "
       Restaurator 1(4):221-231, 1970.   Reprint in English
       of an article first published in Russia in 1961.
3684. _____ .   "Softening Leather Bindings, " Collection of
       Materials on the Preservation of Library Resources.
       Moscow, 1958.   English translation available from
       National Technical Information Service, Springfield,
       Virginia.
3685. _____ .   "The Preservation of Leather Bindings at
       the Lenin State Library in the U. S. S. R. , " UNESCO
       Bulletin for Libraries 13:125-126, 1959.

3686. "Cleaning Buckskin, "Clearing House for (South) Western Museum News Letter No. 192. February 1956.

3687. "Cleaning Deer and Other Skin, " Clearing House for (South) Western Museum News Letter No. 89, July 1947.

3688. Frey, R. W. and F. P. Veitch. Preservation of Leather Book Bindings. Washington: Department of Agriculture, 1933. Leaflet No. 69.

3689. Plenderleith, H. J. "Laboratory Notes: The Preservation of Bookbindings, " British Museum Quarterly 3:77-78, 1927.

3690. "The Problem of Softening Stiffened Leather, " Clearing House for (South) Western Museums News Letter No. 97, March 1948.

3691. Rogers, J. S. and C. W. Beebe. Leather Bookbindings, How to Preserve Them. Washington: U. S. Department of Agriculture, May 1956. Booklet No. 398.

3692. Rohm & Haas Co. "Impregnating and Improving Leather, " USP. 1, 053, 829, May 4, 1964.

3693. Waterer, John W. A Guide to the Conservation and Restoration of Objects Made Wholly or in Part of Leather. London: G. Bell and Sons, 1972.

3694. Werner, A. E. A. "The Conservation of Leather, Wood, Bone and Ivory, and Archival Materials, " The Conservation of Cultural Property. Paris: UNESCO, 1968.

3695. Yates, W. J. "Leather Cleaning Composition, " U. S. P. 2, 064, 285, December 15, 1936.

PARCHMENT AND VELLUM

3696. "A note on the conservation of some parchment documents damaged by fire, " Business Archives, The Journal of the Business Archives Council 33:18-19, 1970. Describes steps taken to salvage the information on damaged documents but not necessarily the material itself.

3697. Audsley, G. A. Guide to Illuminating on Vellum and Paper. London: Rowney, 1911.

3698. Belaya, I. K. "Softening and Restauration of Parchment in Manuscripts and Bookbindings, " Restaurator 1(1):20-51, 1969. Copenhagen.

3699. _____. "Selecting and Testing Adhesives for the
       Restoration of Skinbindings and Parchment,"
       Restaurator 1(4):221-231, 1970. Reprint in English
       of an article first published in Russia in 1961.

3700. Marconi, Bohdan. "Some Tests on the Use of Wax
       for Fixing Flaking Paint on Illuminated Parchment,"
       Studies in Conservation 1:17ff. , 1962.

3701. "Parchment Patients," Newsweek 61:90, 1963. The
       Vatican's institute for the scientific restoration of
       books.

3702. "Parchment Stretcher," American Archivist 1:7, 15,
       1938 and 9:330, 1946.

3703. "Repair of Parchment," American Archivist 1:5, 14,
       52, 60, 73, 1938; 3:212, 213, 1940 and 16:119,
       1953.

3704. Skordas, Gustav. "The Parchment Stretcher at the
       Maryland Hall of Records," American Archivist
       9:330-332, 1946.

3705. Wächter, Otto. "On the Stretching and Flattening of
       Old Parchment," Allgemeiner Anzeiger für Büch-
       bindereien 71(1), 1958. Stuttgart. In German. [3708].

3706. _____. "The Restoration of the Vienna Dioscor-
       ides," Studies in Conservation 7, 1962. Detailed
       report on the repairs to an early 6th-century parch-
       ment. Illustrated manuscript.

BINDING [See also under VIII. Appendices--O.]

3707. Adams, P. "Turkish, Arabic and Persian Bookbind-
       ing," Archiv für Büchbinderei 1904.

3708. Allgemenier Anzeiger für Büchbindereien. Stuttgart:
       Buchbinder-Verlag. 5(14a) Christophstrasse 9,
       Fernruf 94215, 1958. General information for book-
       binding.

3709. All the Kings Horses. Chicago: The Lakeside Press,
       n. d. Description of the work by the Extra Bindery
       of this publishing firm.

3710. Al Sufyani, Abū'l - Abbās Ahmed ibn Muhammed.
       Art of Bookbinding and Guilding, AD 1619. Pub-
       lished in Arabic in Revue Africaine by P. Ricard
       in 1925, and an English translation in Transactions
       of the American Philosophical Society 52(4), 1962.
       This is a detailed account of Arab binding techniques.

3711. A Rod for the Back of the Binder. Chicago: Lakeside Press, 1928. Describes fine binding as done by this company in the 1920's.

3712. Banks, Paul N. "Some Problems in Book Conservation," Library Resources and Technical Services 12(3):330-338, 1968.

3713. Belaya, I. K. "Glue for the Restoration of Leather Bindings," Restoration and Preservation of Library Resources, Documents and Books. London: Oldbourne Press, 1964.

3714. "Bookbinding," American Archivist 3:267, 1940 and 16:115, 1953.

3715. Buck, M. S. Book Repair and Restoration. Philadelphia, 1918. A manual of practical suggestions including some translated sections from Essai sur l'Art de Restaurer les Estampes et les Livres, par. A. Bonnardot.

3716. Chytil, K. and F. A. Borovsky. Bücheinbande vom XVIII, Jahrhundert Bis in Die Neveste Zeit. Prague: Kunstyewerbliches Museum, 1904. Descriptive text on bookbinding in German and Hungarian.

3717. Dana, John C. Bookbinding for Libraries. Chicago: Library Bureau, 1906. The librarians' point of view on bookbinding at the turn of the century.

3718. de Haas, Hendrik. De Boekbinder. Dordrecht: 1806. 'The bookbinder; or complete description of everything related to this art. Complete description of all arts, trades, labors, factories, traffics, their buildings, tools, etc. Partly taken from the best known foreign works and augmented with the theory and practice of the best domestic artists and artisans."

3719. Diehl, Edith. Bookbinding, Its Background and Technique. New York: Rinehart, 1946. Two volumes illustrated. Vol. 1 comprises a history of the craft; Vol. 2 a manual of hand binding.

3720. Domesday Rebound. London: Her Majesty's Stationery Office, 1954. Detailed description of the restoration of two of the Domesday Books.

3721. Foxon, David. The Technique of Bookbinding. London: National Book League, 1955.

3722. Gould, F. C. Mechanization of Bookbinding, Being Lecture Three of the 16th Series of Craft Lectures Given in Stationers' Hall on Friday, 17th December, 1937.

3723. Grimm, Francis W. A Primer to Bookbinding. Boston: Houghton Mifflin Co., 1939.

3724. Halliday, John. Bookcraft and Bookbinding. London: Pitman, 1951. Well illustrated.

3725. Hasluck, P. N. Bookbinding. Philadelphia: David McKay, 1903. A digest of information on binding which originally appeared in the British weekly journal Work. Interesting sections on marbling paper, tree calfing leather, and gold blocking.

3726. Ignatz Wiemeler, Modern Bookbinder. New York: Museum of Modern Art, 1935.

3727. Jennett, Seán. The Making of Books. 2nd ed. London: Faber and Faber, 1956.

3728. Johnson, Pauline. Creative Bookbinding. Seattle: University of Washington Press, 1967.

3729. Lathem, Edward Connery. "Some Personnel Considerations for Binding and Conservation Services," Library Trends 4:321-334, 1956.

3730. Leighton, D. Modern Bookbinding; a Survey and a Prospect. London: School of Printing, 1935.

3731. MacDougall, G. Some Research Problems in Bookbinding. London: 1935.

3732. Mansfield, Edgar. Modern Design in Bookbinding. London: Peter Owen, 1966. A book on the technique and theory of creative bookbinding by the President of the Guild of Contemporary Bookbinders.

3733. _____. "New Directions in Modern Bookbinding," Graphis 15:350-357, 1959.

3734. Middleton, Bernard C. "The Bookbinder's Case Unfolded," The Library 5th Series, 17:66-76, 1962.

3735. Philip, Alex J. The Business of Bookbinding for Librarians, Publishers, Students, Binders, and the General Reader. Gravesend: Philip, 1935.

3736. Schaefer, Ernest Jr. "Hot (Gold) Stamping," Guild of Book Workers Journal 8(1):27-32, 1969. Encouraging report on the quality results obtainable with modern stamping machines, gold foil, and zinc type.

3737. Shipley, Sir A. E. "Bookbinding in the Tropics," Tropical Agriculture 3:141, 1926.

3738. Theory and Practice of Bookbinding. Washington: U.S. Government Printing Office, 1950.

3739. Tomlinson, C. J. Cyclopedia of Useful Arts and Manufactures, 1852. Early methods of bookmaking.

3740. Tribolet, Harold W. "Binding and Related Problems," American Archivist 16:115-126, 1953. Except for

lack of information on deacidification, a good summary of what should and should not be done to
valuable books.

3741.   _____. "Binding Practice as Related to the Preservation of Books," The Library Quarterly
40(1):128-138, 1970. A lucid description of variants in binding and their effect on librarians.

3742. Vaughan, A. J. Modern Bookbinding. Leicester:
Raithby, Lawrence, 1946.

3743. Wheatley, H. B. "The Principles of Design as Applied to Bookbinding," Journal of the Royal Society
of Arts 36(1840):359-377, 1888.

3744. "Why Not Do Your Own Binding?" Reproduction 1:10-
11, 1964.

3745. Williamson, Hugh. Methods of Book Design. London:
Oxford University Press, 1956.

HAND BINDING

3746. Banister, Manly. Pictorial Manual of Bookbinding.
New York: Ronald Press Co., 1958.

3747. Banks, Paul N. "The Treatment of the First British
Edition of Melville's 'The Whale'," Technical Pa-
pers From 1968 Through 1970. New York: IIC
(American Group), 1970.

3748. Battershall, Fletcher. Bookbinding for Bibliophiles.
Greenwich, Conn.: The Literary Collector Press,
1905.

3749. Bean, Florence O. Bookbinding for Beginners. Boston: School Arts Publishing Co., 1914. A teach-
ing manual for use in elementary school handicraft
classes.

3750. "The Binding of the Sherborne Chartuary," British
Museum Quarterly 32(1-2), 1968.

3751. Bookbinders' Complete Instructor in All Branches of
Bookbinding. Peterhead: 1823.

3751a. Bookbinder's Manual. London: 1832.

3752. Brade, L. and E. Winkler. Het Geillustreerde Boek-
bindersboek. Leyden: 1861. The illustrated book
for the bookbinder. Complete instructions in bookbinding, in which is described the latest French,
English, and German accomplishments in this profession. With an extended instruction in the making of various marbled and other edges, also gilding. About the use of the latest machines. With
76 very good recipes and many wood cuts.

3753. Buffam, Clara. Hand Bound Books. Providence, R. I. : Akerman-Standard Co. , 1935.

3754. Buhler, Curt F. "The Binding of Books Printed by William Caxton, " Papers of the Bibliographical Society of America 38:1-9, 1944.

3755. Clements, Jeff. Bookbinding. London: Arco Publications, 1968.

3756. Cockerell, D. Bookbinding and the Care of Books. 5th ed. London: Pitman, 1953.

3757. _____. Some Notes on Bookbinding. London: Oxford University Press, 1929. This small volume is a sequel to Douglas Cockerell's Bookbinding. Hard to find but well worth looking for.

3758. Collins, A. F. Book Crafts for Junior Pupils: A Handbook. New York: Thomas Crowell Co. , 1938.

3759. _____. Book Crafts for Senior Pupils: A Handbook. New York: Thomas Crowell Co. , 1938.

3760. Corderoy, John. Bookbinding for Beginners. New York: Watson-Guptill, 1967. An excellent little book for those who wish to teach themselves.

3761. Cowie, G. The Bookbinder's Manual. London: Cowie & Strange, 1868. Contains a full description of leather and vellum binding. Also, directions for gilding of paper and book-edges, and numerous valuable recipes for sprinkling, colouring, and marbling, together with a scale of bookbinder's charges. A list of book and vellum binders in London, etc.

3762. Crane, W. J. E. Bookbinding for Amateurs. London: Gill, 1885. Descriptions of the various tools and minute instructions for their use. Well illus.

3763. Cushman, E. R. Bookbinding. Boy Scouts of America, Merit Badge Pamphlet, 1930. Includes instructions for simple binding with simple tools.

3764. dé Recy, Georges. Décoration du Cuir. Paris: Ernest Flammarion, 1905.

3765. Diehl, Edith. Bookbinding, Its Background and Technique. New York: Rinehart, 1946.

3766. Diringer, David. The Hand Produced Book. New York: Philosophical Library, 1953.

3767. Domesday Rebound. London: Her Majesty's Stationery Office, 1954. A description of the rebinding of the Domesday Book.

3768. Dudin, René Martin. Arte del Legatore e Doratore di Libri. (Rome?), 1772. An Italian edition of Dudin's "L'Art du Relieur et Doreur de Livres" in Academie Royale des Sciences Descriptions des

3769.   Arts et Metiers, etc. 1772.
                  . Arte del Legatore e Doratore di Libri 1772 con-alcuni estratti di un trattato inedito di Jaques Jaugeon arte di legare i libri (1704). Amsterdam: Graphic, 1964. A reprint edited with notes of 123 pages with 16 plates of Dudin and Jangeon's two 18th century treatises on the art of bookbinding.

3770.   . L'Art du Relieur et Doreur de Livres. Paris: 1772. This early book on bookbinding and gold tooling has 112 pages of text and 16 plates. It was written for the Academie Royale des Sciences.

3771.   . L'Art du Relieur, Nouvelle edition, augmentee de tout ce qui a eta ecrit de mieux sur ces mattieres en Allegmagne, en Angleterre, en Suisse, en Italie par J. E. Betrand. Paris: 1820. Extract from the Description generale des Arts et Metiers, 1772.

3772.   Ede, Charles. "Hand Binding," The Art of the Book. London: Studio Publications, 1951.

3773.   Eggeling, Arthur. Bookbinding by Hand. New York: Eggeling Bookbindery, 1925.

3774.   Fache, J. La Dorure et la Décoration de Reliures. Paris: 1958. Describes tools and techniques for gold tooling.

3775.   Fahey, Herbert and Peter. Finishing in Hand Bookbinding. San Francisco: Printed and published by Herbert and Peter Fahey, 1951.

3776.   Forsyth, K. M. Bookbinding for Teachers, Students and Amateurs. New York: Macmillan, 1932. Simple step-by-step directions.

3777.   Franck, Peter. Die Rundbogen-Heftung. Stuttgart: Buchbinder-Verlag, 1949. Monograph on improved sewing technique to obtain improvement in the shape of the backs of heavy books. Based on technique developed by Swiss bookbinder, Theo. Spiebruch in 1641.

3778.   Grimm, Francis W. A Primer on Bookbinding. Boston: Houghton Mifflin Co., 1939. A basic text of fundamentally correct techniques using the simplest equipment. For juveniles.

3779.   Groneman, Chris H. General Bookbinding. Bloomington, Ill.: McKnight and McKnight, 1946. A high school level manual of instruction. Calls for simplest of tools and equipment.

3780. Halliday, J.   Bookbinding as a Handwork Subject.
        New York: E. P. Dutton and Company, n. d.
3781. Hannett, J.   Bibliopegia or the Art of Bookbinding in
        All Its Branches.   By John Andrews Arnett (pseud.)
        London: Groombridge,   1835.
3782. Harrison, T.   Fragments of Bookbinding Technique.
        London: London School of Printing,   1950.
3783. Hatchards & Zaehnsdorf.   Notes on the Art of Book-
        binding.   London: Hatchards, 1952.   Pamphlet.
3784. Hewitt-Bates, James Samuel.   Bookbinding for
        Schools: A Textbook for Teachers and Students in
        Elementary and Secondary Schools and Training
        Colleges.   Peoria, Ill. :   Manual Arts Press, 1935.
3785. _____ .   Bookbinding.   Leicester: Dryad Press,
        1962.   Presents bookbinding from both a practical
        and educational angle and a series of exercises
        culminating in full leather binding and gold tooling.
3786. Jaugeon, Jacques.   "L'Art de Reliure les Libres, "
        This forms the fifth part and completion of a great
        work, Description et Perfection des Arts et Méti-
        ers.   The manuscript has never been printed.   It
        was begun in 1683 and finished in 1704.   The part
        relating to binding has 42 pages of text, and two
        explanatory plates; these last were used later on
        by Dudin in his "Art du Relieur et Doreur des
        Livres, " which appeared in 1772.   This is the
        first technical work on binding known.
3787. _____ .   Arte di Legare i Libri.   Rome, 1704.
        An Italian edition of Jaugeon's essay on binding in
        Le Jeu du Monde ou l'Intelligence des plus curi-
        euses choses qui se trouvent dans tous les estats,
        les terres et les mers du monde.   Paris: A.
        Auroy, 1684.
3788. Johnson, Pauline.   Creative Bookbinding.   Seattle:
        University of Washington Press, 1965.
3789. _____ .   "Decorative Covers, " Craft Horizons
        45:20-23, 1954.
3790. Kinder, Louis H.   Formulas for Bookbinders.   East
        Aurora, New York: The Roycrofters, 1905.
        Traditional formulas for handbinders.   Many are
        obsolete but the information is important for re-
        storers.
3791. Kitson, Edward.   Bookbinding.   New York: Dover
        Publications, 1954.
3792. Klinefelter, Lee M.   Bookbinding Made Easy.   Mil-
        waukee: Bruce Publishing Co. , 1935.   Revised
        and enlarged in 1960.

3793. Le Moine, Simone. Manual Practique du Reliure.
Paris: Dumod, 1960.

3794. Lenormand, Louis Seb. Nouveau Manuel Complet du
Relieur. Paris: Librairie Encyclopedique du
Roret, 1840. Bookbinding as practiced in France
in mid-19th-century.

3795. Lewis, Arthur William. Basic Bookbinding. New
York: Dover Publications, 1957.

3796. Loubier, Hans. Der Bucheinband. Leipzig: 1926.

3797. "Marbled Paper," American Archivist 1:15, 1938.

3798. Martin, G. The Bookbinder's Complete Instructor in
All Branches of Binding: Particularly Marbling,
Staining, and Gilding the Covers and Edges of
Books: With All the Late Improvements and Discoveries in That Useful Art. By a Practical Bookbinder. Peterhead: P. Buchan, Printer and Publisher, 1823.

3799. Mason, John. Bookbinding. London: Warne, 1936. 36 illustrations in a 62 page pamphlet of the basic steps
in bookbinding.

3800. _____. Gold and Colour Tooling. Leicester,
Eng.: Dryad Press, n.d. Dryad Leaflet No. 105.

3801. _____. Stationery Bookbinding. London: Pitman,
1946.

3802. Matthews, William F. Modern Bookbinding Practically Considered. New York: The Grolier Club,
1889.

3803. _____. Bookbinding. London: V. Gollanez, 1929.
An important text for amateurs by this reknowned
binder.

3804. Nathan, M. The Decoration of Leather. London:
Archibald Constable, 1905. From the French of
Georges de Recy.

3805. Nicholson, James B. A Manual of the Art of Bookbinding. Philadelphia: Baird & Company, 1856.
Contains full instructions in the different branches
of binding and decorating books. Reprinted in
1902.

3806. Oswesley, N. The Whole Art of Bookbinding. London: 1811. This is the earliest English book on
the subject of bookbinding. Contains recipes for
sprinkling, marbling and coloring leather in addition to forwarding and finishing instructions.

3807. Palmer, E. W. A Course in Bookbinding for Voca-
tional Training. New York: Employing Bookbinders of America, 1927. Part 1, Elementary Section, was all that was ever printed.

3808. Parry, Henry. The Whole Art of Bookbinding. London: Craddock & Joy, 1818.

3809. [No entry.]

3810. Paton, James. "Bookbinding," Encyclopaedia Britannica. Edinburgh: Adam and Charles Black, 1876. Discusses the evolution of hand binding, binding styles, and gives a detailed description of quality hand binding as it was practiced at the height of the art. Also includes a discussion of case making with machinery available to the industry in 1875.

3811. Pearce, W. B. Practical Bookbinding. London: Marshall's Practical Manuals, 1906.

3812. Perry, K. F. and C. T. Baab. The Binding of Books. Peoria, Ill.: The Manual Arts Press, 1940. A thorough and practical treatment for both amateurs and skilled craftsmen.

3813. _____. The Binding of Books. Bloomington, Ill.: McKnight & McKnight, 1967. An introduction to binding for vocation high schools and colleges with some comments on binding by machinery.

3814. Pointer, Wallace. "Rebinding the Klencke Atlas," British Museum Quarterly 15, 1961. Discusses problems in handling a book five feet high.

3815. Pratt, Guy A. Let's Bind a Book. Milwaukee: Bruce Publishing Co., 1940.

3816. Regemorter, Berthe van. "La Reliure des Manuscrits Grecs," Scriptorium 8:2-23, 1954. Technical details on binding techniques on early Armenian, Georgian and some Balkan binding.

3817. Robinson, Ivor. Introducing Bookbinding. New York: Watson-Guptill Publications, 1968. Outstandingly illustrated text for those who wish more than a text for a novice.

3818. Smith, F. R. Bookbinding. New York: Pitman Publishing Co., 1929. A small, well illustrated text. One of Pitman's "Craft for All" series by a Fellow of the Royal Society of Arts. Reprinted 1935.

3819. [No entry.]

3820. Town, Laurence. Bookbinding by Hand for Students and Craftsmen. London: Faber & Faber, 1951. The style of presentation and excellent drawings in this book make it of particular value to beginners in the craft.

3821. Watson, Aldren A. Hand Bookbinding: A Manual of Instruction. New York: Reinhold Publishing Corp., 1963.

3822. Wolf-LeFranc, M. and Charles Vermuyse. La Reliure. Paris: Bailliere et Fils, 1957.

3823. Wood, Stacy H. Bookbinding. New York: Boy Scouts of America, 1940.

3824. Woodcock, John. Binding Your Own Books. London: Penguin Books, n. d. Puffin Picture Book 104.

3825. Zaehnsdorf, Joseph W. The Art of Bookbinding. London: Bell, 1880. Republished in 1925. An illustrated manual of forwarding and finishing by one of the great binders.

3826. _____. "Practical Suggestions in Bookbinding, " The Library Chronicle 4:107-111, 1887.

3827. _____. Notes on the Art of Bookbinding. London: Zaehnsdorf Ltd. , 1952.

MARBLING

3828. Adams, Charles. "Some Notes on Marbling Paper, " Bulletin 51(7):411-422, 1947. New York Public Library.

3829. Boeck, Phileas. Bookbinding: The Whole Art of Bookbinding, Containing Valuable Receipts for Sprinkling, Marbling and Colouring of Paper. Owestry: 1811.

3830. Cockerell, Sydney H. Marbling Paper. Hitchin, Herts. , England: Russel Bookcrafts, 1947. Pamphlet.

3831. _____. Marbling Paper as a School Subject. Hitchin, England: July 1934. One specimen of marbled paper. 16 pp.

3832. Combed Pattern Papers. Leicester, England: Dryad Press, n. d. Dryad Leaflet No. 107. Instructions for decorating paper.

3833. Cowie, G. Bookbinders Manual. London: Cowie and Strange, 1868. Full descriptions for leather and velum binding also directions for marbling. Lists bookbinders' charges for the mid-19th century.

3834. Halfer, Joseph. Art of Marbling and Treatment of the New Bronze Colours. 2nd ed. London: 1904.

3835. _____. The Progress of the Marbling Art; With a Supplement on the Decoration of Book Edges. Buffalo: American Bookbinder Co. , 1893. Many specimens of marbled papers.

3836. Hewitt-Bates, James Samuel and J. Halliday. Three Methods of Marbling. Leicester, England: Dryad Press, n. d. Leaflet No. 174.

3837. Hunter, Dard. "A Bibliography of Marbled Paper, "
       The Paper Trade Journal April 28, 1921. Sixty-
       nine titles principally on making marbled paper.
3838. Kantrowitz, M. S. and E. W. Spencer. The Process
       of Marbling Paper. Washington: U. S. Government
       Printing Office, 1953. Bindery Series No. 1.
       Much information on evolution of the process with
       useful formulas and a lengthy bibliography by Dard
       Hunter.
3839. Kinder, Louis H. Formulas for Bookbinders. East
       Aurora, N. Y.: The Roycrofters, 1905. 115
       pages of text including 8 pages of formulas for
       marbling and marbling colors.
3840. Lenormand, Louis Seb. Nouveau Manuel Complet du
       Relieur. Paris: Roret, 1840. Part of the Li-
       brairie Encyclopidique de Roret.
3841. Martin, Thomas. Complete Instructions in all
       Branches of Bookbinding. London: R. Rees, 1813.
       Includes instructions for marbling paper. Also in
       Circle of the Mechanical Arts. [1096]
3842. Mason, John. A Practical Course in Bookcrafts and
       Bookbinding. London: B. T. Batsford, 1935.
       Fuller and more detailed than his elementary
       book, Bookbinding. London: Warne, 1936.
3843. Monk, J. Leonard and W. F. Lawrence. Textbook of
       Stationery Binding. Leicester: Raithby, Lawrence,
       1912. Includes chapters on ruling, marbling,
       leather, paper, etc.
3844. Nicholson, James B. A Manual of the Art of Book-
       binding. Philadelphia: Baird & Company, 1856.
       Reprinted in 1902. A practical manual on fine
       handbinding including marbling, sprinkling, gold
       tooling, etc.
3845. Oswesley, N. The Whole Art of Bookbinding. Lon-
       don: 1811. This early English book on
       binding includes marbling instructions.
3846. Pleger, John J. Bookbinding. Chicago: Inland
       Printer Co., 1924. Contains sections on marbling,
       edge gilding and printed fore edges.
3847. _____. Gilt Edging, Marbling and Hand Tooling.
       Chicago: Inland Printer Co., 1914.
3848. The Process of Marbling Paper. Washington: U. S.
       Government Printing Office, 1953. GPO-PIA Joint
       Research Bulletin B-1. Many recipes, detailed
       instructions, lengthy bibliography.
3849. Thrift, Tim. Modern Methods in Marbling Paper, a
       Treatise for the Layman on the Art of Marbling

Paper for Bookbinding ... Including a Description of
Several Practical Methods with Illustrative Samples
of Marbled Effects. Winchester, Mass.: The
Lucky Dog Press, 1945.

3850. Verstage, K. A. and others. Hints on Marbling. London: London School of Printing, 1940.

3851. Woolnough, C. W. The Whole Art of Marbling as
Applied to Paper and Book Edges. London: A.
Heylin, 1881. Contains a full description of the
nature and properties of the materials used and
the method of preparing them. 82 pages text.
38 examples of surface decorated paper. This and
Halfer's books are the most comprehensive works
on the subject in the English language.

3852. Zaehnsdorf, J. W. The Art of Bookbinding: a Practical Treatise. London: George Bell & Sons, 1903.
A standard work first published in 1880. Marbling
paper included as part of the craft. Reprinted
1925.

LIBRARY BINDING

3853. Alpers, Fred. "Library Binding in Europe - A Summary of the Report to the Council on Library Resources," The Library Binder 9:14-16, 1961.

3854. Atkinson, Kenneth. "Overseas Techniques in Library
Binding," Book Production Magazine 37:80, 86-87,
1961.

3855. Ayer, T. P. "A Schedule for Binding and Rebinding,"
Library Journal 62:621, 856-857, 1937.

3856. Bailey, Arthur L. Library Bookbinding. White
Plains, N.Y.: Wilson, 1916.

3857. Binding for Libraries: Library Handbook No. 5. Chicago: American Library Association, 1915. The
first suggestions for library binding from the ALA's
Bookbinding Committee established in 1905.

3858. Callender, T. E. The Library Bindery and its Ad-
ministration. London: North Western Polytechnic
School of Librarianship, 1954. Occasional Papers
No. 4.

3859. Clough, Eric A. Bookbinding for Librarians. London: Asso. of Assistant Librarians, 1957. A
comprehensive discussion of library binding as it
is done in England. Some materials reported in
"recent developments" are not considered safe for
use on paper.

3860. Coutts, Henry T. and George A. Stephen. Manual of
       Library Book-binding: With Specimens of Leathers
       and Cloths, Forms and Illustrations. London:
       Libraco Limited, 1911.
3861. Dana, J. C. Notes on Bookbinding for Libraries.
       Chicago: Library Bureau, 1906.
3862. Drewery, R. F. Library Binderies. London: Li-
       brary Association, 1950. Library Association
       Pamphlet No. 3.
3863. Feipel, L. N. and Earl Browning. Library Binding
       Manual. Chicago: American Library Association,
       1951.
3864. Handbook for Library Binding. Boston: Library
       Binding Institute, 1972. Advice and assistance for
       librarians.
3865. Mortimer, E. A. Library Books: Their Care and
       Repair. Auckland: The University of Auckland,
       1968. A handbook for library binding instructors
       and librarians prepared as a series of basic lec-
       tures for library workshop apprentices.
3866. Philip, Alex J. The Business of Bookbinding.
       Gravesend: A. Philip, 1935. Glossary. Speci-
       mens of book clothes, 2nd ed.
3867. Preparing Material for the Bindery. Los Angeles:
       Pacific Library Binding Company, 1938.
3868. Reavis, W. Elmo. "Book Sewing Distinguished from
       Book Stitching," Pacific Bindery Talk November
       1937-January 1938. Excellent well illustrated de-
       scription of principal methods of performing each.
       Clarifies differences between machine sewing and
       machine stitching as well as differences between
       hand and machine sewing.
3869. _____ . "The Stream of Bookbinding," Pacific
       Bindery Talk, April, May, June 1938. An histori-
       cal sketch up to and including the concept of "Li-
       brary Binding."
3870. Roberts, Matt. "Oversewing and the Problem of Book
       Preservation in the Research Library," College and
       Research Libraries 28:17-24, 1967. Mr. Roberts
       addresses himself to a practice which is universally
       condemned by persons concerned about books and
       almost universally employed by library binders.
3871. Standard for Library Binding. Boston: Library Bind-
       ing Institute, 1963. This standard for all library
       binding includes prelibrary bound books as well as
       rebinding used books and binding of periodicals.
       Is included in Tauber Library Binding Manual.

Boston, 1972.

3872. Tauber, Maurice F. (ed.). Library Binding Manual: A Handbook of Useful Procedures for the Maintenance of Library Volumes for Reader Useability. Boston: Library Binding Institute, 1972. This outstanding introduction to binding is intended to assist librarians in the preparation of materials for binding and instruct them in the care of their collections. Also much information for students in schools of library science.

3873. Weiss, Dudley A. "Facts and Fallacies on Library Binding," Library Journal 82(1):15-20, 1957.

3874. _____. "Library Binding and the Purchasing Agent," Library Binder 3:15-19, 1955.

3875. _____. "Working With A Library Binder," Science Technology News 19(1), 1965. Recommendations for librarians by the Executive Director of the Library Binding Institute.

EDITION BINDING

3876. Comparato, Frank E. Books for the Millions. Harrisburg, Penn.: The Stackpole Company, 1971. A history of the men whose methods and machines packaged the printed world. The best book available on the industrialization of American binding with excellent descriptions of the development of the machinery.

3877. Darley, Lionel. Introduction to Bookbinding. London: Faber and Faber, 1965.

3878. Ede, Charles. "Commercial Binding," The Art of the Book. London: Studio Publications, 1951.

3879. Esdaile, Arundell. "Binding," Student's Manual of Bibliography. 3rd ed. rev. by R. Stokes. London: George Allen & Unwin and the Library Association, 1954.

3880. Gerring, C. Notes on Bookbinding. Nottingham: Frank Murray, 1899. Illustrations of Birdsall and Chivers' bindings.

3881. Goodwin, Bancroft L. Pamphlet Binding. Chicago: United Typothetae of America, 1925. Typographic technical series for apprentices, part 5, no. 20.

3882. Harrison, T. Bookbinding for Printers. London: Association of Teachers of Printing and Allied Subjects, 1949. ATPAS Handbook for Teachers No. 2.

3883. Helwig, Hellmuth. Handbüch der Einbandkunde. Ham-
      burg: 1953.
3884. Leighton, Douglas. Modern Bookbinding, a Survey
      and a Prospect. London: London School of Print-
      ing, 1935. Fifth annual J. M. Dent Memorial
      Lecture, 1935.
3885. Letterpress Bookbinding Terminology. London: Master
      Bookbinders' Association, 1928.
3886. Madagan, J. R. Bookbinding Methods and Aids for
      the Printing Trade. Charlotte, N. C. : Washburn
      Printing Co. , 1952.
3887. Mason, John. Bookbinding and Ruling. New York:
      Pitman, 1933. The art and practice of printing.
3888. _____ . Edition Case Binding. New York: Pit-
      man, 1946. Printing theory and practice no. 23.
3889. _____ . Letterpress Bookbinding. New York: Pit-
      man, 1946. Printing theory and practice no. 21.
3890. "Methods and Materials for Electronic Case Making, "
      Bookbinding and Book Production 57:32-33, 1953;
      58:33-34, 1953; 58:48-51, 1953; 58:50,
      1953.
3891. "Modern Book Binding, " Times Literary Supplement
      p. 372, June 3, 1949.
3892. Modern Book Production. London: Studio Publica-
      tions, 1928.
3893. Monk, J. Leonard and W. F. Lawrence. Textbook
      of Stationery Binding; A Treatise on the Whole Art
      of Forwarding and Finishing Stationery Books, in-
      cluding Chapters on Ruling, Marbling, Leather and
      Papers. Leicester: Raithby, Lawrence, 1912.
3894. Mordy, C. H. Loose-leaf Binding, Being the Fifth
      Lecture of the 9th Session of Craft Lectures of the
      Stationers' Company and Printing Industry Technical
      Board 1930-1931. London: The Stationers Co. ,
      1931.
3895. Philip, Alex J. The Business of Book-binding: For
      Librarians, Publishers, Students, Binders, and the
      General Reader. 2nd ed. Gravesend, England:
      Alex. J. Philip, 1935. Originally published in
      1912. Entirely rewritten 1934. British practice.
      Includes samples of leather, cloth, and leather-
      cloth.
3896. Plan for a Good Book, An Illustrated Guide Book De-
      scribing the Methods and Equipment Used in Better
      Book Manufacturing. Chicago: John F. Cuneo
      Co. , 1951.

3897. Pleger, J. J. Bookbinding and Its Auxiliary Branches. Chicago: Inland Printer Co., 1914.

3898. _____. "Loose-leaf Binders," Bookbinding. Chicago, Ill.: Inland Printer, 1924.

3899. _____. Pamphlet Binding, Punching, Crimping and Quarter Binding. Chicago: Inland Printer, 1914.

3900. Rollings, Carl Purington. "A Survey of Contemporary Bookmaking," The Dolphin 2:259-329, 1935.

3901. Stephen, G. A. Commercial Bookbinding: A Description of the Processes and the Various Machines Used. London: Stonehill, 1910.

3902. Theory and Practice of Bookbinding. rev. ed. Washington: U.S. Government Printing Office, 1962. U.S. Government Printing Office, Training Series.

3903. Vaughan, A. J. "Letterpress Binding," Practical Printing and Binding. 2nd ed. London: Odhams Press, 1955. Harry Whetton, editor. [3906]

3904. _____. Modern Bookbinding. London: Charles Skilton Ltd., 1929. One of the best 20th century volumes on the combination of hand and machine binding for high quality workmanship.

3905. _____. Modern Bookbinding: A Treatise Covering Both Letterpress and Stationery Branches of the Trade, with a Section on Finishing and Design. rev. ed., London: Charles Skilton Ltd., 1960.

3906. Whetton, Harry. Practical Printing and Binding. London: Odhams Press, 1955.

UNSEWN BINDINGS

3907. Clough, Eric A. Perfect Binding, a New Development. London: Vinyl Products Ltd., 1948. Internal Sales Circular No. 16. Reprinted from the Library Association Record, October 1949.

3908. Flexiback Book Lining Machine. London: Book Machinery Co., 1949.

3909. The Flexiback Thermoplastic Binder. London: Book Machinery Co., Model E Instruction Manual, 1950.

3910. Grove, Lee E. "Adhesive Bookbinding: A Practice Reviewed," Library Resources and Technical Services 6:143-160, 1962.

3911. "New Trends in Vinyl Binding," Book Production 68:40, 1958.

3912. Observations on Library Binding with Special Reference to the Unsewn Method. London: British Federation of Master Printers, 1950. Library Binders

Memorandum No. 1.
3913. Percival, G. S. and R. Graham. Unsewn Binding.
       2nd ed. Leicester: Dryad Press, 1969. 40 pp.
       Clear and concise instructions in a recognized ad-
       junct to the traditional methods of binding.
3914. Siegel, A. "Modern Methods of Loose-Leaf Construc-
       tion, " Bookbinding and Book Production, 1951.
3915. "Summary of 'adhesive' Binding Techniques, " Book-
       binding and Book Production 35-36, 1952.
3916. "Thermoplastic Unsewn Binding, " British Printer
       66:7879, 1954. On the Flexiback binder.
3917. "Unsewn Binders, " Paper & Print 205-206, Summer
       1951.
3918. Upton, P. G. B. and G. E. Busby. The Strength of
       Unsewn Binding. Leatherhead: Printing Associa-
       tion and Allied Trades Research Association, 1951.
       Interim Report No. 63.

BOOK REPAIR

3919. All The King's Horses. Chicago: The Lakeside
       Press, 1954. Also published serially in abridged
       form as H. W. Tribolet's "Arts of Book Repair
       and Restoration, " in Book Production 67(8), 1958.
3920. Banks, Paul N. "Some Problems in Book Conserva-
       tion, " Library Resources and Technical Services
       12(3), 1968.
3921. _____ . "The Treatment of the First Edition of
       Melville's 'The Whale', " Guild of Book Workers
       Journal 7(3):15-21, 1969. A detailed description
       of the restoration of the pages and text and the
       covers of an important 19th century volume printed
       on inferior paper and bound in stamped cloth cov-
       ers.
3922. Belaya, I. K. "Methods of Strengthening the Damaged
       Leather of Old Bindings, " Restaurator 1(2), 1969.
       Copenhagen.
3923. _____ . "Softening and Restoring of Parchment in
       Manuscripts and Book Bindings, " Restaurator 1(1),
       1969. Copenhagen.
3924. Belen'Kaja, N. G. and T. N. Strel'tzova. "Applica-
       tion of Methylolpolyamide Glue PFE-2/10 in the
       Restoration and Seamless Reinforcement of Books

and Documents," New Methods for the Restoration and Preservation of Documents and Books. Moscow: 1960. English translation available from National Technical Information Service, Springfield, Virginia.

3925. _____ and others. "The Use of High Frequency Magnetic Field for the Separation of Stuck-together Documents and Book Pages," Stareniye bumagi 128-131, 1965. Moscow.

3926. Book Mending. New York: Remington Rand, (circa 1948). Remington Rand Library Bureau.

3927. "Books, Care and Repair," American Archivist 1:22, 1938; 10:57, 1947; 11:280, 1948; 18:394, 1955.

3928. (Bro-Dart). Modern Simplified Book Repair. Newark: Bro-Dart Inc., 1969. Simplified instructions for repairs to circulating volumes using the company's supplies.

3929. Buck, Mitchel S. Book Repair and Restoration. Philadelphia: Nicholas L. Brown, 1918. A manual of practical suggestions but now somewhat outdated.

3930. Byrne, Brooke. Mending Books is Fun. Minneapolis: Burgess Publishing Company, 1956. Lightly written but useful for small circulation libraries with limited budgets.

3931. Capell, H. W. "The Preservation and Repair of Old Books," British and Colonial Printer 148(1160):192, 200, 1951.

3932. Chivers, Cedric. "A New Method of Preserving Old Bookbindings, or of Rebinding Old Books," The Library 2nd Series, 6:208-211, 1905.

3933. Cockerell, Sydney M. The Repairing of Books. London: Sheppard Press, 1958. An important manual on book repair by one of England's foremost binders.

3934. Demcobind: A Practical Manual of Mending Books. Madison: Demco Library Supplies, n. d.

3935. Douglas, Clara and Constance Lehde. Book Repairing: New Ideas From the Mendery. Seattle: University of Washington Press, 1940.

3936. Fores, Jean. "How Texts and Bindings are Repaired at the Bibliotheque Nationale," Arts et Metiers Graphiques 63, 1939.

3937. Gardner, A. "The Ethics of Book Repairs," The Library 5th Series, 9(3):194-198, 1954.

3938. Gaylord Bros., Inc. Bookcraft; An Illustrated Manual Describing the Gaylord Unit Method of Book Repair. Syracuse, N. Y.: Gaylord Bros., 1947. Dealer's

catalogue.
3939. Horton, Carolyn. Cleaning and Preserving Bindings
and Related Materials. 2nd ed. Chicago: American Library Association, 1969. Part I of ALA's
Library Technology Program on book preservation.
3940. "How to Use Adhesives Effectively and Economically,"
Book Production March 1935.
3941. Huntting, H. R. Book Mending. Springfield, Mass.:
Huntting Co., n. d.
3942. Hutchins, C. I. "The True Art of Restoration of
Books and Bindings," Bibliophile 1:301-306, 1908.
London.
3943. Lawrence, V. N. "The Case Against Plastic Tape,"
Manuscripts 8, 1956. New York.
3944. Lydenberg, Harry Miller and John Archer. The Care
and Repair of Books. 3rd rev. ed. New York:
R. R. Bowker Company, 1945.
3945. _____ . The Care and Repair of Books. New
York: R. R. Bowker, 1960. An updating of the
1945 edition by John Alden, Keeper of Rare Books,
Boston Public Library.
3946. Meyer, Rosaling. "Volunteer Worker in the Biblioteca
Nazionale in Florence," Guild of Book Workers
Journal 6(1), 1967. Describes keeping of records
of the damaged books.
3947. Middleton, Bernard C. The Restoration of Leather
Bindings. Chicago: American Library Asso.,
1972. (LTP Publication No. 18). This excellent
volume, together with Middleton's History--etc
[358], is all that is necessary for guidance in authentic restoration of early volumes.
3948. Morgana, Mario. Restauro dei libri antichi. Milano:
Hoepli, 1932. Manuali Hoepli. A standard Italian
work.
3949. Mortimer, E. A. Library Books: Their Care and
Repair. Auckland: University of Auckland, 1967.
Basic instruction for librarians.
3950. Muma, Robert. "Conserving the Leather Spines of
Old Books," Guild of Book Workers Journal 8(2),
1969-1970. Describes a method for holding together
the fragile leather with PVA until the repair is
completed.
3951. Nordstrand, O. K. "Chinese Double-leaved Books and
Their Restoration," Libri 17, 1967.
3952. Norton, P. H. Handbook on Book Repairing. rev.
ed. St. John: Red Cross Hospital, Library Department, 1952.

3953. Nyuksha, J. P. "Modern Methods of Restoration of Books and Manuscripts," Bibliotekar 12:64-66, 1958. Moscow.

3954. Patri, Stella. "The Mending Program in Florence," Guild of Book Workers Journal 6(1), 1967. Describes repair of book pages.

3955. Percival, G. S. Repairing Books. Leicester: Dryad Press, n. d. Leaflet No. 150. Sixteen page illustrated leaflet on repairing cloth covered books from torn pages to recasing.

3956. Powell, Roger. "The Lichfield St. Chad's Gospels: Repair and Rebinding," The Library 5th Series, 20:259-275, 1965.

3957. Spawn, Wilman. "The Conservation of Books and Papers," Ontario Library Review February 1962.

3958. Tribolet, Harold W. "Art of Book Repair and Restoration," Book Production 67, March-September, 1958.

3959. _____. Rare Book and Paper Repair Techniques. Nashville, Tenn.: American Association for State and Local History, 1970. Technical Leaflet 13.

3960. Ulman, Charlotte M. "Roger Powell's Talk on the Repair of Early Missles of English and Irish Origin," Guild of Book Workers Journal 2(3), 1964. Report of Powell's description of the rebinding of the Book of Kells.

3961. Wächter, Otto. "The Restoration of Persian Lacquer Bindings," Allgemeiner Anzeiger für Büchbindereien 72(7), 1959. Stuttgart. In German.

3962. Williams, G. R. "The Preservation of Deteriorating Books: An Examination of the Problem With Recommendations for a Solution," Library Journal 91, January 1, 1966; and 91, January 15, 1966.

3963. Yabrova, R. R. "The Effectiveness of Book Reinforcement by Polymethylacrylate Emulsion," Restoration and Preservation of Library Resources Documents and Books. London: Oldbourne Press, 1964.

3964. _____. "The Effectiveness of Book Reinforcement by Polymethylacrylate Emulsion," Collection of Materials on the Preservation of Library Resources (Moscow, 1958). Springfield, Va.: National Technical Information Service, 1964.

3965. Young, Richard. "Experiences at the Biblioteca Nazionale in Florence," Guild of Book Workers Journal 6(3), 1968. Summarizes the entire book restoration process now underway in Florence.

3966. Wendelbo, O. and B. Fosse. "Protein Surgery: A
       Restoring Procedure Applied to Paper, " Restaurator
       1(4):245-248, 1970.   Describes the use of enzymes
       for restoring library and archival material.   Au-
       thors report their success in separating art (coated)
       paper stuck together into solid blocks after water
       damage.   Also describes good results with similarly
       damaged 16th century books.

MAPS

3967. "A New Mounting Cloth for Cloth Backing Maps, Re-
       cords and Charts, " Canadian Surveyor 7(8):21,
       1942.   Illus.   Ottawa.   Describes "Charte Cloth"
       which can be ironed on a map.
3968. Almela Melia, Juan.   Manual de reparacion y con-
       servacion de libros, estampas y manuscriptos.
       Mexico: 1949.   Pan American Institute of Geog-
       raphy and History.   Publication No. 95.   Pages
       65-66 relate specifically to maps, although the
       entire work is applicable to map care and preser-
       vation.
3969. Brown, A. G.   "Protective Surfacing of Maps and
       Charts, " Canadian Chemistry and Process Indus-
       tries 30:27-28, 1946.   Toronto.   Contains several
       formulas for plastic coatings developed during
       World War II.
3970. Brown, Lloyd A.   Notes on the Care and Cataloging
       of Old Maps.   Windham, Conn.: Hawthorne House,
       1940.
3971. Fowler, George Herbert.   "Maps, " British Records
       Association.   Technical Section.   Bulletin 4:4-7,
       January 1939.   London.   Describes the handling
       and mounting of maps in the British Public Record
       Office.   Reprinted in its Bulletin No. 16, pp. 23-
       26, 1946.
3972. (Globes).   "The Repair of Globes, " A lecture first
       given at the meeting of the Internationale Vereinin-
       gung Meister der Einbandkunst held at the Royal
       Library, Stockholm, September 1966.   Reprints
       available from U. K. Group, International Institute
       for Conservation, c /o National Gallery, London.
       Excellent description of the repairing of globes as
       it is done in the British Museum.
3973. Heawood, E.   "The Use of Watermarks in Dating Old

Maps and Documents," Geographical Journal 63:391-412, 1924.

3974. Hirsh, A. A. "Heavy Duty Mounting for Maps," Water and Sewage Works 111:117, 1964.

3975. Kramer, Fritz. "Map Mounting Procedure," Journal of Geography 51:21-23, 1952. Chicago. Gives step-by-step directions for mounting a multi-sheet wall map and lists the equipment needed.

3976. Lynn, Lyman D. "The Care of Special Materials in the U.S. Coast and Geodetic Survey Library," Special Libraries 31:396-400, 1940. Describes the care of charts.

3977. Mackin, J. Hoover. "A Method of Mounting Maps," Science 84:233-234, 1936. New York.

3978. "Maps; Care and Use," American Archivist 1:105; 3:9; 4:190, 283; 9:20, 161; 10:5, 59; 12:283, 425; 13:135, 1937-1949.

3979. "Maps and Globes," Museums Journal 63(2), 1963.

3980. Maughan, Edwin K. "Binding Maps for Easy Reference," American Association of Petroleum Geologists Bulletin 37(2):2051-2054, 1953. Map. Illus. Describes a method of binding large maps into a post binder for convenient reference and storage.

3981. Parsons, D. E. "An experiment with a book of maps," Repairers' News Sheet 18:8, 1971. London, Society of Archivists. Describes an easily separable mounting system for maps in albums.

3982. Schmitz, Julia M. "Mounting Maps on Plywood," Wilson Library Bulletin 15:765-767, 1940-1941. New York.

3983. Spratley, E. "Map repair using soluble nylon," Repairers' News Sheet 18:4, 1971. Society of Archivists, England. Step-by-step description for re-backing large role maps.

3984. Stanford, Edward. Methods of Map Mounting with Illustrations. London: E. Stanford, 1890.

3985. Thiele, Walter. "The Care of Maps," Official Map Publications 294-295, 1938. Chicago. Advocates filing maps in shallow horizontal drawers.

3986. Throop, Vincent M. "A Method of Mounting Maps," Science 78(2016):149-150, 1933. New York. The mounting of maps on cloth at Syracuse University.

3987. Wardle, D. B. Document Repair. London: Society of Archivists, 1971. A small volume presenting document restoration as it is done in England particularly at the Public Records Office. Includes information on map repair.

312 Repair and Restoration

NEWSPRINT

3988. Hill, Frank Pierce. "The Deterioration of Newspaper Paper," ALA Bulletin 4:675-678, 1910.
3989. Kremer, A. W. "The Preservation of Wood Pulp Publications," College and Research Libraries 15:205-209, 1954.
3990. Raux, H. F. "La Restauration des Journaux par Sericollage a la Bibliotheque Nationale," Bulletin des Bibliotheques de France 6(11), 1961. A brief illustrated description of the modification of silk screen printing equipment for use in the reinforcement of newsprint, etc. by laminating with tissue paper and paste.
3991. Scribner, B. W. Preservation of Newspaper Records. Washington: U. S. Government Printing Office, 1934. NBS Miscellaneous Publication No. 145. Deals with repair of damaged newsprint and copying techniques as well as prevention of damage.

MANUSCRIPTS

3992. Alkalaj, Stella. "The Chemical Laboratory for Hygiene, Conservation and Restoration of Damaged Written Materials in the National Library - Sofia," Restaurator 1(2), 1969. Describes the development of the laboratory since its inception in 1956. Details their procedure for mass production in document repair using the pulp process.
3993. Anthony, Donald C. "Caring for Your Collections: Manuscripts and Related Materials," History News 18(6), 1963. Technical Leaflet No. 8.
3994. Bahmer, Robert H. "Recent American Developments in Archival Repair, Preservation and Photography," Archivum 10:59-71, 1960. Abstract in American Archivist 26:256, 1963.
3995. Barrow, Bernard G. Preservation by Restoration of Documents: Part 1, Lamination and Deacidification Procedures. Salt Lake City: The Genealogical Society of the Church of Jesus Christ of Latter Day Saints, 1969. Paper presented at 1969 World Conference on Records and Genealogical Seminar.

3996. Barrow, W. J. Manuscripts and Documents, Their
Deterioration and Restoration. Ann Arbor, Michigan: University Microfilms, Inc. , 1959.

3997. _____ . Method for Preserving Documents and the
Like. Washington: Patent Office, November 17,
1942. U. S. Patent No. 2, 301, 966.

3998. _____ . Procedures and Equipment Used in the
Barrow Method of Restoring Manuscripts and Documents. Richmond, Virginia: W. J. Barrow, 1961.

3999. _____ . "Restoration Methods," (for paper) American Archivist 6:151-154, 1943.

4000. [No entry.]

4001. Belov, G. A. "New Techniques, New Materials and
New Experiences Concerning Restoration of Documents and Seals, Preservation of Maps and Plans
and Photography since 1950," Archivum 10:72-80,
1960.

4002. Bhargava, K. D. Repair and Preservation of Records. New Delhi: National Archives of India,
1959.

4003. Bolsée, J. "La Restauration des Documents aux Archives Générales du Royaume," Archives Bibliothèques et Musées de Belgique 21:3-10, 1950.

4004. Botha, C. Graham. Report of a Visit to Various
Archive Centres in Europe, United States of America and Canada. Pretoria: Government Printing
and Stationery Office, 1921. Contains information
on manuscript repair.

4005. British Records Association. Records Preservation
Section. Report for the year 1948-1949. (n. p. ,
n. d.) Includes a consideration of the preservation,
nature, and uses of records compiled in and preserved by schools and of the preservation of old
diaries, letters and photographs.

4006. Ceccaldi, F. et al. "La Restitution des Documents
Alteres," Gazette des Archives 61, 1968. Deals
not with restoration but rather with the "discovery"
of the original texts in documents that have been
deliberately falsified or accidentally damaged.

4007. Chakravorti, S. "Preservation of Archives," Modern
Librarian 13:101-104, 1943.

4008. Cockerell, Sidney M. "The Binding of Manuscripts,"
The Calligraphers Handbook. (Lamb, C. M. ed.)
London: Faber and Faber Ltd. , n. d.

4009. Csapodi, C. "Conservation of Manuscript and Old
Book Collections at the Library of the Hungarian
Academy of Sciences," Publications Academiae

Scientiarum Hungariae 44:5-21, 1965.   Budapest.
In English.

4010. Devkar, V. L. (ed.).   Museum Bulletin.   Baroda:
       Museum and Picture Gallery, 1969.   This book in-
       cludes a section on the conservation of old paper
       manuscripts.

4011. Duryé, Pierre (ed.).   Pathologie des Documents et
       Leur Protection aux Archives de France.   Paris:
       Archives de France, 1961.   A bulletin of informa-
       tion on restoration, shop outfitting, repairs with
       tissue, protection from sun, conservation, fumiga-
       tion and lamination.   Each article is written by a
       foremost French authority on the subject.

4012. Eckardt, H.   "Restoration of a Manuscript from the
       Halberstadt Cathedral," Neue Museumskunde 10(1):
       25-60, 1967.

4013. Fitzpatrick, John C.   Notes on the Care, Cataloguing,
       Calendaring and Arranging of Manuscripts.   3rd ed.
       Washington: U. S. Government Printing Office,
       1928.   The sections on repairing and mounting ap-
       ply equally to maps as to manuscripts.

4014. Flyate, D. M. (ed.).   Preservation of Documents and
       Papers.   Washington: The National Science Founda-
       tion, 1968.   Translated from the Russian.   Distri-
       buted by the National Technical Information Service,
       Springfield, Virginia.

4015. Guide International des Archives.   Paris: Institut In-
       ternational de Coopération Intellectualle, 1934.   In-
       formation on manuscript repair in France.

4016. Haslam, W.   The Library Handbook of Genuine Trade
       Secrets and Instructions for Cleaning, Repairing
       and Restoring Old Manuscripts, Engravings and
       Books.   London: W. & G. Foyle, Ltd., 1923.

4017. Jenkinson, Sir Hilary.   A Manual of Archives Admin-
       istration.   London: P. Lund Humphries & Co.,
       Ltd., 1937.   Includes manuscript repair.

4018. Khovkina, K. H.   "The Work of a Restorer on Ori-
       ental Manuscripts," Saltykov-Shchedrin 61-66, 1959.
       State Public Library, Leningrad.

4019. Kimberly, Arthur E.   "The Preservation of Records,"
       Tappi 22(1):337-341, 1939.   New York.   Describes
       successive steps in the restoration of manuscripts
       including lamination.

4020. _____ .   "The Repair and Preservation of Records
       in the National Archives," Chemist 15(3):236-244,
       1938.   Early lamination efforts.

4021. Lydenberg, Harry M. "On the Preservation of Manuscripts and Printed Books," Library Journal 53:712-716, 1928.

4022. "Manuscript Preservation in Old Northwest," American Archivist 1:142, 1938.

4023. "Manuscript Repair in European Archives," American Archivist 1(1):1-22, 1938; 1(2):51-77, 1938 and 14:363, 1951.

4024. Minogue, Adelaide E. The Repair and Preservation of Records. Washington: National Archives, Division of Information and Publications, 1943. Reprinted 1970. Also available on microfilm. National Archives Bulletin No. 5.

4025. Nelson, Clark W. Preservation by Restoration of Documents, Part II: Use of Adhesives Tapes, Silking, etc., and Home Repairs, Plastic Folders, etc. Salt Lake City: The Genealogical Society of the Church of Jesus Christ of Latter-Day Saints, 1969. Paper presented at the 1969 World Conference on Records and Genealogical Seminar.

4026. Papritz, J. New Methods, New Materials, and New Results in the Restoration and Conservation of Archives and in Documentary Photo Techniques Since 1950. Report to the International Congress of Archives, Goteborg, 1960.

4027. Plenderleith, H. J. and A. E. A. Werner. "Technical Notes on the Conservation of Documents," Journal Society of Archivists 1, 1955-1959. Advice on latest techniques by two expert authorities.

4028. "Protection of Manuscripts," American Archivist 14:233, 1949 and 19:121, 1954.

4029. "Repair, Checks on," American Archivist 20:326, 1955.

4030. "Repair Methods," American Archivist 1:1, 20, 22, 51, 53, 56, 59, 66, 70, 111; 2:21, 144, 115; 3:212; 6:151; 7:202; 8:120; 9:17, 320; 10:57; 13:404; 14:176, 280, 363; 15:272; 16:118; 17:105; 19:71; 20:319, 327, 329; 25:243, 353; 26:257, 469 (1938-63).

4031. "Restoration of an Ancient Manuscript," The Library of Congress Quarterly Journal 10:13-17, 1952.

4032. "The Restoration of Archive Documents," Figaro Littéraire February 9, 1952. ICOM News 5, August 1952. Report of the salvage of a rare document at Archives of France.

4033. "Restoration Methods," American Archivist 1:16, 147; 6:151; 16:115, 120, 335; 17:370 (1937-   ).

4034. Santucci, L. and C. Wolff. "Rigenerazion dei Documente," Bollettino dell Istituto de Patologia del

Libro 12:69, 1953; 14:45, 1955; 18:146, 1959.   An
excellent review of paper restoration techniques up
to 1959.   Summaries in English.

4035. Tribolet, Harold W.   "Protect Those Documents, "
Autograph Collectors Journal 2(2):3-8, 1950.   A
description of methods to be used in repairing,
framing, binding, and storing documents.

4036. Tribolet, Harold and Gordon Williams.   "More Hints
on the Preservation of Manuscripts, " Manuscripts
13(2), 1961.

4037. Wilson, William K.   "Record Papers and Their Preservation, " Chemistry 43(3), 1970.   Includes a summary with suggested reading of paper chemistry,
diagnostic techniques and treatment.

PRINTS AND DRAWINGS

4038. Andrews, R.   "Polyvinyl acetate, " Repairers' News
Sheet 18:3, 1971.   London: Society of Archivists.
Describes use of P. V. A. for mounting pictures on
ragboard.

4039. Banks, Paul N.   Matting and Framing Documents and
Art Objects on Paper.   Chicago: Newberry Library, 1968.   A useful leaflet for curators.

4040. Beaufort, T. R.   Pictures and How to Clean Them.
London: J. Lane, 1926.   Mostly concerned with
cleaning prints.   Lists tools required.   Also published by Frederick A. Stokes, New York, 1926.

4041. The Beauty and Longevity of an Original Print Depends
Greatly on the Paper That Supports It.   Los Angeles: Tamarind Lithography Workshop, 1969.   Contains samples of some handmade papers used for
printing with a description of fiber content and pH
of each.

4042. Becker, M.   "Documentation of Restoration Operations, " Neue Museumskunde 7(2):156-158, 1964.

4043. Bhowmik, Swarna Kamal.   "A Non-Aqueous Method
for the Restoration of Indian Miniature Paintings, "
Studies in Conservation 12(3), 1967.   A technique
for cleaning water colors.

4044. Bonnardot, Alfred.   Essai sur l'Arte de Restaurer les
Estampes et les Livres.   Paris: Deflorenne, 1858.
First mention of the use of pulp for repairing

damaged paper.

4045. _____ . Essai sur l'Arte de Restaurer les Estampes
et les Livres. New York: Burt Franklin, 1966.
Art History and Reference Series. A modern reprint of Bonnardot's 19th-century classic on book
and print restoration.

4046. Bradley, Morton C. The Treatment of Pictures.
Cambridge, Mass.: Art Technology, 1950.

4047. Branchamp, R. R. "A Simple Layout for the Washing
and Bleaching of Prints and Drawings," Bulletin,
IIC-AG 9(1), 1968. Describes a sink and equipment designed by Canadian National Historic Sites
Service.

4048. Buck, Richard D. "Conservation and Mounting of
Drawings," ICOM News 2:5-6, 1949. In French
and English.

4049. Clarke, Carl D. Pictures, Their Preservation and
Restoration. Butler, Maryland: Standards Arts
Press, 1959. Includes information on ultra-violet
examination.

4050. Eckhardt, E. "Restoration Methods for Drawings and
Prints," Maltechnik 73(1):1-8, 1967.

4051. Gunn, M. J. Print Restoration and Picture Cleaning.
London: L. Upcott Gill, 1911. An illustrated
practical guide. Includes chapter on cleaning water
colors.

4052. _____ . Painting Restoration and Picture Cleaning. London: 1922. This book deals primarily
with cleaning pictures on paper.

4053. Lambert, F. C. Mounts and Frames and How to
Make Them. London: Hazell, Watson and Viney,
1898. A source of information for those who would
restore 19th century frames.

4054. Landon, Edward. Modern Methods of Making and
Finishing Picture Frames. New York: American
Artists Group, 1945.

4055. [No entry.]

4056. Losos, Ludvik. "Questions Concerning Finishing and
Retouching in Museum Conservation," Metodicky
List 36-41, 1967. In Czech with English summary.
The author attempts to work out a theory based on
fundamental aesthetic requirements and current
theories on restoration in order to solve restoration controversies.

4057. Miers, H. A. and S. F. Markham. Conservation of
Prints, Drawings and Manuscripts. Oxford: Oxford

University Press, 1937.

4058. Moyano, L. "The Restoration of a Collection of 16th
       Century Drawings in the Cabinet des Estampes,
       Liege, " Musées di Belgique Bulletin 3:202-205,
       1960-61. Describes technique used for chalk draw-
       ings.

4059. Plenderleigh, H. J. The Conservation of Prints and
       Drawings. London: The Museums Association,
       1937. Compilations and reviews of the most mod-
       ern and approved methods as standardized and
       practiced by their author at the British Museum.
       Written with regard for the requirements of the
       non-professional restorer.

4060. "Protection of Pictures, " American Archivist 17:25,
       1954.

4061. Questions to Ask Your Framer and Answers You
       Should Get. Los Angeles: Tamarind Lithography
       Workshop, 1969.

4062. Rabin, Bernard. "The Conservation of Two Rouault
       Oil Paintings on Paper, " Technical Papers From
       1968 Through 1970. New York: IIC American
       Group, 1970.

4063. "Repairing Engravings, " American Archivist 1:22, 63,
       1938.

4064. Ruhman, Helmut. The Cleaning of Paintings. Lon-
       don: Faber and Faber, 1968. This text on the
       preservation of oil paintings includes much useful
       information on pictures on paper.

4065. Schraubstadter, Carl. Care and Repair of Japanese
       Prints. Cornwall, N.Y.: Idlewild Press, 1948.
       A compendium of safe methods for cleaning, re-
       pairing and remounting of Japanese prints as done
       by Japanese craftsmen.

4066. Sheridan, Jane. "Enzymes, " Exposition of Painting
       Conservation. Brooklyn: Brooklyn Museum, 1962.
       Instructions for removing grease, adhesives, var-
       nish, etc. Brief but important.

4067. Stout, George L. The Care of Pictures. New York:
       Columbia University Press, 1948. Much useful
       information on pictures on paper as well as other
       supports.

4068. Third Report of the Department of Scientific and In-
       dustrial Research on the Cleaning and Restoration
       of Museum Exhibits. London: H.M.S.O., 1926.
       Extremely valuable advice on the cleaning of prints
       and water colors.

4069. Valley Amédée. La Restauration des Tableaux. Paris:
       1930. Only contribution worthwhile in this 40 page
       booklet is a useful paragraph on restoration of
       pastels.

4070. Wächter, Otto. "Das Reihigen und Bleichen von
       Drucken, Graphiken und Agoarellen," Allgemeiner
       Anzieger für Büchbinderein 76(3), 1963. Stuttgart.
       In German.

4071. _____. "The Restoration of a Colour Lithograph,"
       Allgemeiner Anzieger für Büchbindereien 69(10),
       1956. Stuttgart. In German.

4072. Wan-Dan-Chua. "The Conservation of Prints," Blok-
       Notes. Warsaw: Muzeum Mickiewicza, 1955.

4073. Zigrosser, Carl and Christa M. Gaehde. A Guide to
       the Collecting and Care of Original Prints. New
       York: Crown Publishers, 1965. The section on
       the care of prints will be useful and informative
       for anyone concerned with sheet materials: prints,
       drawings, manuscripts, broadsides, maps, etc.

SEALS

4074. Fleetwood, Gustaf. "Sur la Conservation des Seaux
       de Cire du Moyen age Deposes aux Archives du
       Royaume de Suede," Meddelanden fran Svenska
       Riksarkivit 1:59, 1945.

4075. _____. "The Conservation of Medieval Seals in
       the Swedish Riksarkiv," American Archivist 12:166-
       174, 1949. Translated and condensed from Med-
       delanden fran Svenska Riksarkivit 1946.

4076. Galbreich, E. I. "Restoration of a 15th-Century
       Lead Seal," Saltykov-Shchedrin 91-93, 1963. State
       Public Library, Leningrad.

4077. Jenkinson, Sir Hilary. "Some Notes on the Preser-
       vation, Moulding and Casting of Seals," Antiquaries
       Journal 4:338ff, 1926.

4078. Reid of Robertland, David and Anne Ross. The Con-
       servation of Non-Metallic Seals. Glasgow: Uni-
       versity Archives, 1968.

4079. _____. "The Conservation of Non-Metallic Seals,"
       Studies in Conservation 15(1):51-62, 1970. Dis-
       cusses the usual forms of damage and the various
       methods of treatment as practiced at the University

of Glasgow.

4080.   "Repair of Seals," American Archivist 1:9, 55, 1938;
        12:166, 169, 266, 1949.

4081.   Sitwell, H. D. W.   "Matrix of an ancient seal found
        in the Chapel of St. Peter ad Vincula, H. M.
        Tower of London," Archives 5:88-89, 1961.   Ab-
        stract in American Archivist 26:397, 1963.

UNUSUAL MATERIALS

4082.   Kishore, R.   "A Clay Coated Manuscript in the Gilgit
        Collection," Conservation of Cultural Property in
        India 1:74-79, 1960.   Describes treatment of a 4th
        century Chinese document.

4083.   Konrad, Anton J.   "Restoration of a Painted Banner,"
        Technical Papers 1968 Through 1970.   New York:
        IIC (American Group), 1970.

4084.   Plenderleith, H. J.   "Technical Note on Unwrapping
        of Dead Sea Scrolls," in Barthelemy, D. and
        Milik, J. T. Discoveries in the Judean Desert.
        London: Clarendon Press, 1955.

4085.   Scott, Kathryn.   "Conservation of a Third Century
        Fayum Portrait on Linen," Technical Papers 1968
        Through 1970.   New York: IIC (American Group),
        1970.

BARK

4086.   Bosov, N. N. and E. N. Trey.   "Restoration of a
        Manuscript on Birch Bark," Saltykov-Shchedrin 57-
        60, 1965.   Leningrad State Public Library.

4087.   Boustead, W. M.   "The Conservation of Aborigine
        Bark Paintings and Artifacts," Kalori 35, 1968.
        Museums Asso. of Australia.

4088.   Filliozat, Jean.   "Manuscripts on Birch Bark and
        Their Preservation," Indian Archives 1:102-108,
        1947.

4089.   Kumar, Virendra.   "Preservation of Bark and Palm-
        leaf Manuscripts," Herald of Library Science 2:236-
        241, 1963.

4090.   Majumdar, P. C.   "Repair and Conservation of Birch-
        Bark Manuscripts," Conservation of Cultural

Property in India 1:80-88, 1966.

BONE AND IVORY

4091. Baer, N. S. and L. J. Majewski. "Ivory and Related
       Materials in Art and Archaeology: An Annotated
       Bibliography," Art and Archaeology Technical Ab-
       stracts 8(2), 1970-1971. One hundred and ninety
       titles on the care and preservation of ivory, bone
       and horn.
4092. Crawford, V. E. "Ivories from the Earth," Bulletin,
       Metropolitan Museum of Art 21, 1962. Preserva-
       tion techniques.
4093. Gairola, T. R. "Preservation of a Bone Object,"
       Ancient India 10-11, 1954-1955.
4094. Lal, B. B. "Chemical Preservation of Ancient Ob-
       jects," Ancient India 18-19, 1962-1963. Includes
       the problems of treating ivory, horn and bone.
4095. Plenderleith, H. J. "Bone and Ivory," Conservation
       of Antiquities and Works of Art. London: 1962.
       Describes methods for cleaning and preservation.
4096. Todd, Wm. "A Vacuum Process for the Preservation
       of Bone and Similar Material," Technical Studies
       in the Field of Fine Arts 9(4), 1940.

CLAY TABLETS

4097. Chiera, Edward. They Wrote on Clay. Chicago:
       University of Chicago Press, 1938. Edited by
       G. C. Cameron. Background information only.
4098. Organ, R. M. "The Conservation of Cuneiform Tab-
       lets," British Museum Quarterly 23(2):52-57, 1961.
4099. Packard, Eliz. "The Cleaning of a Babylonian Tab-
       let," Technical Studies in the Field of the Fine
       Arts 8(2), 1939.
4100. Parkinson, D. E. "The Preservation of Cuneiform
       Tablets," Museum News 27, 1950. Reviews general
       practices for preheating, firing, washing and coat-
       ing clay tablets.

METAL

4101. Allegro, John M. "The Copper Scroll from Qumran,"
       Restaurator 1(1):13-19, 1969. Copenhagen. Brief

description of the mechanics of unrolling an ancient metal document.

4102. Baker, Wright. "Notes on the Opening of the Bronze Scrolls from Qumran," Bulletin, John Rylands Library 39:45-56, 1956-1957.

4103. Berce, R. "Metal Preservation in Museums," Archeologia Austriaca 18, 1955.

4104. Colton, J. B. "Control of Surface Reactions on Copper by Means of Organic Reagents," Proceedings, National Asso. of Corrosion Engineers 590-596, 1963. Houston, Texas.

4105. Cupr, Vaclav and J. B. Pelikán. "The Principles of Conservation of Metal Objects in Museums," Muzejni Prace 10:1-180, 1963. In Czech.

4106. Giraud, V. C. M. "Removal of Rust and Calamine from Ferrous Metals," Chemical Abstracts No. 20, 19735b, 1961. Washington.

4107. Kaikaris, V. and S. Pilauskiene. Electrochemical Polishing of Silver, USSR Patent 191, 982, January 26, 1967.

4108. Kanwiszer, Andrezej. "Selected Problems in the Conservation of Metals," Prace i Materialy Muzeum Archeologieznegn i Elnograficznego 13:107-130, 1960. Poland. English summary.

4109. Menzhausen, J. "Report on the Conference of Metal Restorers in Dresden," Neue Museumskunde 10(2): 185-187, 1967.

4110. Pelikán, J. B. "Conservation of Iron with Tannin," Studiés in Conservation 2(3), 1966. Reports on a means for preserving rusted iron by painting with chemicals that convert oxides to insoluble protective films.

4111. Peterson, H. Conservation of Metals. Nashville: American Association for State and Local History, 1968. Technical Leaflet No. 10.

4112. Ritornello, V. "Composition for the Removal of Oxide Coatings from Precious Metals and Alloys," Chemical Abstracts 63(13), 17639C, 1963. Washington.

4113. Termansen, N. J. "Note on Polished Gilding," Meddelelser om Konservering 5:33-40, 1967.

PALM LEAVES

4114. Bhowmik, S. "Conservation of Palm-leaf Manuscripts," Baroda Museum and Picture Gallery

Bulletin 19:59-65, 1966.

4115. Crowley, Alfred S. "Repair and Conservation of Palm-leaf Manuscripts," Restaurator 1(2), 1969. Describes the techniques used in the British Museum.

4116. Kishor, Ranbir. "Preservation and Repair of Palm Leaf Manuscripts," Indian Archives 14:73-78, January 1961-December 1962.

4117. Kumar, Virendra. "Preservation of Bark and Palm-leaf Manuscripts," Herald of Library Science 2:236-241, 1963.

4118. Nordstrand, Ove K. "Some Notes on Procedures Used in The Royal Library, Copenhagen, for the Preservation of Palm-leaf Manuscripts," Studies in Conservation 3(3):135-140, 1958.

4119. Schuyler, Montgomery Jr. "Notes on the Making of Palm-leaf Manuscripts in Siam," Journal of the American Oriental Society 29:281-283, 1908.

PAPYRUS

4120. Plenderleith, H. J. and A. E. A. Werner. The Conservation of Antiquities and Works of Art. London: Oxford University Press, 1971. Chapter 3 in this book describes methods for salvaging and cleaning papyrus scrolls.

4121. "Repair of Papyrus," American Archivist 1:14, 62, 1938.

STONE

4122. "Stone Preservative," Building Research Station Digest 128, November 1959. Watford, Herts, England.

4123. Sujanova, O. "Contribution to the Problem of Removal of Black Deposits from Sandstone," Zprávy Pamatkové Pece 74-81, 1963. Prague.

WOOD

4124. Brommelle, N. S. and A. E. A. Werner. Deterioration and Treatment of Wood. New York: ICOM Sub-Committee for the Care of Paintings, 1965.

4125. Bryan, J.   "Methods of Applying Wood Preservatives,"
       Forest Products Research Records 9, 1946.   Great
       Britain, Department of Scientific and Industrial Re-
       search.

4126. Hunt, G. M. and G. A. Garrett.   Wood Preservation.
       New York: McGraw-Hill, 1953.

4127. Jacquiot, C. and Keller-Vaillon.   La Préservation
       des Bois.   Paris: Hermann, 1951.

4128. Kurpik, Wojciech.   "Consolidation of Damaged Wood
       with Synthetic Resins.   Sealing the Missing Parts
       with Sawdust and Resin," Materialy Muzeum
       Budownictwa Ludowego w Sanoku 27-30, 1966.
       Poland.

4129. Nair, G. S.   "Preservation of a Wooden Object From
       the Government of Nepal," Journal Indian Museums
       17-20, 1961-1964.

4130. Van Grenou, B. et al.   Wood Preservation During the
       Last 50 Years.   Leiden: A. W. Sijthoff, 1951.

4131. Wivel, Niels.   "An Apparatus for Rejoining Broken
       or Disjoined Panels," Meddelelser om Konserver-
       ing 2:13-18, 1965.

4132. "Wood Deterioration and Treatment," Technical Studies
       in the Field of Fine Arts 5:64-66, 1936-37.

TEXTILES

4133. Columbus, J. V.   "Washing Techniques Used at the
       Textile Museum," Bulletin of the American Group,
       International Institute for Conservation 7(2), 1967.

4134. Dantyagi, S.   Fundamentals of Textiles and Their
       Care.   Calcutta: Orient Longmans Ltd., 1964.

4135. Delft Conference on the Conservation of Textiles.   2nd
       ed.   London: International Institute for Conserva-
       tion, 1964.

4136. Dudina, V. A.   "Restoration of Archaeological Tex-
       tiles," SOOB. VCNILKR 19:37-54, 1967.

4137. Griffen, Jane C.   Care of Textiles and Costumes:
       Cleaning and Storage Techniques.   Nashville: Amer-
       ican Association for State and Local History, 1970.
       Technical Leaflet No. 2.

4138. Klapthor, Margaret Brown.   Steps in Laundering
       Fragile Cotton and Linen Fabrics.   Washington:
       National Trust For Historic Preservation, n.d.

Expert advice from the Smithsonian Institution's expert on fabrics.

4139. Leene, Dr. J. E. (ed.). Textile Conservation. London: Butterworths & Co., 1971. Nine conservators elucidate on the preservation of all textile materials including tapestries, banners and flags, linen, carpets, lace, gloves, ethuographical collections, etc.

4140. Martin A. R. et al. "Dry Cleaning," Encyclopedia of Chemical Technology, vol. 9. New York: John Wiley and Sons, 1965.

4141. _____. "Dry Cleaning Museum Textiles," Bulletin of the American Group, International Institute for Conservation 7(2), 1967.

4142. _____ and G. P. Fulton. Drycleaning. Technology and Theory. New York: Textile Book Publishers, Inc., 1958.

4143. McHugh, Maureen C. "Conservation Challenge: A 17th Century Linen Handkerchief," Museum News 46(6):47-51, 1968. Technical Supplement.

4144. McLendon, V. I. Removing Stains From Fabrics. Washington: U.S. Government Printing Office, 1959. Department of Agriculture Home and Garden Bulletin No. 62.

4145. The Mothproofing of Wool. London: Scientific and Technical Department of the International Wool Secretariat, 1952.

4146. National Bureau of Standards. Fibers and Fabrics. Washington: U.S. Government Printing Office, 1970. Consumer Information Series C 13.53:2. Hints on caring for home textile products.

4147. Phair, R. A. Protecting Fabric. Washington: U.S. Patent Office, April 9, 1929. U.S. Patent No. 1,708,519.

4148. Randlett, J. C. and W. J. Nicklaw. Spotting. Silver Spring, Maryland: National Institute of Dry Cleaning, 1956. Primarily for the dry cleaning of clothing, but contains good information on removal of many stains occurring in paper.

4149. Removing Stains from Fabrics: Home Methods. Washington: U.S. Department of Agriculture, n.d.

4150. Solovjova, I. I. "Filling in Losses in Moth Damaged Textiles," SOOB. VCNILKR 19:55-61, 1967.

4151. Volgina, T. N. "Cleaning of Museum Textiles," SOOB. VCNILKR 19:5-35, 1967.

FILMS, TAPES, AND DISCS

4152. Calhoun, John M. "The Preservation of Motion-Pic-
        ture Film," American Archivist 30:517-525, 1967.
4153. Chalters, R. M. and C. Jacobs. "Recovery of Faded
        Photographs by Nuclear Techniques," Photo. App.
        Sci. Tech. Med. 4(15), 1970.
4154. Denstman, Hal. "The Invisible Becomes Visible,"
        Industrial Photography 17(4):24-78, 1968. Recovery
        of faded photographs.
4155. Film Preservation. International Federation of Film
        Archivists, 1965.
4156. Gallo, F. "About the Conservation of Microfilm,"
        Bollettino dell Istituto di Patologia del Libro 24(1-
        4):107-110, 1965.
4157. Handling Repair and Storage of 16mm Films. Roches-
        ter: Eastman Kodak Co., 1965. Kodak Pamphlet
        D-23.
4158. Hersh, Seymour. "Washing Photographic Materials,"
        Industrial Photography 19(2), 1970. Discusses
        washing procedures to insure against deterioration
        by chemicals.
4159. Hutchinson, G. L.; L. Ellis and S. A. Ashmore.
        "The Surveillance of Cinematograph Record Film
        During Storage," Journal Applied Chemistry 8:24ff,
        1958.
4160. Keiler, J. A. and G. Pollakowski. "Restoration of
        Silver Images on Black and White Films," East
        German Patent 36,078, May 25, 1965.
4161. Magnetic Recording Tape. Springfield, Va.: National
        Technical Information Service, 1967. Includes re-
        pair data.
4162. "Motion Picture Restoration Printer," American Ar-
        chivist 30:614, 1967; and 31:83, 1968. Description
        of a printer at Ohio State University that will re-
        store historic movies.
4163. "Neutron Activation of Faded Photographs and Docu-
        ments," American Archivist 32:285, 1969. Re-
        ports on studies at Washington State University re
        use of radioactivity to make a new "negative."
4164. Ostroff, E. "Restoration of Photographs by Neutron
        Activation," Science 154(3745):119-123, 1966.
        Washington.
4165. Prevention and Removal of Fungus on Processed
        Films. Rochester: Eastman Kodak Co., 1961.
        Kodak Pamphlet E-22.

4166. Ravensway, Charles van. "An Improved Method for the Restoration of Daguerrotypes," Image 5, 1956. Rochester: Eastman Kodak Co.

4167. Stains on Negatives and Prints. Rochester: Eastman Kodak Co., 1950. Kodak Data Book No. J-18.

4168. Storage and Preservation of Motion-Picture Film. Rochester: Eastman Kodak Co., 1957. Kodak Data Book No. H-8.

4169. Talwar, V. and R. Kishore. "Removal of Stains From Photoprints," Conservation of Cultural Property in India 2:90-91, 1967.

4170. Wagner, Robert. "Motion Picture Restoration," American Archivist 32(2):125-132, 1969. A review of the problem by the Chairman of the Department of Photography at Ohio State University.

4171. West, D. G. and R. W. Henn. "Microscopic Spots in Processed Microfilm - Their Nature and Prevention," Photographic Science and Engineering 7(5):253-261, 1963.

IN THE TROPICS

4172. Blackie, W. J. "Preservation of Books in the Tropics," Agricultural Journal of Fiji 3(2):84-85, 1930.

4173. Boustead, W. M. "The Conservation of Works of Art in Tropical and Sub-Tropical Zones," Recent Advances in Conservation (ed. G. Thomson). London: Butterworths, 1963.

4174. _____. "The Surface pH Measurement and Deacidification of Prints and Drawings in Tropical Climates," Studies in Conservation 9(2), 1964.

4175. Browne, F. "The Preservation of Books in Hot Climates," Scientific American 56, 1903. Supplement.

4176. _____. "Preservation of Books in Hot Climates," Scientific American 65, 1908. Supplement.

4177. Chan Kai Meng. "A De-humidifer for the Personal Library," Malayan Library Journal 1(2):13, 1961.

4178. Cundall, F. "The Preservation of Books in the Tropics," Handbook of Jamaica. Kingston: Government Printing Office, 1926.

4179. Gwam, Lloyd C. The Preservation of Archives in Tropical Countries. Ibadan, Nigeria: National Archives Headquarters, 1964.

4180. Harris, J. "Notes on Book Preservation in West Africa," WALA News 2(4):102-105, 1956.
4181. Instructions for the Preservation of Books. Achimota: University College of Ghana Library, 1956.
4182. Kathpalia, Y. P. "Restoration of Documents," in Yves Pérotin A Manual of Tropical Archivology. Paris: Mouton & Co., 1966. Emphasis on preventive and corrective measures found most suitable for humid countries.
4183. Kennedy, Robert A. Conservation in the Wet Tropics. Technical Bulletin of the Museums Association of Middle Africa, Bulletin No. 1, 1959.
4184. _____. "Conservation in the Humid Tropical Zone," Museum News 38, 1960.
4185. Lefroy, H. M. "Preserving Books in the Tropics," Agricultural News 8:367, 1909. Barbados.
4186. Pérotin, Yves (ed.). A Manual of Tropical Archivology. Paris: Mouton & Co., 1966. Includes some guidance on preservation particularly insect control and enscapulation.
4187. Plumbe, W. J. The Preservation of Books in Tropical and Sub-Tropical Countries. Kuala Lumpur: Oxford University Press, 1964. One of the best sources of information. Lengthy bibliography.
4188. Savage, E. A. "The Preservation of Books in the Tropics," Appendix I in his: The Libraries of Bermuda, the Bahamas, the British West Indies, British Guiana, British Honduras, Puerto Rico, and the American Virgin Islands. London: Library Association, 1934.
4189. Shipley, Sir A. E. "Bookbinding in the Tropics," Tropical Agriculture 3:141, 1926.
4190. UNESCO. The Conservation of Cultural Property With Special Reference to Tropical Conditions. Paris: UNESCO, 1968. This entire manual covering all aspects of museum, library and archives preservation is intended primarily for tropical institutions.
4191. Williams-Hunt, P. D. R. Preserving Books and Prints in the Tropics. Kuala Lumpur: Museums Department, Federation of Malaya, 1953.

LIBRARY WORKSHOPS

4192.   Brommelle, N. S.   "Laboratories and Workshops -
        Conservation Studios," Museums Journal 63(1-2):74-
        79, 1963.
4193.   Hodges, H. W. M.   "Equiping the Laboratory: Basic
        Equipment and Processes," The Conservation of
        Cultural Property.   Paris: UNESCO, 1968.
4194.   Loubier, Jean.   Der Bücheinband in Altes und Neuer
        Zeit.   Berlin, 1903.   A copiously illustrated re-
        view of old and new binding practices.   Section on
        workshops, tools and techniques.
4195.   Millen, Ronald.   "The Kangaroo in the Library,"
        Art and Australia 6(1), 1968.   Describes the de-
        sign and equipping of the print restoration laboratory
        at Florence with Australian help.
4196.   Organ, R. M.   Design for Scientific Conservation of
        Antiquities.   Washington: Smithsonian Institution,
        1968.   Includes advice on workshop and laboratory
        equipment.
4197.   "Repair Center," American Archivist 9:182, 1946.
4198.   Vaccaro, E.   "Restoration Laboratory of the Alfonso
        Gallo Institute of Book Pathology, Rome," UNESCO
        Bulletin for Libraries 20(2):78-82, 1966.
4199.   Vyskocil, Josef.   "The Central Conservation Workshop
        of the State Library of the Czechoslovak Socialist
        Republic," UNESCO Bulletin for Libraries 20:126-
        128, 1966.   Restoration of historical documents and
        other material.
4200.   Werner, A. E. A.   "The British Museum Research
        Laboratory," Museums Journal 62(3):153-159, 1962.

GENERAL

4201. Air Raid Precautions in Museums, Picture Galleries
        and Libraries. London: British Museum, n. d.
4202. The Care of Records in a National Emergency. Wash-
        ington: U. S. Government Printing Office, n. d.
        U. S. National Archives Bulletin No. 3.
4203. Fitzsimmons, N. "Emergency Measures and Muse-
        ums," Museum News 43(6), 1965. Suggested war-
        time measures.
4204. Holmes, Oliver W. "The National Archives and the
        Protection of Records in War Areas," American
        Archivist 9(2):110-127, 1946.
4205. Manual of Hazardous Chemical Reactions, 1968. Bos-
        ton: National Fire Protection Association, 1968.
4206. Noblecourt, Andre. Protection of Cultural Property
        in the Event of Armed Conflict. Museums and
        Monuments - VIII. Paris: UNESCO, 1958. This,
        the eighth of Museums and Monuments Series in
        346 pages with 124 figures and 137 illustrations,
        considers about every aspect of wartime protection
        of buildings and their contents.
4207. Paine, P. M. "What to Save First," Library Journal
        48:509-510, 1923.
4208. Plenderleith, Harold J. "Preservation of Museum
        Objects in War-Time," Nature 152:94-97, 1943.
        London.
4209. Preservation of the Declaration of Independence and
        the Constitution of the United States: A Report by
        the National Bureau of Standards to the Library of
        Congress. Washington: National Bureau of Stand-
        ards, July 2, 1951. NBS Circular No. 505.
4210. [No entry.]
4211. Protecting the Library and its Resources: A Guide
        to Physical Protection and Insurance. Chicago:
        American Library Association, 1963. Library
        Technology Program Publication No. 7.

4212. Rodda, William H. Fire and Property Insurance.
       Englewood Cliffs, N.J.: Prentice Hall, 1956.
4213. Thomas, C. M. "The Protection of War Records at
       the Air Technical Service," American Archivist
       9(2):214-217, 1946.
4214. U. S. Defense Department. Damage from Atomic Ex-
       plosion and Design of Protective Structures. Pre-
       pared for the National Security Resources Board
       by the Department of Defense and the United States
       Atomic Energy Commission. Washington: U. S.
       Government Printing Office, 1950. 32 pp. Pre-
       pared for use by civilian defense planning agencies.

FIRE

4215. A. S. S. I. Engineered High Speed Fire Protection Sys-
       tems. Cambridge, Massachusetts: Advanced Safety
       Systems, Inc. , 1970. Describes design potentials
       of Halon 1301 (Freon) fire suppression systems.
4216. Bahme, C. W. What Firemen Should Know About
       Halon 1301 Systems. Boston: National Fire Pro-
       tection Association, 1969. NFPA F 35-6.
4217. Beers, R. J. "New Fire Control Techniques for Re-
       cords Storage," Records Management Journal 4(3):
       29-32, 1966.
4218. Bond, Horatio. A "First Book" on Fire Safety in the
       Atomic Age. Boston: National Fire Protection As-
       sociation, 1952.
4219. Cummings, James W. ; Alvin C. Hutton, and Howard
       Silfin. "Spontaneous Ignition of Decomposing Cellu-
       lose Nitrate Film," Society of Motion Picture and
       Television Engineers Journal 54:268-274, 1950.
4220. DuPont "Freon" FE 1301 Fire Extinguishing Agent.
       Wilmington: E. I. DuPont Co. , 1969. Description
       of the chemical and physical properties of this im-
       portant halogenated fire extinguishing agent.
4221. "Fire," Museum News 44(9), 1966.
4222. Fire Tests of Library Bookstacks. (film) New York:
       New York Public Library, 1960.
4223. Halogenated Extinguishing Systems. Boston: National
       Fire Protection Association, 1970. This NFPA
       Pamphlet No. 12A establishes standards for total
       flooding Freon based extinguishing systems.

4224. Hamilton, R. M.   "The Library of Parliament Fire,"
       Bulletin of Canadian Library Association 9:73-77,
       1952.   Includes striking photographs showing salvage
       of library materials in this Ottawa disaster.

4225. _____.   "The Library of Parliament Fire," Ameri-
       can Archivist 16:141-144, 1953.   Describes actual
       recovery of books, papers, etc. in this Ottawa
       conflagration.

4226. Hemphill, B. F.   "Lessons of a Fire," Library Jour-
       nal 87, 1962.   Baltimore County, Md. Branch Li-
       brary.

4227. Maddox, Jane.   "The Norwood Book Burning," Wilson
       Library Bulletin 34:412-414, 1960.

4228. "Maximum Fire Protection for High Value Equipment,"
       Modern Plant Operation and Maintenance, 1970.
       Describes installation of Halon 1301 (Freon 1301)
       total flooding systems.

4229. Neilson, George.   "New Fire Protection for High
       Value Areas," DuPont Magazine January-February
       1971.   Describes use of Halon 1301 (Freon 1301)
       in automatic total flooding fire extinguishing sys-
       tems.

4230. Neilson, Harold E.   "Fire Protection for archives
       and records centers," Records Management Quarter-
       ly 2(1):19-23, 1968.

4231. Probst, T.   "Fire Detection-Fire Protection," Muse-
       um News 44(9), 1966.

4232. "Protection From Fire," American Archivist 1:179,
       1938; 11:165, 1948; 14:157, 1951; 16:145-153, 1953.

4233. Protection of Records: Consolidated Reports of the
       Committee on the Protection of Records.   Boston:
       National Fire Protection Association, 1939.

4234. Schaefer, G. L.   "Fire," Library Journal 85:504-505,
       1960.

4235. Schell, H. B.   "Cornell Starts a Fire," Library Jour-
       nal 85:3398, 1961.

4236. Still, John S.   "Library Fires and Salvage Methods,"
       American Archivist 16:145-153, 1953.   Discusses
       means for minimizing causes for fire as well as
       actual salvage of library materials at Ohio State
       Museum fire.

4237. Toxicology of DuPont FE 1301 Fire Extinguishing
       Agent.   Wilmington: E. I. DuPont Co., 1971.
       Laboratory report on bromotrifluoromethane.

4238. U.S. Federal Fire Council.   Committee on Protection
       of Records: Annual Report 1949.   Washington:
       U.S. Federal Fire Council, 1950.   Includes data

relating to the stages of deterioration of nitrate
film.
4239. Windeler, Peter. "Fire: endangers the past - for
the future," Museum Journal 70(2):72-74, 1970.
A review of fire detection equipment and film storage facilities.

PRECAUTIONS AGAINST FIRE

4240. Beers, R. J. "High Expansion Foam Fire Control
for Record Storage," American Archivist 29:563,
1966.
4241. Consumers Union of U.S. "Dry Chemical Fire Extinguishers," Consumers Reports pp. 340-343,
July 1962.
4242. Cunningham, J. K. H. "The Protection of Records
and Documents Against Fire," Journal of the Society of Archivists 3(8):411-417, 1968. An outline
of fire causes, preventive measures, warning devices, fire extinguishing methods and staff training.
4243. Federal Fire Council. Recommended Practices No.
1: Fire Protection for Essential Electronic Equipment. Washington: Federal Fire Council, n.d.
4244. Fire Control Film List. Boston: National Fire Protection Association, 1963. 300 titles of motion
pictures.
4245. Fire Prevention and Extinction: A Reference List.
Boston: Boston Public Library, 1946.
4246. Fireproofing of Wood, 1937-1941. London: Science
Library, 1941.
4247. Fire Protection Handbook. 13th ed. Boston: National Fire Protection Association, 1969. This is
the ultimate word on fire and its control.
4248. Flammable and Combustible Liquids Code 1969. Boston: National Fire Protection Association, 1969.
Primarily for industrial use but principles apply to
small workshops and laboratories.
4249. Guide to Federal Safety Films and Film Strips. Washington: Federal Safety Council, 1963. Lists films
on fire prevention and suppression.
4250. Jenkins, Joseph F. (ed.). Protecting our Heritage:
A Discourse on Fire Protection and Prevention in
Historic Buildings and Landmarks. Boston:

National Fire Protection Association, 1970. Intended to give administrators of historic sites assistance in evaluating the problems they face in
providing fire protection.   It is of equal importance
to librarians, archivists, etc. whose collections are
housed in older buildings.

4251.   Knight, K. C.   "Fire Disrupts the State Library,"
Michigan Librarian 17:7, 1951.

4252.   Layman, Lloyd.   Attacking and Extinguishing Fires.
Boston: National Fire Protection Association, 1952.

4253.   Maintenance and Use of Portable Fire Extinguishers
1969.   Boston: National Fire Protection Association, 1969.   This is the best information available
on this subject.   NFPA No. 10A.

4254.   Manual of Fire Protection for Archives and Record
Centers.   Boston: National Fire Protection Association, 1970.   Covers protection of records in
bulk storage facilities.

4255.   Pomerantz, Louis.   Experiments with Fire Extinguishers.   Unpublished report, The Art Institute
of Chicago, 1958.

4256.   _____.   "Notes on Portable Fire Extinguishers,"
Exposition of Painting Conservation.   Brooklyn:
Brooklyn Museum, 1962.

4257.   Protecting Our Heritage: A Discourse on Fire Protection and Prevention in Historic Buildings.   Nashville: American Association for State and Local
History, 1969.   Prepared by NFPA Committee on
Libraries, Museums and Historic Buildings.

4258.   Protecting Our Heritage: Historic Buildings, Museums
and Libraries.   Boston: National Fire Protection
Association, 1948.

4259.   Protection of Records.   Boston: National Fire Protection Association, 1967.   Minimum fire protection requirements for vaults and records rooms,
treatment of water soaked and charred records,
and the role of records management in achieving
protection against fires.   NFPA No. 232.

4260.   Protection of Library Collections.   Boston: National
Fire Protection Association, 1970.   NFPA No.
910.   Recommended practices for construction,
equipment and facilities, improving existing buildings, operation, maintenance, organization and
training.

4261.   Protection of Museum Collections 1969.   Boston: National Fire Protection Association, 1969.   Covers
construction, facilities, fire equipment, improving

existing buildings and management and organization for fire protection. NFPA No. 911.

4262. [No entry.]

4263. Publications on Fire Prevention and Protection. Boston: National Fire Protection Association, n. d. NFPA No. PL-4 updated frequently.

4264. [No entry.]

4265. Rasbash, D. J. and A. Langford. "The Use of Nets as Barriers for Retaining High Expansion Foam," Fire Technology November 1966.

4266. Recommended Practice for the Protection of Library Collections from Fire. Boston: National Fire Protection Association, 1970. Concerns construction, equipment, operation and maintenance, building alterations, fire protection equipment, organization and training. NFPA No. 910.

4267. [No entry.]

4268. Tentative Manual for Fire Protection for Archives and Record Centers. Boston: National Fire Protection Association, 1970. NFPA No. 232A=M-T. An unofficial compilation, pending formal adoption, of recommendations of useful information needed to intelligently plan for the safeguarding of large collections of records in archives and records centers. It supplements NFPA No. 232. Standard for the Protection of Records.

FLOOD

4269. Barker, Nicolas. "The Biblioteca Nazionale at Florence," The Book Collector Spring 1969. Description of the book restoration effort after the 1966 flood.

4270. First Aid to Flooded Farms and Homes. Washington: U. S. Government Printing Office. U. S. Department of Agriculture Handbook No. 38. Practical hints for salvage of furniture, turning on heat, etc.

4271. "Flood Damage," Connecticut Historical Society Bulletin 20, August 1955.

4272. Fyan, L. D. "The Michigan State Library Fire-- An Account of Water Damage and Salvage Operations," ALA Bulletin 45:164-166, 1951.

4273. Horton, Carolyn. "Saving the Libraries of Florence," Wilson Library Bulletin June 1967.

4274.   Mills, John F.   "Problems and Solutions:10," <u>Con-</u>
        <u>noisseur</u> September 1968.   Comments on book re-
        pair after the Florence floods.
4275.   Nixon, Howard H.   "British Aid for Florence," <u>The</u>
        <u>Book Collector</u> 16(1):29-35, 1967.   An evaluation of
        the entire book restoration program and England's
        contribution to it.
4276.   Rubinstein, Nicolai.   "Book Restoration in Florence,"
        <u>Times Literary Supplement</u> April 17, 1969.
4277.   _____.   "Return to Florence January 1967," <u>The</u>
        <u>Book Collector</u> 16(1):26-28, 1967.   A report on the
        book restoration program.
4278.   Tribolet, Harold.   <u>Restoration in Florence</u>.   Chicago:
        The R. R. Donnelley Co., 1967.   A reprint of
        Tribolet's <u>National Geographic</u> 132(1):1-42, 1967
        article on the aftermath of the flood.
4279.   _____.   "Restoration in Florence," <u>Manuscripts</u>
        <u>20(4),</u> 1968.
4280.   Witt, Mario.   "The Flood of 4 November 1966," <u>The</u>
        <u>Book Collector</u> 16(1):13-25, 1967.   An account of
        the flood at Florence from the point of view of a
        bibliophile.

WINDSTORM

4281.   Organ, R. M. and E. McMillan.   "Aid to a Hurri-
        cane-Damaged Museum," <u>American Group, IIC</u>
        <u>Bulletin</u> 10(1):31-39, 1969.

RECOVERY OPERATIONS

4282.   Ambler, George H.   <u>Water Damaged Files, Papers,</u>
        <u>and Records; What</u> to do <u>About Them</u>.   Royal Oak,
        <u>Mich.:   Document Reclamation Service, Inc.</u>, 1963.
4283.   Arad, A.   "Mass Restoration of Water-damaged Docu-
        ments," <u>Restaurator</u> 1(3), 1970.   Report of a con-
        ference in Bückeburg in February 1970.
4284.   Bendikson, L.   "Charred Documents," <u>The Library</u>
        <u>Journal</u> March 1933.

4285. Davis, R. "Action of Charred Paper on the Photo-
         graphic Plate," Scientific Papers of the National
         Bureau of Standards 18, October 1922.
4286. Doud, D. "Charred Documents, Their Handling and
         Decipherment," Journal of Criminal Law, Criminol-
         ogy and Police Science 43(6), 1953.
4287. First Aid for Flood Damaged Books. London: British
         Museum, 1968. A three-page monograph on emer-
         gency treatment based on the experience in Flor-
         ence.
4288. Grant, J. 'Deciphering Charred Documents," Analyst
         67, 1942.
4289. Hamilton, R. M. "The Library of Parliament Fire,"
         The American Archivist 16(2):141-144, 1953. Dis-
         cusses at considerable length the actual salvage of
         books and records from this fire in Ottawa.
4290. Horton, Carolyn. "Treating Water-Soaked Books,"
         International Institute for Conservation News 2(2):
         14, 1962.
4291. Jordon, Mel. "Hurricane Recovery Efforts--Univer-
         sity of Corpus Christi Library," Texas Library
         Journal 46(4), 1970. How the library recovered
         80% of its water damaged books after Hurricane
         Celia, August 1970.
4292. Matthews, C. G. "Treatment of Parchments Dam-
         aged by Fire," Analyst 49, 1924.
4293. Minogue, Adelaide E. "Treatment of Fire and Water
         Damaged Records," American Archivist 9:17-25,
         1946. Describes methods recommended by National
         Archives for putting remnants of fire damaged re-
         cords in usable condition.
4294. Mitchell, C. A. "The Deciphering of Scorched Docu-
         ments," Discovery 5, 1924.
4295. _____. "The Examination of Charred Documents,"
         Analyst 50, 1925.
4296. Murry, H. D. "Examination of Burned Documents,"
         Nature 148:199, 1941. Describes immersion in
         silver nitrate to salvage information on documents.
4297. Radley, J. A. "Deciphering of Charred Documents,"
         Analyst 75:628-629, 1950.
4298. "Restoring Books and Papers Injured by Fire," Sci-
         entific American Supplement 96:165, 1918.
4299. Rubinstein, N. "Book Restoration in Florence,"
         London Times Literary Supplement April 17, 1969.
         A general description of the work.
4300. Salvaging and Restoring Records Damaged by Fire and
         Water. Washington: Federal Fire Council, 1963.

4301. Still, John S.   "Library Fires and Salvage Methods, "
       The American Archivist 16:145, 1953.
4302. Taylor, W. D. and H. J. Walls.   "A New Method for
       the Decipherment of Charred Documents, " Nature
       147:417, 1941.   A combination of chemical treat-
       ment and photography.
4303. Tyrrel, J. F.   "The Decipherment of Charred Docu-
       ments, " Journal of Criminal Law and Criminology
       30, 1939.
4304. VonNell, Carl C.   Salvaging Book Materials in Li-
       braries Damaged by Fire and Flood from 1936 to
       1953 in the United States and Canada.   M. S. thesis,
       Drexel Institute of Technology, 1954.
4305. "Water and Fire Damaged Books and Records, Treat-
       ment of, " American Archivist 5:129, 1942; 9:17,
       1954; 16:141, 149, 1953.
4306. Williams, Howard D.   "Records Salvage After the
       Fire at Colgate University, " American Archivist
       27:375-379, 1964.

VII. Cooperative Conservation

4307. Boustead, W. M. "Problems of Art Conservation,"
Hemisphere 13(4), 1969. Stresses need for cooperation on mutual problems.
4308. Buck, R. D. "An Experiment in Cooperative Conservation," Studies in Conservation 2(3), 1956. Describes genesis of Intermuseum Conservation Association.
4309. Feller, R. L. "Toward Greater Interdisciplinary
Cooperation," Bulletin American Group-IIC 6(1),
1966.
4310. The First Decade. Rome: International Centre for
the Study of the Preservation and the Restoration
of Cultural Property, 1969. A ten-year progress
report and forecast for the future of the Rome
Centre.
4311. Gettens, R. J. "IIC: An International Association
of Conservators," Museum News 47(10), 1969. A
summary of the history of the activities of the
International Institute for Conservation and its
American Group.
4312. Marijnissen, R. H. The Damaged Work of Art, Its
Conservation and Restoration. Brussels: Arcade
Publishers, 1970. 2 vols. appendix. 332 illus.
Systematical bibliography. This is an inquiry into
the possibility of a discipline of conservation and
restoration.
4313. Philippot, P. "Conservation as an International Problem and the Rome Centre," Institute Royale Patrimoine Artistique Bulletin 10, 1967-68. Explains
work of Rome Centre in coordinating world wide
conservation studies.
4314. Posse, Otto. Handschriften-Konservirung. Dresden:
Verlag des Apollo, 1899. Reprinted in Supplement
No. 1 to Restaurator, Kopenhagen, 1969 in German.
The report of the findings of the first international
conference on the preservation of manuscripts held
in St. Gallen. The conferees agreed among other
things on the need to study the processes of

preservation, deseminate the information on preservation brought to the knowledge of the conference
to put the conference "en rapport" with librarians
and technical experts.   This reprint furthers above.

4315. Rosenquist, Anna M.   "IIC Textile Conference in
       Delft, " Meddelelser om Konservering 2:5-12, 1965.
       English summary.

4316. Schubert, H. and N. Brommelle.   "Co-operation for
       Conservation in Great Britain, " Museums Journal
       61, 1961.

4317. Wallace, Everett L.   Leather Research and Technol-
       ogy at the National Bureau of Standards.   Wash-
       ington: National Bureau of Standards, n. d.   NBS
       Circular No. 560.

C. STANDARDS AND SPECIFICATIONS

4318. Abridgement of Specifications Relating to Books, Portfolios and Card Cases 1768-1866. London: Commissioner of Patents for Inventions, 1870.

4319. Abridgement of Specifications Relating to Cutting, Folding and Ornamenting Papers. London: Commissioner of Patents, 1881. Covers the period 1636-1876.

4320. Abridgement of Specifications Relating to Skins, Hides and Leather AD 1627-1866. London: Commissioners of Patents for Inventions, 1872.

4321. Abridgement of Specifications Relating to the Manufacture of Paper, Pasteboard and Papier Mâché. London: Commissioners of Patents, 1876. Covers the period 1665-1866.

4322. Abridgement of Specifications: Class 40 (ii) Phonographs, etc. London: Patent Office 1909-1930.

4323. Abridgement of Specifications, Class 121, Starch, Gum, Size, Glue, and Other Stiffening and Adhesive Materials 1855-1930. London Patent Office.

4324. American Library Association, Library Technology Program. Development of Performance Standards for Binding Used in Libraries, Phases I & II. Chicago: American Library Association, 1965 & 1967.

4325. Association of Research Libraries, Committee on Preservation of Deteriorating Library Materials. Preparation of Detailed Specifications for a National System for the Preservation of Library Materials. Draft, April 4, 1969. Available from Association of Research Libraries, 1527 New Hampshire Ave., N.W., Washington, D.C. 20036.

4326. "Basic Minimum Standards for Training Paper Conservators by the Apprentice System," IIC-AG Bulletin 2(2):1-7, 1971. A proposal submitted to the annual meeting of the American Group -

International Institute for Conservation.

4327. Binding of Books. London: 1954. Crown Agents for Oversea Governments and Administrations. Standard Specification No. 40.

4328. British Standard Code of Practice CP3 - Chapter X (1950). Precautions Against Vermin and Dust. London: British Standards Institution, 1950.

4329. British Standard Sizes for Paper. London: British Standards Institution, 1937.

4330. Book Cloths, Buckrams, and Impregnated Fabrics for Bookbinding Purposes Except Library Bindings, Commercial Standard CS57-40, 2nd ed. Washington: U.S. Government Printing Office, 1940. U.S. National Bureau of Standards.

4331. Buck, Richard D. "A Specification for Museum Air Conditioning," and Amdur, Elias J. "Humidity Control--Isolated Area Plan," Museum News 43(4), 1964. Technical Supplement No. 6.

4332. Cushman, M. P. "Book Cloths and the Adoption of Standard Tests," Publishers Weekly pp. 1427-1432, April 4, 1936. A talk given at a book-clinic of the American Institute of Graphic Arts.

4333. (Ethics). The Murray Pease Report Code of Ethics for Art Conservators. New York: Conservation Center, Institute of Fine Arts, NYU, 1968. Presents the code of ethics adopted by the American Group, International Institute for Conservation in 1967, plus the Articles of Association of IIC and the Bylaws of the American Group.

4334. Feller, R. L. "Standards of Exposure to Light," Bulletin American Group, International Institute for Conservation 4(1), 1963.

4335. (Film). U.S.A. Standard Specifications for Photographic Films for Permanent Records, PH1.28-1957. Obtainable from the USA Standards Institute, Inc. 10 East 40th St., New York, N.Y. 10016.

4336. (Film). U.S.A. Standard Specifications for Safety Photographic Film. PH1.25-1965. Obtainable from the USA Standards Institute, Inc., 10 East 40th St., New York, N.Y. 10016.

4337. (Film Storage). Standards of the National Board of Fire Underwriters for Storage and Handling of Cellulose Nitrate Motion Picture Film as Recommended by the National Fire Protection Association. New York: National Board of Fire Underwriters, 1963. NBFU Pamphlet No. 40.

4338. (Fire Extinguishers). Standard for the Installation, Maintenance and Use of Portable Fire Extinguishers. Boston: National Fire Protection Association, 1969. NFPA No. 10A.

4339. (Fire Protection). Standard for the Protection of RECORDS. Boston: National Fire Protection Association, 1967. NFPA No. 232. Being primarily concerned with the protection of relatively small collections of records, this pamphlet is inappropriate for guidance in fire protection of large collections in records buildings. (For protection of large collections in archives, etc. see NFPA No. 232 A-M-T.)

4340. (Library Binding). Development of Performance Standards for Library Binding, Phase I. Chicago: American Library Association, 1965. Library Technology Program Publication No. 2.

4341. (Library Binding.) Development of Performance Standards for Binding Used in Libraries, Phase II. Chicago: American Library Association, 1967. Presents three provisional standards (i.e. durability, workmanship and openability) developed by the ALA Library Technology Program to develop performance standards.

4342. (Microfilm). U.S.A. Standard Practice for Storage of Microfilm, USAS No. PH5.4. Approved July 2, 1957. New York: American Standards Association, 1957.

4343. _____. "Standard for Permanent Record Photographic Microcopying Film," American Archivist 9(3):229-232, 1946.

4344. [No entry.]

4345. _____. Microfilm Norms. Chicago: American Library Association, 1966. Contains pertinent standards of American Standards Association, National Microfilm Association and U.S. Government.

4346. _____. Standards for Reproduction of Documents in Micronegative Form. Springfield, Va.: Clearinghouse for Federal Scientific and Technical Information, 1967. Publication Pf-16763 is now distributed by National Technical Information Service, Springfield, Virginia.

4347. (Paper Testing). Indian Standard Institution Specification. IS:1060 (Part II) Methods of Sampling and Tests for Paper and Allied Products. New Delhi, 1960.

344 Appendices

4348. Poole, F. G. "Performance Standards in Library
Binding, " Book Production Magazine 75:67-68, 1962.
Comments on some of the results of the Barrow
Laboratory's examination of the effects of age and
use on library bindings.

4349. _____ . "Preservation Costs and Standards, " Special Libraries 59:614-619, 1968.

4350. (Records Protection). Standard for the Protection of
Records. Boston: National Fire Protection Association, 1967. Incorporates the changes prepared
by the Committee of Records Protection and adopted
by NFPA in 1967. Supercedes 1963 edition. NFPA
No. 232.

4351. Salmon, Stephen R. Specifications for Library of
Congress Microfilming. Washington: Library of
Congress, 1964.

4352. Schneider, A. H. "Some Practical Suggestions Regarding Specifications for Rebinding Public Records, " American Archivist 9(3):226-228, 1946.

4353. Standards for the Storage and Handling of Cellulose
Nitrate Motion Picture Film. Boston: National
Fire Protection Association, 1967. NFPA No. 40.

4354. TAPPI Standards. Atlanta: Technical Association of
the Pulp and Paper Industry. This trade organization devises and publishes widely accepted procedures for the testing of paper, several of which
are listed hereafter.

4355. USA Standard Specifications for Photographic Films
for Permanent Records PH1.28-1957. Obtainable
from USA Standards Institute, Inc., 19 East 40th
Street, New York, N.Y. 10016.

4356. USA Standard Specifications for Safety Photographic
Film, PH1.25-1965. Obtainable from the USA
Standards Institute, Inc., 10 East 40th Street, New
York, N.Y. 10016.

4357. White, Lucien W. "Library Lighting Standards, " Wilson Library Bulletin 33:297-301, 1958.

4358. Wilson, William K. "Development of Specifications
for Archival Record Materials, " American Archivist 33(2):219-223, 1970. The Chief of the Paper
Evaluation Section at the National Bureau of Standards summarizes progress on the paper research
project being sponsored by the Society of American
Archivists in cooperation with the National Archives
and the Bureau of Standards.

E. FORMULA SOURCES

4359. Alcherius. "On Various Colours," in M. P. Merri-
        field's Original Treatises. New York: 1849.
        Gold writing, silver writing, brass writing, gild-
        ing parchment, paper, wood, grinding gold, ink,
        dying leather, making eracing paper.
4360. Alexander, S. M. "Medieval Recipes Describing the
        Use of Metals in Manuscripts," Marsyas 12:34-51,
        1966. New York.
4361. Bennett, H. et al. Practical Emulsions II, Applica-
        tions. New York: Chemical Publishing Company,
        1968. A useful compilation of basic formulations
        of emulsions. Includes a chapter on leather and
        paper treatment emulsions.
4362. Bolz von Rufach, Valentin. Illuminir-Büch Kunstlich
        alle Farben zu machen und zu bereiten. Basel:
        1549. Book of Illuminating. The manufacture and
        preparation of colors.
4363. A Book of Secrets. Shewing divers waies to make
        and prepare all sorts of Inke, and Colours; as
        Blacke, white Blew, Greene, Red, Yellow and oth-
        er Colours. Also to write with Gold, and Silver,
        or any kind of Mettall out of the Pen: with many
        other profitable Secrets, as to colour Quils and
        Parchment of any colour: and to grave with strong
        Water in Steele and Iron. Necessarie to be knowne
        of all Scriveners, Painters and others that delight
        in such Arts. London: 1592. Translated out of
        the Dutch (i.e. German) into English by W. P.
4364. Book of Trade Secrets. London: J. Haslam & Co., Ltd.,
        1909. Recipes and instructions for renovating old
        books and prints. Almost all now outdated.
4365. Cennini, Cennino D'Andrea. Il Libro dell' Arte
        translated by D. V. Thompson in The Craftsman's
        Handbook. New Haven: Yale University Press,
        1933. Book 5, adhesives, glues, cements, for
        stone, glass, fish glue, goat glue size for gesso
        cheese glue. Book 9, illuminating. Book 12, pa-
        per. Republished New York: Dover Publications,
        Inc., 1954.
4366. Colwall, Daniel. "An Account of the Way of Making
        English Green-Copperas," Philosophical Transac-
        tions 12:1056-1059, 1678. Royal Society of London.
4367. "Compositiones Variae," L. A. Muratori, Antiquitates
        Italicae Medii Aevi 42(2):365-392, 1738. Milan.

In Latin.   A collection of over one hundred technical recipes: gold leaf, refining of gold, gold
solder, gold thread, gold writing (Manufacture of
gold ink).   Method of preparation of various types
of adhesives, with detailed descriptions of adhesives for stone and for wood.   Fish glue, hide
glue, casein glue.   Preparation of parchment.

4368.   "De arte illuminandi, On the Art of Illuminating, "
in D. V. Thompson and G. H. Hamilton, De arte-
illuminandi.   The Technique of Manuscript Illumination.   New Haven: Yale University Press, 1933.
32 recipes devoted to the illumination of manuscripts, adhesives.

4369.   Eraclius.   "De coloribus et artibus romanorum Books
1 and 2, " Original Treatises 1:166-203, 1849.
Published by M. P. Merrifield.   Of the three
Books which make up this work, the first two are
datable perhaps to the 10th century.   Book 3 is
considered to be 13th century (q. v.).   Books 1 and
2 contain 21 recipes including inks.

4370.   Ettliche Kunste, auff mancherley weisz Dinten und
allerhand Farven zu bereyten.   Strasburg, 1593.
Divers arts, many ways of preparing inks and all
sorts of colours.   A German version of the Kunst-
buchlein in 1531.

4371.   "Fragmentary Manuscript in the Biblioteca Capitolare
of Ivrea, " Noted by G. Carbonelli.   Sulle Fonti
Storiche della Chimica e dell'.   Recipes for gold and
silver writing and dyeing of skins.

4372.   Gabb, M. H. and W. E. Latchem.   A Handbook of
Laboratory Solutions.   New York: Chemical Publ. ,
1968.

4373.   Gerrarde, John.   The Herball or Generall Historie
of Plantes Gathered by John Gerrarde of London.
London: 1597.   Ink from galls and soot saffron
for illumination.

4374.   Hiscox Gardner, D. (ed.).   Henley's Twentieth Century Book of Formulas, Processes and Trade Secrets.   New York: N. W. Henley, 1946.

4375.   [No entry.]

4376.   Hopkins, Albert A. (ed.).   The Scientific American
Cyclopedia of Formulas.   New York: Scientific
American Publishing Company.   Periodically re-
vised and enlarged.

4377.   Kinder, Louis H.   Formulas for Bookbinders.   East
Aurora, New York: The Roycrofters, 1905.

4378. The Laboratory or School of Arts. London: 1739.
Contains curiosities relating to gold and silver;
secrets for jewellers, experiments for making
casts in metal, wax, and other materials; glass-
making; secrets for the use of cutlers, joiners,
japanners, bookbinders and other handicraftsmen.

4379. Laurie, A. P. Pigments and Mediums of the Old
Masters. New York: MacMillan, 1914. Ink
recipes.

4380. Le Begue, Jehan. "Experimenta de Coloribus. Experiments on Colors," in M. P. Merrifield's
Original Treatises, New York, 1849. Gold writing
(substitute for gold), silver writing, gilding parchment, gilding, inks, adhesives for parchment, eras-
letters from parchment, making seal impressions.

4381. Leyden, Papyrus X. 3rd century A. D. From Egypt.
Written in Greek. Fifteen formulae on the manufacture of gold ink.

4382. Lucas, A. Ancient Egyptian Materials and Industries.
3rd ed. London: Edward Arnold & Co., 1948.

4383. Madrid Codex A. 16. c. 1130. in J. M. Burnam,
Recipes from Matritensis. Cincinnati: University
of Cincinnati Press, 1912. A craftsman's handbook written in Catalonia, c. 1130. The recipes
on writing in gold and silver are comparable to
those of the Papyrus X of Leyden and the Compositiones Variae, 8th century.

4384. Petrus De Sancto Audemaro. "De coloribus pictorum
et illuminatiorum liborum Faceidis," in M. P.
Merrifield's Original Treatises 1:112-165, New
York: 1849. On making colours for painters and
illuminators of books. Gilding copper vessels
(gold substitute), gilding tin, gilding parchment and
walls tempering gums for gilding. Inks. Green
ink adhesives: hide glue, glue from cheese.

4385. "A Receipt for Making Writing Ink," Gentleman's
Magazine 23:212, 1753.

4386. Recipes on miscellaneous subjects, 15th century.
Published in Th. Wright and J. O. Halliwell,
Reliquiae Antiquae. Scraps from ancient manu-
scripts, illustrating chiefly early English literature.
London: 1841. 2 vols. Reprinted by AMS Press,
Inc., New York: 1966. Removing writing from
parchment, making glue, cleaning a book with
bread, gum for making ink, making ink.

4387. Singer, D. W. "Michael Scot and Alchemy," Isis
13:5-15, 1929. Gold writing, gilding.

4388.   "Segreti per Colori," in M. P. Merrifield, Original
        Treatises 2:325-600, 1849.   Making parchment,
        making a window from parchment, varnishes, lin-
        seed oil, gums and gum water.

4389.   Standage, H. C. Cements, Pastes, Glues and Gums--
        With Recipes and Formulas.   London: Crosby
        Lockwood & Co. , 1893.

4390.   The Stockholm Papyrus.   3rd century A. D. ?   May
        form the counter part to the Leydon Papyrus X.
        One recipe on the removal of writing from papyrus.

4391.   Thompson, Daniel V. Jr.   Il Libro dell'Arte (The
        Craftsman's Handbook).   New Haven: Yale Univer-
        sity Press, 1933.   An English translation of a
        classical medieval text useful for source material
        on the arts and crafts.

4392.   Tottill, Richard.   A very proper treatise wherein is
        briefly sett forthe the arts of Limming, which
        teacheth the order in drawing and tracing of letters,
        vinets, flowers armes and Imagery, and the maner
        how to make Sundry Sises or grounds to laye silver
        or golde uppon, and how silver or golde layed or
        limmed uppon the sise,.. etc.   London: 1573.   Re-
        printed Ann Arbor, Mich. :   Edwards Bros. , 1932
        as The Art Of Limming.   Preparation of parchment
        for writing, ink making, making sealing wax, re-
        moving grease.

4393.   Virgil, Polydore.   De Inventoribus Rerum.   Venice:
        1498.   An early attempt to write the history of in-
        ventions in the arts and sciences, and to trace the
        growth of religious ceremonies.   Book 2, Ch. 6,
        early history of books and printing, libraries, writ-
        ing materials, inks, soot from varnish for black
        ink.

J.   EXAMINATION OF PAPER

4394.   Arad, A.   "A Simple Measurement of Torsional Rigid-
        ity in Paper," Restaurator 1(2), 1969.   Suggests
        an inexpensive physical testing device for paper in
        lieu of expensive laboratory equipment.

4395.   _____.   "Tear-resistance Instrument," Restaurator
        1(3), 1970.   Describes a simple, easily made, low
        cost device for comparative tests of paper samples.

4396. "Artificially Aged Documents, " The Analyst 50, 1925.
4397. Baillie, W. J. H. Direct Ultra-violet Photography and the Technical Examination of Museum Objects. London: International Institute for Conservation (UK Group), n. d.
4398. Barrow, W. J. "Hot vs. Cold Extraction Methods for Making a pH Determination, " Tappi 46:468-472, 1963.
4399. _____. Spot Testing for Unstable Modern Book and Record Papers. Richmond: W. J. Barrow Research Laboratory, 1969. Permanence/Durability of the Book - VI. Simple procedures for spot testing for groundwood, acid, alum and rosin in paper.
4400. Baynes-Cope, A. D. Methods of Testing New Materials. Paper presented at meeting of IIC-UK Group, 29 February 1968. Simple tests for evaluating acidity in paper, adhesives.
4401. Bessemans, A. "Triple Verification of the Age of a Questioned Document, " International Criminal Police Review 84, January 1955.
4402. Blum, Andre. On The Origin of Paper. New York: R. R. Bowker, 1934. Includes information on the evolution of water marks.
4403. Brewster, F. Contested Documents and Forgeries. Calcutta: The Book Company Ltd. , 1932.
4404. Briquet, Charles M. "De la Valeur des Filigranes de Papier Comme Moyen de Déterminer l'Age et la Provenance des Documents non Datis, " Bulletin de la Societé d'Histoire et d'Archeologie de Genève 1:192-202, 1892. Geneva.
4405. _____. Les Filigranes 1281-1600. Paris: 1907. 4 volumes. Watermarks provide valuable evidence of the makeup of a book and are often evidence of alterations to an early volume. This book reprinted in Leipzig in 1923 has 16,112 facsimiles.
4406. Brown, J. T. "The Detection of Faked Literary MSS, " The Book Collector 2(1):6-23, 1953. London. Discusses some of the points to be considered when examining a suspect document.
4407. Browning, B. L. Analysis of Paper. New York: Marcel Dekker, Inc. , 1969. Includes the detection and determination of the components of paper with special attention to the nonfibrous adhesives. Qualitative and quantitative methods of analysis are described. Much excellent information on paper but the laboratory methods outlined are too complicated for use by librarians and archivists.

4408. Browning, B. L. and R. W. K. Ulm. "The Nature
       and Measurement of Paper Acidity," Paper Trade
       Journal 102:69-86, 1936.
4409. Buck, R. D. and others. "An Investigation of the
       Use of pH Indicators on Paper," ICA Newsletter
       7(1), 1969. Recommends low cost chemical indi-
       cators for checking the pH of paper in small mu-
       seum workshops.
4410. Burton, D.; J. B. Poole, and R. Reed. "A New
       Approach to the Dating of the Dead Sea Scrolls,"
       Nature 184:533-534, 1959.
4411. Carter, John and Graham Pollard. An Enquiry into
       the Nature of Certain Nineteenth-Century Pamphlets.
       London: Constable, 1934.
4412. "Chromatographic Analysis of Dyes in Paper," Color
       Engineer 6(1):41-42, 1968.
4413. Conway, J. V. P. Evidential Documents. Spring-
       field, Ill.: Thomas, 1959.
4414. The Dictionary of Paper, 3rd ed. New York: Amer-
       ican Pulp and Paper Association, 1965. Primarily
       for papermakers but of great value to librarians
       and archivists.
4415. Easby, Dudley T. Jr. and Ralph R. Colin. "The
       Legal Aspects of Forgery and the Protection of the
       Expert," Metropolitan Museum Art Bulletin 26(6):
       257-261, 1968.
4416. Edlin, C. H. "A Case of an Altered Document,"
       Police Journal 11, 1938.
4417. Erastov, D. P. "Additional Data on the Investigation
       of Experimental Paper Samples by Means of Optical
       Methods," Stareniye bumagi 153-6, 1965. Moscow.
4418. _____. "Potentialities of Electronographic Methods
       in Document Investigation," Stareniye bumagi 133-
       44, 1965.
4419. Farrer, J. A. Literary Forgeries. London: Long-
       mans, Green & Co., 1907.
4420. "Fiber Analysis of Paper and Paperboard, Tappi T
       401 M-60," Atlanta: Technical Association of the
       Pulp and Paper Industry, 1960.
4421. (Fiber Identification). "Identification of Wood and
       Fibers. Tappi T8 SM61," Atlanta: Technical As-
       sociation of the Pulp and Paper Industry, 1961.
4422. Flieder, Françoise. "Techniques of Identification for
       Pigments and Media Used in the Picture Layer of
       Manuscript Illuminations," Studies in Conservation
       13(2):49-86, 1968.

4423. Flynn, Joseph H. and Leslie E. Smith. "Comparative pH Measurements on Papers by Water Extraction and Glass Electrode Spot Tests," Tappi 44(3), March 1961.

4424. "Frauds and Imperfections in Paper-making," Annals of Philosophy 6:68, 1823.

4425. Graff, J. H. A Color Atlas of Fiber Identification. Appleton, Wis.: The Institute of Paper Chemistry, 1940.

4426. _____. Pulp and Paper Microscopy. 2nd ed. Appleton, Wis.: The Institute of Paper Chemistry, 1942.

4427. Grant, Julius. Books and Documents, Dating, Permanence and Preservation. London: Grafton and Co., 1937. Sound information on the determination of the age, history and origin of book materials.

4428. _____. "The Conception of pH Values and Its Background in the Development of Paper Manufacture," Paper-Maker and British Trade Journal 113:17-22, 1947.

4429. _____. Examination of Documents. London: Paper presented to a meeting of IIC-UK Group, n.d.

4430. Grant, R. L.; F. L. Hudson, and J. A. Hockey. "A New Method of Detecting Fingerprints on Paper," Journal of Forensic Science Society 4:85-86, 1963.

4431. _____. "Detecting Fingerprints on Paper," Nature 200:1348, 1963.

4432. Gray, G. G. "An Accelerated Aging Study Comparing Kinetic Rates vs. Tappi Method 453," Tappi.

4433. Harrison, W. R. Forgery Detection. New York: Frederick A. Praeger, 1964. A simplified introduction to forgery detection written for the layman but with much basic information on how to recognize document forgeries. Not to be confused with the same author's highly scientific treatment of the subject in Suspect Documents, 1958. [4434].

4434. _____. Suspect Documents, Their Scientific Examination. New York: Frederick A. Praeger, 1958.

4435. Haselden, R. B. Scientific Aids to the Study of Manuscripts. London: The Bibliographical Society, 1935.

4436. Heawood, Edward. "The Use of Watermarks in Dating Old Maps and Documents," The Geographical Journal 63:391-412, 1924.

4437. Hilton, O. "Pitfalls in the Use of Ultra-violet Examination to Differentiate Between Writing Papers," Journal of Criminal Law and Criminology 40(4), 1949.

4438. _____ . The Scientific Examination of Documents.
Chicago: Callaghan & Co., 1956.

4439. Hoving, Thomas P. F. "The Game of Duplicity,"
Bulletin, Metropolitan Museum of Art 26(6):241-
246, 1968.

4440. Hudson, F. L. and C. J. Edwards. "Some Direct
Observations on the Aging of Paper," Paper Technology 7:27-28, 1966.

4441. _____ and W. D. Milner. "The Use of Flat Headed
Glass Electrodes for Measuring the pH of Paper,"
Svensk Papperstidning 62(3):83-84, 1959.

4442. Infra-red and Ultra-violet Photography. Rochester,
N. Y.: Eastman Kodak Co., 1963. Kodak Advanced Data Book No. M-3.

4443. Isenberg, I. H. Pulp and Paper Microscopy. 3rd
ed. Appleton, Wis.: The Institute of Paper Chemistry, 1967. First and second editions were by
J. H. Graff. [4426]

4444. _____ and J. D. Hankey. "The Microsectioning of
Fibers and Papers," Tappi 49(8):373-376, 1966.

4445. Jarrell, T. D.; J. M. Hankins, and F. P. Veitch.
Deterioration of Paper as Indicated by Gas Chamber
Tests. Washington: U. S. Dept. of Agriculture,
1938. Technical Bulletin No. 605.

4446. Jayme, G. and E. M. Rohmann. "Use of Infra-red
Spectroscopy in Examining Pulp and Paper," Papier
19(10A):719-728, 1965. Darmstadt.

4447. Johnson, Virginia C. "Differentiating Between Cotton
and Flax Fibers in Paper," Richmond: Unpublished
report to the W. J. Barrow Research Laboratory,
1966.

4448. Journal of Forensic Science. Chicago: Callaghan &
Co., a quarterly. Frequently includes articles on
document examination, forgeries, etc.

4449. King, A.; A. Pelikan, and W. E. Faulkner. "The
Use of the Archivists' Pen and Universal pH Solution for Estimating the Surface pH of Paper,"
Studies in Conservation 15(1):63-64, 1970. This
study shows that inexpensive pens or the equally
inexpensive universal pH solution will give reason-
able estimates of the pH of paper.

4450. Lacy, George. "Questioned Documents," American
Archivist 9(4):267-275, 1946. Written originally
for attorneys, this data is also of much interest
to archivists.

4451. Launer, Herbert F. Determination of the pH Value
of Papers. Washington: U. S. Government Printing

Office, 1939. U. S. National Bureau of Standards Research Paper RP1205.

4452. _____. "Retention of Aluminum Ion and Hydrogen Ion in Papers," Paper Trade Journal 110:30-34, 1940.

4453. Lee, H. N. "Established Methods for Examination of Paper," Technical Studies in the Field of the Fine Arts 4(1), 1935. Descriptions of the commonly used methods by which the constituents of paper may be determined.

4454. _____. "Improved Methods for the Examination of Paper," Technical Studies in the Field of the Fine Arts 4(2), 1935.

4455. Mitchell, Ainsworth. Documents and Their Scientific Examination. London: Chas. Griffin & Company, 1935.

4456. _____. The Expert Witness and the Applications of Science and of Art to Human Identification, Criminal Investigation, Civil Actions and History. Cambridge, England: W. Heffer & Sons, Ltd., 1923.

4457. Morland, Nigel. An Outline of Scientific Criminology. New York: Philosophical Library, Inc., 1950. Contains a useful chapter on identification of inks, paper, erasures, document identification, etc.

4458. Neimo, L. "Accelerated Heat Aging of Cellulose," Paperi ja Puu--Papper och Tra 46:7-9, 11-14, 1964. Available in translation from the Institute of Paper Chemistry, Appleton, Wis.

4459. O'Hara, C. E. and J. W. Osterburg. An Introduction to Criminalistics. New York: The MacMillan Co., 1952. Excellent material on ink identification and revival, document examination, infra-red and ultra-violet applications. Fully footnoted and lengthy bibliographies at end of each section.

4460. Osborne, A. S. The Problem of Proof. 2nd ed. Newark, N. J.: The Essex Press, 1926.

4461. _____. Questioned Documents. 2nd ed. Toronto: Boyd Printing Co., 1929.

4462. _____. Questioned Documents Problems. 2nd ed. Albany: Boyd Printing Co., 1946.

4463. Paper and Paper Boards: Characteristics, Nomenclature and Significance of Tests. Philadelphia: American Society for Testing & Materials, 1963. Special Technical Publication No. 60-B.

4464. (Paper testing). Indian Standard Institution Specification, 15:1060-1956. Part 1, Methods of Sampling and Test for Paper and Allied Products.

4465.   Petrova-Zavgorodnyaya, A. P. and D. P. Erastov.
        "Determination of Mould Contamination of Paper
        by Luminescence," Bulletin, Academy of Science
        of the USSR 403-411, 1959.

4466.   Pierce, J. H. and I. D. Ratee.   "The Concept of In-
        ternal pH in Acid-Base-catalyzed Hydrolysis in
        Heterogeneous Systems," Journal of the Society of
        Dyers and Colourists 81:317-319, 1965.

4467.   Plitt, T. M.   Microscopic Methods Used in Identify-
        ing Commercial Fibers.   Washington: U. S. Gov-
        ernment Printing Office.   National Bureau of
        Standards Circular C-423.

4468.   Pravilova, T. A.   "On pH of Water Extraction of Pa-
        per," Causes of Decay of Written and Printed
        Monuments 143-146, 1967.   Leningrad, U. S. S. R.:
        Laboratory for Preservation and Restoration of
        Documents.   Demonstrates advantages of cold ex-
        traction over heat extraction.   Available from Na-
        tional Technical Information Service, Springfield,
        Virginia.

4469.   (Questioned Documents).   "Characteristics of Pigments
        in Early Pencil Writing," Nature 105:12-14, 1920.

4470.   Quirke, A. J.   Forged Anonymous and Suspect Docu-
        ments.   London: George Routledge & Sons, Ltd.,
        1930.

4471.   Rasch, R. H.   "Accelerated Aging Test for Paper,"
        U. S. National Bureau of Standards Journal Research
        7:465-475, 1931.

4472.   and B. W. Scribner.   "Comparison of Natur-
        al Aging of Paper with Accelerated Aging by Heat-
        ing," Journal of Research of the National Bureau
        of Standards 11:727-732, 1933.

4473.   .   "Accelerated Aging Tests for Determining
        Permanence of Papers," Industrial and Engineering
        Chemistry 26:1154-1157, 1934.

4474.   Richter, G. A.   "Durability of Purified Wood Fibers:
        Accelerated Aging Tests of Various Types of Paper-
        Making Fibers," Industrial and Engineering Chem-
        istry 23:371-380, 1931.

4475.   .   "Relative Permanence of Papers Exposed
        to Sunlight," Industrial and Engineering Chemistry
        27:177-185, 1935.

4476.   .   "Relative Permanence of Papers Exposed
        to Sunlight, II," Industrial and Engineering Chemis-
        try 27:432-439, 1935.

4477. _____ and F. L. Wells. "Influence of Moisture
       in Accelerated Aging of Cellulose, " Tappi 37:603-
       608, 1956.

4478. Rorimer, J. Examination of Works of Art with Ultra-
       violet. New York: Metropolitan Museum of Art,
       n. d.

4479. Royen, A. H. van. "Comparison of Artificial Aging
       of Pulp at 100° C with Natural Aging at Room
       Temperature, " Association Technique del'Industrie
       Papètiere Bulletin 6:223-226, 1957.

4480. Standard Method for the Determination of the Thick-
       ness and Bulk of Paper. Paper Makers Associa-
       tion, 1936.

4481. Séve, R. "Examen Microscopique de la Surface du
       Papier, " Association Tech. Ind. Papetiere Bull.
       19(2), 1965.

4482. Stevenson, Allan H. "Chain-indentations in Paper as
       Evidence, " Bibliographical Society Papers 6, 1954.
       University of Virginia.

4483. _____. Observations on Paper as Evidence. Law-
       rence, Kansas: University of Kansas, 1961. The
       Annual Public Lectures on Books and Bibliography,
       1961. Observations also on watermarks.

4484. _____. "Paper as Bibliographical Evidence, "
       Transactions of the Bibliographical Society 197-
       212, 1962.

4485. Technical Association of the Pulp and Paper Industry,
       Standards and Methods. "Fiber Analysis of Paper
       and Paperboard, " T-401, m-60, 1960.

4486. _____. "Folding Endurance of Paper, " T-423, su-
       68 1968.

4487. _____. "Hydrogen Ion Concentration (pH) of Paper
       Extracts, " T-435, su-68 1968.

4488. _____. "Internal Tearing Resistance of Paper, "
       T-414, ts-65, 1965.

4489. _____. "Starch in Paper, " T-419 su-70, 1970.

4490. _____. Qualitative Analysis of Synthetic Fibers.
       Atlanta: Technical Association of the Pulp and
       Paper Industry, 1969. CA Report No. 21. A
       simplified system for identifying eight synthetic
       fibers used in the production of wet-laid, non-
       woven papers.

4491. "Tests Made on Old Papers, " Paper Mill 53(29):14,
       1930.

4492. Tholl, J. "Short Wave Ultra-violet Radiation. Its
         Use in the Questioned Document Laboratory," Po-
         lice 11(4):21-28, 1967.
4493. Trillat, J. J. and G. Martin. "Application of
         Electron Microscopy and X-ray Microscopy to the
         Study of Paper," Papeterie 9:1136-1146, 1965.
4494. Tydeman, P. A. "A Simple Method for Contact Beta-
         Radiography of Paper," Paper Maker 153(6):42-48, 65
         1967.
4495. Venter, J. S. M. The Aging and Preservation of
         Paper--a Development Study. Pretoria: Council
         for Scientific and Industrial Research, 1966.
4496. Vilars, J. "Measurement of Humidity in Paper,"
         A. T. I. P. Bulletin 19(4):167-178, 1965.
4497. Webber, R. B. The Book of pH. London: George
         Newnes Ltd., 1957. A simple description of the
         theory of pH measurements.
4498. Wehmhoff, B. L. "The Determination of pH Values
         and Total Acidity of Paper," Technical Association
         Papers 13:230, May 1930; and 14:387, May 1931.
4499. Wilson, Norval F. "A New stain for Identifying Pa-
         permaking Fibers," Pap. Industry and Paper World
         27:215-216, 1945.
4500. Wilson, William K.; Jack L. Harvey; John Mandel,
         and Thelma Worksman. "Accelerated Aging of
         Record Papers Compared with Normal Aging,"
         Tappi 38:543-548, 1955.
4501. Wooding, W. M. "pH Measurement and Control,"
         Paper Trade Journal 135:19-27, 1952.

K.   SOLVENTS (AND PRECAUTIONS)

4502. Allan, H. "Safe Practice with Solvents," Chemical
         Age 73, 1955.
4503. Amor, A. J. "The Toxicity of Solvents, I-II," Paint
         Mfg. 20, 1950.
4504. Brommelle, N. S. Toxic Chemicals. London: Vic-
         toria & Albert Museum, 1969. A short minute dis-
         tributed to the museum's staff outlining policy for
         the use of toxic chemicals. Sound advice for all
         who use solvents. [See page 338, vol. 1 this book.]
4505. Burrell, Harry. "A Solvent Formulating Chart," Of-
         ficial Digest of the Federation of Societies for Paint

Technology 1159-1173, November 1, 1957.

4506. Doolittle, Arthur K. Technology of Solvents and Plasticizers. New York - London: John Wiley, 1954.

4507. Durrans, Th. Solvents. 6th ed. rev. Princeton: Van Nostrand, 1950. Also London: Chapman Hall, Ltd., 1950.

4508. "Exit Carbon Tetrachloride from the Home," Chemistry 41(9):9, 1968.

4509. Fuller, W. R. Solvents. Philadelphia: Federation of Societies for Paint Technology, 1967. Unit No. 6 of a series of pamphlets on coating technology. An excellent, condensed, up-to-date discussion of the properties of solvents.

4510. "Hygenic Guide Series," Detroit: American Industrial Hygiene Association, n.d. Gives details on toxicity and other hazards of industrial chemicals.

4511. Jasser, A. "Without Knowing it, You May be Killing Yourself," Graphic Arts Monthly 1962. Hazards of solvents.

4512. Jordan, Otto. Technology of Solvents. London: Leonard Hill, 1937.

4513. Millan, Ibert. Industrial Solvents Handbook. Park Ridge, N.J.: Noyes Data Corp., 1970. The nature of solvents. Safe handling of solvents.

4514. Plunkett, E. F. Handbook of Industrial Toxicology. New York: Chemical Publishing Co., 1966. Discusses hazards, tolerances, symptoms and precautions.

4515. (Precautions). "The Editor's Column," Analytical Chemistry 38(12):93A-95A, 1966. Washington. Discusses importance of precautions in use of common solvents particularly benzene and carbontetrachloride.

4516. Scheflan, L. and M. B. Jacobs. The Handbook of Solvents. Princeton: Van Nostrand, 1953. Text and also data on each solvent in tabular form.

4517. Stolow, Nathan. "Physical, Commercial, Toxicology of Solvents Used or Proposed for Conservation of Paintings," Exposition of Painting Conservation. Brooklyn: The Brooklyn Museum, 1962. This data is also of value to library conservators.

4518. [No entry.]

4519. Wood, W. S. "Use, Storage and Disposal of Flammable Solvents," Industrial Engineering Chemistry 51, 1959.

L. EXAMINATION OF INK

4520. Barrow, W. J. "New Non-Acid Permanent Iron Ink, "
        American Archivist 10(4):338, 1947.
4521. Brackett, J. W. and L. Bradford. "Comparison of
        Ink Writing on Documents by Paper Chromatog-
        raphy, " Journal of Criminal Law and Criminology
        43(4), 1952.
4522. Brown, C. and P. L. Kirk. "Horizontal Paper
        Chromatography in the Identification of Ball Point
        Inks, " Journal of Criminal Law and Criminology
        vol. 43, 1952.
4523. Coldwell, A. "The Comparison of Inks and Writings by
        Paper Chromatography, " Analyst 80, 1955.
4524. Feigl, Fritz and E. Hans. "Sensitive and Selective
        Test for Gallontannin (Tannic Acid) and Other Tan-
        nins, " Industrial and Engineering Chemistry 18,
        1946.
4525. Harrison, W. R. Forgery Detection. New York:
        Frederick A. Praeger, 1960.
4526. _____. Suspect Documents: Their Scientific Ex-
        amination. New York: Frederick A. Praeger,
        1958.
4527. Hasledon, R. B. Scientific Aids for the Study of
        Manuscripts. London: Bibliographical Society,
        1935.
4528. Hilton, O. "Restoring Erased Ink Writing, " Police
        Journal October-December 1956.
4529. _____. The Scientific Examination of Documents.
        Chicago: Callaghan & Co. , 1956.
4530. Longhetti, A. and P. L. Kirk. "Restoration and
        Decipherment of Erasures and Obliterated or In-
        dented Writing, " Journal of Criminal Law and
        Criminology 41(4), November-December 1950.
4531. Martin. "Further Developments in the Chromatographic
        Analysis of Dried Ink, " International Criminal Po-
        lice Review 91, 1955.
4532. Mitchel, C. A. Documents and Their Scientific Ex-
        amination. London: C. Griffin and Co. , 1937.
4533. _____. "Erasures and Ultra-violet Light, " Analyst
        58, 1933.
4534. _____. "Ink and Ultra-violet Light, " Analyst
        55:746-747, 1930.
4535. _____. Inks, Their Composition and Manufacture.
        4th ed. Philadelphia: Lippincott, 1937.

4536. _____. "The Use of Infra-red Rays in the Examination of Inks and Pigments," Analyst 60:454-461, 1935.

4537. Munson, L. S. "The Testing of Writing Inks," Journal of the American Chemical Society 28:512-516, 1906.

4538. O'Hara, C. E. and J. W. Osterburg. An Introduction to Criminalistics. New York: The MacMillan Company, 1952. Includes excellent chapters on inks, the examination of questioned documents and ultra-violet and infra-red examinations.

4539. O'Neill, M. E. "Restoration of Obliterated Ink Writing," Journal Criminal Law and Criminology 27:574-577, 1936.

4540. Quirke, A. J. Forged, Anonymous and Suspect Documents. London: George Routledge & Sons, Ltd., 1930.

4541. Rupert, F. F. "Examination of Writing Inks," Industrial Engineering Chemistry 15:489-493, 1923.

4542. Sannie, C. "Recherches sur l'analyse de L'encre des documents manuscripts," Revue de Criminologie et de la Police Technique 6(2), 1952.

4543. Söderman, H. and J. J. O'Connell. Modern Criminal Investigation. New York: Funk & Wagnalls Co., 1935. Contains section on ink and paper analysis for document authentication.

4544. Somerford, W. "The Comparison of Writing Inks by Chromatography," International Criminal Police Review 59, 1952.

4545. Susumu, I. "Identification of Inks by Paper Chromatography," Science and Crime Detection 8(3), 1955. Japan.

4546. Ward, T. J. "The Microchemical Identification of Ink in Handwriting," Analyst 59, 1934.

4547. Waters, C. E. "Blue Dye as Evidence of the Age of Writing," Industrial Engineering Chemist and Chemistry 25:1034, 1933.

4548. Williams, T. I. Introduction to Chromatography. Brooklyn: Chemical Publishing Company, 1947.

M.   EXAMINATION OF ADHESIVES

4549.   Clark, R. G.   "Waterproof Starch Adhesives, " Cana-
        dian Pulp and Paper Industry 14(4):88-90, 93, 1961.
4550.   DeBruyne, Norman Adrian and Roelof Houwink, Edi-
        tors.   Adhesion and Adhesives.   New York: Else-
        vier Publishing Co. , 1951.
4551.   Delmonte, J.   The Technology of Adhesives.   New
        York: Reinhold Publishing Corp. , 1947.
4552.   Lucas, A.   "Chemical Tests for Adhesives, " Forensic
        Chemistry.   4th ed.   Pontiac, Mich. :   Arnold,
        1945.
4553.   Phelan, W. H. et al.   "An Evaluation of Adhesives
        for Use in Paper Conservation, " Bulletin American
        Group - IIC 11(2):58-75, 1971.   Progress report on
        work underway at the Conservation Center of the
        Institute of Fine Arts at New York University.
4554.   Skeist, Irving.   Handbook of Adhesives.   New York:
        Reinhold Publishing Co. , 1962.   Technical informa-
        tion on composition and end use of a wide variety
        of adhesives.
4555.   Testing Adhesives.   Atlanta: Technical Association of
        the Pulp and Paper Industry, 1963.

N.   PRECAUTIONS IN THE USE OF PESTICIDES

4556.   Barnes, J. M.   "Control of Health Hazards Associ-
        ated with the Use of Pesticides, " in Metcalf, R. L. ,
        Advances in Pest Control Research.   New York:
        John Wiley & Sons, 1957.
4557.   _____ .   "Toxic Hazards of Certain Pesticides to
        Man, " Bulletin World Health Organization 8:419-
        490, 1953.
4558.   Christol, S. J. and H. L. Haller.   "The Chemistry
        of DDT--A Review, " Chemical Engineering News
        23, 1945.
4559.   Deker, G. C.   "Pros and Cons of Insecticides, "
        Agricultural Chemistry 18(3):22, 112, 1963.
4560.   Durham, W. F. and H. R. Wolfe.   "Measurement of
        the Exposure of Workers to Pesticides, " Bulletin
        World Health Organization 26:75, 1962.

4561.   Edson, E. F.   "Applied Toxicology of Pesticides, "
        Pharmacy Journal 185:361-367, 1960.

4562.   Film Guide on Chemicals, Chemistry and the Chemical
        Industry, 1967-68.   Washington: Manufacturing
        Chemists Association, 1967.   Includes titles on
        pesticides and safety.

4563.   Foulger, J. H.   "A Practical Approach to Protection
        of Laboratory Personnel From Toxic Materials, "
        Journal Chemical Education 42(4):A285-A289, 1965.
        Washington.

4564.   Fulton, R. A.; F. F. Smith, and R. L. Bushey.
        Respiratory Devices for Protection Against Certain
        Pesticides.   Washington: United States Department
        of Agriculture, 1964.   D. A. Publication ARS 33:1.

4565.   Gallo, Fausta.   "Biological Agents Which Damage Pa-
        per Materials in Libraries and Archives, " Recent
        Advances in Conservation.   London: Butterworths,
        1963.

4566.   Gallo, Piero.   "Problems in the Use of Insecticides
        on Occupied Premises, " Recent Advances in Con-
        servation.   London: Butterworths, 1963.

4567.   Graham, Frank Jr.   Since Silent Spring.   Boston:
        Houghton Mifflin Co. , 1970.   Contains an appendix
        of guidance for safe use of pesticides.

4568.   Hayes, W. J.   "The Toxicity of Dieldrin to Man, "
        Bulletin World Health Organization 20:891-912, 1959.

4569.   Mass, A. A.   "DDT, " Museum Journal 46, 1946.

4570.   U. S. Dept. of Agriculture & U. S. Dept. HEW (Food
        and Drug Dept.).   Regulations of Pesticides in the
        United States.   Washington: U. S. Government
        Printing Office, 1968.

4571.   U. S. Dept. of H. E. W.   Report of the Secretary's
        Commission on Pesticides and Their Relationship
        to Environmental Health, Pts. I and II.   Washing-
        ton: U. S. Government Printing Office, 1969.   Con-
        tains realistic recommendations for pesticide con-
        trol based on compromise between health consider-
        ations and desired effect.

4572.   Use of Pesticides.   The United States President's
        Science Advisory Committee Report.   Washington:
        U. S. Government Printing Office, 1963.

4573.   Weber, C. G. et al.   "Effects of Fumigants on Pa-
        per, " Journal of Research, National Bureau of
        Standards 15(3):271, 1935.

4574.   Whitney, W. K.   "Fumigation Hazards as Related to
        the Physical Chemical and Biological Properties of
        Fumigants, " Pest Control 29(7):16, 1961.

4575. World Health Organization. Toxicité des pesticides
      pour l'homme. Geneva: World Health Organiza-
      tion, 1956. Group Report No. 114.

4576. _____. "Select Bibliography on the Toxicity of
      Pesticides to Man and Animals 1953-55," Bulletin
      World Health Organization 16:1219-1241, 1957.

4577. Zavon, M. R. "A Doctor's Prescription for Safety,"
      Pest Control 31(1):16, 1963.

O. HOW TO EXAMINE BINDINGS

4578. Barrow, W. J. "New Device Tests Performance of
      Library Bindings," Book Production Magazine 79:60-
      62, 1964. Describes machine built to simulate in
      a laboratory the effects of age and use on library
      bindings.

4579. "Binders Learn Objectives and Goals of Book Testing
      Programs," Book Production Industry 42(11):66-67,
      1966.

4580. Birrell, Augustine. Three Essays: I, Book Buying;
      II, Book Binding; III, The Office of Literature.
      New York: 1924.

4581. Donnelley, R. R. & Sons. Extra Binding at the Lake-
      side Press. Chicago: Lakeside Press, 1925.

4582. _____. A Rod for the Back of the Binder. Chi-
      cago: Lakeside Press, 1929.

4583. _____. All the Kings Horses and All the Kings
      Men Couldn't Put Humpty-Dumpty Together Again.
      Chicago: Lakeside Press, 1954.

4584. Harrison, T. "What to Look for in a Modern Bind-
      ing," The Book-Collector's Quarterly 13:31-41,
      January-March, 1934.

4585. McNamee, John J. The Essentials of Good Binding.
      A lecture delivered before the Massachusetts Li-
      brary Club, 1896.

ENCYCLOPEDIAS

4586.   Bennett, H. (ed.).   Concise Chemical and Technical
        Dictionary.   New York: Chemical Publishing Co.,
        1962.

4587.   Besterman, Theodore.   Bibliography of Bibliographies.
        Lausanne: Societas Bibliographica, 1965-1966.

4588.   Carter, John.   ABC For Book Collectors.   4th ed.
        rev.   New York: Alfred A. Knopf, 1966.   Con-
        tains a wealth of information on the physical
        makeup of a book, the language of librarianship
        and book collecting and the rewards and pitfalls of
        book buying and selling.

4589.   Day, F. T.   Paper and Printing Manual.   London:
        Trade Journals, 1950.

4590.   The Dictionary of Paper.   New York: American Pulp
        and Paper Association, 1965.   Highly technical
        reference for paper makers.   Contains much infor-
        mation for others.

4591.   Geyer's American Paper Trade Directory.   Contains
        a complete list of all paper, fiber and wood pulp
        mills in the United States and Canada.   vol. 1,
        18-? New York: 1884.
        Title changed: 1885, Geyer's Directory of the
        American Paper Trade.
        1886-1891, Geyer's Reference Directory of the
        Booksellers and Stationers of the United States and
        Canada.
        1893, Geyer's Directory of the American Paper
        Trade.
        1894, Geyer's American Paper Trade Directory.

4592.   Glaister, G. A.   Glossary of the Book.   London:
        George Allen and Unwin, 1960.   Terms used in
        paper making, printing, book binding and publish-
        ing with notes on illuminated manuscripts.

4593.   Grant, Julius.   Hackh's Chemical Dictionary.   4th ed.
        New York: McGraw-Hill, 1969.   American and

British usage.

4594. Hertzberger, Menno. (ed.). Dictionary for the Antiquarian Book-trade. International League of Antiquarian Booksellers, 19-?. In eight languages it
is of inestimable value for perusing foreign cata-
logs.

4595. Labarre, E. J. Dictionary and Encyclopedia of Paper and Paper Making. Amsterdam: Swets &
Zeitlinger, 1967. A technical reference of great
importance. Contains a ten page bibliography on
paper and is indexed in English, French, German,
Dutch, Italian, Spanish and Swedish. Reprinted in
1969.

4596. Lockwood's Directory of the Paper and Allied Trades.
New York: 1875 to present (annually).

4597. Loeber, E. G. Supplement to Labarre's Dictionary
and Encyclopedia of Paper. [4595] Amsterdam:
Swetz and Zeitlinger, 1967.

4598. Lyon, Mary. "Glossary of Craft Terms," Craft Horizons 27:14-15, 1968. A short list of basic craft
terms in English, Spanish, German and French.

4599. _____. "Tools: A Four Language Glossary of
Implements for Craftsmen," Craft Horizons pp. 22-
23, July-August 1969. A short list in four languages (English, Spanish, German and French) of
terms for basic craft tools. Bookbinding and paper
included.

4600. Mayer, Ralph. Dictionary of Art Terms and Techniques. New York: Thomas Y. Crowell Co.,
1970. Includes every major art form of the Western world except architecture with chief emphasis
on materials and methods.

4601. Phillips Paper Trade Directory of the World. London:
S. C. Phillips and Co. Revised frequently.

4602. "Purchasing Guide," Library Journal 93(7), yearly. An
annual listing of over 600 types of products, equipment and service of interest to librarians. Includes a directory of suppliers.

4603. (Technical Dictionary - Leather). Freudenberg, W.
International Dictionary of Leather and Allied Trades.
New York: Springer, 1968. Technical terms in
Dutch, English, French, Italian, Spanish.

4604. Technical Studies in the Field of Fine Arts. 10 vols.
Cambridge, Mass.: Harvard University Press,
1932-1942. This important, long out-of-print,
reference is now available on microfilm from Intermuseum Conservation Association, Allen Art Bld.,

Oberlin, Ohio 44074.
4605. Wheelwright, W. B. Paper Trade Terms: A Glossary for the Allied Trades. Boston: Callaway
Associates, 1947. Illustrated.

ABSTRACTS

4606. "Abstracts, " Technical Studies in the Field of the
Fine Arts. Cambridge, Mass. : Harvard Press,
1932-1942.
4607. Abstracts of the Technical Literature on Archaeology
and the Fine Arts. London: International Institute
for the Conservation of Historic and Artistic Works,
1955 to 1966. (IIC Abstracts) Includes author and
subject indices.
4608. APCA Abstracts. Pittsburgh, Pa. : Air Pollution
Control Association, in cooperation with the U. S.
Public Health Service and the Library of Congress,
1956 to present.
4609. Art and Archaeology Technical Abstracts. (Formerly
IIC Abstracts) New York: Institute of Fine Arts,
New York University, 1966 to present.
4610. Gettens, R. J. and Bertha M. Usilton. Abstracts of
Technical Studies in Art and Archaeology. Washington: Freer Gallery of Art, 1955. Information
on world literature from 1943 to 1952. Includes
sections on paper, papyrus, books, leather, parchment, ink, adhesives, solvents, agencies of deterioration, protection and fire prevention.
4611. Preservation from Deterioration Abstracts. Washington: Prevention of Deterioration Center, Division
of Chemistry and Chemical Technology, National
Academy of Sciences, National Research Council,
1946 to 1961-62.

BIBLIOGRAPHIES

GENERAL

4612. Beerstecher, Louise. A Reading List on Library
       Buildings. Boston: Bulletin of Bibliography Pam-
       phlet No. 5, 1898.
4613. Besterman, Theodore. A World Bibliography of Bibli-
       ographies. Lausanne: Societas Bibliographica,
       1965, 1966. Five volumes of bibliographical cata-
       logs, calendars, abstracts, digests, indexes, etc.
4614. Bibliography on Magnetic Recording Systems. Wash-
       ington: U. S. Department of Commerce, 1963.
       Office of Technical Services SB-471, revised.
4615. Blanchet, Jules Adrien. Sigillography Francaise.
       Paris: Académie des Inscriptions et Belles Let-
       tres, 1962.
4616. Blanck, Jacob. Bibliography in America. New Haven:
       Yale University Press, 19--. Includes the Bibliog-
       raphical Society of America's key to identification
       of early binders cloths.
4617. Books and Pamphlets on Lighting. Pretoria: South
       African Council for Scientific and Industrial Re-
       search, 1954.
4618. (Buildings). Brief List of References on Library
       Buildings, Their Design and Construction. Wash-
       ington: Library of Congress, 1932.
4619. (Buildings). Recent Books and Periodical Articles on
       Library Architecture. Washington: Library of
       Congress, 1947.
4620. Burr, Nelson R. Safeguarding Our Cultural Heritage,
       a Bibliography on the Protection of Museums, Works
       of Art, Monuments, Archives and Libraries in Time
       of War. Washington: U. S. Library of Congress,
       General Reference and Bibliography Division, 1952.
4621. Catalogue of Books Printed in the Fifteenth Century.
       London: British Museum, 1908. The first volume
       was printed in 1908 and it is still in progress.
       An indispensable reference for incunabula. First
       eight volumes reprinted with corrections in 1963.
4622. Deuel, Leo. Testaments of Time. New York: Al-
       fred A. Knopf, 1965. Includes a lengthy bibliog-
       raphy of sources of information on early records.
4623. Disc Recording Apparatus. Adelaide: Public Library
       of South Australia, 1956.

4624. Esdaile, A. J. K. A Student Manual of Bibliography, rev. Roy Stokes, 3d rev. ed. London: George Allen & Unwin and Library Association, 1954.

4625. Films and Film Strips on Forestry. Nocogdoches, Texas: Austin State College, 1965. Lists films on paper and paper utilization.

4626. Fire Prevention and Extinction: A Reference List. Boston: Public Library, 1946.

4627. Gandilhow, René. Bibliographie de la Sigillographie Française. Paris: 1955.

4628. Gesamtkatalog der Wiegendrucke. Leipzig: 1925, etc. This exhaustive catalog of 15th century printed books reached volume eight (the letter F) in 1940. It is edited by Germans but with assistance from incunabulists all over the world. Text in German. Arranged by authors.

4629. Godlove, I. H. Intersociety Color Council. Bibliography on Color. Cleveland: Braden-Sulphin Ink Co., 1957.

4630. Howard, C. L. A Descriptive Bibliography of the Most Important Books in the English Language Relating to the Art and History of Engraving, 1912-1913. Only 350 copies printed. The author's copy containing extensive notes and additions is in the Library of Congress.

4631. Grenberg, Yurili. Bibliographic Index of Russian Literature on Restoration and Conservation. Moscow: Central Laboratory of Restoration and Conservation of Works of Art, 1961-1965. 2467 abstracts of articles from the Russian literature including paintings, drawings, printed books, manuscripts, sculpture, etc.

4632. Hain, Ludwig. Repertorium Bibliographicum. 2 vols. 1826-1838. (Reprinted) An alphabetical list by author of 16,311 books printed before 1501. A convenient first reference for incunabula. [See also 4633.]

4633. Hain, (supplements to). Prepared by Copinger, W. A. 3 vols, 1895-1902. K. Burger published indices to Hain in 1891 and D. Reichling did a series of appendices beginning in 1905.

4634. Hills, T. H. A Selected Annotated Bibliography of the Humid Tropics. Montreal: International Geographical Union, 1960.

4635. Ivory: A Selected List of References. Washington: Library of Congress, 1919. Supplemented in 1946.

4636. Kirk, Albert. A Selected List of Graphic Arts Liter-
       ature, Books and Periodicals. London: British
       Federation of Master Printers, 1948.
4637. A List of Books and Pamphlets in the National Art
       Gallery South Kensington Museum Illustrating Seals.
       London: 1886.
4638. A List of References of Archives and Their Care in
       the United States. Washington: Library of Con-
       gress, 1915.
4639. The Literature of Library Technical Services. Ur-
       bana, Ill.: University of Illinois Library School,
       1960. Forty-eight page survey of publications in
       the fields of interest of the Resources and Techni-
       cal Services Division of the school.
4640. Perrella, Renato. Bibliographia delle Pubblicazioni
       Italiane Relative all Archivistica. Roma, 1963.
       Confined to works published in Italy and primarily
       of interest to archivists, but it contains a section
       on conservation and restoration of archives as
       practiced in Italy.
4641. Plastics. Arlington, Va.: Armed Services Technical
       Information Agency, 1962.
4642. (Plastics). Books on Plastics. Boston: Boston Pub-
       lic Library, 1946.
4643. _____ . Select List of Books on Plastics, 1940-
       1954. London: Science Library, 1955. Biblio-
       graphical Series Nos. 732-733.
4644. Plumbe, Wilfred. Storage and Preservation of Books,
       Periodicals and Newspapers in Tropical Climates.
       Paris: UNESCO, 1964. A select bibliography.
4645. Publications on the Subjects of Fire Prevention. Bos-
       ton: National Fire Protection Association, updated
       frequently.
4646. Rath, F. L. and M. Rogers. NYSA Selective Guide
       to Historic Preservation. Cooperstown, N.Y.:
       New York State Historical Association, 1966. New
       edition 1968. An excellent list of sources of infor-
       mation about the many aspects of historic preser-
       vation. Many hundreds of references in seven
       general categories.
4647. [No entry.]
4648. Rufsvold, M. and C. Guss. Guides to Newer Educa-
       tional Media. Chicago: American Library Asso-
       ciation, 1967. A bibliography of bibliographies on
       films, tapes, etc. including some on conservation
       subjects.

4649. Safeguarding Our Cultural Heritage.   Washington: U. S.
      Government Printing Office, 1952.   A bibliography
      on the protection of museums, works of art, monu-
      ments, archives, and libraries in time of war.
      Compiled by Nelson R. Burr.
4650. A Selected List of References on the Administration
      and Care of Public Archives in the United States.
      Washington: Library of Congress, 1934.
4651. Select List of References on the Prevention of Fire.
      Washington: Library of Congress, 1912.
4652. Select List of References on Wood Preservation.
      Washington: Library of Congress, 1911.   (aug-
      mented 1918)
4653. Spencer, K. S.   High-fidelity Sound Reproduction.
      London: Library Association, 1956.
4654. _____ .   High-fidelity: A Bibliography of Sound
      Reproduction.   London, 1958.
4655. Weitenkampf, Frank.   "List of Works in the New York
      Public Library Relating to Prints and Their Pro-
      duction, " Bulletin 19:847-935 and 959-1002, 1915.
      New York Public Library.   A bibliography of ap-
      proximately 2400 entries on the literature of print
      making processes, the applications of the repro-
      ductive arts, previous bibliographies, the care of
      prints, the history of print making, artists, etc.
      Includes the photo-mechanical processes.
4656. _____ .   Prints and Their Production.   New York:
      N. Y. Public Library, 1916.   A list of 2750 refer-
      ences in the New York Public Library.   Supple-
      mented in 1917 with 100 items.

ADHESIVES

4657. (adhesives for book repair).   American Archivist 1:3,
      1938 and 13:318, 1950.
4658. Adhesives.   Adelaide, Australia: Public Library of
      South Australia, 1958.
4659. Books on the Manufacture of Adhesives, 1920-1936.
      London: Science Library, 1937.   Bibliographical
      Series No. 339.
4660. List of Publications on Glue and Plywood.   Washing-
      ton: U. S. Department of Agriculture, 1945.
4661. Pressure Sensitive Adhesives.   Adelaide: Public Li-
      brary of South Australia, 1959.
4662. Smith, Lee T. and R. M. Hamilton.   "Starch Adhe-
      sives, " Chemical Engineering News 22, 1944.   A

review. Bibliography of one hundred forty-seven
references.

4663. Weiner, Jack and Lillian Roth. Adhesives. Appleton,
Wis.: Institute of Paper Chemistry. Bibliographic
Series No. 205. Four volumes. General Application, 1963. Paper, 1963. Boards, plastics, textiles, 1964. Tapes and machinery, 1964.

AIR POLLUTION

4664. Air Conditioning: Catalog of Technical Reports. Washington: U.S. Department of Commerce, Office of
Technical Services, 1958.

4665. Air Pollution Publications - A Selected Bibliography,
1955-1963. Washington: U.S. Department of
Health, Education and Welfare, 1963. rev. 1964.
Excellent source of titles subdivided under eleven
major headings. Author indexed.

4666. Air Pollution Publications - A Selected Bibliography,
1963-1966. Washington: U.S. Department of
Health, Education and Welfare, 1966. Contains
approximately 900 entries including some inadvert-
ently omitted from the 1955-63 bibliography on
same subject by HEW's Public Health Service.

4667. Air Pollution Study: Technical Literature Abstracts.
Chicago: Department of Smoke Inspection and
Abatement, 1940.

4668. Bibliography on Air Pollution and Purification. Wash-
ington: U.S. Department of Commerce, 1963.
Office of Technical Services SB-448. Revised with
Supplement 1.

4669. Davenport, S. J. and G. G. Morgan. Air Pollution:
A Bibliography. Washington: Bureau of Mines,
1954. Bulletin No. 537. 3,902 titles.

4670. Gibson, Jack R. et al. The Air Pollution Bibliography. Washington: Library of Congress, 1957-
1959. 1,550 items.

4671. Grogan, D. J. Clean Air. London: Library Association, 1956. Special Subject List No. 8.

4672. Heiman, H. (and others). Biological Aspects of Air
Pollution: An Annotated Bibliography. Washington:
U.S. Public Health Service, 1950.

4673. Kingsley, K. "Air Pollution Review, 1956-1957,"
Industrial Engineering Chemistry 50, 1958. 261
references.

4674. Micrometeorology, Aerosols and Air Pollution Bibliography. Washington: U. S. Library of Congress, 1963.

4675. Murk, Janet B. "Sources of Air Pollution Literature," Industrial Engineering Chemistry 47, 1955.

4676. Richardson, Marie S. "Bibliography on Air and Water Pollution," Special Libraries 57, 1966.

BOOKS AND RELATED SUBJECTS

4677. "Bibliography of Book Production," Book Production Magazine 78:76a, 1963.

4678. Bookbinding Bibliography in Edith Diehl's Bookbinding, Its Background and Technique. New York: Rinehart & Co., 1946.

4679. Books about modern bookmaking and in Publisher's Weekly which occasionally has articles on present day bookmaking practices including binding, etc.

4680. Catalogue of Works on Printing, Bookbinding, Papermaking and Related Industries. Leicester: Municipal Library, 1927.

4681. Course on the History of Bookbinding: The Literature of Bookbinding. Oxford: Bodleian Library, 1960.

4682. Dühmert, Anneliese. Buchpflege. Stuttgart: Max Hettler, 1964. A bibliography of over two thousand items in several languages on the care and repair of bindings.

4683. Freer, Percy. Bibliography on Modern Book Production. Johannesburg: Witwaterstrand University, 1954.

4684. Hobson, A. R. A. The Literature of Bookbinding. London: National Book League, 1954.

4685. Hobson, G. D. "Books on Bookbinding," Book Collector's Quarterly 7:70-84, 1932. A well annotated list.

4686. Kyriss, Ernst. Research in Bookbinding. Lexington: University of Kentucky Library, 1951. Fifty titles in bibliography.

4687. Lehmann-Haupt, H. One Hundred Books About Bookmaking. New York: Columbia University Press, 1949.

4688. Library Literature (1921-), "Books--Conservation and Restoration," A Bibliography.

4689. List of Books and Articles Relating to Bookbinding to be Found in the Library. New York: Grolier Club, 1907.

4690. London College of Printing Library Book List: Book-
       binding and Warehouse Work. London: College of
       Printing, 1959. A guide to literature available up
       to 1957 at the College of Printing, National Book
       League, and St. Bride Printing Library.

4691. McMurtrie, Douglas. The Book. New York: Oxford
       University Press, 1957. Includes selective bibliog-
       raphies on all phases of the book and book making.

4692. Mejer, Wolfgang. Bibliographie der Buchbindereiliter-
       atur. Leipzig: Verlag K. Hiersemann, 1925.
       Lists 2,691 titles in seven languages on binding
       history and technique; the enemies of books; and
       bookbinding materials.

4693. _____. Erganzungsband, 1924-1932. Leipzig:
       1933. This supplement by Herman Herbst to
       Mejer's 1925 list adds 2,224 titles to the original
       2691.

4694. Mullins, J. D. Bibliography: or Books about Books,
       Their Making, etc. Birmingham: Free Library,
       1884.

4695. Nelson, C. A. Catalog Raisonnée: Works on Book-
       binding--from the Collection of Samuel Putnam
       Avery. New York: Columbia University Library,
       1903.

4696. Payne, John R. "An Annotated List of Works on Fine
       Bindings," American Book Collector 16(1), 1967.
       A list of works on fine bindings held by the North
       Texas State University plus a check list of about
       300 works on fine bindings identified by compiler
       through secondary sources.

4697. Peddie, R. A. Catalogue of Works on Practical
       Printing, Processes of Illustration and Bookbinding.
       London: St. Bride Foundation, 1911.

4698. Pratt, R. D. A Thousand Books on Books. London:
       The Merrythought Press, 1967. A selection of
       English books on book-making, book-selling.

4699. Prideaux, Sarah Treverbian. "A Bibliography of
       Bookbinding," The Library First Series, 4:15-24;
       50-56; 90-95, 1892.

4700. _____. An Historical Sketch of Bookbinding. Lon-
       don: Lawrence & Bullen, 1893. Excellent bibliog-
       raphy of early French, German and English sources.
       She contends that marbled paper is of Turkish
       origin.

4701. Selected List of Books on Printing, Book Illustration
       and Bookbinding. Sydney: Public Library of New
       South Wales, 1919.

4702. Simoni, P. K. Opyt Shornika Svedenni po Istori i
Tekhnike Knigoperepletnogo Khudozkestva ma Rusi.
Moscow: 1903. An attempt at a corpus of source
materials relating to the history and technique of
the art of bookbinding in Russia.

4703. St. Bride Foundation Institute. Catalogue of the periodicals relating to printing and allied subjects in
the technical library of the St. Bride Institute with
an introduction by Ellic Howe. London: St. Bride
Institute, 1951. This publication lists twenty-seven
periodicals which relate wholly or partly to bookbinding.

4704. Thoinan, Ernest. Les Reliures Francais, 1500-1800.
Paris: Paul, Huard & Guillemin, 1893. An annotated and critical biography of binders in Renaissance France together with a study of bookbinding styles and a history of the community of
binders and gold toolers.

4705. Walker, Violet. Catalogue of Books on Printing--
Bookbinding, Papermaking, Lithography, Photo-en-
graving. Nottingham: Public Library, 1930.

4706. Walton, R. P. "Causes and Prevention of Deterioration in Book Materials, " Bulletin 33(4), 1929.
New York Public Library. A compendium of much
of the published data (1858-1929) on book preservation, deterioration of leather, leather preservation recipes, and acidity in leather. Out of date
but still important.

INK

4707. Books on Ink 1916-1936. London: Science Library,
1937. Bibliographical Series No. 321.

4708. Gamble, W. B. and H. M. Lydenberg. "Chemistry
and Manufacture of Writing and Printing Inks, "
Bulletin 29:579-591; 625-677; 706-741, 1925. New
York Public Library. A list of 2,167 references,
728 of which are books and articles in journals and
the remaining 1,439 are American and European
patents. The patents are subject indexed.

4709. Manufacture of Writing Inks 1927-1936. London: Science Library, 1937. Bibliographical Series No.
335.

4710. A Select List of References on Printing Machinery
and Printing Inks. Washington: Library of Congress, 1924.

4711. Selected Books on Paints, Inks, Glues and Varnishes.
       Sydney: Public Library of New South Wales, 1919.

LEATHER

4712. Bibliography on Leather, Hides and Shoes. Washing-
       ton: U. S. Department of Commerce, 1961. Office
       of Technical Services SB-483.
4713. Horigan, F. D. and R. S. Cary. The Mycology of
       Leather: A Bibliography. Philadelphia: QM Re-
       search and Development Laboratories, 1948. The
       fungi found in leather.
4714. Leather and the Leather Industry: A List of Recent
       Books. Washington: Library of Congress, 1940.
4715. Leather and Tanning Industry; List of Works Avail-
       able. Bermondsey, Eng. : Public Library, 1952.
4716. List of References on the Leather Industry. Washing-
       ton: Library of Congress, 1918. Includes history,
       production, uses, chemistry and economics.
4717. List of References on Tanning Materials. Washington:
       Library of Congress, 1920.
4718. Parchment. London: Science Library, 1938. Biblio-
       graphical Series No. 425. Excludes references to
       vegetable parchment.

PAPER

4719. (Aging and Preservation of Paper). Venter, J. S. M.
       (C. S. I. R.) Development Study, U. D. C. 676. 33. 017 /
       019. Pretoria, South Africa: September 1966.
       146 references with a general description complete
       to 1965.
4720. Banks, Paul N. An Annotated Reading List of the
       Most Important Current Material on the Chemical
       Deterioration and the Chemical and Physical Pres-
       ervation of Paper. Chicago: Newberry Library,
       1965.
4721. Bibliography on Paper. Washington: U. S. Depart-
       ment of Commerce, 1963. Office of Technical
       Services SB 515.
4722. Books on Paper-making, 1929-1939. London: Sci-
       ence Library, 1940. Bibliographical Series No.
       523.
4723. Byrne, Jerry and Jack Weiner. Permanence. Apple-
       ton, Wis. : Institute of Paper Chemistry, 1964.

The Institute of Paper Chemistry's paper bibliography.

4724. Calkin, J. B. Microscopy of Paper. Atlanta: Technical Asso. of the Pulp and Paper Industry, 1937. TAPPI Special Bibliographic Series No. 1.

4725. Dumercy, Charles. Bibliographie de la Papeterie. Bruxelles: 1888. Privately printed, only 103 copies made.

4726. Graff, J. H. Microscopy of Pulp and Papers. Appleton, Wis.: Institute of Paper Chemistry, 1952. Bibliographic Series No. 177.

4727. Grove, L. E. "Conservation of Paper," Museum News 42:15-20, 1963. Includes bibliography.

4728. Hunter, Dard. Hand Made Paper and Its Watermarks: A Bibliography. New York: Technical Association of the Pulp and Paper Industry, 1917.

4729. _____. Handmade Paper and Its Watermarks: A Bibliography. New York: Burt Franklin, 1968. A must in any research on early tests on paper. Reprint of 1917 edition.

4730. _____. The Literature of Papermaking, 1390-1800. Chillicothe, Ohio: The Mountain House Press, 1925.

4731. _____. Literature of Papermaking: 1390-1800. New York: Burt Franklin, 1969. Reprint of the 1925 edition. This and Hunter's Handmade Paper and Its Watermarks must be points of departure on any search for early titles on paper.

4732. Kantrowitz, Morris; Ernest W. Spencer, and Robert H. Simmons. Permanence and Durability of Paper, an Annotated Bibliography of the Technical Literature from 1885 A.D. to 1939 A.D. Washington: U.S. Government Printing Office, 1940. Division of Tests and Technical Control, Technical Bulletin, No. 22.

4733. A List of References on the Repair and Restoration of Manuscripts and Documents. Washington: Library of Congress, 1924.

4734. Lydenberg, Harry Miller. "Bibliography of Paper Deterioration," Paper 8:12-13, 1918.

4735. Macek, Karel (and others). Bibliography of Paper Chromatography 1957-1960. Prague: Academy of Sciences, 1962.

4736. Minogue, A. E. The Repair and Preservation of Records. Bulletin of the National Archives No. 5. Washington: 1943. Includes a bibliography on causes and prevention of deterioration of paper, leather and bindings.

4737. Overton, John. Paper for Book Production. A Bib-
       liography. London: National Book League, 1955.
       The Book No. 3.

4738. Padfield, Tim. The Deterioration of Cellulose: A
       Literature Review. London: Victoria and Albert
       Museum, 1965. A paper presented to 1965 Wash-
       ington Meeting of ICOM Committee for Museum
       Laboratories. Lengthy bibliography keyed to the
       text.

4739. "Paper, Bibliography, " American Archivist 4:50, 1941
       and 10:187, 1947.

4740. Paper in Its Relation to Printing. Appleton, Wis. :
       The Institute of Paper Chemistry, 1962. Almost
       2,000 references on paper in the world of books.

4741. Permanence of Paper, A Bibliography. Appleton,
       Wis. : The Institute of Paper Chemistry, 1964.
       Bibliography Series 213. Lists 470 references to
       permanence with short abstracts and criticisms,
       complete to 1962.

4742. "Repair Bibliography, " American Archivist 1:22, 59,
       61, 70, 77, 1938.

4743. Santucci, L. "Report on Paper Stability, " Bollettino
       dell Istituto di Patologia del Libro 22:67-104,
       1963. A survey of literature (120 references), a
       discussion of the problem and some experimental
       contributions.

4744. Schlosser, Leonard B. "Books on the History of Pa-
       per Making, " Guild of Book Workers Journal 8(1):
       20-23, 1969. Describes 54 old and rare volumes
       from the author's collection.

4745. Surface, H. E. United States Government Publica-
       tions Pertaining to Pulp and Paper. New York:
       1910. Reprinted from Paper, October 4, 1916.
       [4746]

4746. Surface, H. E. "U. S. Government Publications Per-
       taining to Pulp and Paper, " Paper 19(4), 1916.

4747. Weiner, Jack. Bibliography of Papermaking, 1951-
       1955. Atlanta: Technical Association of the Pulp
       and Paper Industry, 1957.

4748. _____ and Lillian Roth. Protective and Decorative
       Coatings for Paper. Appleton, Wis. : Institute of
       Paper Chemistry, 1962. Bibliographic Series No.
       199.

4749. West, C. J. Bibliography of Paper Making and United
       States Patents on Paper Making and Related Sub-
       jects, 1931-1933. Atlanta: Technical Association

of the Pulp and Paper Industry, 1932-34.
4750. _____. Bibliography of Pulp and Paper Making. 1900-1928. New York: Lockwood Trade Journal Co., 1928.
4751. _____. Papermaking Materials. Appleton, Wis.: Institute of Paper Chemistry, 1949-1950. Bibliographic Series Nos. 171 and 176, 1949-1950.
4752. _____. Paper Testing. Appleton, Wis.: Institute of Paper Chemistry, 1961. Bibliographic Series No. 139. I, Strength testing, 1961; II, Properties, 1943; III, Optical Properties, 1943.
4753. _____. Reading List on Papermaking Materials. New York: Lockwood Trade Journal Co., 1928.
4754. _____. Sizing of Paper. Appleton, Wis.: Institute of Paper Chemistry, 1948. Bibliographic Series No. 165.

PEST CONTROL

4755. Action of High Frequency Fields on Insects and Bacteria. London: Science Library, 1949. Bibliographical Series No. 676.
4756. Bibliography on Pest Control. Washington: U.S. Department of Commerce, 1962. Office of Technical Services SB-486.
4757. Carruthers, R. H. and H. B. Weiss. "Insect Pests of Books," Bulletin 40:829-836, 985-995, 1049-1063, 1936. New York Public Library. 493 entries from classical times to 20th century.
4758. Colcord, M.; I. L. Hawes, and J. Carabelli. Check List of Publications on Entomology Issued by the U.S. Department of Agriculture Through 1927. Washington: U.S. Department of Agriculture, 1930.
4759. Hawes, Ina L. Bibliography of the Effect of Light on Insects. Washington: U.S. Department of Agriculture, 1935.
4760. Horigan, F. D. and F. H. Cozzi. The Persistency of Insecticidal Residues on Various Surfaces. Philadelphia: QM Research and Development Laboratories, 1952. Technical Library Bibliographic Series No. 23.
4761. _____ and C. R. Sage. Fungal Growth on Painted Surfaces: A Bibliography. Philadelphia: QM Research and Development Laboratories, 1947. Technical Library, Bibliographic Series No. 1.

4762.   ___ : The Mycology of Leather: A Bibliography.
            Philadelphia: QM Research and Development Labor-
            atories, 1948. Technical Library Bibliographic
            Series No. 4.
4763.   ___ . The Technology of Fungi, Mold and Mil-
            dew: A Literature and Patent Survey. Philadel-
            phia: QM Research and Development Laboratories,
            1950. Technical Library, 1950.
4764.   Houlbert, C. V. Les Insectes Ennemis des Livres.
            Paris: Picardetfils, 1903. Includes a bibliography
            of ninety-four references (1724-1902) to insects
            and books as well as footnote references in body
            of text.
4765.   List of Publications of the Division of Insecticide In-
            vestigations. Washington: U. S. Department of
            Agriculture, 1947. Irregular supplements have
            been issued.
4766.   References on Animals Injurious to Books. London:
            Science Library, 1938. Bibliographical Series No.
            377.
4767.   "Select Bibliography on the Toxicity of Pesticides to
            Man and Animals 1953-1955, " Bulletin World Health
            Organization 16:1219-1241, 1957.
4768.   Snyder, T. E. Bibliography of Termites. Washing-
            ton: Smithsonian Institution, 1956.

PERIODICALS

INTERNATIONAL

4769.   Art and Archaeology Technical Abstracts. New York:
            Institute of Fine Arts, 1966+. Quarterly publication
            formerly appeared as IIC Abstracts, London. Cov-
            ers the whole field of technical literature.
4770.   ICOM News, Bi-monthly. International Council of
            Museums, Maison de l'Unesco, 6, rue Franklin,
            Paris XVIe, France. 1948+
4771.   IIC News. Membership. London: International In-
            stitute for Conservation, 608 Grand Buildings,
            Trafalgar Square. 1960-1969 as a twice yearly
            hand duplicated newssheet. From 1970 on as part
            of Studies in Conservation.

4772. International Bookbinder. Washington: International
      Brotherhood of Bookbinders of North America,
      1910 to 1942. This was devoted to the interest of
      bookbinders and women bindery workers in the
      United States and Canada.
4773. International Lighting Review. Amsterdam, The Neth-
      erlands.
4774. Journal of International Association of Leather Trades
      Chemists. London: International Association of
      Leather Trades Chemists.
4775. Museum. Quarterly. UNESCO, 6 rue Franklin,
      Paris XVIe, France or UNESCO, Publications
      Center, 801 Third Avenue, New York, N.Y. 10022.
      Surveys the activities and means of research in
      museography. Much of interest to librarians and
      archivists. 1948+
4776. Restaurator: International Journal for the Preserva-
      tion of Library and Archival Material. Published
      by Restaurator Press, Copenhagen. 1969+. Twice
      annually with occasional supplements.
4777. Studies in Conservation. The quarterly journal of the
      International Institute for Conservation, 608 Grand
      Buildings, Trafalgar Square, London. 1956+
4778. UNESCO Bulletin for Libraries. UNESCO, Place de
      Fontenoy, Paris VII. Many articles on preserving
      books and other library materials.

      AMERICAN

4779. American Archivist. The quarterly journal of the So-
      ciety of American Archivists. 1938+
4780. American Book Collector. Published monthly (except
      July and August) since 1949. Publication office
      1822 School Street, Chicago, Ill. 60657. Contains
      occasional articles on conservation.
4781. American Leather Chemists Association Journal.
      American Leather Chemists Association, Easton,
      Pa.
4782. Annual Report of the Council on Library Resources,
      Inc. Council on Library Resources, 1025 Con-
      necticut Ave., N.W., Washington, D.C. Much
      information on preservation studies supported by
      the council.
4783. Bookbinding Magazine. New York, 1925 to 1936.
      This was continued as Bookbinding and Book Pro-
      duction, 1936 to 1954.

4784. Bookbinding and Book Production. 1936 to 1954.
         This was continued as Book Production Magazine.
4785. Book Production Magazine. 1955 to 1965. This was
         continued as Book Production Industry.
4786. Book Production Industry, 1965 to present.
4787. Boston Museum of Fine Arts, Bulletin. Museum of
         Fine Arts, Boston, Mass.
4788. Bulletin of the American Group, International Institute
         for Conservation. Twice Year. Conservation Cen-
         ter, Institute of Fine Arts, New York University.
4789. Bulletin of the New York Public Library. Discont. 1972.
4790. Building Research. Building Research Institute, 1725
         DeSales Street, N. W., Washington, D. C. 20036.
         1964 + bi-monthly.
4791. Chemical Abstracts. American Chemical Society,
         Washington, D. C.
4791a. College and Research Libraries. Chicago: American
         Library Association and Association of College and
         Research Libraries. Includes occasional articles
         on preservation.
4792. Colophon: A Quarterly for Bookmen. Emphasized
         collected and collectable books, first editions, fine
         printing, incunabula, Americana, bibliography and
         manuscripts. Volumes of the first and final series
         were composed of individual signatures separately
         printed by the finest presses of the day. New
         York, 1930-1940.
         Series 1: Vols. 1-5 (i. e. pts. 1-20),   1930-1935
                                                  (all publ.).
         Series 2: Vols. 1-3 /# 4,   1935-1938
                                                  (all publ.).
         Series 3: Nos. 1-4,   1939-1940
                                                  (all and
                                                  last publ.).
4793. Craft Horizons. American Craftsman's Council, 16
         East 52nd Street, New York, N. Y. 10022.
4794. The Dolphin: A Journal of the Making of Books. No.
         1-4. New York: Limited Editions Club, 1933-
         1941. 4 nos. in 6. No. 3, 1938 is a history of
         printed books.
4795. Forest Products Journal. Forest Products Research
         Society, Madison, Wis.
4796. Guild of Book Workers Journal. Published three
         times a year by the Guild of Book Workers, 1059,
         3rd Avenue, New York, N. Y.
4797. Hiscox, G. D. (ed.). Henley's 20th Century Book of
         Formulas, Processes and Trade Secrets. New

York: Norman W. Henley Publishing Co.   Periodically revised.

4798. Historic Preservation. Washington: National Trust for Historic Preservation. 1948+. A quarterly journal primarily concerned with architectural preservation but some articles are of interest to librarians.

4799. History News. Nashville, Tenn.: American Association for State and Local History. A monthly journal containing frequent references to conservation and restoration primarily architectural.

4800. Intermuseum Conservation Association Bulletin. Oberlin, Ohio. Occasional newsletter of brief but interesting and useful information.

4801. Journal of the Air Pollution Control Association. Air Pollution Control Association, 4400 Fifth Avenue, New York, N. Y.

4802. Journal of Research of the National Bureau of Standards. U. S. Government Printing Office, Washington.

4803. The Library Binder. Boston: The Library Binding Institute. This semi-annual publication of the LBI has much interest to the library profession as well as to its membership - high caliber commercial binderies throughout the United States and Canada. 1953-1971. Continued as The Library Scene.

4804. Library of Congress Information Bulletin. Beginning with vol. 29, No. 22, June 1970, will include from time to time a "preservation supplement" on news items, etc. relating to the conservation of books and documents.

4805. Library Journal. 1876 to present. New York. R. R. Bowker Co. Nearly every number in early issues had something on book binding. Modern issues include many articles on conservation of library materials.

4806. Library Quarterly. University of Chicago Press. A journal of investigation and discussion in the field of library science.

4807. Library Resources and Technical Services. Richmond, Virginia. American Library Association. This quarterly official publication of the Resources and Technical Services Division of the ALA contains frequent information of conservation interest.

4808. Library Scene. Boston: The Library Binding Institute, Vol. I no. 1, 1972 onward twice yearly.

4809. Library Technology Reports. Chicago: American
       Library Association. Bi-monthly coverage by Li-
       brary Technology Program of equipment and sys-
       tems of interest to librarians.
4810. Library Trends. Published by Graduate School of
       Library Science, University of Illinois, Urbana,
       Ill.
4811. Lockwood's Directory of the Paper and Allied Trades.
       1875 to present annually.
4812. Manuscripts. Manuscript Society quarterly, 1023
       Amherst Drive, Tyler, Texas 75701.
4813. Museum News. Journal of the American Association
       of Museums, Washington, D. C. Published monthly,
       September through June. Has frequent articles on
       conservation.
4814. The Paper Maker. First published in Kalamazoo,
       Mich. by the Paper Makers Chemical Corporation
       (1932-36) and the Hercules Powder Company (1936-
       40), thereafter by the Hercules Powder Company
       at Wilmington, Del. Frequency varies, currently
       issued biannually.
4815. Paper Trade Journal. New York: Lockwood Trade
       Journal Co. , 1872-? Weekly.
4816. The Paper World. A monthly journal of information,
       discussion and recital as to paper. 1880-1898.
       Holyoke, Mass.
4817. Philadelphia Museum of Art, Bulletin. Philadelphia
       Museum of Art, Philadelphia, Pa.
4818. Preservation News. National Trust for Historic Pres-
       ervation, 815 - 17th St. , N. W. , Washington, D. C.
       20006. Monthly.
4819. Print Connoisseur. Was devoted exclusively to prints
       and drawings. For 13 years it illustrated virtually
       every category of print: aquatint, etching, litho-
       graphy, pencil drawings, mezzotint, drypoint, wood
       engraving, and woodcut. New York, 1920-1932.
4820. Prologue. The journal of the National Archives,
       General Services Administration, Washington, D. C.
       20408. Published three times yearly. Occasional
       articles of conservation interest.
4821. Special Libraries. Special Libraries Association, New
       York. 1910 + . Includes occasional articles on
       preservation.
4822. Tappi. Technical Association of the Pulp and Paper
       Industry, Atlanta, Georgia. Many important tech-
       nical articles on paper, paper durability, testing,
       etc.

4823. <u>Technical Studies in the Field of the Fine Arts</u>. Cambridge, Mass. : Fogg Art Museum. Quarterly from
1932 to 1942. Original contributions included articles on paper, adhesives, vellum, ink, leather,
conservation techniques, etc. Also abstracted over
450 articles in other journals. Now available on
microfilm from Intermuseum Conservation Asso. ,
Oberlin, Ohio.

4824. <u>Textile Museum Journal</u>. Textile Museum, Washington, D. C.

4825. <u>U. S. National Museum, Bulletin</u>. Smithsonian Institution, Washington, D. C.

4826. <u>Wilson Library Bulletin</u>. Published monthly by the
H. W. Wilson Company, 950 University Ave. ,
Bronx, New York 10452. Indexed in <u>Readers
Guide</u> and <u>Library Literature</u> and abstracted in <u>Li-
brary Science Abstracts</u>.

BRITISH

4827. <u>Annual Reports of the Master Bookbinders Association</u>.
London. 19th century.

4828. <u>Atmospheric Environment</u>. London: Pergamon Press,
bimonthly. This journal deals with all aspects of
air pollution research including control and measurement of emissions, detection and effects of emissions and transport and modification of pollutants.

4829. <u>Bibliographica</u>. Emphasized illuminated manuscripts
and early printed books of England. The journal
was particularly noted for its studies on rare
books, woodcuts, bindings, and the early book
trade. Vols. 1-3 (all pub.). London, 1895-1897.

4830. <u>The Bibliographical Journal</u>. Worcester College, Oxford, England.

4831. <u>The Bookbinder</u>. London, 1887 to 1890. A trade
journal continued as the <u>British Bookmaker</u>. [4836]

4832. <u>Bookbinders' Trade Circular</u>. London. October 1850
to November 1877. This was the organ of the
London Consolidated Society of Journeymen Bookbinders.

4833. <u>Bookbinding Trades Journal</u>. Manchester, 1910 to
1912.

4834. <u>The Book Collector</u>. A series commencing in 1952,
successor to <u>The Book Handbook</u> published between
1947-1951. Contains frequent articles on book
preservation, bindings and related subjects.

4835. The Book Handbook, vol. 1, nos. 1-9 and vol. 2,
       nos. 1-4, 1947-1951. (All published.) This jour-
       nal directly preceeded The Book Collector into
       which it was incorporated.
4836. British Bookmaker. 1890 to 1894. This was absorbed
       by the British Printer in 1894.
4837. The British Museum Quarterly. Published by Trustees
       of British Museum. Occasional articles on books,
       prints and maps.
4838. Ex Libris Society Journal. The journal presented de-
       tailed studies of owners, libraries, designs, mot-
       toes, and methods of production and reproduction
       of bookplates. Vols. 1-18 (all publ.). London,
       1891-1908.
4839. Forensic Science Society Journal. Forensic Science
       Society, Harrogate, Yorkshire, England.
4840. IIC (UK Group) Reports of Meetings. Mimeographed
       reports of lectures and discussions are circulated
       to members of group.
4841. Journal of the Society of Archivists. Society of Ar-
       chivists, London.
4842. The Library. Series 1-3, London. 1889-1919. Con-
       tinued as Series 4 Transactions of the Bibliographi-
       cal Society, London, 1920+.
4843. Museums Association Monthly Bulletin. The Museums
       Association, London, England.
4844. Museums Journal. London. The Museums Associa-
       tion, 87 Charlotte St. , W1. Quarterly publication
       since 1902 on general museology but some articles
       on lighting, air conditioning, picture restoration,
       etc.
4845. The Penrose Annual. London, Percy Lund Humphries
       & Co. , Ltd. , 1906 to the present. An annual re-
       view of the graphic arts including bookmaking,
       prints, materials, etc.
4846. Transactions of the British Bibliographical Society.
       1920+.
4847. Transactions of the Royal Society of Arts. London.
4848. Occasional articles also appear in Bowater Papers,
       The British Printer, Graphis, Paper and Print,
       Print in Britain, and Printing World.

OTHER COUNTRIES

4849. Allgemeiner Amzeiger für Buchbindereien. Quarterly
       since 1887. West Germany.

4850. Archiv für Buckbinderei. Halle: 1902+.
4851. Baroda Museum and Picture Gallery, Bulletin.   Baro-
       da Museum, Baroda, India.
4852. Le Bibliophile: Revue Artistique et Documentaire du
       Livre Ancien et Modern. 1931-33. The fifteen
       volumes included some material on preservation.
4853. Biblioteka Muzealnictwa i Ochrony Zabytkow. Minis-
       terstwo Kultury Isztuki, Warsaw, Poland.
4854. Bibliotekar. Moscow, U. S. S. R.
4855. CIBA Review. CIBA, Ltd., Basel, Switzerland.
4856. Bollettino dell Istituto Centrale del Restauro. Istituto
       Centrale del Restauro, Rome.
4857. Bollettino dell Istituto di Patologia del Libro. Istituto
       di Patologia del Libro, Rome. Always has articles
       of importance to librarians and archivists. English
       summaries, sometimes all in English.
4858. Conservation of Cultural Property in India. Proceed-
       ings of the annual meetings of the Indian Associa-
       tion for the Study of Conservation. New Delhi:
       National Museum, 1966+.
4859. Das Felzbein. Monalsschrift für den Nachwuchs in
       Buchbindergewerb. Stuttgart: Buchbinder-Verlag,
       April 1948 to March 1951 (all printed). (The
       "Bonefolder" - Guidance for Young Men in Book-
       binding.)
4860. Gazette des Beaux - Arts. Presses Universitaires
       de France, Paris.
4861. Gigiena i Sanitariya (Hygiene and Sanitation). Trans-
       lations of this Russian periodical, beginning with
       the January 1964 issue which contains frequent
       articles on air pollution, are available from the
       National Technical Information Service, Springfield,
       Virginia.
4862. The Indian Archives. A quarterly journal, New Del-
       hi, 1947+.
4863. Institute Royal du Patrimoine Artistique, Bulletin.
       Institute Royal du Patrimoin Artistique, Brussels,
       Belgium.
4864. Istoricheskii Arkhiv. Institut Istorii, Akademiia Nauk
       SSSR, Moscow, USSR.
4865. Japan Academy Proceedings. Japan Academy, Tokyo.
4866. Jardin des Arts. 17 rue Remy-Dumoucel, Paris.
4867. Journal of Indian Museums. Museums Association of
       India, Prince of Wales Museum, Bombay.
4868. Juhrbuch der Einbandkunst. 4 vols. Leipzig, 1927-
       37.

4869. Kalori. Journal of the Museums Association of Aus-
       tralia.
4870. Kniga: issleclovaniya i materialy. Moscow, 1959 to
       the present. A journal of research and materials
       relating to the book.
4871. Laboratoire du Musée du Louvre, Bulletin. Musée
       National du Louvre, Paris. Mainly articles on
       technical examination of works of art and in parti-
       cular examination by radiation.
4872. Maltechnik. Munich: Verlag. George D. W. Call-
       wey, 1955 onward. Technical articles on tech-
       niques and materials for bookbinding.
4873. Microbiologiya. Moscow-Leningrad, USSR.
4874. Mitteilungen der Internationalen Arbeitsgemeinschaft
       der Archiv, Bibliotheks und, Graphik Restauratoren.
       Frieburg im Breslau, German Federal Republic is
       devoted entirely to records preservation.
4875. Museum. Tokyo National Museum, Tokyo, Japan.
4876. Neue Museumskunde. Leipzig, German Democratic
       Republic.
4877. Das Papier. Der Papiermacherberufsgenossenschaft.
       Darmstadt, German Federal Republic.
4878. Proceedings: Indian Association for the Study of the
       Conservation of Cultural Property. New Delhi Na-
       tional Museum. Contains articles of interest to
       library conservators.
4879. La Reliure. Paris. Dedicated to the furtherance of
       bookbinding in France.
4880. Science for Conservation. Department of Conservation
       Science, Tokyo National Research Institute for Cul-
       tural Properties, Tokyo, Japan.
4881. Scientific Papers on Japanese Antiques and Arts Crafts.
       Tokyo National Research Institute for Cultural
       Properties, Tokyo, Japan.
4882. Staub-Reinhaltung der Luft (Dust - Clean Air Mainten-
       ance). Translations of this German periodical
       beginning with the January 1965 issue are available
       from National Technical Information Service, Spring-
       field, Virginia.

Author Index

to

CONSERVATION OF LIBRARY MATERIALS

Volume II: A Bibliography

[Numerals in this index are to entry numbers in this volume, not to page numbers.]